About the Author

Dr. Paul Kurowski obtained his M.Sc. and Ph.D. in Applied Mechanics from Warsaw Technical University. He completed postdoctoral work at Kyoto University. Dr. Kurowski is an Assistant Professor in the Department of Mechanical and Materials Engineering, at the University of Western Ontario. His teaching includes Finite Element Analysis, Product Design, Kinematics and Dynamics of Machines and Mechanical Vibrations. His interests focus on Computer Aided Engineering methods used as tools of product design.

Dr. Kurowski is also the President of Design Generator Inc., a consulting firm with expertise in Product Development, Design Analysis, and training in Computer Aided Engineering.

Dr. Kurowski has published many technical papers and taught professional development seminars for the Society of Automotive Engineers (SAE), the American Society of Mechanical Engineers (ASME), the Association of Professional Engineers of Ontario (PEO), the Parametric Technology Corporation (PTC), Rand Worldwide, SolidWorks Corporation and others.

Dr. Kurowski is a member of the Association of Professional Engineers of Ontario and the Society of Automotive Engineers. He can be contacted at www.designgenerator.com.

Acknowledgements

This book is in its twelfth edition counting from the first one "Engineering Analysis with COSMOSWorks 2003." In the 2009 edition, the book title was changed to "Engineering Analysis with SolidWorks Simulation 2009" to address the product re-naming implemented by the SolidWorks Corporation. The book takes a unique approach by bridging introductory theory with examples showing the theory's practical implementations.

The book evolves together with **SolidWorks Simulation** software and I hope that every year it offers better value to students who use it in the introductory courses of Finite Element Analysis and **SolidWorks Simulation**.

Writing and updating this book every year following the new software release has been a very substantial effort that would not have been possible without the help and support of my professional colleagues. I would like to thank the students attending my various courses for their valuable comments and questions. I would like to thank Tom Kurowski for editing and proof reading the text and the exercises. I thank my wife Elżbieta for her support and encouragement that made it possible to write this book.

Paul Kurowski

Table of contents

Before You Start

Notes on hands-on exercises and functionality of Simulation

This book goes beyond a standard software manual because its unique approach concurrently introduces you to **SolidWorks Simulation** software and the fundamentals of Finite Element Analysis (FEA) through hands-on exercises. We recommend that you study the exercises in the order presented in the book. As you go through the exercises, you will notice that explanations and steps described in detail in earlier exercises are not repeated in later chapters. Each subsequent exercise assumes familiarity with software functions discussed in previous exercises and builds on the skills, experience, and understanding gained from previously presented problems. Exceptions to the above are chapters 23, 24 and 25 which do not include hands-on exercises.

The functionality of **SolidWorks Simulation** depends on which software **Simulation** product is used. The functionality of different products is explained in the following **Simulation** Product Matrix:

	SOLIDWORKS PREMIUM	SOLIDWORKS SIMULATION PROFESSIONAL	SOLIDWORKS SIMULATION PREMIUM	SOLIDWORKS FLOW SIMULATION
Tolerance Stack-Up Analysis	■	■	■	
Assembly Simulation	■	■	■	
Mechanism Analysis		■	■	
Event-Based Motion		■	■	
Compare and Optimize Design		■	■	■
Simulate Natural Frequencies		■	■	
Predict Buckling or Collapse		■	■	
Simulate Heating or Cooling		■	■	■
Simulate Drop Test		■	■	
Simulate Fatigue		■	■	
Simulate Plastic and Rubber Components			■	
Simulate Composites			■	
Simulate Forced Vibrations			■	
Nonlinear Dynamics			■	
Fluid Flow Simulation			■	■

The following **Simulation** studies are available in different **SolidWorks** and **SolidWorks Simulation** products:

SolidWorks Standard
Simulation Xpress

SolidWorks Premium
Stress
Motion

Simulation Professional
Stress
Fatigue
Optimization
Frequency
Buckling
Drop test
Pressure Vessel
Thermal
Motion
Event Based Motion

Simulation Premium
All capabilities of Simulation Professional
Nonlinear material
Dynamics (Vibration Analysis)

This book deals with structural analysis using **SolidWorks Simulation**. Therefore, **Motion** analysis won't be covered. **SimulationXpress** is a simplified version of **SolidWorks Simulation** and will not be covered either.

Information on **SolidWorks** and **Simulation** bundles is available at: www.solidworks.com/sw/products/10169_ENU_HTML.htm

Most exercises in this book will require **SolidWorks Simulation Professional**. Exercises limited to static analysis can be completed in **SolidWorks Premium**. Some exercises in chapter 15 and all exercises in chapters 19 and 20, require **SolidWorks Simulation Premium**. All exercises in this book use **SolidWorks** models, which can be downloaded from www.sdcpublications.com. These exercises do not contain any **Simulation** studies; you are expected to create all studies, results plots, and graphs yourself. The only exceptions are exercises in chapters 21 and 22 which come with **Simulation** studies fully or partially defined. All problems presented here have been solved with **SolidWorks Simulation Premium** running on Windows 7 in a 64 bit operating environment.

We encourage you to explore each exercise beyond its description by investigating other options, other menu choices, and other ways to present results. You will soon discover that the same simple logic applies to all functions in **SolidWorks Simulation**.

Finally, "Engineering Analysis with SolidWorks 2013" is an introductory text. The focus is more on understanding Finite Element Analysis than presenting all software capabilities. This book is not intended to replace software manuals. Therefore, not all **Simulation** capabilities will be covered, especially those of design studies, optimization, nonlinear and dynamic analyses. The knowledge acquired by the reader will not be strictly software specific. The same concepts, tools and methods in an FEA project will apply to any FEA software.

Prerequisites

The following prerequisites are recommended:

❑ An understanding of Statics, Kinematics and Dynamics

❑ An understanding of Mechanics of Materials

❑ An understanding of Heat Transfer

❑ An understanding of Mechanical Vibrations

❑ Experience with parametric, feature based solid modeling using SolidWorks

❑ Familiarity with the Windows Operating System

Selected terminology

The mouse pointer plays a very important role in executing various commands and providing user feedback. The mouse pointer is used to execute commands, select geometry, and invoke pop-up menus. We use Windows terminology when referring to mouse-pointer actions.

Item	Description
Click	Self-explanatory
Double-click	Self-explanatory
Click-inside	Click the left mouse button. Wait a second, and then click the left mouse button inside the pop-up menu or text box. Use this technique to modify the names of folders and icons in **SolidWorks Simulation** Manager.
Drag and drop	Use the mouse to point to an object. Press and hold the left mouse button down. Move the mouse pointer to a new location. Release the left mouse button.
Right-click	Click the right mouse button. A pop-up menu is displayed. Use the left mouse button to select a desired menu command.

All **SolidWorks** file names appear in CAPITAL letters, even though the actual file names may use a combination of capital and small letters. Selected menu items and **SolidWorks Simulation** commands appear in **bold**, **SolidWorks** configurations, **SolidWorks Simulation** folders, icon names and study names appear in *italics* except in captions and comments to illustrations. **SolidWorks** and **Simulation** also appear in bold font. Bold font may also be used to draw reader's attention to particular term.

1: Introduction

What is Finite Element Analysis?

Finite Element Analysis, commonly called FEA, is a method of numerical analysis. FEA is used for solving problems in many engineering disciplines such as machine design, acoustics, electromagnetism, soil mechanics, fluid dynamics, and many others. In mathematical terms, FEA is a numerical technique used for solving field problems described by a set of partial differential equations.

In mechanical engineering, FEA is widely used for solving structural, vibration, and thermal problems. However, FEA is not the only available tool of numerical analysis. Other numerical methods include the Finite Difference Method, the Boundary Element Method, and the Finite Volume Method to mention just a few. However, due to its versatility and numerical efficiency, FEA has come to dominate the engineering analysis software market, while other methods have been relegated to niche applications. When implemented into modern commercial software, both FEA theory and numerical problem formulation become completely transparent to users.

Finite Element Analysis used by Design Engineers

FEA is a powerful engineering analysis tool useful in solving many problems ranging from very simple to very complex. Design engineers use FEA during the product development process to analyze the design-in-progress. Time constraints and limited availability of product data call for many simplifications of computer models. On the other hand, specialized analysts implement FEA to solve very complex problems, such as vehicle crash dynamics, hydro forming, and air bag deployment.

This book focuses on how design engineers use FEA, implemented in **SolidWorks Simulation**, as a design tool. Therefore, we highlight the most essential characteristics of FEA as performed by design engineers as opposed to those typical for FEA performed by analysts.

FEA for Design Engineers: Another design tool

For design engineers, FEA is one of many design tools that are used in the design process and include CAD, prototypes, spreadsheets, catalogs, hand calculations, text books, etc.

FEA for Design Engineers: Based on CAD models

Modern design is conducted using CAD, so a CAD model is the starting point for analysis. Since CAD models are used for describing geometric information for FEA, it is essential to understand how to prepare CAD geometry in order to produce correct FEA results, and how a CAD model is different from an FEA model. This will be discussed in later chapters.

FEA for Design Engineers: Concurrent with the design process

Since FEA is a design tool, it should be used concurrently with the design process. It should drive the design process rather than follow it.

Limitations of FEA for Design Engineers

An obvious question arises: would it be better to have a dedicated specialist perform FEA and let design engineers do what they do best – design new products? The answer depends on the size of the business, type of products, company organization and culture, and many other tangible and intangible factors. A general consensus is that design engineers should handle relatively simple types of analysis, but do it quickly and of course reliably. Analyses that are very complex and time consuming cannot be executed concurrently with the design process, and are usually better handled either by a dedicated analyst or contracted out to specialized consultants.

Objectives of FEA for Design Engineers

The ultimate objective of using FEA as a design tool is to change the design process from repetitive cycles of "design, prototype, test" into a streamlined process where prototypes are not used as design tools and are only needed for final design validation. With the use of FEA, design iterations are moved from the physical space of prototyping and testing into the virtual space of computer simulations (Figure 1-1).

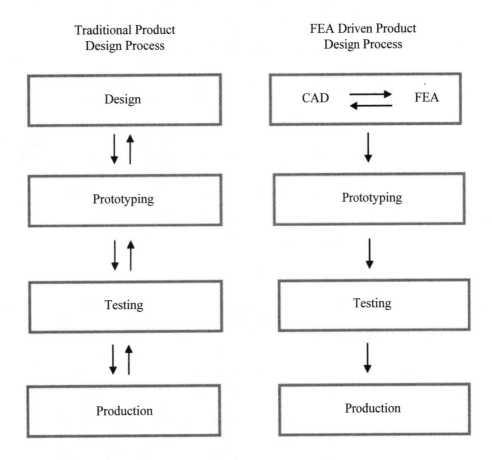

Figure 1-1: Traditional and FEA-driven product development.

Traditional product development needs prototypes to support a design in progress. The process in FEA-driven product development uses numerical models, rather than physical prototypes to drive development. In an FEA driven product design process, the prototype is no longer a part of the iterative design loop.

What is SolidWorks Simulation?

SolidWorks Simulation is a commercial implementation of FEA capable of solving problems commonly found in design engineering, such as the analysis of displacements, stresses, natural frequencies, vibration, buckling, heat flow, etc. It belongs to the family of engineering analysis software products originally developed by the Structural Research & Analysis Corporation (SRAC). SRAC was established in 1982 and since its inception has contributed to innovations that have had a significant impact on the evolution of FEA. In 1995 SRAC partnered with the **SolidWorks** Corporation and created COSMOSWorks, one of the first **SolidWorks** Gold Products, which became the top-selling analysis solution for the **SolidWorks** Corporation. The commercial success of COSMOSWorks integrated with **SolidWorks** CAD software resulted in the acquisition of SRAC in 2001 by Dassault Systèmes, parent of **SolidWorks** Corporation. In 2003, SRAC operations merged with the **SolidWorks** Corporation. In 2009, COSMOSWorks was re-named **SolidWorks Simulation**.

SolidWorks Simulation is integrated with **SolidWorks** CAD software and uses **SolidWorks** for creating and editing model geometry. **SolidWorks** is a solid, parametric, feature-driven CAD system developed specifically for the Windows Operating System. Many other CAD and FEA programs were originally developed in a UNIX environment and only later ported to Windows, and therefore are less integrated with Windows than **SolidWorks** and **SolidWorks Simulation**.

Fundamental steps in an FEA project

The starting point for any **SolidWorks Simulation** project is a **SolidWorks** model, which can be a *part* or an *assembly*. First, material properties, loads, and restraints are defined. Next, as is always the case with using any FEA-based analysis tool, the model geometry is split into relatively small and simply shaped entities called finite elements. The elements are called "finite" to emphasize the fact that they are not infinitesimally small, but relatively small in comparison to the overall model size. Creating finite elements is commonly called meshing. When working with finite elements, the **SolidWorks Simulation** solver approximates the sought solution (for example stress) by assembling the solutions for individual elements.

From the perspective of FEA software, each application of FEA requires three steps:

❑ Preprocessing of the FEA model, which involves defining the model and then splitting it into finite elements

❑ Solving for desired results

❑ Post-processing for results analysis

We will follow the above three steps in every exercise. From the perspective of FEA methodology, we can list the following FEA steps:

❑ Building the mathematical model

❑ Building the finite element model by discretizing the mathematical model

❑ Solving the finite element model

❑ Analyzing the results

The following subsections discuss these four steps.

Building the mathematical model

The starting point to analysis with **SolidWorks Simulation** is a **SolidWorks** model. Geometry of the model needs to be meshable into a correct finite element mesh. This requirement of meshability has very important implications. We need to ensure that the CAD geometry will indeed mesh and that the produced mesh will provide the data of interest (e.g. stresses, displacements or temperature distribution) with acceptable accuracy.

The necessity to mesh often requires modifications to the CAD geometry, which can take the form of defeaturing, idealization, and/or clean-up:

Term	Description
Defeaturing	The process of removing geometry features deemed insignificant for analysis, such as outside fillets, chamfers, logos, etc.
Idealization	A more aggressive exercise that may depart from solid CAD geometry by, for example, representing thin walls with surfaces and beams with lines.
Clean-up	Sometimes needed because geometry must satisfy high quality requirements to be meshable. To clean-up, we can use CAD quality control tools to check for problems like, for example, sliver faces, multiple entities, etc. that could be tolerated in the CAD model, but would make subsequent meshing difficult or impossible.

It is important to mention that we do not always simplify the CAD model with the sole objective of making it meshable. Often we must simplify a model even though it would mesh correctly "as is", because the resulting mesh would be large (in terms of the number of elements) and consequently, the meshing and the analysis would take too long. Geometry modifications allow for a simpler mesh and shorter meshing and computing times.

Sometimes, geometry preparation may not be required at all. Successful meshing depends as much on the quality of geometry submitted for meshing as it does on the capabilities of the meshing tools implemented in the FEA software.

Having prepared a meshable, but not yet meshed geometry, we now define material properties (these can also be imported from a CAD model), loads and restraints, and provide information on the type of analysis that we wish to perform. This procedure completes the creation of the mathematical model (Figure 1-2). Notice that the process of creating the mathematical model is not FEA specific. FEA has not yet entered the picture.

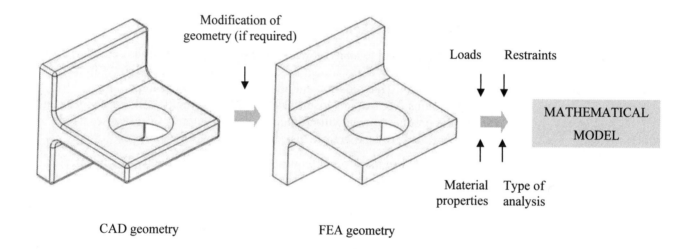

Figure 1-2: Building the mathematical model.

The process of creating a mathematical model consists of the modification of CAD geometry (here removing outside fillets), definition of loads, restraints, material properties, and definition of the type of analysis (for example linear static) that is to be performed.

You may review the differences between CAD geometry and FEA geometry using part model BRACKET DEMO.

Building the finite element model

The mathematical model now needs to be split into finite elements using the process of discretization, more commonly known as meshing (Figure 1-3). Geometry, loads, and restraints are all discretized. The discretized loads and restraints are applied to the nodes of the finite element mesh.

Solving the finite element model

Having created the finite element model, we now utilize a solver provided in **SolidWorks Simulation** to produce the desired data of interest (Figure 1-3).

Analyzing the results

Often the most difficult step of FEA is analyzing the results. Proper interpretation of results requires that we understand all simplifications (and errors they introduce) in the first three steps: defining the mathematical model, meshing, and solving.

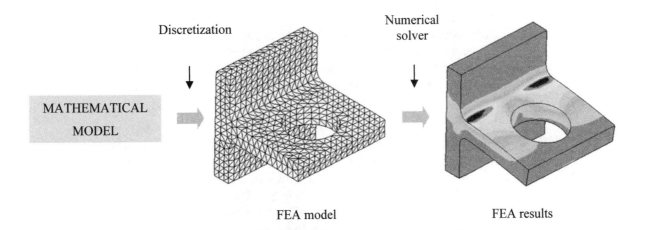

Figure 1-3: Building the finite element model.

The mathematical model is discretized into a finite element model. This completes the pre-processing phase. The FEA model is then solved with one of the numerical solvers available in SolidWorks Simulation.

Errors in FEA

The process illustrated in Figure 1-2 and Figure 1-3 introduces unavoidable errors. Formulation of a mathematical model introduces modeling errors (also called idealization errors), discretization of the mathematical model introduces discretization errors, and solving introduces solution errors. Of these three types of errors, only discretization errors are specific to FEA. Modeling errors affecting the mathematical model are introduced before FEA is utilized and can only be controlled by using correct modeling techniques. Solution errors are caused by the accumulation of round-off errors.

A closer look at finite elements

Meshing splits continuous mathematical models into finite elements. The type of elements created by this process depends on the type of geometry meshed. **SolidWorks Simulation** offers three types of three dimensional (3D) elements: solid elements for meshing solid geometry, shell elements for meshing surface geometry and beam elements for meshing wire frame geometry. SolidWorks Simulation also works with two dimensional (2D) elements: plane stress elements, plane strain elements, and axi-symmetric elements.

Before proceeding, we need to clarify an important terminology issue. In CAD terminology, "solid" denotes the type of geometry: solid geometry (as opposed to surface or wire frame geometry). In FEA terminology, "solid" denotes the type of element used to mesh the solid CAD geometry.

Solid elements

The type of geometry that is most often used for analysis with **SolidWorks Simulation** is solid CAD geometry. Meshing of this geometry is accomplished with tetrahedral solid elements, commonly called "tets" in FEA jargon. The tetrahedral solid elements in **SolidWorks Simulation** can either be first order elements ("draft quality"), or second order elements ("high quality"). The user decides whether to use draft quality or high quality elements for meshing. However, as we will soon prove, only high quality elements should be used for an analysis of any importance. The difference between first and second order tetrahedral elements is illustrated in Figure 1-4.

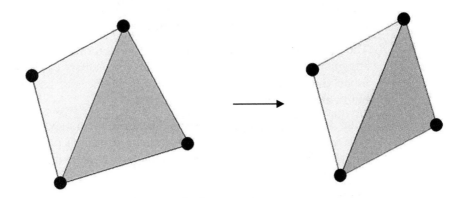

First order tetrahedral element
before deformation

First order tetrahedral element
after deformation

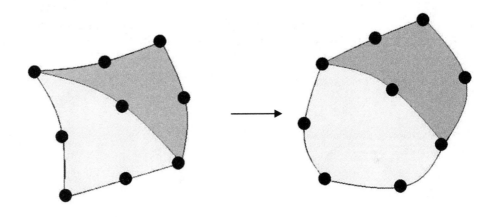

Second order tetrahedral element
before deformation

Second order tetrahedral
elementafter deformation

Figure 1-4: Differences between first and second order tetrahedral elements.

First and second order tetrahedral elements are shown before and after deformation. Notice that the first order element has corner nodes only, while the second order element has both corner and mid-side nodes (one mid-side node is not visible for the second order element in this illustration). Single elements seldom experience deformations of this magnitude, which are exaggerated in this illustration.

In a first order element, edges are straight and faces are flat. After deformation the edges and faces must retain these properties.

The edges of a second order element before deformation may either be straight or curvilinear, depending on how the element has been mapped to model the actual geometry. Consequently, the faces of a second order element before deformation may be flat or curved.

After deformation, edges of a second order element may either assume a different curvilinear shape or acquire a curvilinear shape if they were initially straight. Consequently, faces of a second order element after deformation can be either flat or curved.

First order tetrahedral elements model the linear field of displacement inside their volume, on faces, and along edges. The linear (or first order) displacement field gives these elements their name: first order elements.

If you recall from Mechanics of Materials, strain is the first derivative of displacement. Since the displacement field is linear, the strain field is constant. Consequently the stress field is also constant in first order tetrahedral elements. This situation imposes a very severe limitation on the capability of a mesh constructed with first order elements to model the stress distribution of any complex model. To make matters worse, straight edges and flat faces cannot map properly to curvilinear geometry, as illustrated in Figure 1-5, left.

Second order tetrahedral elements have ten nodes (Figure 1-4) and model the second order (parabolic) displacement field and first order (linear) stress field in their volume, on faces and along edges. The edges and faces of second order tetrahedral elements can be curvilinear before and after deformation, therefore these elements can be mapped precisely to curved surfaces, as illustrated in Figure 1-5 right. Even though these elements are more computationally demanding than first order elements, second order tetrahedral elements are used for the majority of analyses with **SolidWorks Simulation** because of their better mapping and stress modeling capabilities.

A tetrahedral solid element is the only type of solid element available in **SolidWorks Simulation**.

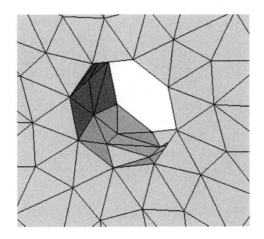

First order solid tetrahedral elements

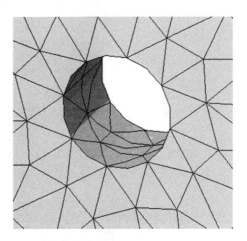

Second order solid tetrahedral elements

Figure 1-5: Failure of straight edges and flat faces to map to curvilinear geometry when using first order elements (left), and precise mapping to curvilinear geometry using second order elements (right).

Notice the imprecise first order element mapping of the hole; flat faces approximate the face of the curvilinear geometry. Second order elements map well to curvilinear geometry.

Shell elements

Shell elements are created by meshing surfaces or faces of solid geometry. Shell elements are primarily used for analyzing thin-walled structures. Since surface geometry does not carry information about thickness, the user must provide this information. Similar to solid elements, shell elements also come in draft and high quality with analogous consequences with respect to their ability to map to curvilinear geometry, as shown in Figure 1-6.

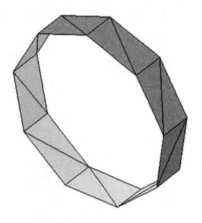 

First order triangular shell elements   Second order triangular shell elements

Figure 1-6: First order shell elements (left) and second order shell elements (right).

The shell element mesh on the left was created with first order elements. Notice the imprecise mapping of the mesh to curvilinear geometry. The shell element mesh on the right was created with second order elements, which map correctly to curvilinear geometry.

We need to make two important comments about Figure 1-5 and Figure 1-6. First, a mesh should never be that coarse (large size of elements compared to the model). We use a coarse mesh only to show the differences between first and second order elements clearly. Second, notice the "kinks" on the side of the second order elements; they indicate locations of mid side nodes. The second order element does map precisely to second order geometry.

As in the case of solid elements, first order shell elements model linear displacements and constant strain and stress. Second order shell elements model second order (parabolic) displacement and linear strain and stress.

The assumptions of modeling first or second order displacements in shell elements apply only to in-plane directions. The distribution of in-plane stresses across the thickness is assumed to be linear in both first and second order shell elements.

Triangular elements are the only type of shell elements available in **SolidWorks Simulation**.

Certain classes of shapes can be modeled using either solid or shell elements, such as the plate shown in Figure 1-7. Often the nature of the geometry dictates what type of element should be used for meshing. For example, a part produced by casting would be meshed with solid elements, while a sheet metal structure would be best meshed with shell elements.

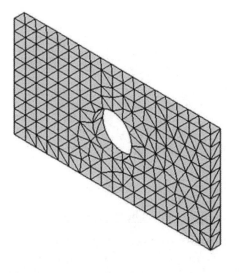
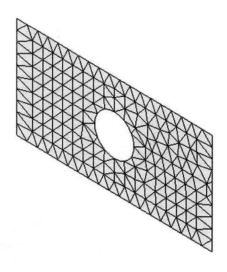

Second order tetrahedral solid elements   Second order triangular shell elements

Figure 1-7: Plate modeled with solid elements (left) and shell elements (right).

The actual choice between solids and shells depends on the particular requirements of analysis and sometimes on personal preferences.

Beam elements

Beam elements are created by meshing curves (wire frame geometry). They are a natural choice for meshing weldments. Assumptions about the stress distribution in two directions of the beam cross section are made.

A beam element does not have any physical dimensions in the directions normal to its length. It is possible to think of a beam element as a line with assigned beam cross section properties (Figure 1-8).

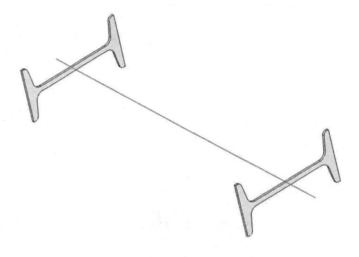

Figure 1-8: Conceptual representation of a beam element.

A beam element is a line with assigned properties of a beam cross section as required by beam theory. This illustration conceptualizes how a curve (here a straight line) defines an I-beam but does not represent actual geometry of beam cross-section.

Before we proceed with the classification of finite elements we need to introduce the concept of nodal degrees of freedom which are of paramount importance in FEA. The degrees of freedom (DOF) of a node in a finite element mesh define the ability of the node to perform translation and rotation. The number of degrees of freedom that a node possesses depends on the element type. In **SolidWorks Simulation**, nodes of solid elements have three degrees of freedom, while nodes of shell elements have six degrees of freedom.

This is because in order to describe the transformation of a solid element from the original to the deformed shape, we only need to know three translational components of nodal displacement. In the case of shell and beam elements, we need to know the translational components of nodal displacements and the rotational displacement components.

Using solid elements we study how a 3D structure deforms under a load. Using shell elements we study how a 3D structure with one dimension "collapsed" deforms under a load. This collapsed dimension is thickness which is not represented explicitly in the model geometry. Beam elements are intended to study 3D structures with two dimensions removed from the geometry and not represented explicitly by model geometry. It is important to point out that solids, shells and beams are all 3D elements capable of deformation in 3D space.

2D elements

There are also cases where a structure's response to load can be fully described by 2D elements that have only two in-plane degrees of freedom. These are plane stress, plane strain and axi-symmetric elements.

Plane stress elements are intended for the analysis of thin planar structures loaded in-plane, where out-of-plane stress is assumed to be equal zero. Plane strain elements are intended for the analysis of thick prismatic structures loaded in-plane, where out-of-plane strain is assumed to be equal zero. Axi-symmetric elements are intended for the analysis of axi-symmetric structures under axi-symmetric load. In all of these special cases, the structure deformation can be fully described using elements with only two degrees of freedom per node. For plane stress and plane strain, these are two components of in-plane translation. For axi-symmetric elements these are radial and axial displacements.

2D elements are summarized in Figure 1-9.

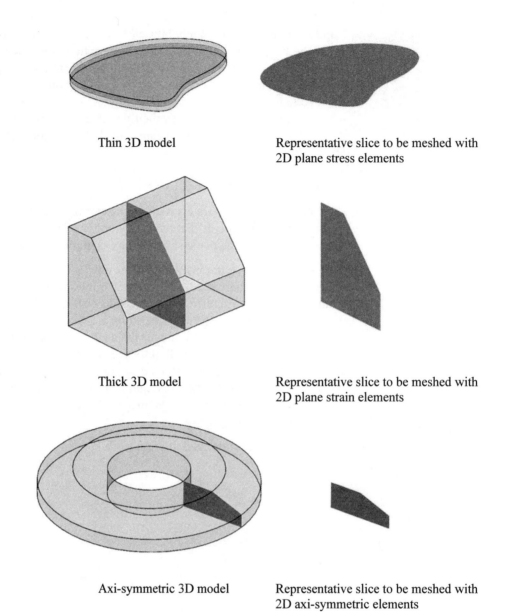

Thin 3D model

Representative slice to be meshed with 2D plane stress elements

Thick 3D model

Representative slice to be meshed with 2D plane strain elements

Axi-symmetric 3D model

Representative slice to be meshed with 2D axi-symmetric elements

Figure 1-9: Application of 2D elements: plane stress (top), plane strain (middle), and axi-symmetric (bottom).

Just like solids and shells, 2D elements may be of first or second order.

Figure 1-10 presents the basic library of elements in **SolidWorks Simulation**. Solid elements are tetrahedral, shell elements and 2D elements are triangles and beam elements are lines. Elements such as hexahedral solids or quadrilateral shells are not available in **SolidWorks Simulation**.

	3D elements			2D elements
	Solid elements	**Shell elements**	**Beam elements**	**Plate elements**
First order element Linear (first order) displacement field Constant stress field	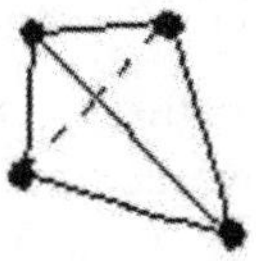	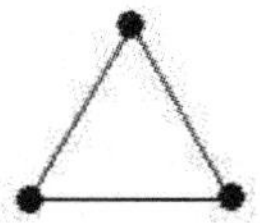	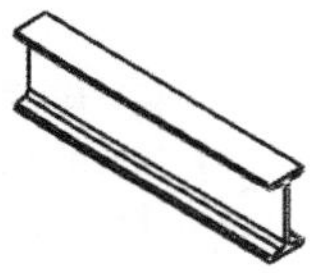	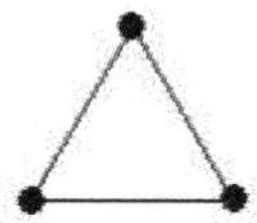
Second order element Parabolic (second order) displacement field Linear stress field	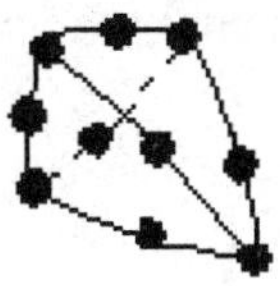	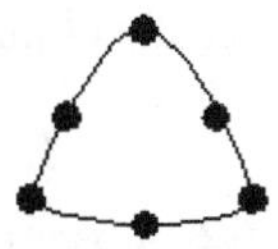		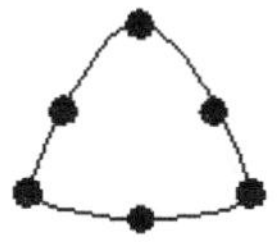

Figure 1-10: Basic element library of SolidWorks Simulation.

The majority of analyses use the second order tetrahedral element. Element order is not applicable to a beam element. 2D elements are commonly referred to as Plate elements.

What is calculated in FEA?

Each degree of freedom of a node in a finite element mesh constitutes an unknown. In structural analysis, nodal degrees of freedom represent displacement components, while in thermal analysis they represent temperatures. Nodal displacements and nodal temperatures are the primary unknowns for structural analysis and thermal analysis, respectively.

Structural analysis finds displacements, strains and stresses. If solid elements are used, then three displacement components (three translations) per node must be calculated. With shell and beam elements, six displacement components (six translations) must be calculated. 2D elements require calculations of two displacement components. Strains and stresses, are calculated based on the nodal displacement results.

Thermal analysis finds temperatures, temperature gradients, and heat flow. Since temperature is a scalar value (unlike displacements, which are vectors), then regardless of what type of element is used, there is only one unknown (temperature) to be found for each node. All other thermal results such as temperature gradient and heat flux are calculated based on temperature results. The fact that there is only one unknown to be found for each node, rather than three or six, makes thermal analysis less computationally intensive than structural analysis.

How to interpret FEA results

Results of structural FEA are provided in the form of displacements and stresses. But how do we decide if a design "passes" or "fails"? What constitutes a failure?

To answer these questions, we need to establish some criteria to interpret FEA results, which may include maximum acceptable displacements, maximum stress, or the lowest acceptable natural frequency.

While displacement and frequency criteria are quite obvious and easy to establish, stress criteria are not. Let us assume that we need to conduct a stress analysis in order to ensure that stresses are within an acceptable range. To judge stress results, we need to understand the mechanism of potential failure. If a part breaks, what stress measure best describes that failure? **SolidWorks Simulation** can present stress results in any desired form, but it is up to us to decide which stress measures should be used to analyze results.

Discussion of various failure criteria is out of the scope of this book. Any textbook on the Mechanics of Materials provides information on this topic. Here we will limit our discussion to commonly used failure criteria: Von Mises Stress failure criterion and Maximum Normal Stress failure criterion.

Von Mises Stress failure criterion

Von Mises stress, also known as Huber stress, is a stress measure that accounts for all six stress components of a general 3-D state of stress (Figure 1-11).

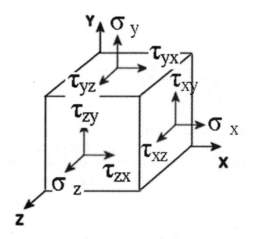

Figure 1-11: General state of stress represented by three normal stresses: σ_x, σ_y, σ_z and six shear stresses.

Two components of shear stress and one component of normal stress act on each side of this elementary cube. Due to symmetry of shear stresses, the general 3D state of stress is characterized by six stress components: σ_x, σ_y, σ_z and $\tau_{xy} = \tau_{yx}$, $\tau_{yz} = \tau_{zy}$, $\tau_{xz} = \tau_{zx}$

Von Mises stress σ_{vm}, can be expressed either by six stress components as:

$$\sigma_{vm} = \sqrt{0.5 \times \left[(\sigma_x - \sigma_y)^2 + (\sigma_y - \sigma_z)^2 + (\sigma_z - \sigma_x)^2\right] + 3 \times \left(\tau_{xy}{}^2 + \tau_{yz}{}^2 + \tau_{zx}{}^2\right)}$$

Von Mises stress σ_{vm}, can be also expressed three principal stresses (Figure 1-12) as:

$$\sigma_{vm} = \sqrt{0.5 \times \left[(\sigma_1 - \sigma_2)^2 + (\sigma_2 - \sigma_3)^2 + (\sigma_3 - \sigma_1)^2\right]}$$

Notice that von Mises stress is a non-negative, scalar stress measure. Von Mises stress is commonly used to present results because the structural safety for many engineering materials showing elasto-plastic properties (for example, steel or aluminum alloy) can be evaluated using von Mises stress.

The maximum von Mises stress failure criterion is based on the von Mises-Hencky theory, also known as the shear-energy theory or the maximum distortion energy theory. The theory states that a <u>ductile</u> material starts to yield at a location when the von Mises stress becomes equal to the stress limit. In most cases, the yield strength is used as the stress limit. According to the von Mises failure criterion, the factor of safety (FOS) is expressed as:

$$FOS = \sigma_{limit} / \sigma_{vm}$$

where σ_{limit} is yield strength.

Maximum Normal Stress failure criterion

By properly adjusting the angular orientation of the stress cube in Figure 1-11, shear stresses disappear and the state of stress is represented only by three principal stresses: σ_1, σ_2, σ_3, as shown in Figure 1-12. In **SolidWorks Simulation**, principal stresses are denoted as P1, P2, P3.

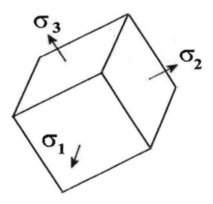

Figure 1-12: The general state of stress represented by three principal stresses: σ_1, σ_2, σ_3.

The Maximum Normal Stress Failure criterion is used for <u>brittle</u> materials. Brittle materials do not have a specific yield point. This criterion assumes that the ultimate tensile strength of the material in tension and compression is the same. This assumption is not valid in all cases. For example, cracks considerably decrease the strength of the material in tension while their effect is not significant in compression because the cracks tend to close.

This criterion predicts failure will occur when σ_1 exceeds the stress limit, usually the ultimate tensile strength. According to the maximum principle stress failure criterion, the factor of safety FOS is expressed as:

$$FOS = \sigma_{limit}/\sigma_1$$

where σ_{limit} is ultimate tensile strength.

Units of measure

Internally, **SolidWorks Simulation** uses the International System of Units (SI). However, for the user's convenience, the unit manager allows data entry in any of three systems of units: SI, Metric, and English. Results can be displayed using any of the three systems. Figure 1-13 summarizes the available systems of units.

	International System (SI)	Metric (MKS)	English (IPS)
Mass	kg	kg	lb
Length	m	cm	in
Time	s	s	s
Force	N	Kgf	lbf
Gravitational acceleration	m/s^2	G	in/s^2
Mass density	kg/m^3	kg/cm^3	lbf/in^3
Temperature	K	°C	°F

Figure 1-13: Unit systems available in SolidWorks Simulation.

SI, Metric, and English systems of units can be interchanged when entering data and analyzing results in SolidWorks Simulation.

As **SolidWorks Simulation** users, we are spared much confusion and trouble with systems of units. However, we may be asked to prepare data or interpret the results of other FEA software where we do not have the convenience of the unit manager. Therefore, we will make some general comments about the use of different systems of units in the preparation of input data for FEA models. We can use any consistent system of units for FEA models, but in practice, the choice of the system of units is dictated by what units are used in the CAD model. The system of units in CAD models is not always consistent; length can be expressed in [*mm*], while mass density can be expressed in [kg/m^3]. Contrary to CAD models, in FEA all units must be consistent. Inconsistencies are easy to overlook, especially when defining mass and mass density and can lead to serious errors.

In the SI system, based on meters [*m*] for length, kilograms [*kg*] for mass, and seconds [*s*] for time, all other units are easily derived from these base units. In mechanical engineering, length is commonly expressed in millimeters [*mm*], force in Newtons [*N*], and time in seconds [*s*]. All other units must then be derived from these basic units: [*mm*], [*N*], and [*s*]. Consequently, the unit of mass is defined as a mass which, when subjected to a unit force equal to 1N, will accelerate with a unit acceleration of 1 mm/s^2. Therefore, the unit of mass in a system using [*mm*] for length and [*N*] for force, is equivalent to 1000 kg or one metric ton. Therefore, mass density is expressed in metric tonnes [*tonne/mm^3*]. This is critically important to remember when defining material properties in FEA software without a unit manager. Review Figure 1-14 and notice that an erroneous definition of mass density in [*kg/m^3*] rather than in [*tonne/mm^3*] results in mass density being one trillion (10^{12}) times higher.

System SI	[m] [N] [s]
Unit of mass	kg
Unit of mass density	kg/m^3
Density of aluminum	2794 kg/m^3

System of units derived from SI	[mm] [N] [s]
Unit of mass	tonne
Unit of mass density	tonne/mm^3
Density of aluminum	2.794 x 10^{-9} tonne/mm^3

English system (IPS)	[in] [lbf] [s]
Unit of mass	slug/12
Unit of mass density	slug/12/in^3
Density of aluminum	2.614 x 10^{-4} slug/12/in^3

Figure 1-14: Mass density of aluminum in the three systems of units.

Comparison of numerical values of mass densities of 1060 aluminum alloy defined in the SI system of units with the system of units derived from SI, and with the English (IPS) system of units.

Using online help

SolidWorks Simulation features very extensive online Help and Tutorial functions, which can be accessed from the Help menu in the main **SolidWorks** tool bar or from the **Simulation** menu. The Study advisor can be accessed from the Study drop down menu (Figure 1-15).

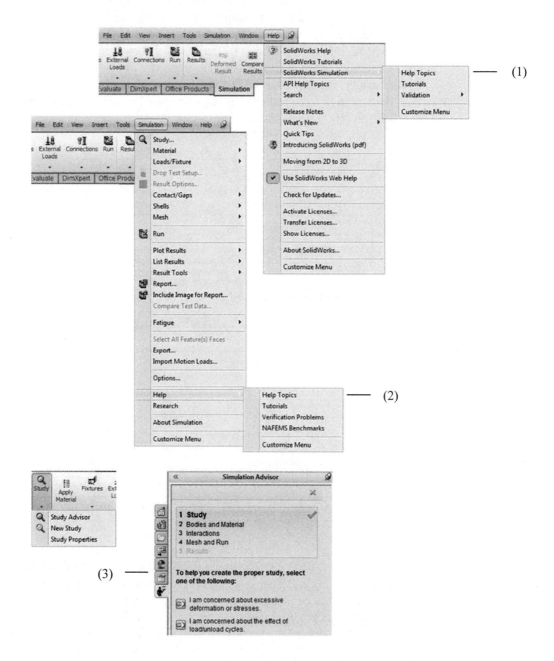

Figure 1-15: Accessing online Help, and Study Advisor.

Online Help, Tutorials, and Validation can be accessed from the main SolidWorks toolbar (1) or from the Simulation menu (2). The Study Advisor can be accessed from the Study drop down menu (3).

Limitations of SolidWorks Simulation Professional

We need to appreciate some important limitations of **SolidWorks Simulation** Professional: material is assumed as linear, and loads are static.

Linear material

Whatever material we assign to the analyzed parts or assemblies, the material is assumed to be linear, meaning that stress is proportional to the strain (Figure 1-16).

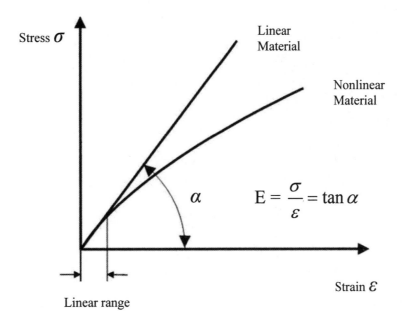

Figure 1-16: The linear material model assumed in SolidWorks Simulation.

With a linear material, stress is linearly proportional to strain. The linear range is where the linear and nonlinear material models are not significantly different.

Using a linear material model, the maximum stress magnitude is not limited to yield or to ultimate stress as it is in reality. Material yielding is not modeled, and whether or not yield may in fact be taking place can only be established based on the stress magnitudes reported in results. Most analyzed structures experience stresses below the yield stress, and the factor of safety is most often related to the yield stress. Therefore, the limitations imposed by linear material seldom impede **SolidWorks Simulation** Professional users.

Static loads

All structural loads and restraints are assumed not to change with time. Dynamic loading conditions cannot be analyzed with **SolidWorks Simulation Professional** (the only exception is a **Drop Test** analysis). This limitation implies that loads are applied slowly enough to ignore inertial effects.

Nonlinear material analysis and dynamic analysis can be performed with **SolidWorks Simulation Premium.**

2: Static analysis of a plate

Topics covered

- ❏ Using the **SolidWorks Simulation** interface
- ❏ Linear static analysis with solid elements
- ❏ Controlling discretization error with the convergence process
- ❏ Finding reaction forces
- ❏ Presenting FEA results in a desired format

Project description

A steel plate is supported and loaded, as shown in Figure 2-1. We assume that the support is rigid (this is also called built-in support, fixed support or fixed restraint) and that a 100000N tensile load is uniformly distributed along the end face, opposite to the supported face.

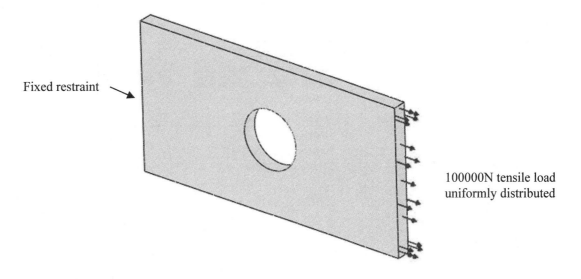

Fixed restraint

100000N tensile load uniformly distributed

Figure 2-1: SolidWorks model of a rectangular plate with a hole.

We will perform a displacement and stress analysis using meshes with different element sizes. Notice that repetitive analysis with different meshes does not represent standard practice in FEA. However, repetitive analysis with different meshes produces results which are useful in gaining more insight into how FEA works.

Procedure

In **SolidWorks**, open the model file called HOLLOW PLATE. Verify that **SolidWorks Simulation** is selected in the **Add-Ins** list (Figure 2-2).

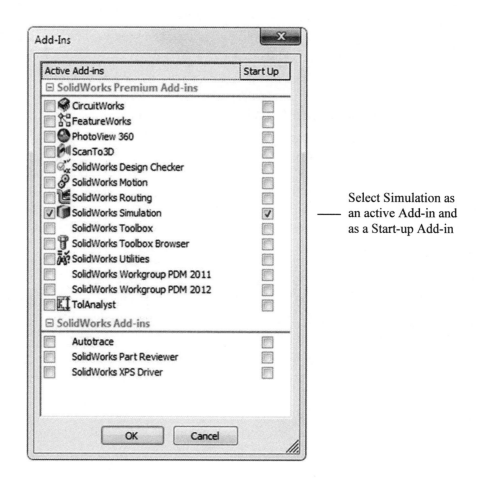

Select Simulation as ——— an active Add-in and as a Start-up Add-in

Figure 2-2: Add-Ins list in SolidWorks.

Verify that SolidWorks Simulation is selected in the list of Add-Ins.

Once **Simulation** has been added, it shows in the main **SolidWorks** menu and in the Command Manager.

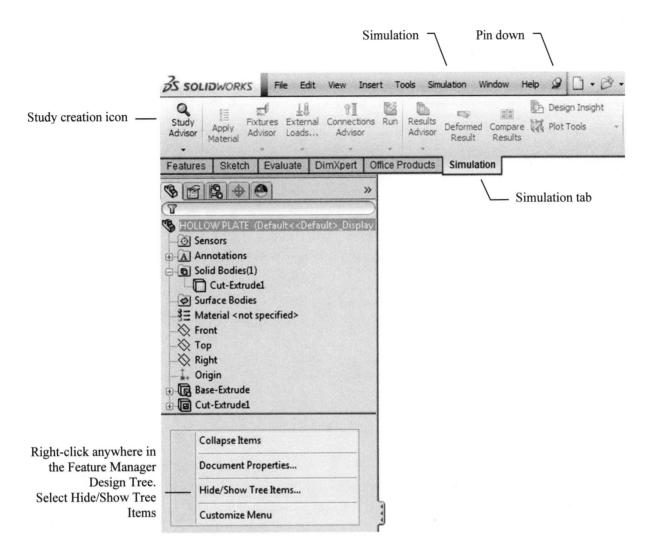

Figure 2-3: The Simulation tab is a part of the SolidWorks Command Manager.

Selecting the Simulation tab in the Command Manager displays Simulation menu items (icons). Since no study has been yet created, only the Study creation icon is available, all others are grayed-out. For convenience, pin down the top tool bar as shown.

Notice that **Feature Manager Design Tree** shown in Figure 2-3 displays **Solid Bodies** and **Surface Bodies** folders. These folders can be displayed by right-clicking anywhere in **Feature Manager Design Tree** to bring up the pop- up menu and selecting **Hide/Show Tree Items**. This will invoke **System Options- Feature Manager** (not shown here). From there, **Solid Bodies** and **Surface Bodies** folder can be selected to show. We will need to distinguish between these two different bodies in later exercises. In this exercise these two folders do not need to show.

Before we create a study, let's review the **Simulation** main menu (Figure 2-4) along with its **Options** window (Figure 2-5).

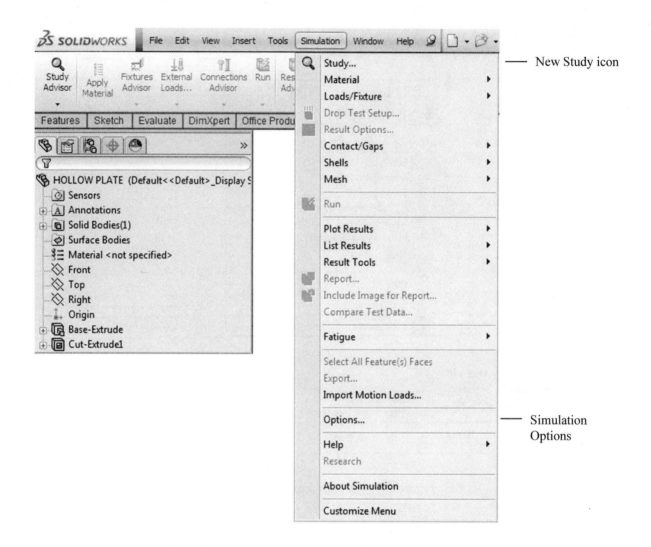

Figure 2-4: Simulation main menu.

Similar to the Simulation Command Manager shown in Figure 2-3, only the New Study icon is available. Notice that some commands are available both in the Command Manager and in the Simulation menu.

Simulation studies can be executed entirely from the **Simulation** drop down menu shown in Figure 2-4. In this book we will use the **Simulation** main menu and/or Command Manager to create a new Study. Everything else will be done in the Study Property Manager window.

Now click on the **Simulation** options shown in Figure 2-4 to open the **Simulation** System Options window shown in Figure 2-5

Default Options

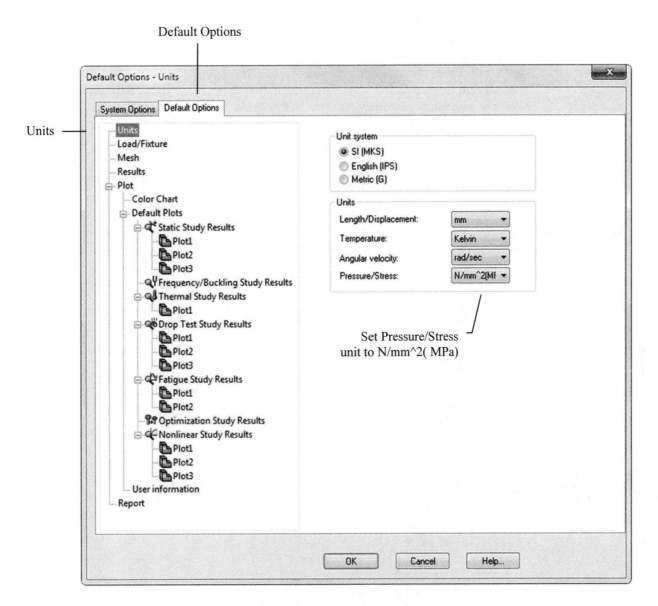

Units

Figure 2-5: Simulation Options window.

*The Options window has two tabs. In this example; **Default Options** and **Units** are selected and shown.*

Please spend time reviewing all of the options in both System Options and Default Options shown in Figure 2-5 before proceeding with the exercise. In the **Units** options, make the choices shown in Figure 2-5. In this book we will mostly use the SI system of units using MPa rather than Pa as a unit of stress and pressure. Occasionally we will switch to the IPS system.

Notice that **Default Plots** can be added, modified, deleted or grouped into sub-folders which are created by right-clicking on the results folders, for example; **Static Study Results** folder, **Thermal Study Results** folder, etc.

Creation of an FEA model starts with the definition of a study. To define a new study, select **New Study** in either the **Simulation** tab in the Command Manager (Figure 2.3) or **Simulation** main menu (Figure 2-4). This will open the **Study Property Manager**. Notice that the **New Study** icon in the **Simulation** Command Manager can be also used to open the **Study Advisor**. We won't be using the **Study Advisor** in this book. Name the study *tensile load 01* (Figure 2-6).

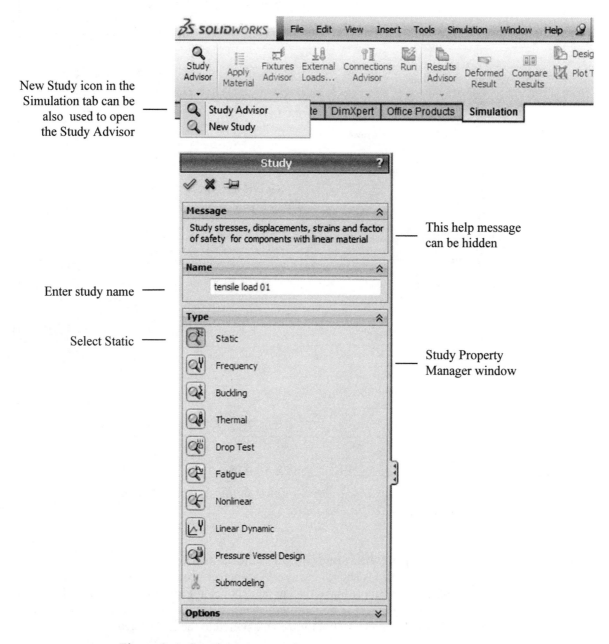

Figure 2-6: Creating a new study.

The study definition window offers choices for the type of study, here we select Static.

Once a new study has been created, **Simulation** Commands can be invoked in three ways:

❑ From the Simulation Command Manager (Figure 2-3)

❑ From the Simulation main menu (Figure 2-4)

❑ By right-clicking appropriate items in the **Study Property Manager** window. In this book, we will most often use this method.

When a study is defined, **Simulation** creates a study window located below the **Feature Manager Design Tree** and places several folders in it. It also adds a study tab located next to **Model** and **Motion Study** tabs. The tab provides access to the study (Figure 2-7).

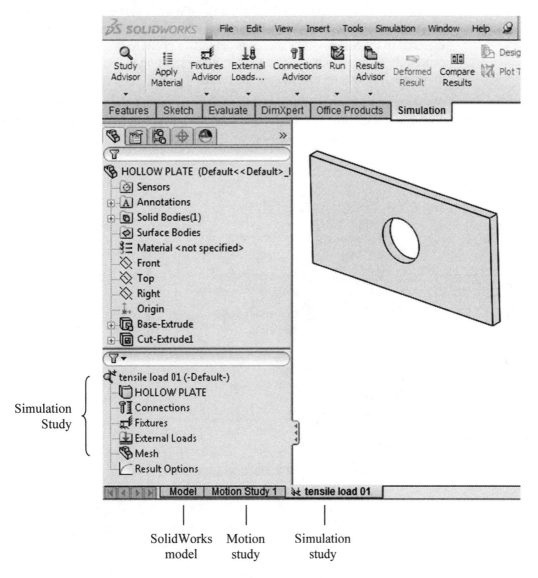

Figure 2-7: The Simulation window and Simulation tab.

You can switch between the SolidWorks Model, Motion Studies and Simulation Studies by selecting the appropriate tab.

We are now ready to define the analysis model. This process generally consists of the following steps:

❑ CAD geometry idealization and/or simplification in preparation for analysis. This is usually done in **SolidWorks** by creating an analysis specific configuration and making your changes there

❑ Material properties assignment

❑ Restraints application

❑ Load application

In this case, the geometry does not need any preparation because it is already very simple, therefore we can start by assigning material properties.

Notice that if a material is defined for a **SolidWorks** part model, the material definition is automatically transferred to the **Simulation** model. Assigning a material to the **SolidWorks** model is actually a preferred modeling technique, especially when working with an assembly consisting of parts with different materials. We will do this in later exercises.

To apply material to the **Simulation** model, right-click the HOLLOW PLATE folder in the *tensile load 01* simulation study and select **Apply/Edit Material** from the pop-up menu (Figure 2-8).

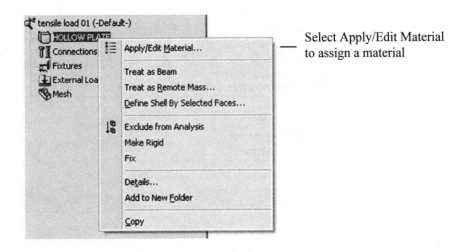

Select Apply/Edit Material to assign a material

Figure 2-8: Assigning material properties.

The action in Figure 2-8 opens the **Material** window shown in Figure 2-9.

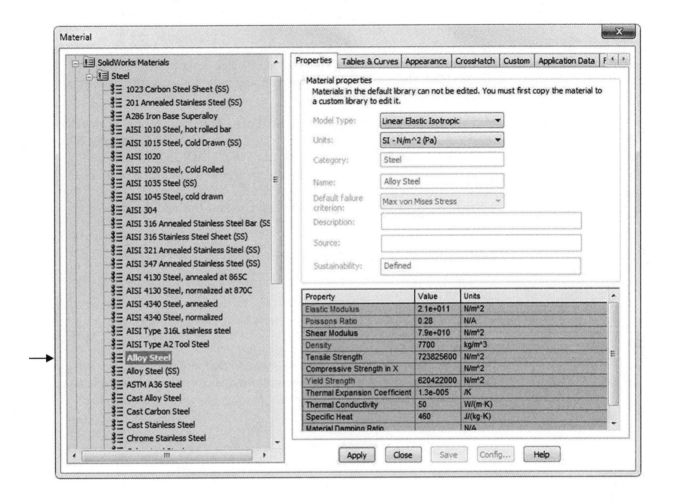

Figure 2-9: Material window.

Select Alloy Steel to be assigned to the model. Click Apply, and then click Close.

In the **Material** window, the properties are highlighted to indicate the mandatory and optional properties. A red description (Elastic modulus, Poisson's ratio) indicates a property that is mandatory based on the active study type and the material model. A blue description (Mass density, Tensile strength, Compressive strength, Yield strength, Thermal expansion coefficient) indicates optional properties. A black description (Thermal conductivity, Specific heat, Material damping ratio) indicates properties not applicable to the current study.

In the **Material** window, open the **SolidWorks Materials** menu, followed by the **Steel** menu. Select **Alloy Steel.** Select **SI** units under the **Properties** tab (other units could be used as well). Notice that the HOLLOW PLATE folder in the *tensile load 01* study now shows a check mark and the name of the selected material to indicate that a material has been assigned. If needed, you can define your own material by selecting **Custom Defined** material.

Defining a material consists of two steps:

❑ Material selection (or material definition if a custom material is used)
❑ Material assignment (either to all solids in the model, selected bodies of a multi-body part, or to selected components of an assembly)

Having assigned the material, we now move to defining the restraints. To display the pop-up menu that lists the options available for defining restraints, right-click the *Fixtures* folder in the *tensile load 01* study (Figure 2-10).

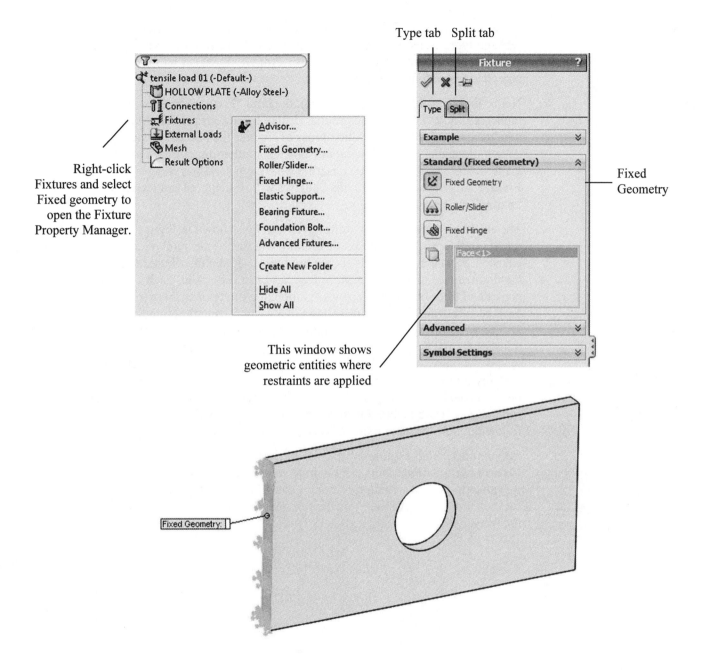

Type tab   Split tab

Right-click
Fixtures and select
Fixed geometry to
open the Fixture
Property Manager.

This window shows
geometric entities where
restraints are applied

Fixed
Geometry

Figure 2-10: Pop-up menu for the Fixtures folder and Fixture definition
window (Fixture Property Manager).

*All restraints definitions are done in the Type tab. The Split tab is used to
define a split face where a restraint is to be defined. The same can be done in
SolidWorks by defining a Split Face.*

Once the **Fixtures** definition window is open, select the **Fixed Geometry** restraint type. Select the end-face entity where the restraint is to be applied. Click the green check mark in the Fixture Property manager window to complete the restraint definition.

Notice that in **SolidWorks Simulation,** the term "Fixture" implies that the model is firmly "fixed" to the ground. However, aside from **Fixed Geometry,** which we have just used, all other types of fixtures restrain the model in certain directions while allowing movements in other directions. Therefore, the term "restraint" may better describe what happens when choices in the **Fixture** window are made. In this book we will switch between the terms "fixture" and "restraint" freely.

The existence of restraints is indicated by symbols shown in Figure 2-10. In the **Symbol** Settings of the Fixture window the size of the symbol can be changed. Notice that symbols shown in Figure 2-10 are distributed over the highlighted face meaning the entire face has been restrained. Each symbol consists of three orthogonal arrows symbolizing directions where translations have been restrained. Each arrow has a disk symbolizing that rotations have also been restrained. The symbol implies that all six degrees of freedom (three translations and three rotations) have been restrained. However, the element type we will use to mesh this model (second order solid tetrahedral element) has only translational degrees of freedom. Rotational degrees of freedom can't be restrained because they don't exist in this type of element. Therefore, disks symbolizing restrained rotations are irrelevant in our model. Please see the following table for more explanations.

Before proceeding, explore other types of restraints accessible through the **Fixture** window. Restraints can be divided into two groups: **Standard** and **Advanced**. Review animated examples available in the **Fixture** window and review the following table. Some less frequently used types of restraints are not listed here.

Standard Fixtures	
Fixed	Also called built-in or rigid support. All translational and all rotational degrees of freedom are restrained.
Immovable (No translations)	Only translational degrees of freedom are restrained, while rotational degrees of freedom remain unrestrained. If solid elements are used (like in this exercise), **Fixed** and **Immovable** restraints would have the same effect because solid elements do not have rotational degrees of freedom. Therefore, the **Immovable** restraint is not available if solid elements are used alone.
Roller/Slider	Specifies that a planar face can move freely on its plane but not in the direction normal to its plane. The face can shrink or expand under loading.
Fixed Hinge	Applies only to cylindrical faces and specifies that the cylindrical face can only rotate about its own axis. This condition is identical to selecting the **On cylindrical face** restraint type and setting the radial and axial components to zero.
Advanced Fixtures	
Symmetry	Applies symmetry boundary conditions to a flat face. Translation in the direction normal to the face is restrained and rotations about the axes aligned with the face are restrained.
Circular symmetry	Allows analysis of a model with circular patterns around an axis by modeling a representative segment. The geometry, restraints, and loading conditions must be identical for all other segments making up the model. Turbine, fans, flywheels, and motor rotors can usually be analyzed using circular symmetry.
Use Reference Geometry	Restrains a face, edge, or vertex only in certain directions, while leaving the other directions free to move. You can specify the desired directions of restraint in relation to the selected reference plane or reference axis.
On Flat Faces	Provides restraints in selected directions, which are defined by the three directions of the flat face where restraints are being applied.
On Cylindrical Faces	This option is similar to **On flat face**, except that the three directions of a cylindrical face define the directions of restraints.
On Spherical Face	Similar to **On Flat Faces** and **On Cylindrical Faces**. The three directions of a spherical face define the directions of the applied restraints.

When a model is fully supported (as it is in our case), we say that the model does not have any rigid body motions (the term "rigid body modes" is also used), meaning it cannot move without experiencing deformation.

Notice that the presence of restraints in the model is manifested by both the restraint symbols (showing on the restrained face) and by the automatically created icon, **Fixture-1**, in the *Fixtures* folder. The display of the restraint symbols can be turned on and off by either:

❑ Right-clicking the *Fixtures* folder and selecting **Hide All** or **Show All** in the pop-up menu shown in Figure 2-10, or

❑ Right-clicking the fixture icon and selecting **Hide** or **Show** from the pop-up menu.

Use the same method to control display of other **Simulation** symbols.

Now define the load by right-clicking the *External Loads* folder and selecting **Force** from the pop-up menu. This action opens the **Force** window as shown in Figure 2-11.

Right-click External Loads, select Force to open Force/Torque Property Manager

Force

This window shows geometric entities where loads are applied

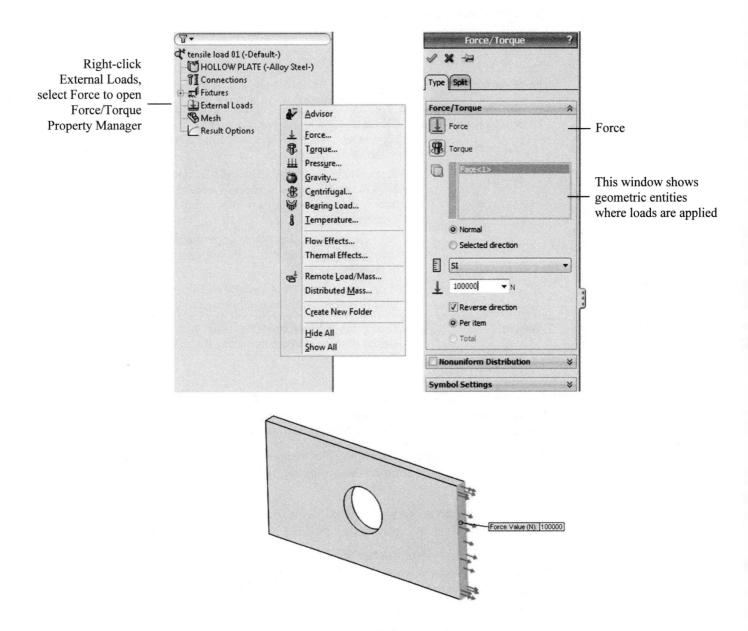

Figure 2-11: Pop-up menu for the External Loads folder and Force window.

The Force window displays the selected face where the tensile force is applied. If only one entity is selected, there is no distinction between Per Item and Total. In this illustration, load symbols have been enlarged by adjusting the Symbols Settings. Symbols of previously defined restraints have been hidden.

In the **Type** tab, select **Normal** in order to load the model with a 100000N tensile force uniformly distributed over the end face, as shown in Figure 2-11. Check the **Reverse direction** option to apply a tensile load.

Generally, forces can be applied to faces, edges, and vertices using different methods, which are reviewed below:

Force normal	Available for flat faces only, this option applies load in the direction normal to the selected face.
Force selected direction	This option applies a force or a moment to a face, edge, or vertex in the direction defined by the selected reference geometry. Moments can be applied only if shell elements are used. Shell elements have six degrees of freedom per node: three translations and three rotations, and can take a moment load. Solid elements only have three degrees of freedom (translations) per node and, therefore, cannot take a moment load directly. If you need to apply moments to solid elements, they must be represented with appropriately applied forces.
Torque	This option applies torque (expressed by traction forces) about a reference axis using the right-hand rule.

Try using the click-inside technique to rename the **Fixture-1** and **Force/Torque-1** icons. Notice that renaming using the click-inside technique works on all items in **SolidWorks Simulation**.

The model is now ready for meshing. Before creating a mesh, let's make a few observations about defining the geometry, material properties, loads and restraints.

Geometry preparation is a well-defined step with few uncertainties. Geometry that is simplified for analysis can be compared with the original CAD model.

Material properties are most often selected from the material library and do not account for local defects, surface conditions, etc. Therefore, the definition of material properties usually has more uncertainties than geometry preparation.

The definition of loads is done in a few menu selections, but involves many assumptions. Factors such as load magnitude and distribution are often only approximately known and must be assumed. Therefore, significant idealization errors can be made when defining loads.

Defining restraints is where severe errors are most often made. For example, it is easy enough to apply a fixed restraint without giving too much thought to the fact that a fixed restraint means a rigid support – a mathematical abstraction. A common error is over-constraining the model, which results in an overly stiff structure that underestimates displacements and stresses. The relative level of uncertainties in defining geometry, material, loads, and restraints is qualitatively shown in Figure 2-12.

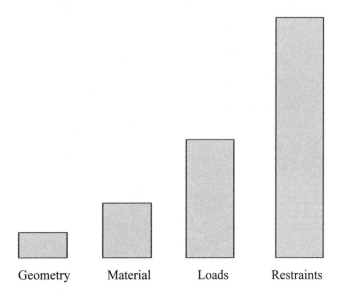

Figure 2-12: Qualitative comparison of uncertainty in defining geometry, material properties, loads, and restraints.

The level of uncertainty (or the risk of error) has no relation to time required for each step, so the message in Figure 2-12 may be counterintuitive. In fact, preparing CAD geometry for FEA may take hours, while applying restraints and loads takes only a few clicks.

In all of the examples presented in this book, we assume that definitions of material properties, loads, and restraints represent an acceptable idealization of real conditions. However, we need to point out that it is the responsibility of the FEA user to determine if all those idealized assumptions made during the creation of the mathematical model are indeed acceptable.

Before meshing the model, we need to verify under the **Default Options** tab, in the **Mesh** properties, that **High** mesh quality is selected (Figure 2-13). The **Options** window can be opened from the **SolidWorks Simulation** menu as shown in Figure 2-4.

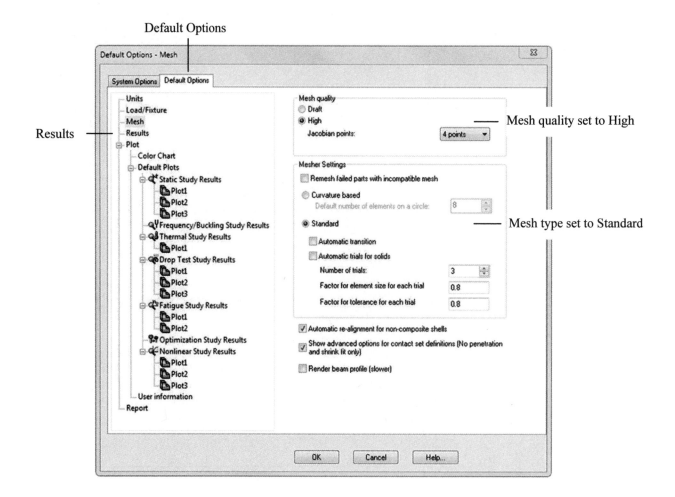

Figure 2-13: Mesh settings in the Options window.

Use this window to verify that the mesh quality is set to High and the mesh type is set to Standard. Use these settings for other exercises unless indicated otherwise.

The difference between **High** and **Draft** mesh quality is:

❑ Draft quality mesh uses first order elements

❑ High quality mesh uses second order elements

Differences between first and second order elements were discussed in chapter 1.

The difference between **Curvature based** mesh and **Standard** mesh will be explained in chapter 3. Now, right-click the *Mesh* folder to display the pop-up menu (Figure 2-14).

Right-click Mesh to display mesh pop up menu ———

——— Create Mesh

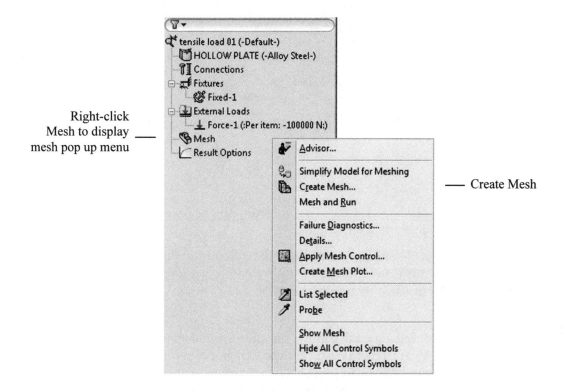

Figure 2-14: Mesh pop-up menu.

Select Create Mesh from the pop-up menu.

In the pop-up menu, select **Create Mesh**. This opens the **Mesh** window (Figure 2-15) which offers a choice of element size and element size tolerance.

This exercise reinforces the impact of mesh size on results. Therefore, we will solve the same problem using three different meshes: coarse, medium (default), and fine. Figure 2-15 shows the respective selection of meshing parameters to create the three meshes.

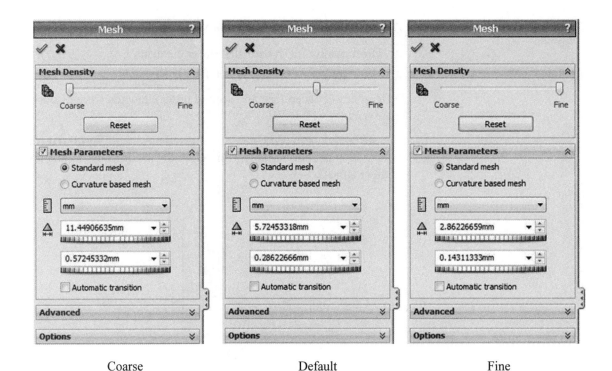

| Coarse | Default | Fine |

Figure 2-15: Three choices for mesh density from left to right: coarse, medium (default), and fine.

Show Mesh Parameters to see the element size. In all three cases use Standard mesh. Notice the different slider positions in the three windows. Verify that standard mesh is used.

The medium mesh density, shown in the middle window in Figure 2-15, is the default that **SolidWorks Simulation** proposes for meshing our model. The element size of 5.72 mm and the element size tolerance of 0.286mm are established automatically based on the geometric features of the **SolidWorks** model. The 5.72 mm size is the characteristic element size in the mesh, as explained in Figure 2-16. The default tolerance is 5% of the global element size. If the distance between two nodes is smaller than this value, the nodes are merged unless otherwise specified by contact conditions (contact conditions are not present in this model).

Mesh density has a direct impact on the accuracy of results. The smaller the elements, the lower the discretization error, but the meshing and solving time both take longer. In the majority of analyses with **SolidWorks Simulation**, the default mesh settings produce meshes that provide acceptable discretization errors, while keeping solution times reasonably short.

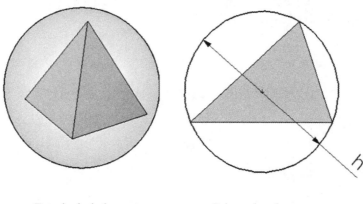

Tetrahedral element   Triangular element

Figure 2-16: Characteristic element size for a tetrahedral element (left) and triangular element (right)

The characteristic element size of a tetrahedral element is the diameter h of a circumscribed sphere (left). This is easier to illustrate with the 2D analogy of a circle circumscribed on a triangle (right).

Right-click the Mesh folder again and select **Create...** to open the **Mesh** window. With the **Mesh** window open, set the slider all the way to the left (as illustrated in Figure 2-15, left) to create a coarse mesh, and click the green checkmark button. The mesh will be displayed as shown in Figure 2-17.

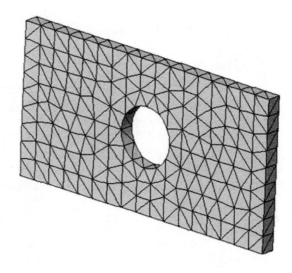

Figure 2-17: A coarse mesh created with second order, solid tetrahedral elements.

You can control the mesh visibility by selecting Hide Mesh or Show Mesh from the pop-up menu shown in Figure 2-14.

The presence of a mesh is reflected in the appearance of the solid folder in a **Simulation** study (Figure 2-18).

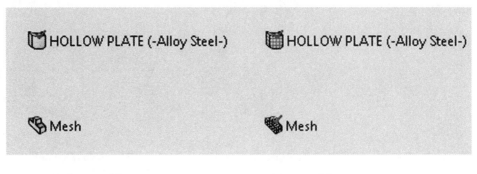

Before meshing   After meshing

Figure 2-18: Solid and mesh folders in a Simulation study before and after meshing.

Cross hatching is added to the Solid folder and to the Mesh folder in a Simulation study to show that a mesh has been created.

To start the solution, right-click the *tensile load 01* study folder which displays a pop-up menu (Figure 2-19). Select **Run** to start the solution.

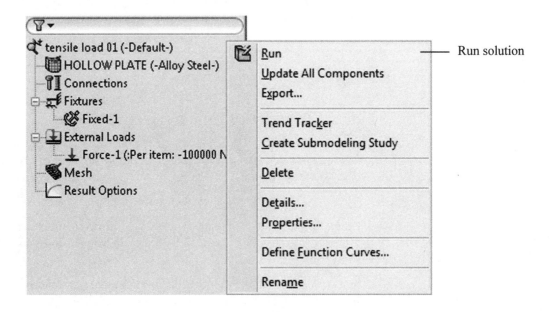

Figure 2-19: Pop-up menu for the *tensile load 01* folder.

Start the solution by right-clicking the tensile load 01 folder to display a pop-up menu. Select Run to start the solution.

The solution can be executed with different properties, which we will investigate in later chapters. You can monitor the solution progress while the solution is running (Figure 2-20).

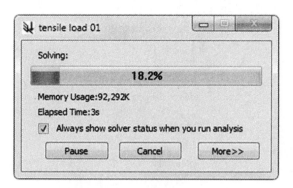

Figure 2-20: Solution Progress window.

The solver reports solution progress while the solution is running.

If the solution fails, the failure is reported as shown in Figure 2-21.

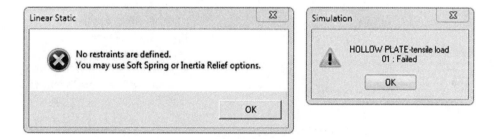

Figure 2-21: Failed solution warning window.

Here, the solution of a model with no restraints was attempted. Once the error message has been acknowledged (left), the solver displays the final outcome of the solution (right).

When the solution completes successfully, **Simulation** creates a *Results* folder with result plots which are defined in **Simulation Default Options** as shown in Figure 2-5.

In a typical configuration three plots are created automatically in the Static study; make sure that the above plots are defined in **Simulation** options, if not, define them:

- ❑ *Stress1*   showing von Mises stresses
- ❑ *Displacement1*   showing resultant displacements
- ❑ *Strain1*   showing equivalent strain

Once the solution completes, you can add more plots to the *Results* folder. You can also create subfolders in the *Results* folder to group plots (Figure 2-22).

Right-click to display **Results Option** window shown below —

Three plots are automatically — created if **Results Options** include Stresses and strains

Right-click **Results** folder to invoke this pop-up window

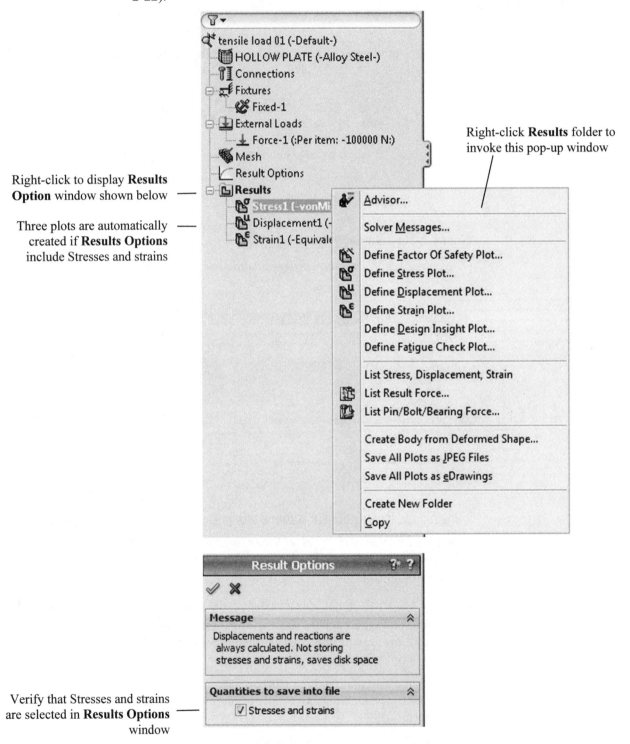

Verify that Stresses and strains are selected in **Results Options** — window

Figure 2-22: More plots and folders can be added to the *Results* folder.

Right-clicking on the Results folder activates this pop-up menu from which plots may be added.

The **Result Options** window shown in Figure 2-22 has different choices depending on the type of study. In a **Static** study, deselecting **Stress and strain** disables calculation of stress and strain which reduces calculation time and the size of solution data base. This may be important in analysis of very large models.

To display stress results, double-click on the **Stress1** icon in the *Results* folder or right-click it and select **Show** from the pop-up menu. The stress plot is shown in Figure 2-23.

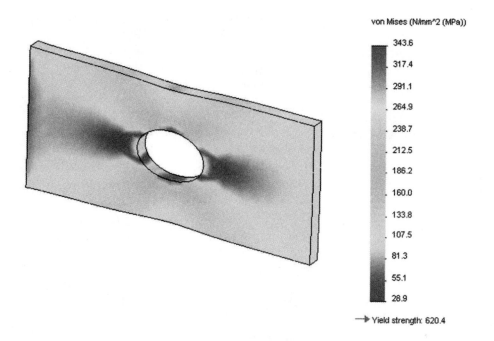

Figure 2-23: Stress plot displayed using default stress plot settings.

Von Mises stress results are shown by default in the stress plot window. Notice that results are shown in [MPa] as was set in the Default Options tab (Figure 2-5). The highest stress 340 MPa is below the material yield strength, 620 MPa. The actual numerical results may differ slightly depending on the solver used, software version, and service pack used.

Once the stress plot is showing, right-click the stress plot icon to display the pop-up menu featuring different plot display options (Figure 2-24).

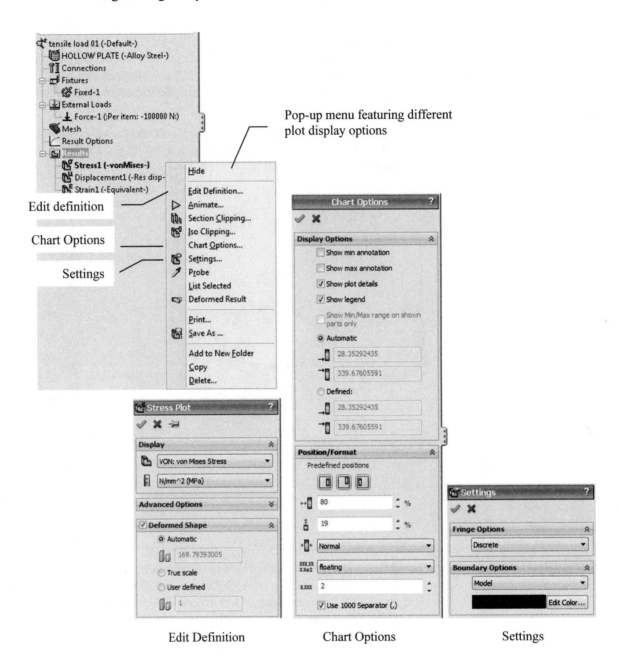

Edit definition

Chart Options

Settings

Pop-up menu featuring different plot display options

Edit Definition

Chart Options

Settings

Figure 2-24: Pop-up menu with plot display options.

Plots can be modified using selections from the pop-up menu (top). Callouts relate selections in the pop-up menu to the invoked windows.

Explore all selections offered by these three windows. In particular, explore scientific, floating and general format options in Chart Options and color Options also in Chart Options. Color Options are not shown in the above illustration.

Use **Edit Definition** to change units if necessary. **Chart Options** offers control over the format of numerical results, such as scientific, floating, and general, and also offers a different number of decimal places. Explore these choices. In this book, results will be presented using different choices, most suitable for the desired plot.

The default type of **Fringe Options** in the **Settings** window is **Continuous** (Figure 2-24). Change this to **Discrete** through the **Default Options** window, by selecting **Plot** (Figure 2-5). This way you won't have to modify the future plots individually. In this book we will be using **Discrete Fringe Options** to display fringe plots. The plots from the current study will not change after changing the default options.

Since the above change does not affect already existing plots, we now examine how to modify the stress plot using the **Settings** window shown in Figure 2-25. In **Settings,** select **Discrete** in **Fringe options** and **Mesh** in **Boundary options** to produce the stress plot shown in Figure 2-25.

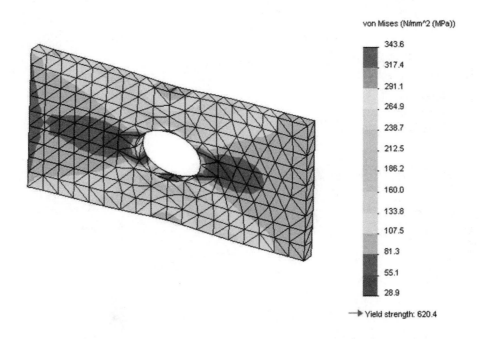

Figure 2-25: The modified stress plot is shown with discrete fringes and the mesh superimposed on the stress plot.

The stress plot in Figure 2-25 shows node values, also called averaged stresses. Element values (or non-averaged stresses) can be displayed by proper selection in the **Stress Plot** window in **Advanced Options**. Node values are most often used to present stress results. See chapter 3 and the glossary of terms in chapter 23 for more information on node values and element values of stress results.

Before you proceed, investigate this stress plot with other selections available in the windows shown in Figure 2-24.

We now review the displacement and strain results. All of these plots are created and modified in the same way. Sample results are shown in Figure 2-26 (displacement) and Figure 2-27 (strain).

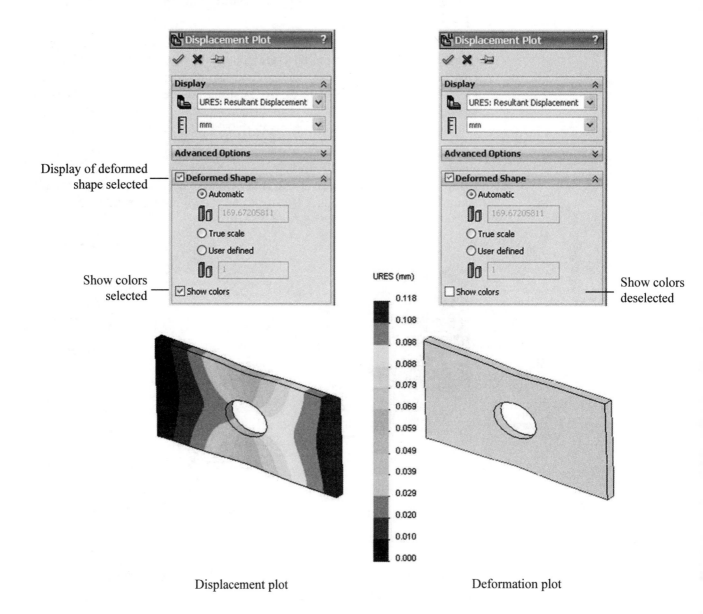

Display of deformed shape selected

Show colors selected

Show colors deselected

Displacement plot

Deformation plot

Figure 2-26: Displacement plot (left) and Deformation plot (right).

A Displacement plot can be turned into a Deformation plot by deselecting Show Colors in the Displacement Plot window. The same window has the option of showing the model with an exaggerated scale of deformation as shown above.

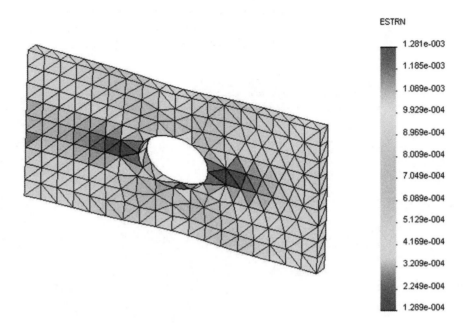

ESTRN

1.281e-003
1.185e-003
1.089e-003
9.929e-004
8.969e-004
8.009e-004
7.049e-004
6.089e-004
5.129e-004
4.169e-004
3.209e-004
2.249e-004
1.289e-004

Figure 2-27: Strain results.

Strain results are shown here using Element values. The mesh is also shown.

The plots in Figures 2-23, 2-25, 2-26, 2-27 all show the deformed shape in an exaggerated scale. You can change the display from deformed to undeformed or modify the scale of deformation in the **Displacement Plot**, **Stress Plot**, and **Strain Plot** windows, activated by right-clicking the plot icon, then selecting **Edit Definition**.

Now, construct a **Factor of Safety** plot using the menu shown in Figure 2-22. The definition of the **Factor of Safety** plot requires three steps. Follow steps 1 through 3 using the selection shown in Figure 2-28. Refer to chapter 1 and review Help to learn about failure criteria and their applicability to different materials.

Click right arrow to move
through windows

Review Help (question mark) to
learn more about failure criteria

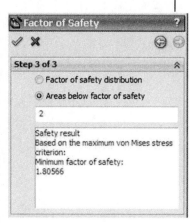

Step 1
Use von Mises Stress criterion.
Review Property options to
insert text and/or use specific
views for the plot.

Step 2
Select multiplication factor

Step 3
Select "Areas below a factor
of safety" and enter the
number 2.

Figure 2-28: Three windows show the three steps in the Factor of Safety plot
definition. Select the Max von Mises Stress criterion in the first window.

*To move through steps, click on the right and left arrows located at the top of
the Factor of Safety dialog.*

Step 1 *selects the failure criterion,* ***step 2*** *selects display units, sets the stress
limit and sets multiplication factor,* ***Step 3*** *selects what will be displayed in
the plot. Here we select areas below the factor of safety 2.*

The factor of safety plot in Figure 2-29 shows the area where the factor of safety is below the specified.

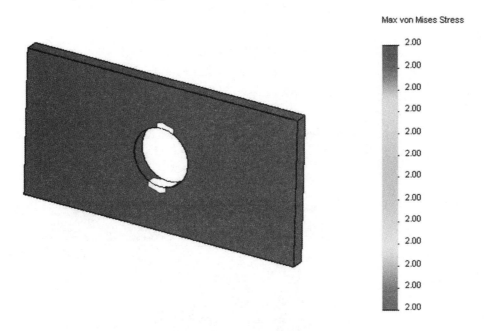

Figure 2-29: The red color (shown as white in this grayscale illustration) displays the areas where the factor of safety falls below 2.

Color scale in this case shows only the selected factor of safety.

We have completed the analysis with a coarse mesh and now wish to see how a change in mesh density will affect the results. Therefore, we will repeat the analysis two more times using medium and fine density meshes respectively. We will use the settings shown in Figure 2-15. All three meshes used in this exercise (coarse, medium, and fine) are shown in Figure 2-30.

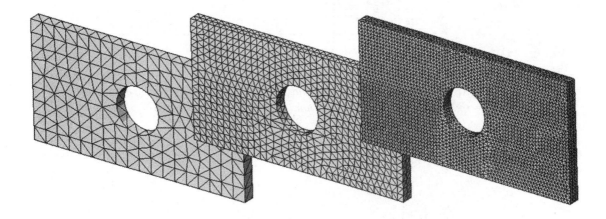

Figure 2-30: Coarse, medium, and fine meshes.

Three meshes used to study the effects of element size on results.

To compare the results produced by different meshes, we need more information than is available in the plots. Along with the maximum displacement and the maximum von Mises stress, for each study we need to know:

❑ The number of nodes in the mesh.

❑ The number of elements in the mesh.

❑ The number of degrees of freedom in the model.

The information on the number of nodes and number of elements can be found in **Mesh Details** accessible from the menu in Figure 2-14. The mesh Details window is shown in Figure 2-31.

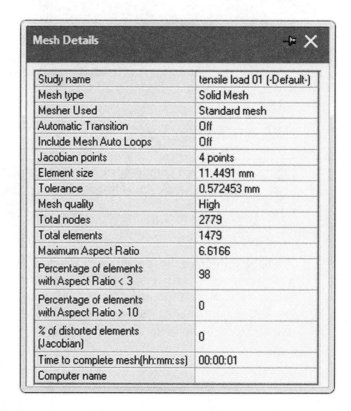

Study name	tensile load 01 (-Default-)
Mesh type	Solid Mesh
Mesher Used	Standard mesh
Automatic Transition	Off
Include Mesh Auto Loops	Off
Jacobian points	4 points
Element size	11.4491 mm
Tolerance	0.572453 mm
Mesh quality	High
Total nodes	2779
Total elements	1479
Maximum Aspect Ratio	6.6166
Percentage of elements with Aspect Ratio < 3	98
Percentage of elements with Aspect Ratio > 10	0
% of distorted elements (Jacobian)	0
Time to complete mesh(hh:mm:ss)	00:00:01
Computer name	

Figure 2-31: Mesh details window.

Right-click the Mesh folder and select Details from the pop-up menu to display the Mesh Details window. Notice that information on the number of degrees of freedom is not available here.

Another way to find the number of nodes and elements and also the number of degrees of freedom is to use the pop-up menu shown in Figure 2-32. Right-click the *Results* folder and select **Solver Messages** to display the window shown in Figure 2-32.

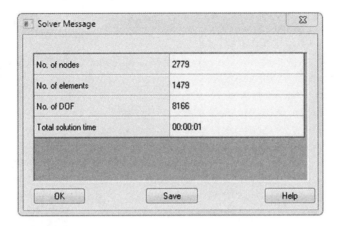

Figure 2-32: The Solver Message window lists information pertaining to the solved study.

Total solution time was too short to register. To save this solver message, click the Save button.

Now create and run two more studies: *tensile load 02* with the default element size (medium), and *tensile load 03* with a fine element size, as shown in Figure 2-15 and Figure 2-30. To create a new study we could just repeat the same steps as before but an easier way is to copy the original study. To copy a study, follow the steps in Figure 2-33.

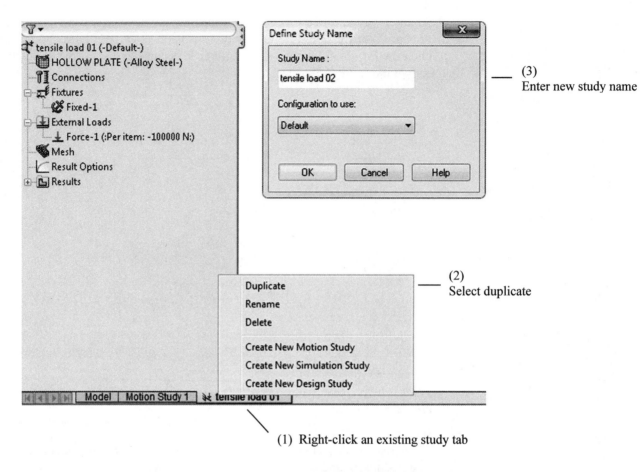

(3)
Enter new study name

(2)
Select duplicate

(1) Right-click an existing study tab

Figure 2-33: A study can be copied into another study in three steps as shown.

Notice that all definitions in a study (material, restraints, loads, mesh) can also be copied individually from one study to another by dragging and dropping them into a different study tab.

A study is copied complete with results and plot definitions. Before remeshing with default element size, you must acknowledge the warning message shown in Figure 2-34.

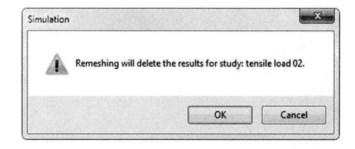

Figure 2-34: Remeshing deletes any existing results in the study.

The summary of results produced by the three studies is shown in Figure 2-35.

Study	Element size [mm]	Number of nodes	Number of elements	Number of DOF	Max. result. displ. [mm]	Max. von Mises stress [MPa]
tensile load 01	11.45	2779	1479	8166	0.117824	344
tensile load 02	5.72	12208	7028	36069	0.118033	370
tensile load 03	2.86	83769	54741	249903	0.118072	377

Figure 2-35: Summary of results produced by the three meshes.

Notice that these results are based on the same problem. Differences in the results arise from the different mesh densities used in studies tensile load 01, tensile load 02, and tensile load 03.

The actual numbers in this table may vary slightly depending on the type of solver and release of the software used for solution.

Figure 2-36 shows the maximum resultant displacement and the maximum von Mises stress as a function of the number of degrees of freedom. The number of degrees of freedom is in turn a function of mesh density.

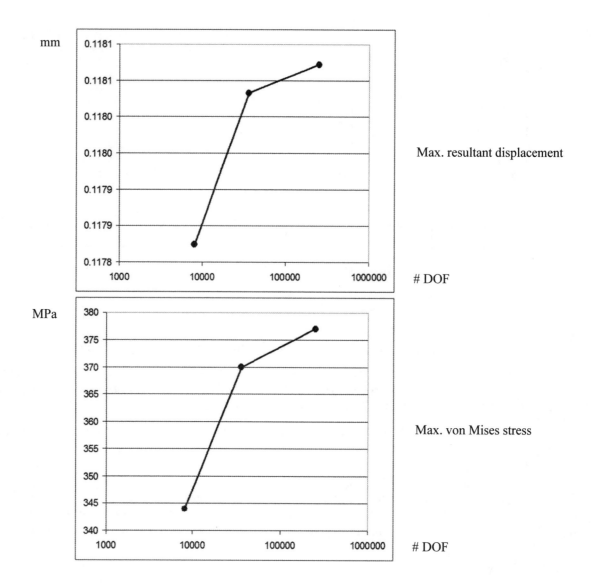

Figure 2-36: Maximum resultant displacement (top) and maximum von Mises stress (bottom).

Both are plotted as a function of the number of degrees of freedom in the model. The three points on the curves correspond to the three models solved. Straight lines connect the three points only to visually enhance the graphs.

Having noticed that the maximum displacement increases with mesh refinement, we can conclude that the model becomes "softer" when smaller elements are used. With mesh refinement, a larger number of elements allows for better approximation of the real displacement and stress field. Therefore, we can say that the artificial restraints imposed by element definition become less imposing with mesh refinement.

Displacements are the primary unknowns in structural FEA, and stresses are calculated based on displacement results. Therefore, stresses also increase with mesh refinement. If we continued with mesh refinement, we would see that both the displacement and stress results converge to a finite value which is the solution of the mathematical model. Differences between the solution of the FEA model and the mathematical model are due to discretization errors, which diminish with mesh refinement.

We will now repeat our analysis of the HOLLOW PLATE by using prescribed displacements in place of a load. Rather than loading it with a 100000N force that caused a 0.118 mm displacement of the loaded face, we will apply a prescribed displacement of 0.118 mm to this face to see what stresses this causes. For this exercise, we will use only one mesh with the default (medium) mesh density.

Define a fourth study, called *prescribed displ*. The easiest way to do this is to copy one of already completed studies, for example study *tensile load 02*. The definition of material properties, the fixed restraint to the left-side end-face and mesh are all identical to the previous design study. We need to delete the current **External Loads** (right-click the load icon and select **Delete**) and apply in its place a prescribed displacement.

To apply the prescribed displacement to the right-side end-face, right-click the **Fixtures** folder and select **Advanced Fixtures** from the pop-up menu. This opens the **Fixture** definition window. Select **On Flat Face** from the **Advanced** menu and define the displacement as shown in Figure 2-37. Check **Reverse direction** to obtain displacement in the tensile direction. Notice that the direction of a prescribed displacement is indicated by a restraint symbol.

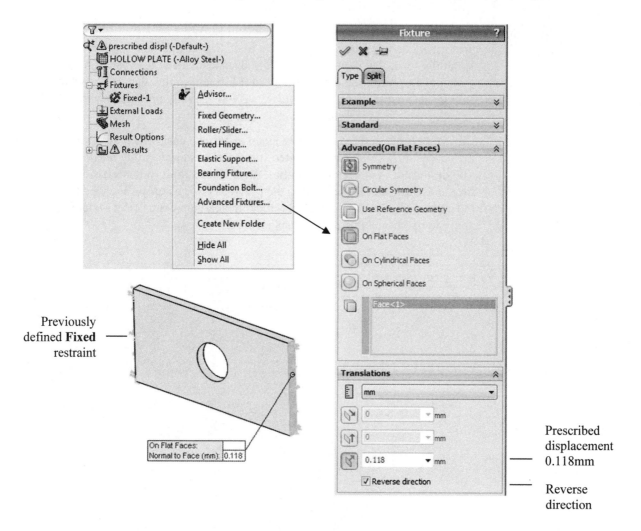

Figure 2-37: Restraint definition window.

The prescribed displacement of 0.118 mm is applied to the same face where the tensile load of 100000N had been applied. Select Reverse Direction and verify that the arrows are pointed away from the selected face.

Once again, notice that the visibility of all loads and restraints symbols is controlled by right-clicking the symbol and making the desired choice (**Hide/Show**). All load symbols and all restraint (fixture) symbols may also be turned on/off all at once by right-clicking the **Fixtures** or **External loads** folders and selecting **Hide all/ Show all** from the pop-up menu.

Once a prescribed displacement is defined to the end face, it overrides any previously applied loads to the same end face. While it is better to delete the load in order to keep the model clean, the load has no effect if a prescribed displacement is applied to the same entity in the same direction.

Figures 2-38 compares stress results for the model loaded with force to the model loaded with prescribed displacement.

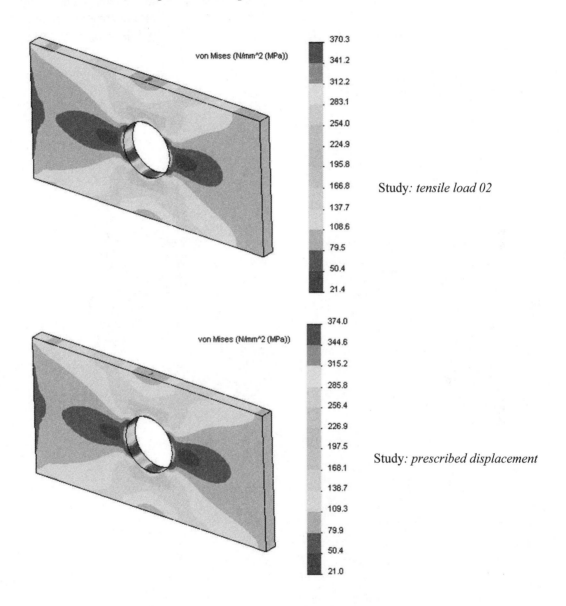

Figure 2-38: Comparison of von Mises stress results.

Von Mises stress results with a load applied as a force (top) and von Mises stress results with a load applied as a prescribed displacement (bottom).

Results produced by applying a force load and by applying a prescribed displacement load are very similar, but not identical. The reason for this discrepancy is that in the model loaded by force, the loaded face does not remain flat. In the prescribed displacement model, this face remains flat, even though it experiences displacement as a whole. Also, while the prescribed displacement of 0.118 mm applies to the entire face in the prescribed displacement model, it is only seen as a maximum displacement in one point in the force load model. You may plot the displacement along the edge of the end face in study *tensile load 02* by following the steps in Figure 2-39.

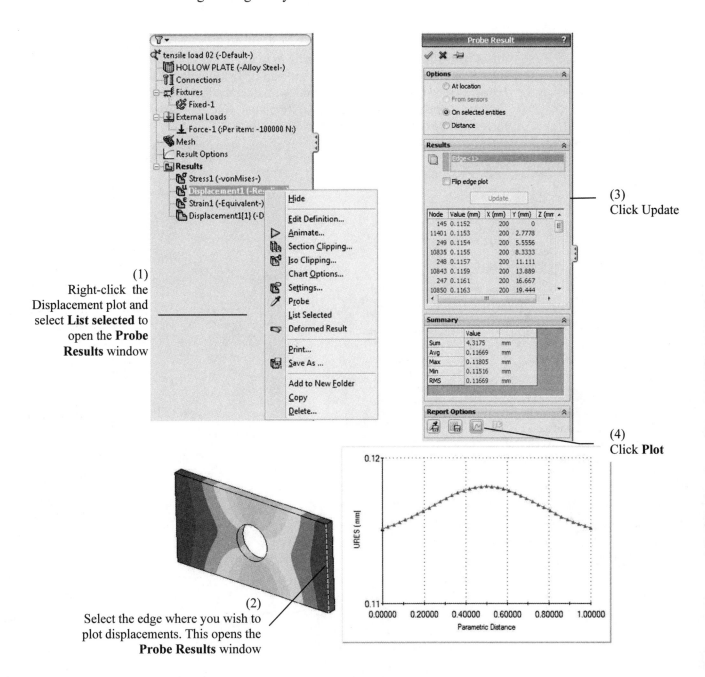

(1)
Right-click the
Displacement plot and
select **List selected** to
open the **Probe
Results** window

(3)
Click Update

(4)
Click **Plot**

(2)
Select the edge where you wish to
plot displacements. This opens the
Probe Results window

Figure 2-39: Plotting displacement along the edge of the force loaded face in study
tensile load 02.

*Right click the resultant displacement plot in the tensile load 02 study to invoke a
pop-up menu shown in the top left corner. Follow steps 1 through 4 to produce a
graph of displacements along the loaded edge. Repeat this exercise for a model
loaded with a prescribed displacement to verify that the displacement is constant
along the edge.*

We conclude the analysis of the HOLLOW PLATE by examining the reaction forces using the results of study *tensile load 02*. In the study *tensile load 02*, right-click the *Results* folder. From the pop-up menu, select **List Result Force** to open the **Result Force** window. Select the face where the fixed restraint is applied and click the **Update** button. Information on reaction forces will be displayed as shown in Figure 2-40.

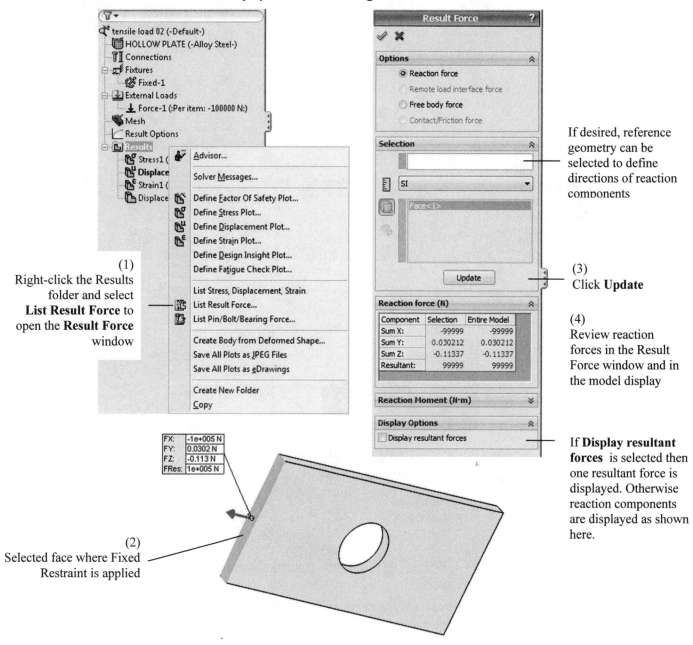

Figure 2-40: Result Force window.

Right-click the Results folder and follow steps 1 through 4 to analyze and display reaction forces. Reaction forces can also be displayed in components other than those defined by the global reference system. To do this, reference geometry such as a plane or axis must be selected.

A note on where **Simulation** results are stored: By default, all study files are saved in the same folder with the **SolidWorks** part or assembly model. Mesh data and results of each study are stored separately in *.CWR files. For example, the mesh and results of study tensile load 02 have been stored in the file: HOLLOW PLATE-tensile load 02.CWR

When the study is opened, the CWR file is extracted into a number of different files depending on the type of study. Upon exiting **SolidWorks Simulation** (which is done by means of deselecting **SolidWorks Simulation** from the list of add-ins, or by closing the **SolidWork**s model), all files are compressed allowing for convenient backup of **SolidWorks Simulation** results.

The location of CWR files is specified in the **Default Options** window (Figure 2-5). For easy reference, the **Default Options** window is shown again in Figure 2-41.

The size of CWR file may be significantly reduced if stresses and strains are deselected in the Results Options (Figure 2-22). We will work with simple models, therefore we won't use this option.

Default Options

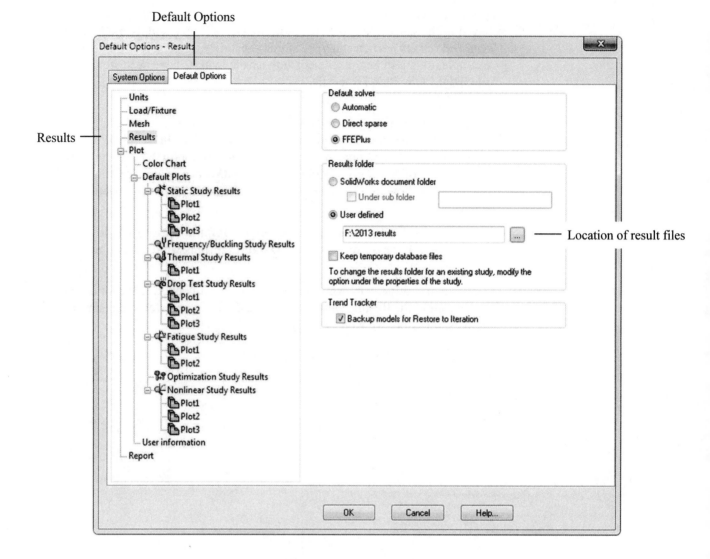

Results

Location of result files

Figure 2-41: Location of solution database files.

*You may use the **SolidWorks** document folder or a user defined folder.*

Using the settings shown in Figure 2-41, *.CWR files are located in folder F:\2013 results. The default location is the **SolidWorks** document folder.

3: Static analysis of an L-bracket

Topics covered

- Stress singularities
- Differences between modeling errors and discretization errors
- Using mesh controls
- Analysis in different **SolidWorks** configurations
- Nodal stresses, element stresses

Project description

An L-shaped bracket (part L BRACKET) is supported and loaded as shown in Figure 3-1. We would like to find the displacements and stresses caused by a 1000N bending load. In particular, we are interested in stresses in the corner where the 2mm fillet is located. Since the radius of the fillet is small compared to the overall size of the model, we decide to suppress it. As will be proven, suppressing the fillet is a bad mistake.

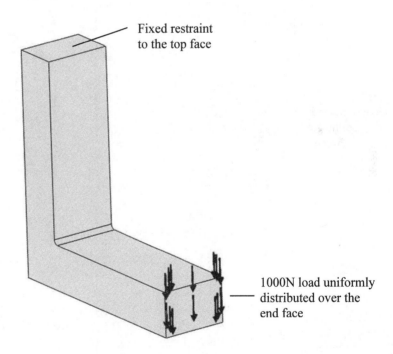

Figure 3-1: Loads and supports applied to the L BRACKET model.

The geometry of the L BRACKET includes a fillet, which will be mistakenly suppressed, leaving in its place a sharp re-entrant edge.

The L BRACKET model has two configurations: *01 sharp edge* and *02 round edge*. The material (Alloy steel) is applied to the **SolidWorks** model and is automatically transferred to **Simulation**.

Procedure

Make sure the model is in configuration *01 sharp edge*. Following the same steps as those described in chapter 2, define a study called *mesh 1* and define a **Fixed** restraint to the top face shown in Figure 3-1. Define the load using the **Force/Torque** window choices shown in Figure 3-2.

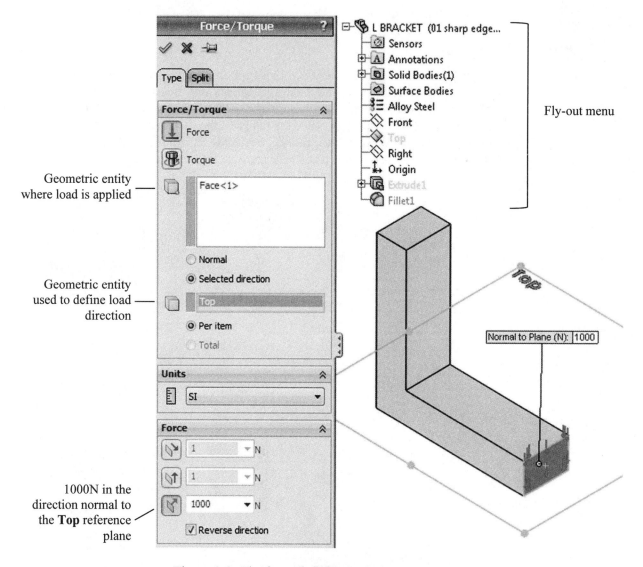

Figure 3-2: The force definition window specifies force in a selected direction. The direction is specified as normal to the Top reference plane.

The Top reference plane is used as a reference to determine the force direction. The reference plane can be conveniently selected from the fly out SolidWorks menu to the right of the Force/Torque window.

Next, make sure the mesh setting is **Standard mesh** and mesh the model with second order tetrahedral elements, accepting the default element size. The finite element mesh is shown in Figure 3-3.

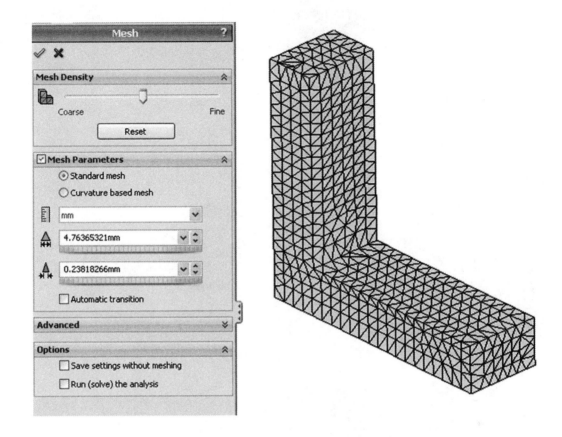

Figure 3-3: The finite element mesh created with the default settings of the automesher.

To show the Mesh menu, right-click the mesh folder. In this mesh, the global element size is 4.76 mm.

The displacement and stress results obtained in the *mesh 1* study are shown in Figure 3-4.

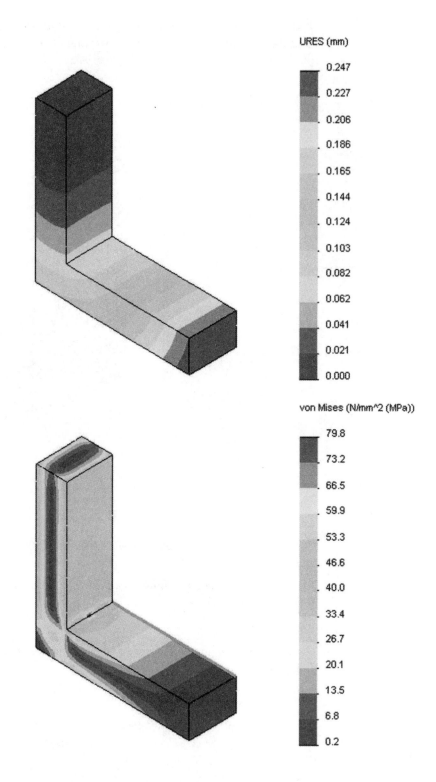

Figure 3-4: Displacement results (top) and von Mises stress results (bottom) produced using study *mesh 1*.

The maximum displacement is 0.247 mm and the maximum von Mises stress is 80 MPa. As explained later, these stress results are meaningless.

Now we will investigate how using smaller elements affects the results. In chapter 2, we did this by refining the mesh uniformly so that the entire model was meshed with elements of a smaller size. Here we will use a different technique. Having noticed that the stress concentration is located near the sharp re-entrant edge, we will refine the mesh locally in that area by applying mesh controls. The element size everywhere else will remain the same as defined previously: 4.76mm.

Copy the *mesh 1* study into a new study, naming it *mesh 2*. Select the edge where mesh controls will be applied, then right-click the *Mesh* folder in the *mesh 2* study dialog (this folder is currently empty) to display the pop-up menu shown in Figure 3-5.

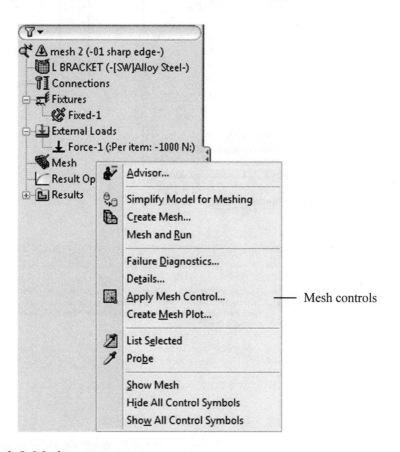

Figure 3-5: Mesh pop-up menu.

Select **Apply Mesh Control…**, which opens the **Mesh Control** window (Figure 3-6). It is also possible to open the **Mesh Control** window first and then select the desired entity or entities (here the re-entrant edge) where mesh controls are being applied.

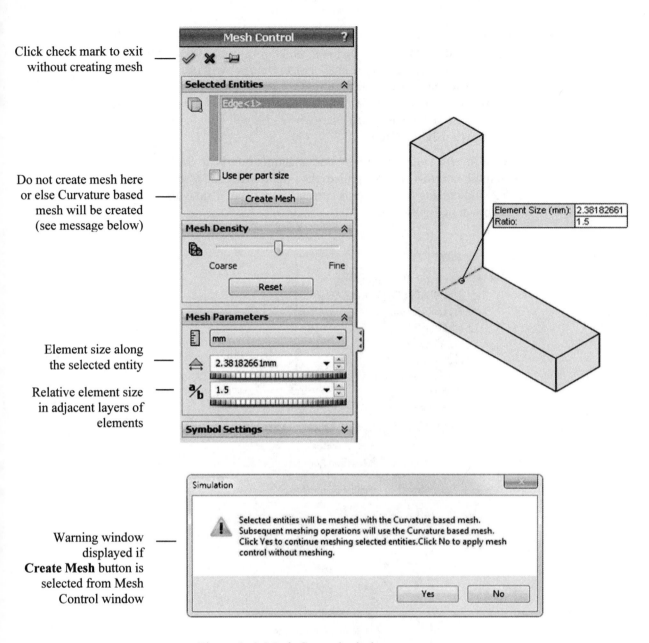

Click check mark to exit without creating mesh

Do not create mesh here or else Curvature based mesh will be created (see message below)

Element size along the selected entity

Relative element size in adjacent layers of elements

Warning window displayed if **Create Mesh** button is selected from Mesh Control window

Figure 3-6: Mesh Control window.

Mesh controls allow for the definition of a local element size on selected entities. Accept the default values of the Mesh Control window.

Click the check mark to exit without creating a mesh.

The element size along the selected edge is now controlled independently of the global element size. **Mesh Control** can also be applied to vertices, faces and to entire components of assemblies. Having defined a **Mesh Control**, create a mesh with the same global element size as before (4.76 mm), while making elements along the specified edge to be 2.38 mm. The added mesh controls display as the **Control-1** icon in the *Mesh* folder and can be edited using the pop-up menu displayed by right-clicking the mesh control icon (Figure 3-7).

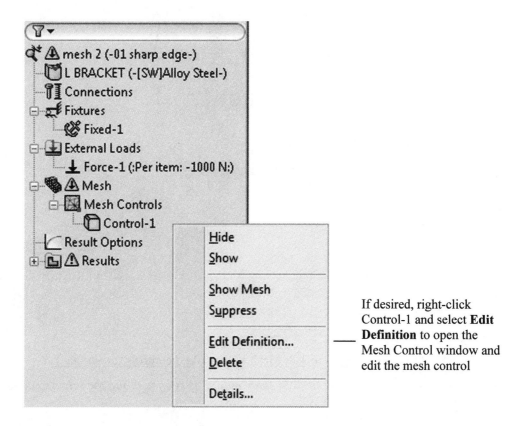

Figure 3-7: Pop-up menu for the mesh control icon.

If desired, right-click Control-1 and select **Edit Definition** to open the Mesh Control window and edit the mesh control

The mesh with applied control (also called mesh bias) is shown in Figure 3-8.

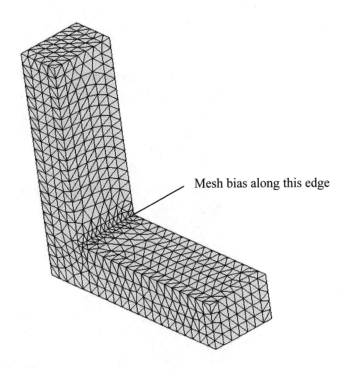

Mesh bias along this edge

Figure 3-8: Mesh with applied controls (mesh bias).

The mesh in study mesh 2 is refined along the selected edge.

The maximum displacements and stress results obtained in study *mesh2* are 2.478 mm and 74.1 MPa respectively. The number of digits shown in a result plot is controlled using **Chart Options** (right-click on a plot and select **Chart Options)**.

Now repeat the same exercise three more times using progressively smaller elements along the sharp re-entrant edge. Create three studies with an element size along the sharp reentrant edge as shown in Figure 3-9.

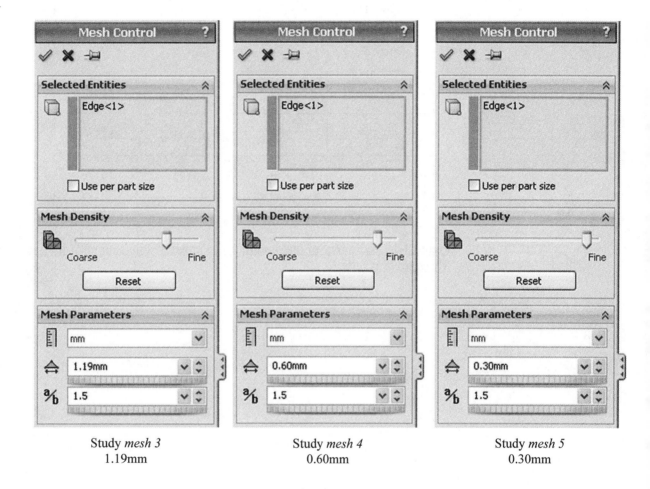

Study *mesh 3*
1.19mm

Study *mesh 4*
0.60mm

Study *mesh 5*
0.30mm

Figure 3-9: Mesh Control windows in studies *mesh3*, *mesh4*, and *mesh5*, defining the element size along the sharp re-entrant edge.

The summary of results of all five studies is shown in Figures 3-10 and 3-11.

Study	Element size along the edge [mm]	Max. resultant displacement [mm]	Max. von Mises stress [MPa]
mesh 1	4.76	0.2478	85.7
mesh 2	2.38	0.2478	73.5
mesh 3	1.19	0.2482	110.6
mesh 4	0.60	0.2484	143.9
mesh 5	0.30	0.2485	197.0

Figure 3-10: Summary of maximum displacement results and maximum von Mises stress results.

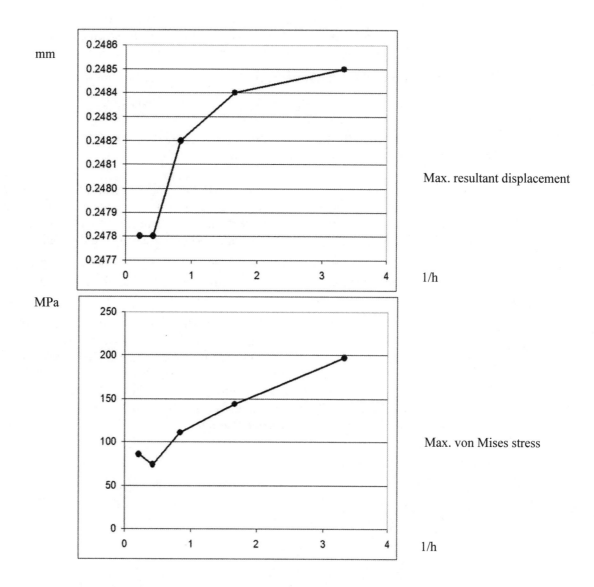

Figure 3-11: Max. resultant displacement (top) and max. von Mises stress (bottom) as a function of 1/h, where h is the element size (Figure 2-16) along the sharp re-entrant edge where the mesh controls were applied.

The local drop in stress magnitude for study mesh 2 is caused by shifting the maximum stress location between studies mesh1 and mesh 2.

Upon examining Figure 3-11, we notice that while each mesh refinement brings about an increase in the maximum displacement, the difference between consecutive results decreases. The increase of displacement in results is so minute that the results need four decimal places to show the difference. The first study, without any mesh refinement provides accurate displacement results.

The stress behaves very differently. Each mesh refinement brings about an increase in the maximum stress. The difference between consecutive results increases, proving that the maximum stress result is divergent.

We could continue with this exercise of progressive mesh refinement either:

❑ Locally, near the sharp re-entrant, as we have done here by means of mesh controls, or

❑ Globally, by reducing the global element size, as we did in chapter 2.

Given enough time and patience, we can produce results showing any stress magnitude we want. All that is necessary is to make the element size small enough! We should avoid a temptation to make any conclusions based on the stress graph in Figure 3-11 because all of these results are meaningless.

The reason for divergent stress results is not that the finite element model is incorrect, but that the finite element model is based on the wrong mathematical model.

According to the theory of elasticity, stress in a sharp re-entrant corner is infinite. A mathematician would say that stress in a sharp re-entrant edge is singular. Stress results along sharp re-entrant edges are completely dependent on mesh size: the smaller the element, the higher the stress. Therefore, we must repeat this exercise after un-suppressing the fillet, which is done by changing from configuration *01 sharp edge* to *02 round edge* in the **SolidWorks Configuration Manager**.

Notice that after we return from the **SolidWorks Configuration Manager** window to the **SolidWorks Simulation** window, all studies pertaining to the model in configuration *01 sharp edge* are not accessible. They can be accessed only if the model configuration is changed back to *01 sharp edge* (Figure 3-12).

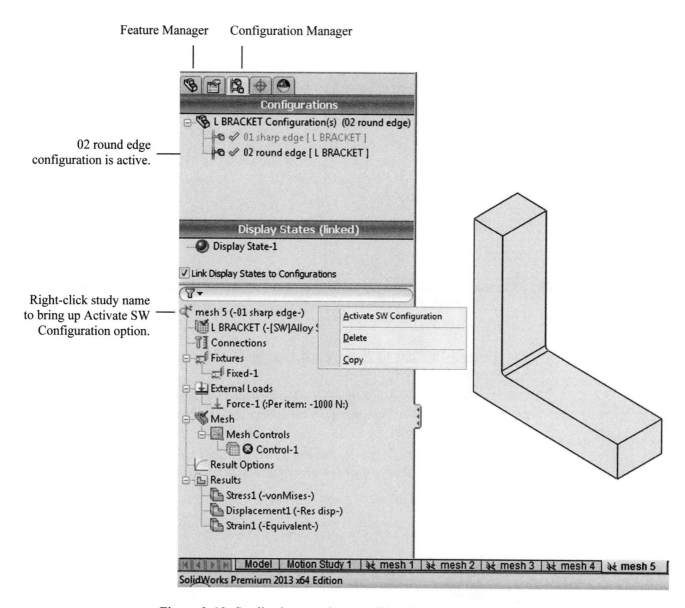

Figure 3-12: Studies become inaccessible when the model configuration is changed to a configuration other than that corresponding to the now grayed-out studies.

Studies mesh 1, mesh 2, mesh 3, mesh 4, and mesh 5 have all been created in configuration 01 sharp edge and are now inaccessible.

The SolidWorks model can be changed to a configuration corresponding to a given study by right-clicking the study icon and selecting Activate SW configuration.

To analyze the bracket with the round fillet, define a study named *round edge*. Copy the *Fixtures* and *External Loads* folders from any inactive studies to the *round edge* study by clicking them and dragging them to the new study tab (Figure 3-13).

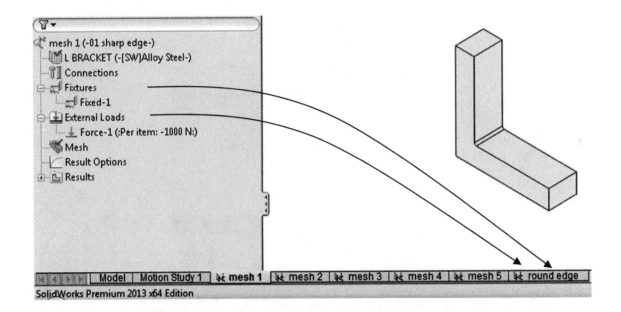

Figure 3-13: Copying *Fixtures* and *External Loads* from study *mesh 2* to *study round edge.*

Entities can be copied between studies by dragging them and dropping them into a study tab as shown, even if the source information is from an inaccessible study.

In some cases, the entire Fixtures or External Loads folders can't be copied but you may still copy the contents of these folders individually.

Meshing with the default element size and **Standard Mesh** properties produces elements with an excessive turn angle in the area where it is particularly important to have a correct mesh (Figure 3-14).

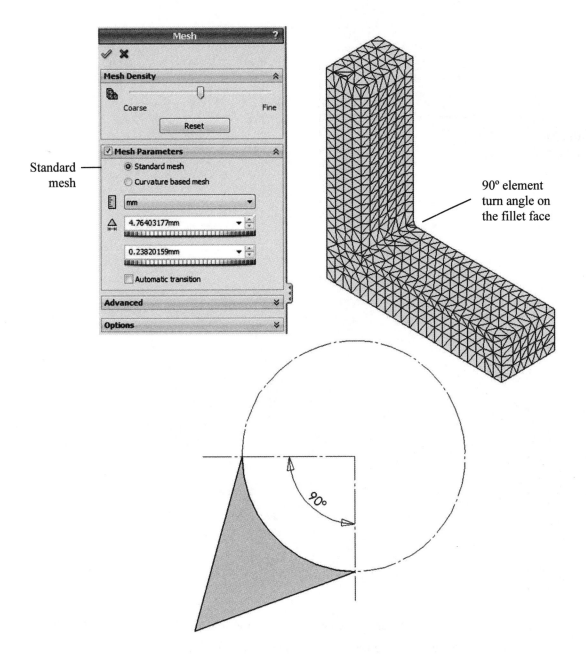

Figure 3-14: A mesh created as a Standard Mesh with a default element size is not acceptable because of the high turn angle.

Here, the turn angle of the element meshing the fillet is 90°. Just one element covers the 90° angle, as shown.

To eliminate excessive turn angles from areas where stresses are of particular interest we use the **Curvature based mesh** option and enter values shown in Figure 3-15.

Curvature based mesh

Maximum element size 5mm

Minimum element size 1mm

Minimum number of elements in a circle 12

Element size growth ratio 1.6

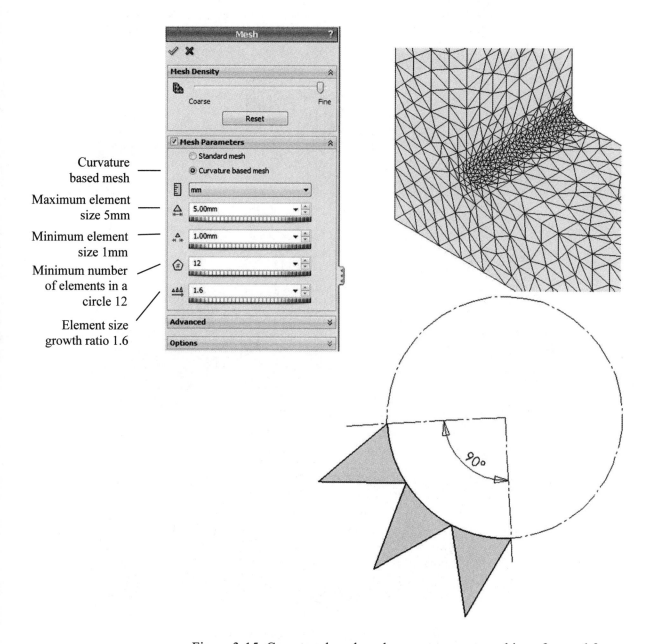

Figure 3-15: Curvature based mesh assures correct meshing of curved faces.

Using the above settings, a minimum of 3 elements are created on a 90° fillet.

With the minimum number of elements in a circle (360°) set to 12, an element turn angle is no more than 360°/12=30°.

The element size growth ratio controls the transition between the refined mesh on curved faces and the coarser mesh on flat faces.

It is generally recommended that the turn angle does not exceed 30° in "sensitive" locations where stresses must be correctly modeled.

The L-BRACKET example is a good place to review the different ways of displaying stress results. Stresses can be presented either as **Node Values** or **Element Values**. To select either node values or element values, right-click the plot icon and select **Edit Definition**. This will open the **Stress Plot** window. Figure 3-16 shows the node values of von Mises stress results produced in the study *02 round edge*.

Node values —

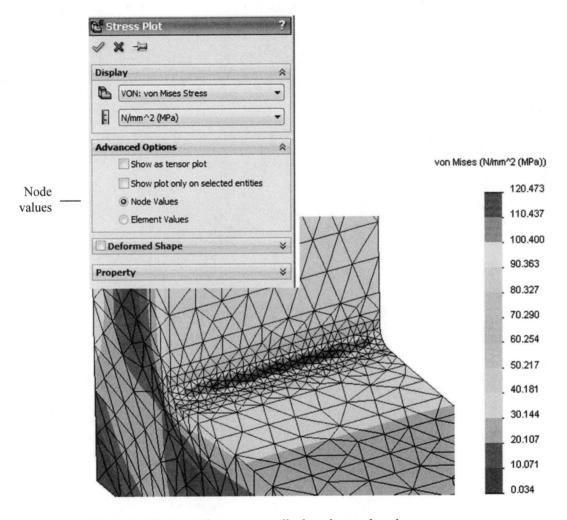

Figure 3-16: Von Mises stresses displayed as node values.

The irregularities in the shape of discrete fringes showing nodal stress results (left) may be used to decide if more mesh refinement is needed in the area of a stress concentration. Here, fairly regular shapes indicate sufficient mesh refinement.

The maximum stress (120MPa) is now bounded. In the convergence process it will converge to a finite value, close to the one shown in Figure 3-16. Again, we must resist temptation to compare this result to the maximum stress results produced by the studies using the sharp re-entrant edge because those results are all meaningless.

Figure 3-17 shows the element values of von Mises stress results produced in the study *02 round edge*.

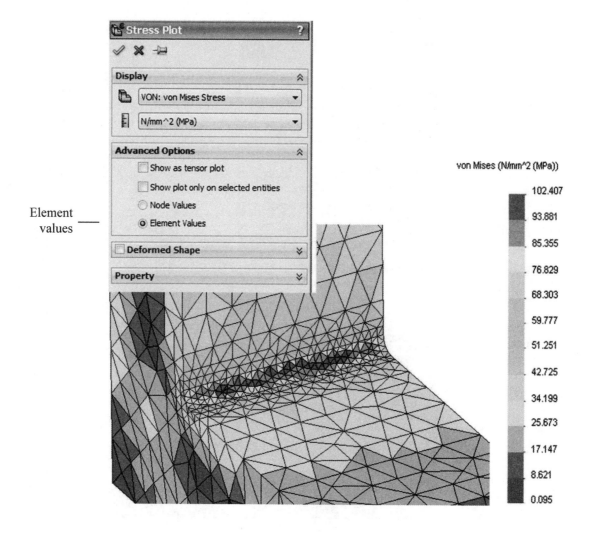

Figure 3-17 Von Mises stresses displayed as element values.

Element values are not averaged across different elements. A single stress value is assigned to each element.

As was explained in chapter 1, nodal displacements are computed first, from which strains and then stresses are calculated. Stresses are first calculated inside the element at certain locations, called Gauss points. Next, stress results are extrapolated to all of the elements' nodes. If one node belongs to more than one element (which is always the case unless it is a vertex node), then the stress results from all the elements sharing a given node are averaged and one stress value, called a node value, is reported for each node. This stress value is called a nodal stress.

An alternate procedure to present stress results is by obtaining stresses at Gauss points, then averaging them in between themselves. This means that one stress value is calculated for the element. This stress value is called an element stress.

Nodal stresses are used more often because they offer smoothed out, continuous stress results. However, examination of element stresses provides important feedback on the quality of the results. If element stresses in two adjacent elements differ too much it indicates that the element size at this location is too large to properly model the stress gradient. By examining the element stresses, we can locate mesh deficiencies without running a convergence analysis.

To decide how much is "too much" of a difference requires some experience. As a general guideline, we can say that if the element values of stress in adjacent elements are apart by several colors on the default color chart (12 colors), then a more refined mesh should be used. You are encouraged to perform a convergence analysis using a **Curvature Based mesh**.

Notes:

4: Static and frequency analyses of a pipe support

Topics covered

- ❑ Use of shell elements
- ❑ Frequency analysis
- ❑ Bearing load

Project description

We will analyze a support bracket (Figure 4-1) with the objective of finding stresses and the first few modes of vibration. This will require running both static and frequency analyses. Open the PIPE SUPPORT model with assigned material properties of Galvanized Steel. Open a new **Static** study and name it *01 static*.

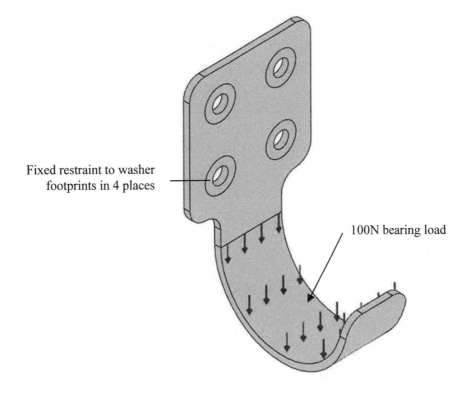

Fixed restraint to washer footprints in 4 places

100N bearing load

Figure 4-1: PIPE SUPPORT model.

Notice that the model has been designed in SolidWorks as sheet metal.

Procedure

Before defining the study, consider that thin wall geometry would be difficult to mesh with solid elements. Generally it is recommended that two layers of second order tetrahedral elements be used across the thickness of a wall undergoing bending. Therefore, a large number of solid elements would be required to mesh this thin model.

A sheet metal model has inherently thin walls. Therefore, when a sheet metal model is presented to **SolidWorks Simulation**, it is by default designated for meshing with shell elements. Having created **Simulation** study *01 static* notice that the familiar *Solid* folder is replaced with a *Shell* folder (Figure 4-2).

 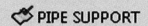

Solid folder from chapter 2   Shell folder in this exercise

Figure 4-2: The solid folder in the study from chapter 2, and the shell folder in the present study.

The presence of the Shell folder indicates that the model will be meshed with shell elements.

If solid elements are preferred after all, the default designation **Shell** can be changed to **Solid** as shown in Figure 4-3.

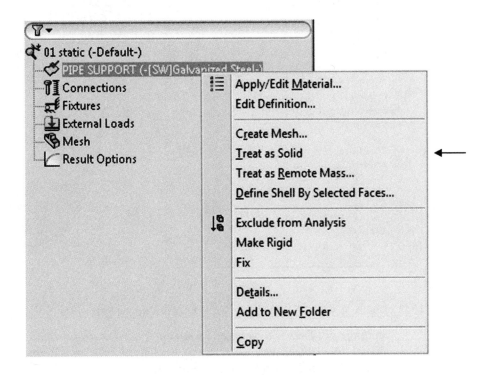

Figure 4-3: Changing from Shell elements to Solid elements.

If you would prefer to mesh the sheet metal model with solid elements, right click the Shell folder and select Treat as Solid. This exercise uses shell elements and this illustration is for information only.

Apply a fixed restraint to the four washer footprints, as shown in Figure 4-1. Review the split lines in the **SolidWorks** model that define split faces where restraints are applied. Split faces are commonly used in preparation of CAD models for analysis with **SolidWorks Simulation**.

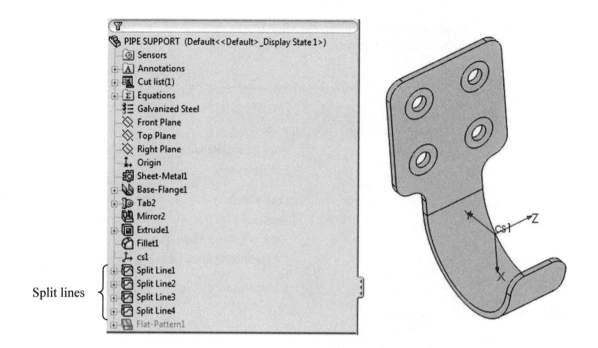

Split lines

<u>Figure 4-4: Split lines and a local coordinate system in the SolidWorks model.</u>

Adding split lines is a technique frequently used in preparation of a CAD model for analysis with FEA. In this model, the split lines define the faces where the bearing load and restraints are applied.

Apply the **Fixed** restraints as shown in Figure 4-1.

The total load carried by the hanger is 100N in the *x* direction of the local coordinate system **cs1**. We will approximate the load of a pipe onto the hanger by applying a **Bearing Load**. Right-click the *External Loads* folder and select **Bearing Load** from the pop-up menu. Select the cylindrical face where the load is to be applied, and then select **cs1** as the reference coordinate system using the *fly-out* menu (shown previously in figure 3-2) and apply 100N in the *x* direction of that coordinate system (Figure 4-5).

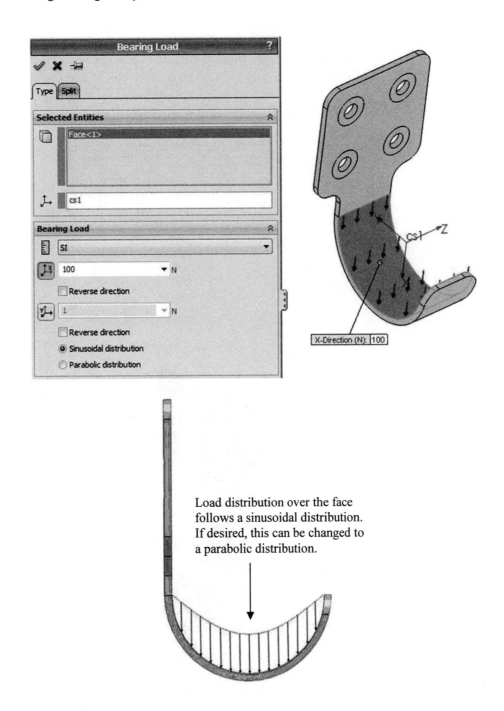

Figure 4-5: Bearing Load definition.

A bearing load can only be applied to a cylindrical face. It is not uniformly distributed over the face but follows a sinusoidal or parabolic distribution. A typical application of a Bearing Load is modeling interactions between shafts and housings.

The model is now ready for meshing (right-click the *Mesh* folder, **Create Mesh**). Use the default element size. The shell element mesh is shown in Figure 4-6.

System Options

Shell bottom face color

Figure 4-6: A shell element mesh. Mesh elements have been placed on a mid-surface defined between the outer faces defining the thin wall.

Different colors distinguish between the top and bottom of the shell elements. The bottom face color is specified in the System Options window as shown above. The top face color is the same as the color of the SolidWorks model.

In this model the side opposite to where the load is applied is meshed with shell element tops. The side where the load is applied is meshed with the bottoms of shell elements. The side where the load is applied appears with a color specified in **Shell bottom face color** in the **Simulation Options** window.

Review the mesh colors to ensure that the shell elements are aligned. Try reversing the shell element orientation: select the face where you want to reverse the orientation, right-click the Mesh folder to display a pop-up menu, and select **Flip shell elements** (Figure 4-7).

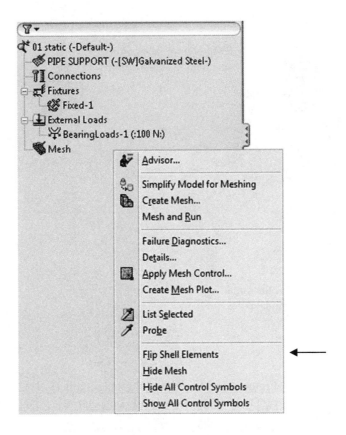

Figure 4-7: The pop-up menu for modifying shell element orientation.

If desired, you may reverse shell element orientation with this menu choice. In this exercise reversing shell element orientation is not required.

Misaligned shell elements lead to the creation of erroneous plots like the one shown in Figure 4-8, which shows a rectangular plate undergoing bending; this is unrelated to the PIPE SUPPORT exercise, however is brought to the reader's attention.

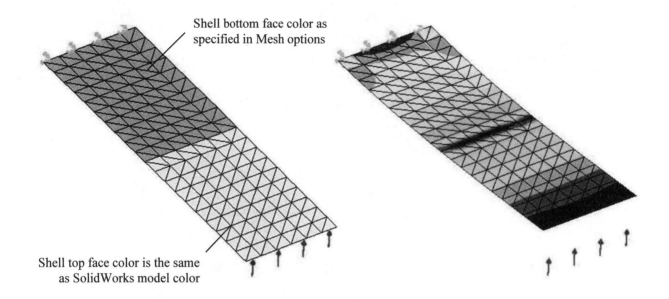

Shell bottom face color as specified in Mesh options

Shell top face color is the same as SolidWorks model color

Figure 4-8: Misaligned shell elements (left) and erroneous von Mises Stress plot (right) resulting from shell element misalignment.

The misaligned shell element mesh (left) and erroneous von Mises Stress plot are the result of shell element misalignment.

Obtain the solution and display the displacement results. Select the **Superimpose model on the deformed shape** option. This option is available in plot settings (Figure 4-9).

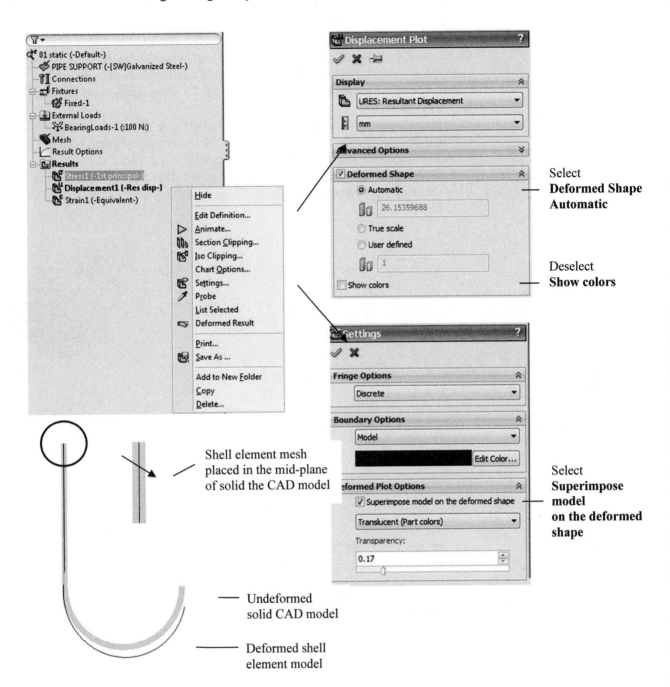

Shell element mesh placed in the mid-plane of solid the CAD model

Undeformed solid CAD model

Deformed shell element model

Figure 4-9: The undeformed model is superimposed on the deformed shape.

This plot clearly shows that the shell element mesh has been placed in the mid-plane of the solid in the CAD model. The plot shows the deformation of the model. The Show color option has been deselected, therefore the color legend is not showing.

Shell elements differentiate between stress results on the top and bottom of the element. In the case of bending, one side will show tensile stress, the other compressive stress. For correct interpretation of results we must know on which side of the element results are presented. To illustrate this, we prepare two stress plots:

P1 stress (maximum principal stress) on the tensile side of the model. The tensile side corresponds to the bottom of the shell elements (Figure 4-10)

P3 stress (minimum principal stress) on the compressive side of the model. The compressive side corresponds to the top of the shell elements. Notice that P3 is the maximum compressive stress (Figure 4-11).

Bottom
selected

Figure 4-10: Maximum principle stress (P1) results for the bottom faces of the shell elements - on the tensile side of the model. This is the visible side.

Information on the element side is shown in Plot details. This can be turned off in Chart Options.

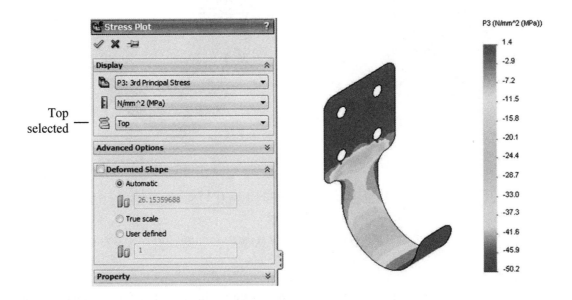

Top
selected

Figure 4-11: Minimum principle stress (P3) results for the top faces of the shell elements - on the compressive side of the model. This is the back side, invisible in this illustration.

In Figure 4-10 we are looking at the bottom faces of the shell elements. Still, stress results are displayed for the top side (which is "underneath" the model) of the elements, as if the shells were transparent. What stress is visible (top or bottom) does not depend on view direction (which side is visible) but only on the selection made in the **Stress Plot** window. Stress plots showing results produced by shell element models may be confusing because the model behaves as if it was transparent; results pertaining to top side of elements can be seen from the bottom side and vice versa.

This confusion may be avoided if shell thickness is rendered on the stress plot. This option is available in **Advanced Options** of the stress plot. Figure 4-12 demonstrates this using the P1 stress plot as an example.

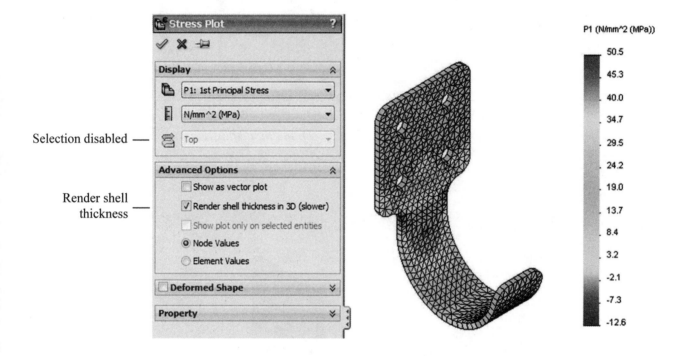

Figure 4-12: Maximum principle stress (P1) shown with shell thickness rendered.

Rotate the stress plot to see that results are now shown differently on the inside and the outside of the model.

Figure 4-12 now shows P1 stress results with a rendered thickness of the shell element mesh. Notice that the elements look like prisms because the mesh shown in this illustration has an appearance of a 3D mesh. In reality this is the result of 3D rendering on the shell element mesh.

Remember that the stress distribution through that rendered thickness shown in Figure 4-12 does not show a distribution of bending stress, it shows the distribution of P1 stress. To see how bending stress changes across the thickness would require a plot of directional stresses such as SX, SY, SZ. These directional stresses are aligned by default with the global coordinate system. To show the distribution of bending stresses in the curved portion of the model we need to align them with an axis that defines the local cylindrical coordinate system. After the alignment, SX becomes radial stress, SY becomes circumferential stress and SZ becomes axial stress (Figure 4-13).

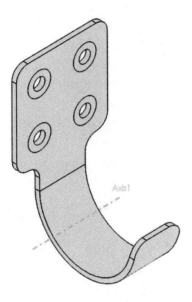

Default	Aligned with axis
SX	Radial
SY	Circumferential
SZ	Axial

Figure 4-13: Alignment of directional stresses with an axis defining a local cylindrical system.

Directional stresses may be also aligned with a coordinate system or a reference plane in which case stress components are defined in a local Cartesian coordinate system.

To show the distribution of bending stress in the curved portion of the model, use SY stress and align the plot with Axis1 as shown in Figure 4-14.

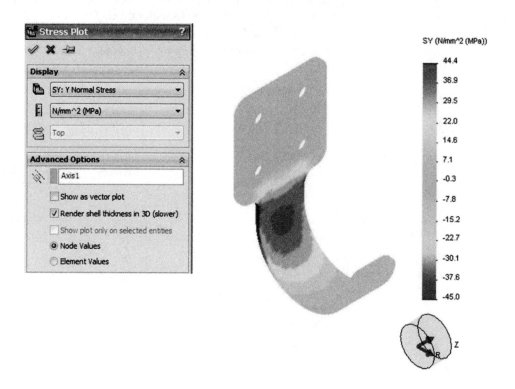

Figure 4-14: Stress plot SY aligned with Axis1, shell thickness is rendered. Circumferential stress can be seen as changing from compressive -45MPa on the back of side the model to tensile 44.4Mpa on the front side of the model.

Notice the symbol in the lower right corner; it indicates that stresses have been aligned with a local cylindrical coordinate system.

The distribution of bending stress across the shell element thickness may also be shown without rendering shell element thickness but that requires two plots as shown in Figure 4-15 and Figure 4-16. These plots use vectors to show the line and direction of stress. Remember that as opposed to von Mises stress which is a scalar entity, directional stresses are vectors.

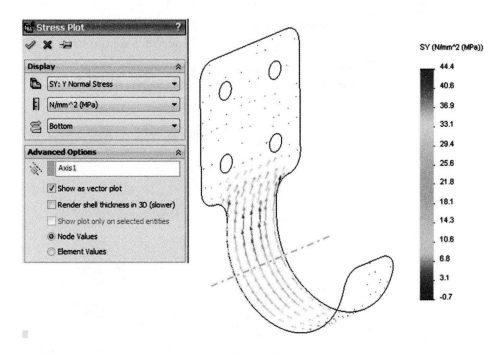

Figure 4-15: Stress plot SY aligned with Axis1, shown on the front side of the model. This is the tensile side, so stresses are positive.

The cylindrical coordinate system symbol is not shown.

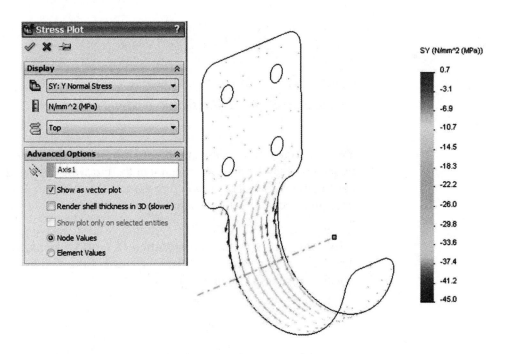

Figure 4-16: Stress plot SY aligned with Axis1, shown on the back side of the model. This is the compressive side, so stresses are negative.

The cylindrical coordinate system symbol is not shown.

The structural analysis of the support bracket has been completed. We now proceed to calculate natural frequencies for the same bracket.

This requires a frequency analysis also known as modal analysis. Create a new study and name it *02 modal* (Figure 4-17).

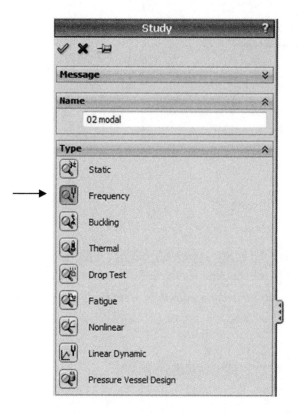

Figure 4-17: Frequency study definition.

This type of analysis is also known as Modal analysis.

You can copy restraints and mesh definitions from the static study to the frequency study by dropping them into the frequency study tab. No loads are defined in this frequency study. We assume that loads, if any are present, will not significantly affect the natural frequencies.

In the properties of the **Frequency** study, verify that five modes will be calculated (Figure 4-18). In **Simulation Default Options**, verify that displacement plots are automatically created in the *Results* folder for all calculated modes (Figure 4-19).

Specify five frequencies ————

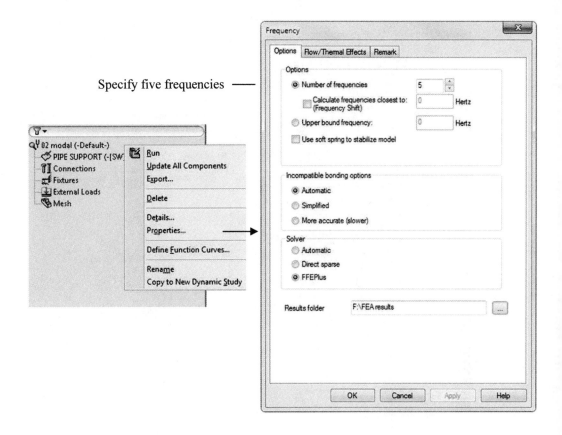

Figure 4-18: Properties of a frequency study.

Five frequencies are calculated by default, meaning that five frequencies and five corresponding shapes of vibration will be calculated. Frequency and the corresponding shape are jointly called a mode of vibration.

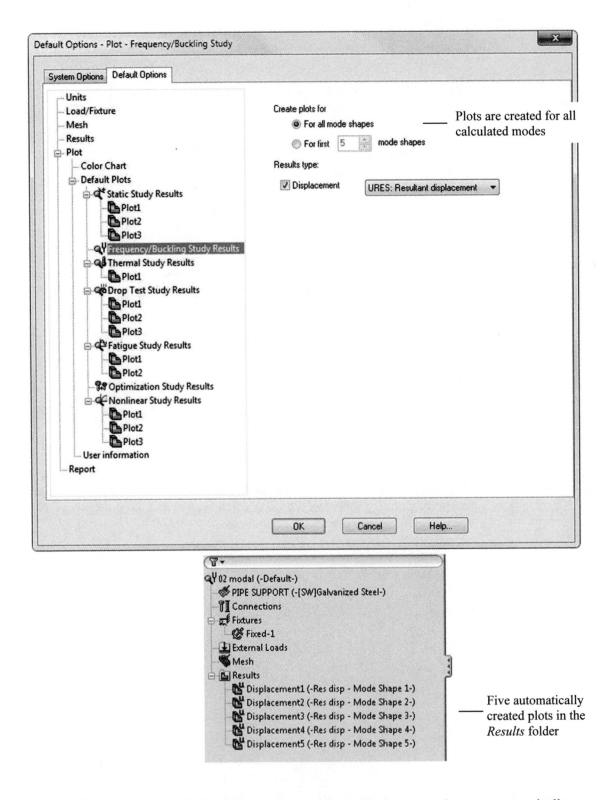

Run the solution and verify that five displacement plots are in the *Results* folder. Right-click any displacement plot and select **Edit Definition** to open the **Mode Shape/Displacement Plot** panel. Try displaying the mode shape plot with and without colors by making the appropriate selection shown in Figure 4-20.

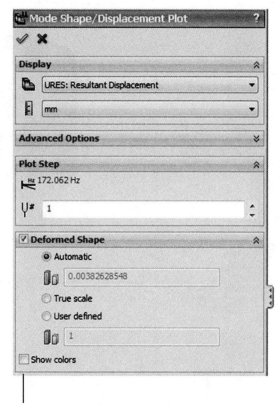

It is better not to show colors in frequency analysis results to avoid displaying confusing information

Figure 4-20: Mode Shape/Displacement Plot definition window.

You can switch between Mode Shape and Displacement plot showing or hiding colors. However, you must remember that absolute displacements values are meaningless. Only ratios between displacements in the same mode are valid.

Figure 4-21 shows the first mode of vibration presented as a mode shape and as a displacement plot.

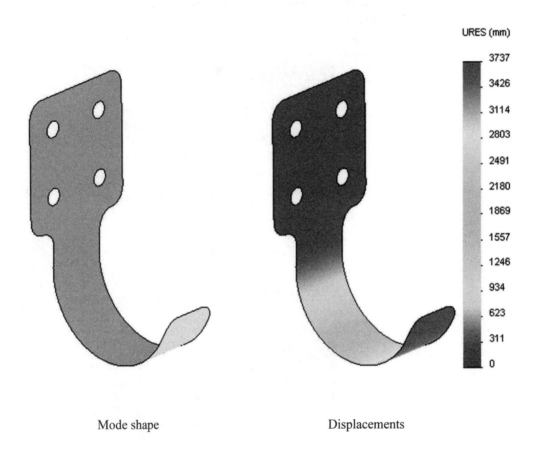

Mode shape   Displacements

Figure 4-21 Mode shape plot and Displacement plot.

Both plots show the vibration frequency associated with this mode, here 172Hz. Numerical results shown in the displacement plot are meaningless, therefore displacements plots have little use in presenting results of frequency analyses.

Even though the displacement plot does show displacement magnitude, the absolute displacement results are meaningless. Displacement results are purely qualitative and can be used only for a comparison of displacements within the same mode of vibration. Relative comparisons of displacements between different modes is invalid.

One of the worst errors an FEA user can make is to take displacement results from a modal analysis for their face value!

Examine deformation plots of higher modes (Figure 4-22) to notice that higher modes are associated with more deformation. The best way to analyze the results of a frequency analysis is by examining the animated deformation plots.

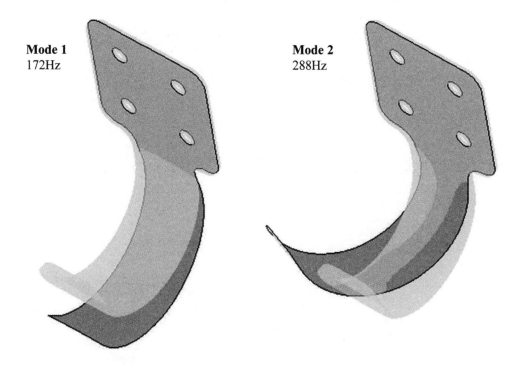

Mode 1
172Hz

Mode 2
288Hz

Figure 4-22: Deformation plots showing the shape of deformation (mode shape) of the first two modes.

SolidWorks Simulation results plots can be viewed more than one at a time using the SolidWorks split window technique. The deformation scale in these plots has been adjusted to better show the deformed shape superimposed on the undeformed shape.

To animate any plot, right-click an active plot icon to display an associated pop-up menu, and then select **Animate**.

To **List Resonance Frequencies**, right-click the *Results* folder and make the selection as shown in Figure 4-23.

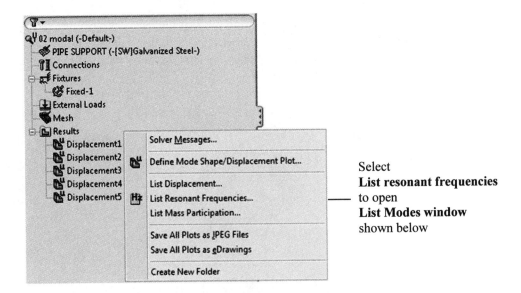

Select
List resonant frequencies
to open
List Modes window
shown below

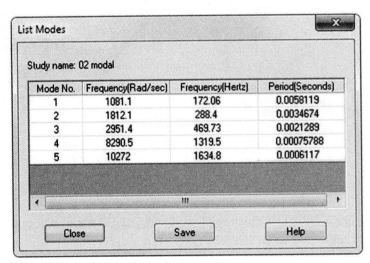

Figure 4-23: The summary of frequency results includes the list of all calculated modal (resonant) frequencies.

The **List Modes** window in Figure 4-18 presents results of the calculated frequencies in three different ways:

❑ ω - circular (or angular) frequency [rad/s]

❑ f - frequency (cycles per second) [Hz]

❑ T - vibration period [s]

Circular frequency, frequency and period are related as follows:

$$f = \frac{1}{T} \qquad \omega = 2\pi f \qquad T = \frac{1}{f}$$

Notes:

5: Static analysis of a link

Topics covered

- ❏ Symmetry boundary conditions
- ❏ Preventing rigid body motions
- ❏ Limitations of the small displacements theory

Project description

We need to calculate displacements and stresses of the link shown in Figure 5-1. The link is supported by tight-fitting pins in the two end holes and is loaded by a loose fitting pin at the central hole with a force of 30000N. The other two holes are not loaded. Open part file LINK. It has been assigned the material properties of Chrome Stainless Steel.

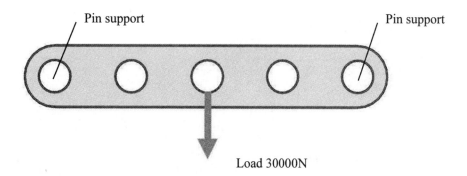

Figure 5-1: CAD model of the link.

Notice that the supporting pins and the loaded pin are not present in the model. All chamfered edges have no structural significance and will be suppressed to simplify meshing.

Procedure

One way to conduct this analysis would be to model both the link and all three pins, and then conduct an analysis of the assembly. However, we are not interested in the contact stresses that will develop between the pins and the link. Our focus is on displacements and stresses that will develop in the link. Therefore the analysis can be simplified; instead of modeling the pins, we can simulate their effects by properly defining restraints and loads. Notice that the link geometry, restraints, and loads are all symmetrical. We can take advantage of this symmetry and analyze only half of the model, replacing the other half with symmetry boundary conditions.

To work with half of the model, switch to the *02 half model* configuration using the **Configuration Manager**. This also suppresses all the small chamfers in the model. The chamfers have negligible structural effect and would unnecessarily complicate the mesh. Removing geometric details deemed unnecessary for analysis is called defeaturing.

Finally, notice a split face in the middle hole that defines the area where the load will be applied. The geometry in FEA-ready form is shown in Figure 5-2. Figure 5-2 also explains how the restraints should be applied.

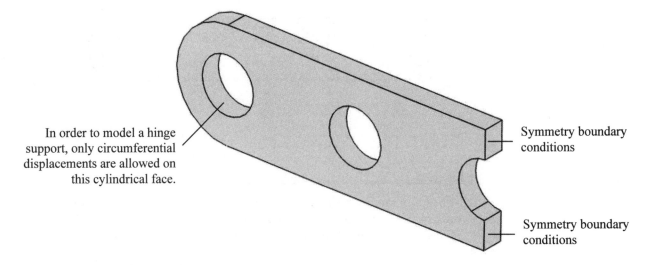

In order to model a hinge support, only circumferential displacements are allowed on this cylindrical face.

Symmetry boundary conditions

Symmetry boundary conditions

Figure 5-2: Half of the link with restraints explained.

The applied restraints: a hole where the pin support is simulated and two faces in the plane of symmetry where symmetry boundary conditions are required.

The model is ready for the definition of restraints – the highlight of this exercise. Move to **SolidWorks Simulation** and define a static study.

Right-click the *Fixtures* folder and select **Fixed Hinge** from the pop-up menu. This opens the **Fixture** window with the **Fixed Hinge** button already selected (Figure 5-3). This restraint simulates hinge support.

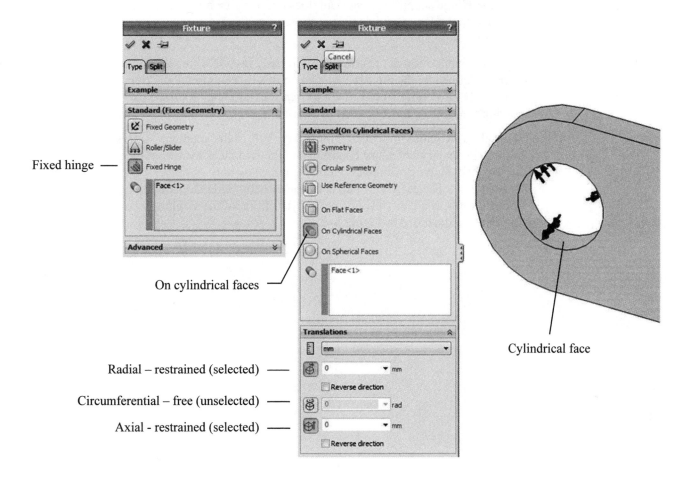

Fixed hinge

On cylindrical faces

Radial – restrained (selected)

Circumferential – free (unselected)

Axial - restrained (selected)

Cylindrical face

Figure 5-3: The fixture window defining hinge support.

An identical restraint can be obtained using either Hinge or On Cylindrical Face (with suppressed radial and axial directions). Once the Fixture definition window has been opened, you can move between different types of restraints. You are not committed by the selection made in the pop-up menu choice.

When the **Fixture** definition window specifies the restraint type as **Hinge** or **On cylindrical face**, the restraint directions are associated with the directions of the cylindrical face (radial, circumferential, and axial), rather than with global directions x, y, and z.

To simulate a pin support that allows the link to rotate about the pin axis, radial displacements need to be restrained and circumferential displacements allowed. Furthermore, displacements in the axial direction need to be restrained in order to avoid any rigid body motions of the entire link along this direction.

Using the **Hinge** support is easier but does not describe how the restraint functions, so the **On cylindrical face** restraint method is used here instead for clarification.

Notice that while we must restrict the rigid body motion of the link in the direction defined by the pin axis, we can do this by restraining any point of the model. It is simply convenient to remove rigid body motions by applying the axial restraints to this cylindrical face.

To simulate the entire link, even though only half of the geometry is present, we apply symmetry boundary conditions to the two faces located in the plane of symmetry. Symmetry boundary conditions allow only in-plane displacements. The easiest way to define symmetry boundary conditions is to use **Symmetry** as a type of restraint. The definition of the symmetry boundary conditions is illustrated in Figure 5-4.

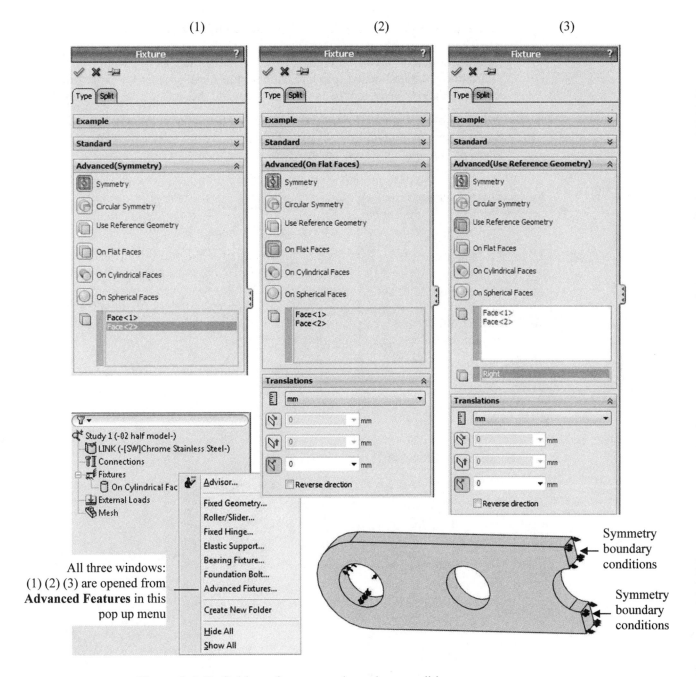

Figure 5-4: Definition of symmetry boundary conditions.

Three ways of defining the same symmetry condition are shown (the user may select which option he/she prefers):

(1) Symmetry restraint.

(2) On Flat Face restraint where both in-plane displacements are allowed, but displacement in the direction normal to the face is set to zero.

(3) Use Reference Geometry where free and restrained directions are defined with reference to selected reference geometry (here, the Right reference plane). The reference plane can be selected from the fly-out menu which is not shown here.

Recall from Figure 5-1 that the link is loaded with 30000N. Since we are modeling half of the link, we must apply a 15000N load to a portion of the cylindrical face, as shown in Figure 5-5. The size of the load application area is arbitrarily created with a split line. It should be close to what we expect the contact area to be between the loose fitting pin and the link.

When defining the load (Figure 5-5), take advantage of **SolidWorks'** fly-out menu visible in the **SolidWorks Simulation** window to select the reference plane required in the **Force/Torque** definition window.

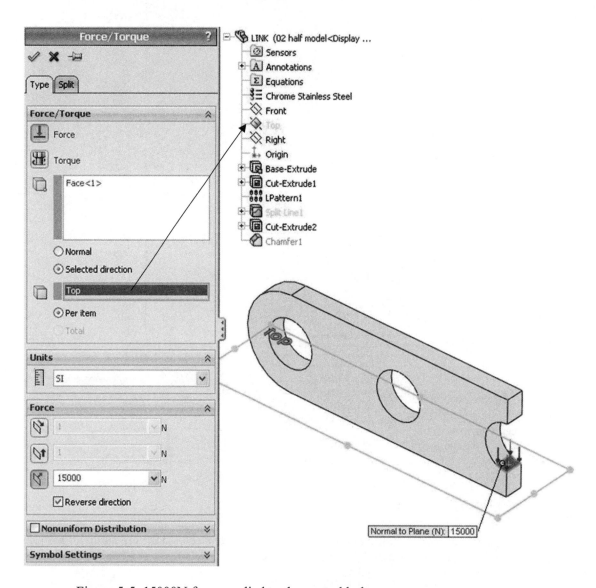

Figure 5-5: 15000N force applied to the central hole.

Force is applied in the selected direction. The Top reference plane is used to determine the load direction. Notice that the load is distributed uniformly. We are not trying to simulate a contact stress problem.

The final task of model preparation is meshing. Right-click the *Mesh* folder to display the related pop-up menu, and then select **Create Mesh...** Verify that the mesh preferences are set on high quality (meaning that second order elements will be created) and mesh the geometry using the default element size. For more information on the created mesh, you may wish to review the **Mesh Details** (Figure 5-6).

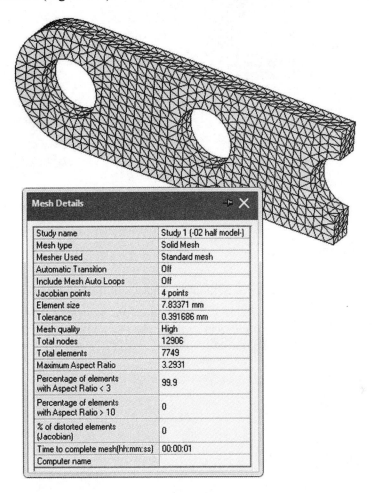

Mesh Details	
Study name	Study 1 (-02 half model-)
Mesh type	Solid Mesh
Mesher Used	Standard mesh
Automatic Transition	Off
Include Mesh Auto Loops	Off
Jacobian points	4 points
Element size	7.83371 mm
Tolerance	0.391686 mm
Mesh quality	High
Total nodes	12906
Total elements	7749
Maximum Aspect Ratio	3.2931
Percentage of elements with Aspect Ratio < 3	99.9
Percentage of elements with Aspect Ratio > 10	0
% of distorted elements (Jacobian)	0
Time to complete mesh(hh:mm:ss)	00:00:01
Computer name	

Figure 5-6: The meshed model shown together with the Mesh Details window.

After solving the model, we first need to check if the pin support and symmetry boundary conditions have been applied properly. This includes checking whether the link can rotate around the pin and whether it behaves as a half of the whole link. This is best done by examining the animated displacements, preferably with the undeformed shape visible (Figure 5-7).

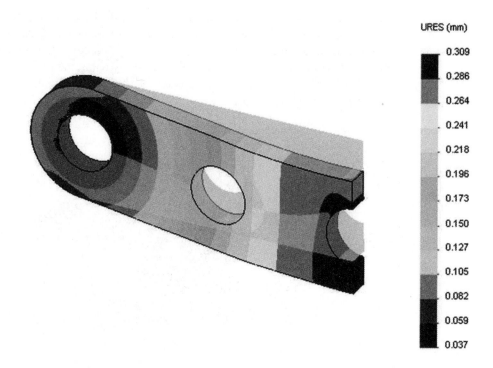

Figure 5-7: Comparison of the deformed and undeformed shapes.

Comparison of the deformed and undeformed shapes verifies the correctness of the applied restraints; the link rotates around the imaginary pin while faces in the plane of symmetry remain flat and perform only in-plane translations.

To conclude this exercise, review the stress results. Examine the different stress components, including the maximum principal stresses, minimum principal stresses, etc.

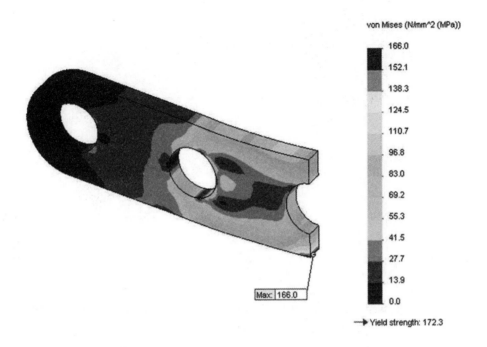

Figure 5-8: Sample of stress results: von Mises stress.

In this plot, the location of the maximum stress is shown, as requested in the Chart Options window.

Repeat this exercise using the full model to perform an analysis of the complete model without using symmetry boundary conditions.

Before finishing the analysis of LINK, we should notice that the link supported by two pins as modeled in this exercise corresponds to the configuration shown in Figure 15-23, where one of the hinges is supported by rollers and is free to move horizontally.

Since linear analysis does not account for changes in model stiffness during the deformation process (nor does it account for material yielding), linear analysis is unable to model stresses that would have developed if both pins were in a fixed position. If both pins were fixed, a nonlinear geometry analysis would be required to analyze the model. Refer to chapter 15 for more information on non-linear analyses.

Notes:

6: Frequency analysis of a tuning fork and a plastic part

Topics covered

- ❑ Frequency analysis with and without supports
- ❑ Rigid body modes
- ❑ The role of supports in frequency analysis
- ❑ Symmetric and anti-symmetric modes

Project description

Structures have preferred frequencies of vibration, called resonant frequencies. A mode of vibration is the shape in which a structure will vibrate at a given natural frequency. The only factor controlling the amplitude of vibration in resonance is damping. While any structure has an infinite number of resonant frequencies and associated modes of vibration, only a few of the lowest modes are important when analyzing response to dynamic loading. A frequency analysis is used to calculate these resonant frequencies and their associated modes of vibration.

Open the part file called TUNING FORK. It has material properties already assigned (Chrome Stainless Steel). The model is shown in Figure 6-1.

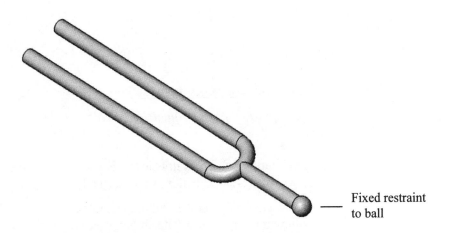

Fixed restraint to ball

Figure 6-1: The TUNING FORK model.

A fixed restraint is applied to the surface of the ball. Do not apply an "On spherical face" restraint.

A quick inspection of the CAD geometry reveals a sharp re-entrant edge. This condition renders the geometry unsuitable for stress analysis, but is acceptable for frequency analysis unless the omitted fillet significantly changes the model stiffness.

Procedure

Define a **Frequency** study called *tuning fork*. Once the study has been created right-click it to open a pop-up menu and select Properties (Figure 6-2).

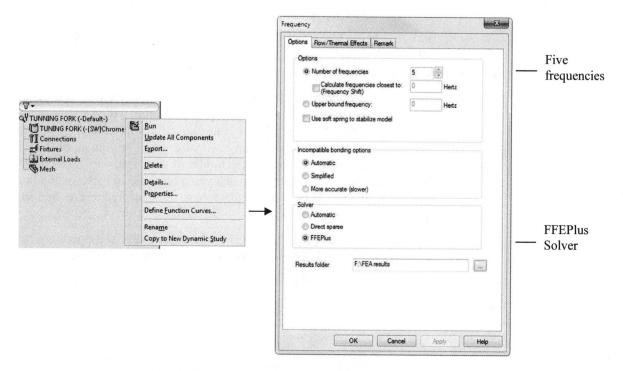

Figure 6-2: Frequency study definition (left) and study properties (right).

We request that five frequencies be calculated using the FFEPlus solver.

Next, define fixed restraints to the ball surface, as shown in Figure 6-1. This approximates the situation when the TUNING FORK is held with two fingers.

Finally, mesh the model with the default element size. The meshed model is shown in Figure 6-3. The automesher selects the element size to satisfy the requirements of a stress analysis. A frequency analysis is less demanding on the mesh, so generally, a less refined mesh is acceptable. Nevertheless, since this is a very simple model, we accept the mesh without making any attempt at simplify it.

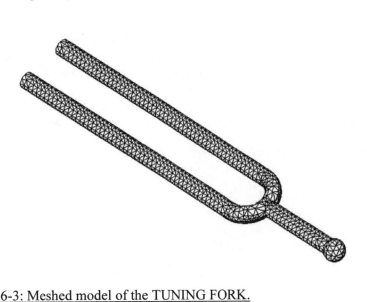

Figure 6-3: Meshed model of the TUNING FORK.

Sharp re-entrant edges are present in the model which is acceptable for frequency analysis if their omission does not significantly change the model's stiffness. Sharp reentrant edges will not cause a singularity in the solution for modes of vibration.

After the solution is complete, **SolidWorks Simulation** automatically creates displacement plots (Figure 6-4). For reasons already explained in chapter 4, we ignore displacement results. Using the **Mode Shape/ Displacement** window we deselect colors, turning the displacement plot into a deformation plot. We call the **Displacement** plot without colors a **Mode Shape** plot.

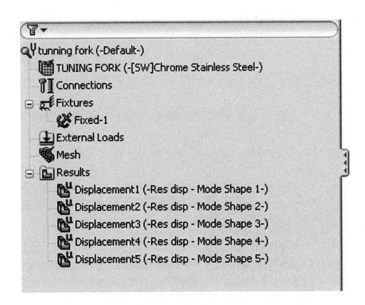

Figure 6-4: Five Displacement plots are created automatically.

Plot Displacement1 shows Mode Shape 1 etc.

The **Mode Shape** plot in the modal analysis shows the associated modal shape of vibration and lists the corresponding natural frequency. The first four modes of vibration are presented in Figure 6-5.

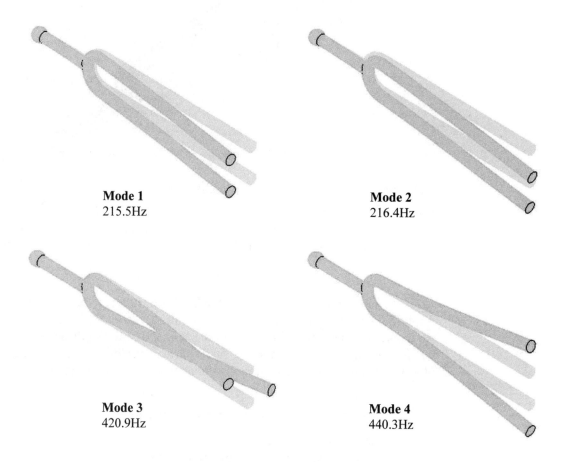

Mode 1
215.5Hz

Mode 2
216.4Hz

Mode 3
420.9Hz

Mode 4
440.3Hz

Figure 6-5: The first four modes of vibration and their associated frequencies.

The undeformed model is superimposed on the mode shape plots.

The analyzed TUNING FORK is the most common type of tuning fork and as any musician will tell us, should produce a lower A sound, with a frequency of 440 Hz.

However, the lower A frequency of 440 Hz which is expected to be the first mode, is actually the fourth mode. Before explaining why this occurs, let's run the frequency analysis once more, this time without any restraints. Define a new frequency study, called *tuning fork no supports*.

The easiest way is to do this is to copy the existing *TUNING FORK* study and either delete or suppress the restraint (right-click the restraint icon and make the proper selection).

As we will soon explain, in the absence of restraints the model has six Rigid Body Modes. Therefore if we still want to calculate five modes of vibration, which for consistency should now be called **Elastic Modes**, we must specify a total of 11 modes in the properties of the frequency study.

After the solution has been completed, right-click the *Deformation* folder and select **List Resonant Frequencies** (Figure 6-6).

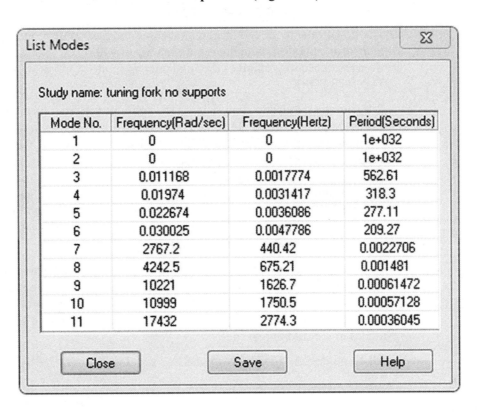

List Modes

Study name: tuning fork no supports

Mode No.	Frequency(Rad/sec)	Frequency(Hertz)	Period(Seconds)
1	0	0	1e+032
2	0	0	1e+032
3	0.011168	0.0017774	562.61
4	0.01974	0.0031417	318.3
5	0.022674	0.0036086	277.11
6	0.030025	0.0047786	209.27
7	2767.2	440.42	0.0022706
8	4242.5	675.21	0.001481
9	10221	1626.7	0.00061472
10	10999	1750.5	0.00057128
11	17432	2774.3	0.00036045

Close   Save   Help

Figure 6-6: The **List Modes** window in the analysis of TUNING FORK.

Modes 1-6 are rigid body modes with frequency equal to, or very close to 0Hz. Numerical error is the reason why not all rigid body modes have a frequency exactly equal to 0Hz.

Mode 7 is the first elastic mode of vibration. This illustration has been modified to show all calculated modes without scrolling. Many other illustrations in this book have been modified in a graphics program to improve their clarity.

We notice that the first six modes have the associated frequency 0Hz or very close to 0Hz. Why? The first six modes of vibration correspond to rigid body modes. Because the TUNING FORK is not supported, it has six degrees of freedom as a rigid body: three translational and three rotational.

SolidWorks Simulation detects these rigid body modes and assigns them with a frequency of zero (0Hz). Modes 3, 4, 5, and 6 do not have a frequency of exactly zero due to numerical error.

The first elastic mode of vibration, meaning the first mode requiring the fork to deform is mode 7, which has a frequency of 440.4 Hz. This is close to what we were expecting to find as the fundamental mode of vibration for the TUNING FORK.

Why did the frequency analysis with the restraint not produce the first mode with a frequency near to 440 Hz? If we closely examine the first three modes of vibration of the supported TUNING FORK, we notice that they all need the support in order to exist. The support is needed to sustain these modes, but while this support makes these first three modes possible, in reality it also provides damping. After modes 1, 2, and 3 have been damped out, the TUNING FORK vibrates the way it was designed to: in mode 4 (as calculated in the analysis with supports) or mode 7 (as calculated in the analysis without supports). These two modes are identical.

To learn more about modes of vibration of an unsupported elastic model (all models in FEA are considered elastic), calculate six elastic modes of the unsupported model PLASTIC PART. **Mode Shape** results corresponding to the first six elastic modes are shown in Figure 6-7. You'll need to request 12 modes in the study properties.

All 12 modes: six rigid body modes and six elastic modes are listed in Figure 6-8.

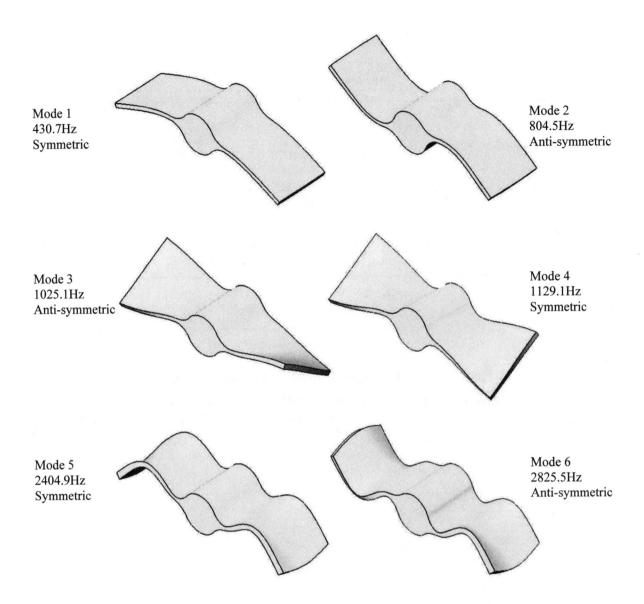

Mode 1
430.7Hz
Symmetric

Mode 2
804.5Hz
Anti-symmetric

Mode 3
1025.1Hz
Anti-symmetric

Mode 4
1129.1Hz
Symmetric

Mode 5
2404.9Hz
Symmetric

Mode 6
2825.5Hz
Anti-symmetric

Figure 6-7: The first six elastic modes of vibration of the unsupported model PLASTIC PLATE.

Based on the deformation results of PIPE SUPPORT, TUNING FORK and PLASTIC PLATE, we can make an interesting observation about the nature of the modes of vibration. If a model is symmetric and has symmetric restraints (or no restraints at all), then its modal shapes are either symmetric or anti-symmetric.

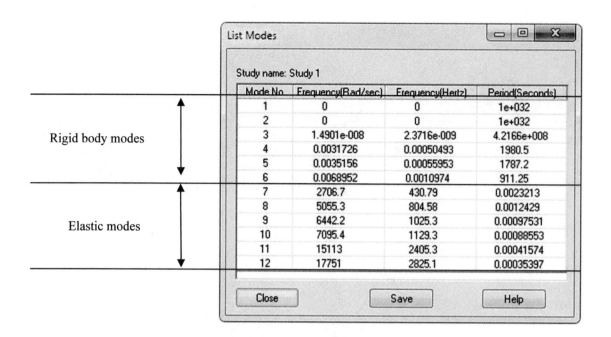

Figure 6-8: The **List Modes** window in the analysis of PLASTIC PART.

Modes 1-6 are rigid body modes with frequency equal or very close to 0Hz. Modes 7-12 are elastic modes shown in Figure 6-7 where they are numbered from 1 to 6.

7: Thermal analysis of a pipe connector and a heater

Topics covered

- Analogies between structural and thermal analysis
- Steady state thermal analysis
- Analysis of temperature distribution and heat flux
- Thermal boundary conditions
- Thermal stresses
- Vector plots

Project description

So far, we have performed static analyses and frequency analyses, which both belong to the class of structural analyses. Static analysis provides results in the form of displacements, strains, and stresses, while frequency analysis provides results in the form of natural frequencies and associated modes of vibration. We will now examine a thermal analysis example. Numerous analogies exist between thermal and structural analyses. The most direct analogies are summarized in Figure 7-1.

Structural Analysis	Thermal Analysis
Displacement [m]	Temperature [K]
Strain [dimensionless]	Temperature gradient [K/m]
Stress [N/m^2]	Heat flux [W/m^2]
Load [N] [N/m] [N/m^2] [N/m^3]	Heat source [W] [W/m] [W/m^2] [W/m^3]
Prescribed displacement [m]	Prescribed temperature [K]

Figure 7-1: Selected analogies between structural and thermal analysis with corresponding units in the SI system.

A negative heat source is a heat sink.

137

Procedure

Open part model PIPE CONNECTOR. Our objective is to find the steady state temperature and heat flux in the part when prescribed temperatures are applied to the end faces as shown is Figure 7-2. As indicated in Figure 7-1, prescribed temperatures are analogous to prescribed displacements in structural analyses.

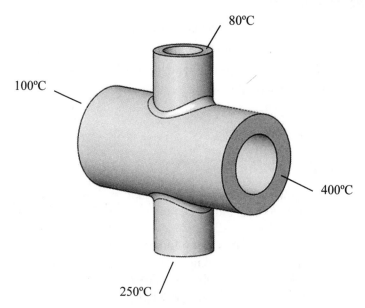

Figure 7-2: CAD model of pipe connector.

Shown are the prescribed temperatures, applied to the end faces as temperature boundary conditions. Notice that the units given are in degrees Celsius, however units of degrees Fahrenheit or degrees Kelvin may also be used.

Since no convection coefficients are defined on any surfaces, heat can enter and leave the model only through the end faces with the prescribed temperatures assigned. Even though the problem has little relevance to real heat transfer problems, it helps us understand the basics of thermal analysis.

The first step in thermal analysis is the study definition. Call this study *crossing pipes* and define it as shown in Figure 7-3.

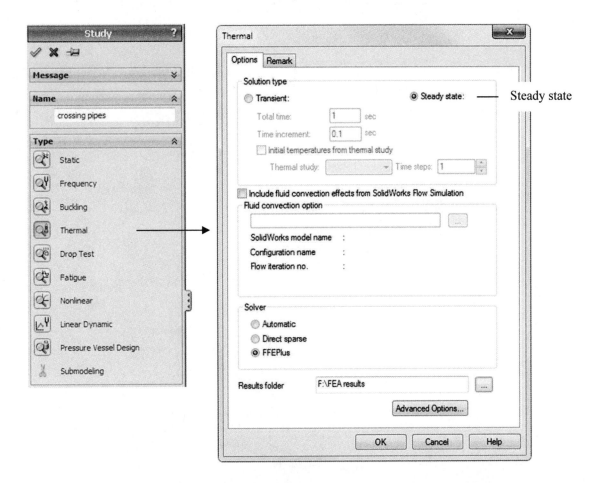

Figure 7-3: Definition of *crossing pipes* thermal study (left). Also shown is the study properties window (right).

Steady state is the default option in study properties.

In a **Steady state** thermal analysis, it is assumed that enough time has passed since the thermal conditions have been applied, and therefore all parameters characterizing heat flow no longer vary with time.

To define the prescribed temperature, right-click the *Thermal Loads* folder and select **Temperature** to open the **Temperature** definition window. Define prescribed temperatures to the four faces in four separate steps as shown in Figure 7-2.

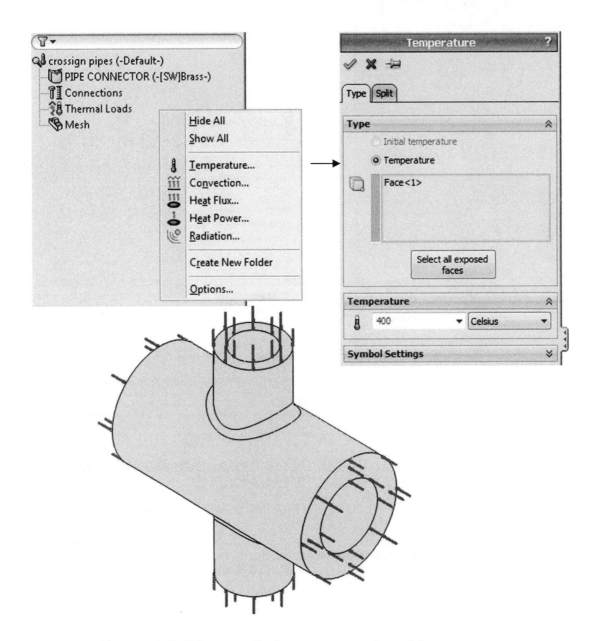

Figure 7-4: Defining prescribed temperature on the end face.

Right-click the Thermal Loads folder and select Temperature from the pop-up menu. Define the prescribed temperatures in the Temperature definition window. The bottom illustration shows Temperature symbols on all four faces.

Mesh the model using the settings shown in Figure 7-5.

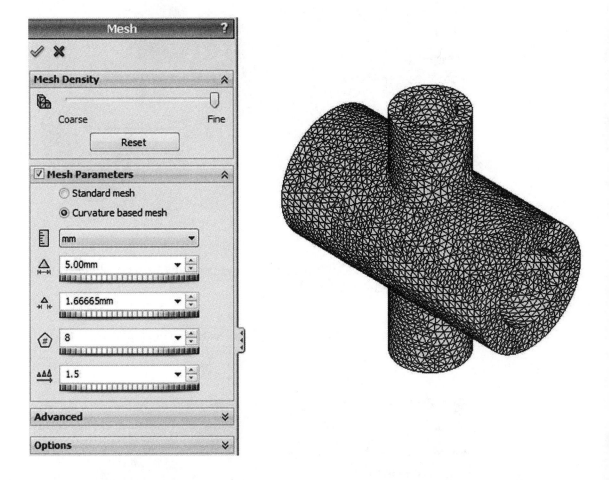

Figure 7-5: Curvature based mesh is used to assure correct meshing of fillets.

A 5mm element size gives two elements across the wall of thinner pipe. Eight elements in a circle are specified to assure low element turn angle.

After solving the model, notice that only one result folder called *Thermal1* is present. By default, it shows the temperature distribution (Figure 7-6).

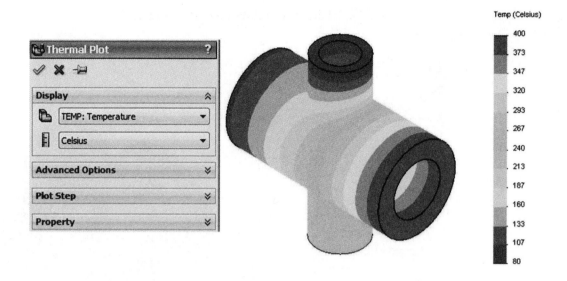

Figure 7-6: **Thermal Plot** window defining temperature distribution and corresponding plot.

Create a plot showing resultant heat flux (Figure 7-7).

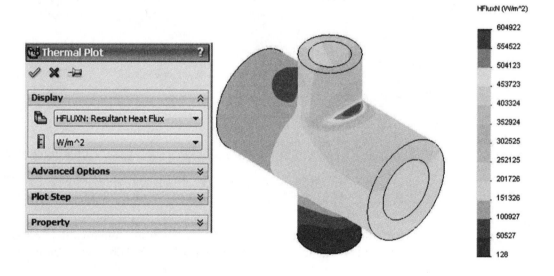

Figure 7-7: **Thermal Plot** window defining a heat flux plot and the corresponding plot.

Since heat flux is a vector quantity, it lends itself well to be presented as a vector plot. Follow the steps in Figure 7-8 to redefine Figure 7-7 into a vector plot and edit it appropriately.

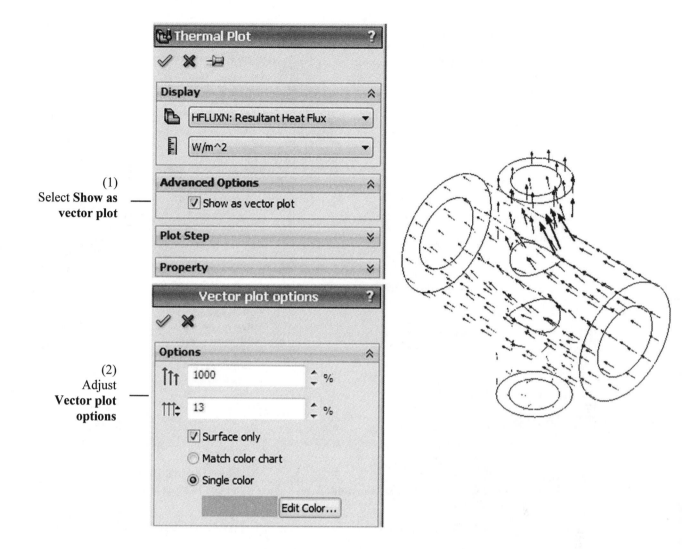

Figure 7-8: Heat flux result presented as a vector plot.

Proceed as explained below to produce a heat flux vector plot.

To create a vector plot, right-click the existing heat flux plot and select **Edit definition** to open the **Thermal Plot** window. In **Advanced Options**, select **Show as vector plot** (1). Once the vector plot is showing, right-click its icon again and select **Vector Plot Options** to open the **Vector plot options** **window** (2). Adjust the settings to have a clear plot. In particular, select **Surface only** in **Vector plot options**.

The non-uniform temperature field that establishes itself in the model (Figure 7-6) produces thermal stress due to non-uniform thermal expansion of different portions of the model. We will now analyze those thermal stresses. Define a static study, *thermal stresses*, with the properties shown in Figure 7-9.

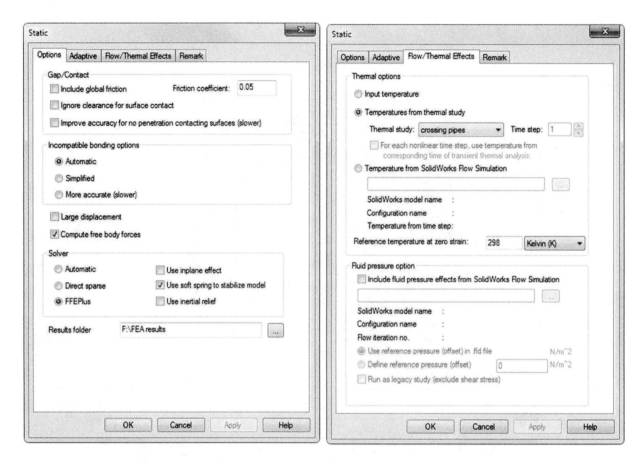

Options tab:
Select **Use soft springs to stabilize the model**

Flow/Thermal Effects tab:
Select **Temperatures from thermal study**

Figure 7-9: Properties of the study intended for analysis of thermal stresses are defined under two tabs.

Proceed as explained below to define Options and Flow/Thermal Effects.

In the **Options** tab select **Use soft springs to stabilize model**. This is because in a static analysis, the model will not be subjected to any structural loads or restraints. This way the pure effect of temperature is shown. The model is under internally balanced loads, but due to numerical errors, would experience rigid body movement. Soft springs eliminate those rigid body movements by attaching springs of very low stiffness to all nodes.

In the **Flow/Thermal Effects** tab specify **Temperature from thermal study**, *crossing pipes*. This will import temperature results from the previously completed thermal study *crossing pipes*.

A static study with temperatures imported from a thermal study must use a mesh that is identical to the one used in the thermal study. To make sure the mesh is identical, copy the mesh from the thermal study *crossing pipes* to the static study *thermal stresses*. To copy the mesh, click and drag it from the *crossing pipes* study onto the *thermal stresses* study tab.

Run the thermal stresses study and display a von Mises stress plot (Figure 7-10).

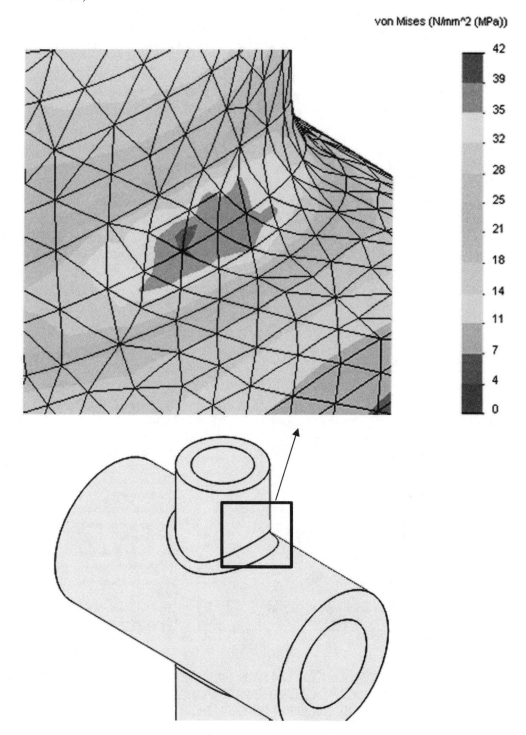

Figure 7-10: Thermal stresses develop due to non-uniform temperature distribution.

Notice the irregular shape of fringes.

Analysis of the results in Figure 7-10 reveals irregularly shaped fringes. This is due to a coarse mesh. As it turns out, the mesh was adequate for the analysis of temperature and heat flux, but not sufficiently refined for an analysis of thermal stresses. Repeat the analyses (both thermal and static) with a more refined mesh to see the effect of element size on "regularity" of fringe plots (Figure 7-11).

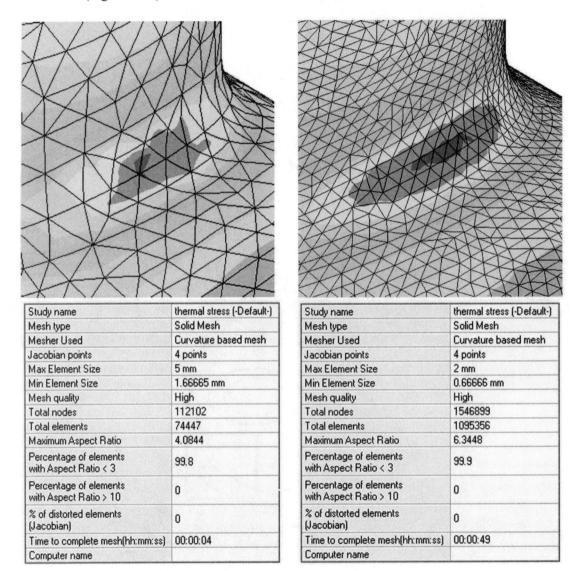

Study name	thermal stress (-Default-)		Study name	thermal stress (-Default-)
Mesh type	Solid Mesh		Mesh type	Solid Mesh
Mesher Used	Curvature based mesh		Mesher Used	Curvature based mesh
Jacobian points	4 points		Jacobian points	4 points
Max Element Size	5 mm		Max Element Size	2 mm
Min Element Size	1.66665 mm		Min Element Size	0.66666 mm
Mesh quality	High		Mesh quality	High
Total nodes	112102		Total nodes	1546899
Total elements	74447		Total elements	1095356
Maximum Aspect Ratio	4.0844		Maximum Aspect Ratio	6.3448
Percentage of elements with Aspect Ratio < 3	99.8		Percentage of elements with Aspect Ratio < 3	99.9
Percentage of elements with Aspect Ratio > 10	0		Percentage of elements with Aspect Ratio > 10	0
% of distorted elements (Jacobian)	0		% of distorted elements (Jacobian)	0
Time to complete mesh(hh:mm:ss)	00:00:04		Time to complete mesh(hh:mm:ss)	00:00:49
Computer name			Computer name	

Figure 7-11: Thermal stress results produced by a mesh used in this study (left) and by a more refined mesh (right). The corresponding mesh information is shown below the plots.

The left plot is a repetition of Figure 7-10. You can use the "regularity" of fringe plots to decide if a mesh needs to be refined. The original mesh uses a 5mm elements size. The refined mesh uses 2mm.

Complete this exercise by reviewing the animated displacements results.

We will now conduct a thermal analysis of a pipe with cooling fins. The objective of this analysis is to find how much heat is dissipated by a 50mm long section (Figure 7-12). Open part model HEATER, make sure it is in *01 full model* configuration, and create a **Thermal** study.

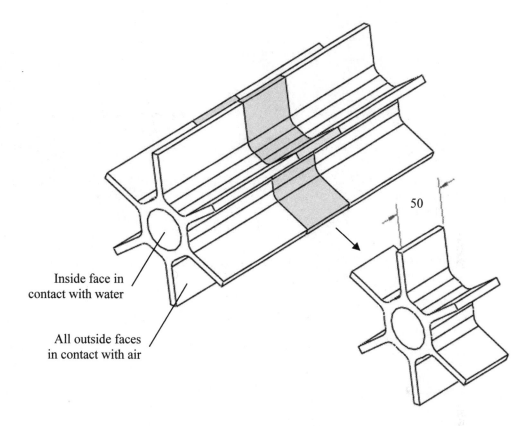

Figure 7-12: Analysis of a pipe with cooling fins (left) is conducted on a section 50mm long (right).

Hot water at 100°C (373K) flows inside the heater. The coefficient of thermal convection between the water and the inside heater face is 1000 W/m²K, meaning that each 1m² of the inside face exchanges (gains or losses) 1000J of heat per second if the temperature difference between the face and water is 1K. The coefficient of thermal convection between the outside faces and the air is 20 W/m²K meaning that each 1m² of the outside face exchanges (gains or losses) 20J of heat per second if the temperature difference between the face and air is 1K. The ambient air temperature is 27°C (300K).

Notice that we are using somewhat arbitrary values of convection coefficients. Finding convection coefficients that correctly describe the problem is often the most difficult part of a thermal analysis.

Define convection coefficients and bulk temperatures as shown in Figures 7-13 and 7-14.

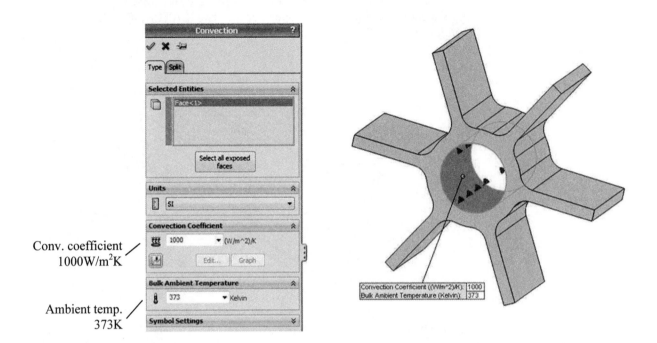

Conv. coefficient 1000W/m²K

Ambient temp. 373K

Figure 7-13: Convection coefficient and bulk temperature on the water side (inside the tube).

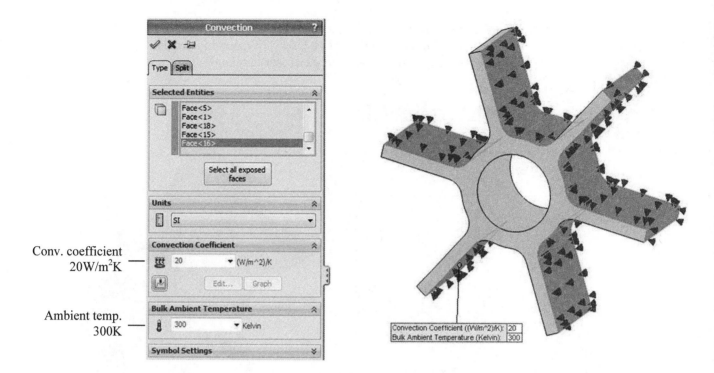

Figure 7-14: Convection coefficient and bulk temperature on the air side (outside).

Since the model represents a section of a longer pipe, we assume that there is no heat exchange through the end faces. Therefore we do not define any convection coefficients on the end faces, treating them as insulated.

Use a **Curvature based mesh**. Specify a 2.5mm global element size to create two elements across the fin thickness. Use 8 for the minimum number of elements on a circle to produce a low element turn angle (Figure 7-15)

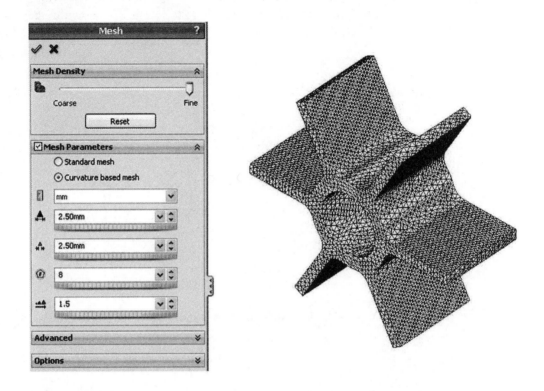

Figure 7-15: A curvature based mesh type is used to control the element turn angle in round fillets.

Use 2.5mm for element size and 8 elements over 360°.

Solve the study and display the resultant heat flux plot. Right-click the results folder and select **List Heat Power** (1) from the pop-up menu to open the **Heat Power** window. In the model window select the inside face (water side) (2), then click the **Update** button (3) in the **Probe Result** window. The total heat entering the model through the selected face is shown in the lower portion of the **Probe Result** window (4) as shown in Figure 7-16.

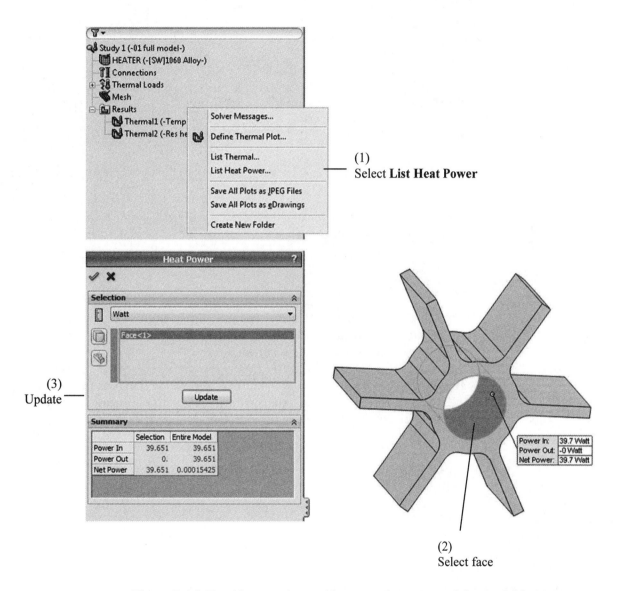

Figure 7-16: Total heat exchanged between the water and the model is 39.7W.

The positive sign of net power indicates that the model gains heat from the water. This can be visualized by constructing a vector plot of resultant heat flux.

Alternatively we can obtain the same results by selecting all faces on the air side (Figure 7-17).

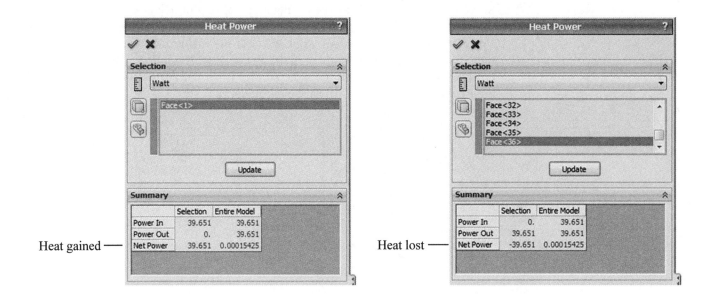

Heat gained ——

Heat lost ——

Figure 7-17: Total heat exchanged between water and the model (left), and between air and the model (right).

The heat gained from the water is +39.65W. The heat lost by the model to the air is -39.65W.

Since this is a steady state thermal analysis, the amount of heat entering the model and the amount of heat dissipated by the model must be equal. Any small discrepancies are due to numerical error.

The analysis can be significantly simplified by noticing that heat flow through the model has the property of axial symmetry. Therefore, instead of analyzing the entire model, we can analyze just one angular section (Figure 7-18).

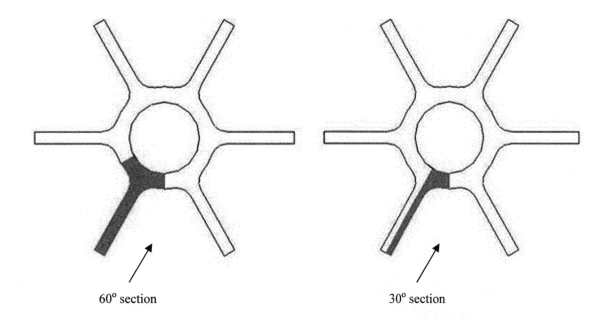

60° section   30° section

Figure 7-18: The model can be simplified to a radial section. While a 60°
section (left) appears the most obvious at first sight, the smallest repeatable
section is 30° (right).

You are encouraged to repeat the analysis in model configuration *60 degrees
section* or *30 degrees section*. Do not apply any convection conditions on
faces created by radial cuts and remember to multiply the total heat either by 6
or by 12 depending on which configuration you use for analysis (Figure 7-19).

Notice that symmetry boundary conditions in a thermal analysis correlate to
no heat flow through the plane of symmetry. Therefore, to construct thermal
symmetry boundary conditions on a face, do not define a convection
coefficient, prescribed temperature or anything other condition. In summary,
do not apply any conditions to the face where thermal symmetry boundary
conditions exist.

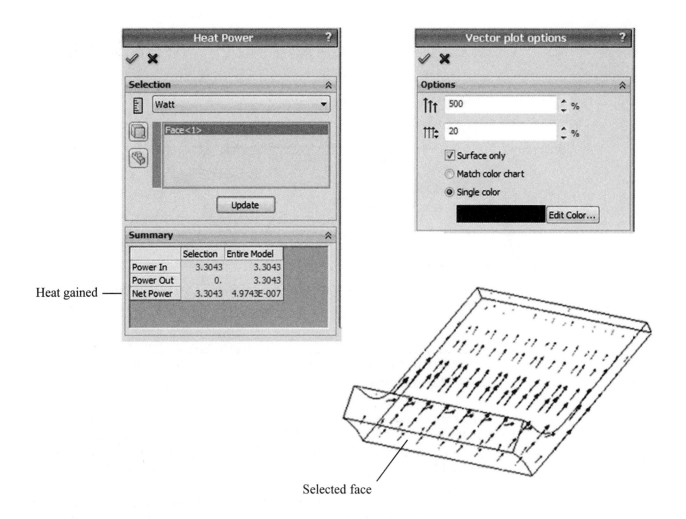

Heat gained

Selected face

Figure 7-19: Total heat exchanged between water and the selected face of the 30° section.

Total heat gained from the water by the model is 3.3 x 12 = 39.6W.

Heat flow is presented using a vector plot with the above shown settings.

8: Thermal analysis of a heat sink

Topics covered

- Analysis of an assembly
- Global and local Contact conditions
- Steady state thermal analysis
- Transient thermal analysis
- Thermal resistance layer
- Use of section views in result plots

Project description

In this exercise, we continue with thermal analysis. However, this time we will analyze an assembly rather than a single part. Open the assembly HEAT SINK (Figure 8-1).

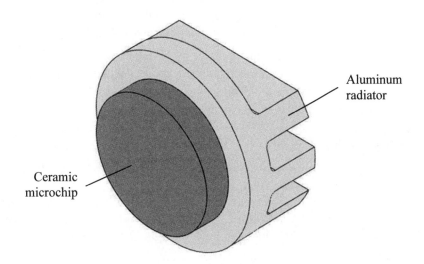

Aluminum
radiator

Ceramic
microchip

Figure 8-1: Assembly model of a heat sink using a radiator.

HEAT SINK assembly consists of two components: a ceramic microchip and an aluminum radiator. All heat generated by the microchip dissipates through the radiator. The two faces of microchip visible in this illustration do not dissipate heat.

Analysis of an assembly allows assignment of different material properties to each assembly component. Notice that the *Solids* folder contains two icons corresponding to the two assembly components with material properties already assigned. This is because material has been assigned to each part that the assembly consists of: Ceramic Porcelain material to the microchip and 1060 Alloy to the radiator.

The ceramic microchip generates a heat power of 25W and the aluminum radiator dissipates this heat. The ambient temperature is 27°C (300K). Heat is dissipated to the environment by convection through all exposed faces of the radiator. We assume that the microchip is insulated, meaning it cannot dissipate heat directly to ambient air, but only through the face touching the radiator. The convection coefficient (also called the film coefficient) is assumed to be 25 (W/m^2)/K in this model. This value of the convection coefficient corresponds to natural convection taking place without a cooling fan.

Heat flowing from the microchip to the radiator encounters thermal resistance on the boundary between the microchip and radiator. Therefore, a thermal resistance layer must be defined on the interface between these two components.

Our first objective is to determine the temperature and heat flux of the assembly in steady state conditions (after enough time has passed for temperatures to stabilize). This will require steady state thermal analysis.

The second objective is to study the temperature in the assembly as a function of time in a transient process when the assembly is initially at room temperature and the power is turned on at time t = 0. This will require transient thermal analysis.

Procedure

Create a thermal study called *heat sink steady state*. Before proceeding, we need to investigate the folder called *Connectors* which is found in the *heat sink steady state* study. By default, the **Global Contact** between parts in an assembly is **Bonded**. As the name implies, all parts in assembly behave as one. We need to change it by defining a **Contact Set**.

Right-click the *Connectors* folder and select **Contact Set** to open the **Contact Set** window shown in Figure 8-2. Select **Thermal Resistance** with **Node to surface** as the contact type. This contact condition overrides the global **Bonded** contact condition. Select the contacting faces and enter **Distributed Thermal Resistance** as $0.001 \text{Km}^2/\text{W}$. This value is quite high; we use it to demonstrate clearly the effect of a thermal resistance layer. The magnitude of thermal resistance is usually obtained by testing. Notice that the units of thermal resistance are the reciprocal of units of thermal convection.

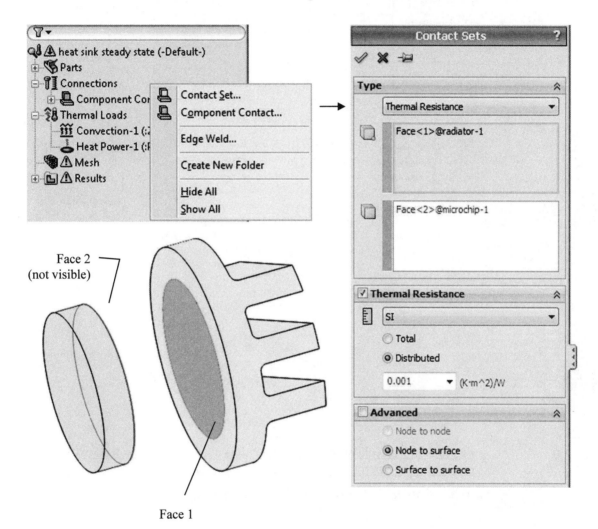

Figure 8-2: Definition of Thermal Resistance Contact Set.

We need to define a local Contact Set for contacting faces in order to introduce a thermal resistance layer between the contacting faces. This can only be done as a local Contact Set using the Node to surface option in Advanced settings. Use the exploded model view to define the Contact Set.

Next, specify the heat power generated in the microchip. To do this, right-click the *Thermal loads* folder to open the pop-up menu. Select **Heat Power...** to open the **Heat Power** window (Figure 8-3), and then from the **SolidWorks** fly-out menu select the *MICROCHIP* assembly component and define a 25W heat power. This applies heat power to the entire volume of the selected component.

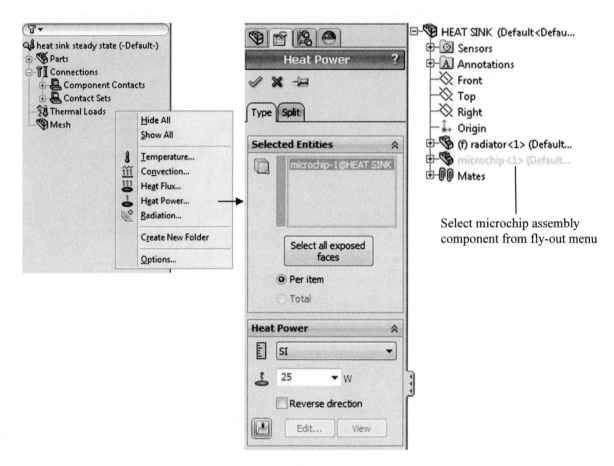

Select microchip assembly component from fly-out menu

Figure 8-3: The SolidWorks fly-out menu is used to make a selection of the part (here a microchip) necessary to define Heat Power.

Notice that MICROCHIP-1 appears in the Selected Entities field.

So far we have assigned material properties to each component, and also defined a heat source and a thermal resistance layer. In order for heat to flow, we must also establish a mechanism for heat to escape the model. This is accomplished by defining convection coefficients.

Right-click the *Thermal Loads* folder to open a pop-up menu and select **Convection...** to open the **Convection** window (Figure 8-4). Select all faces of the RADIATOR except the one touching the MICROCHIP. Do not select any face of the MICROCHIP. Enter 25 (W/m^2)/K as the value of the convection coefficient for all selected faces and enter the **Bulk Ambient Temperature** as 300K.

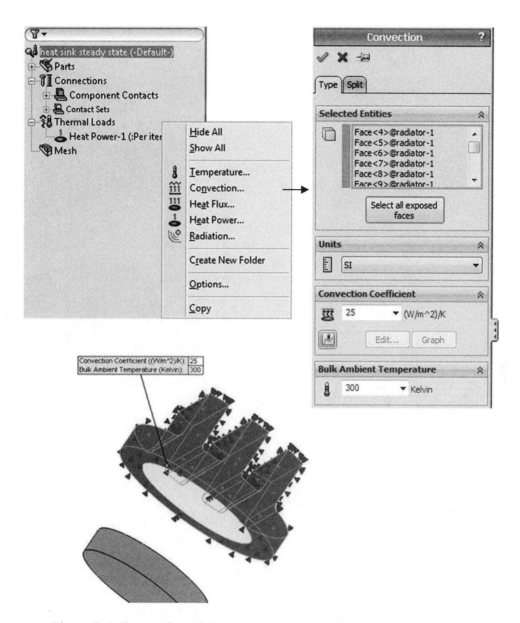

Figure 8-4: Convection window.

Use this window to specify both the Convection Coefficient and the Bulk Temperature. Instead of selecting the faces one by one, you may click Select all exposed faces and then deselect those faces where convection is not occurring.

The last step before solving is creating the mesh. For accurate heat flux results we need several elements modeling the fillet curvature. This can be done either using a **Standard Mesh** with mesh controls applied to all six fillets or using a **Curvature based mesh** shown in Figure 8-5. We will use this method.

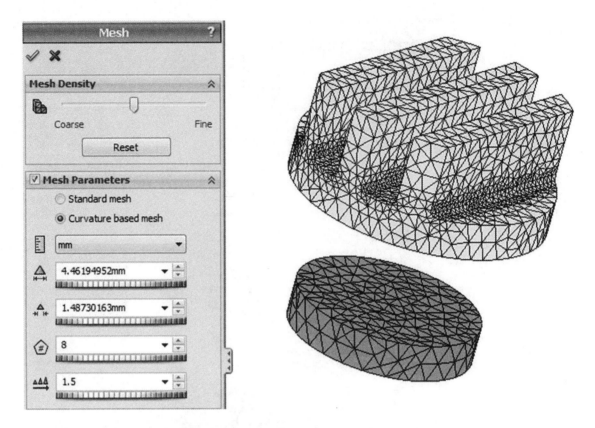

Figure 8-5: Curvature based mesh assures correct meshing of fillets without the use of mesh controls.

Notice that the Curvature based mesh produces a low element turn angle at the base of each fin.

Once the solution is ready, examine the two plots: temperature and resultant heat flux. The temperature plot is created automatically in the *Results* folder. The required choices for both plots are shown in Figure 8-6.

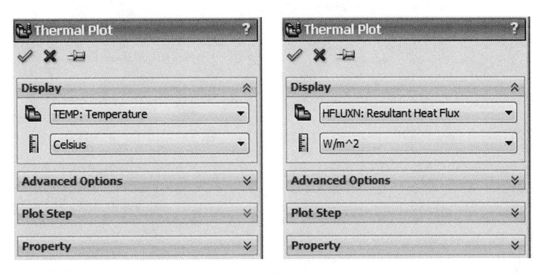

Temperature distribution   Heat flux

Figure 8-6: Thermal Plot definition window for temperature distribution plot (left) and heat flux plot (right).

Both temperature and heat flux result plots are more informative if presented using section views. **SolidWorks Simulation** offers a multitude of options for sectioned plots which are easier to practice than to read about. Here we describe the procedure of creating a flat section result plot using one of the default reference planes in **SolidWorks**, but any reference plane can be used.

To show the section view of the temperature distribution plot, right-click the plot icon and select **Section Clipping** from the pop-up menu to open the **Section** window. By default, the cutting surface is aligned with the **Front** reference plane. To select another cutting plane select it from the **SolidWorks** fly-out menu.

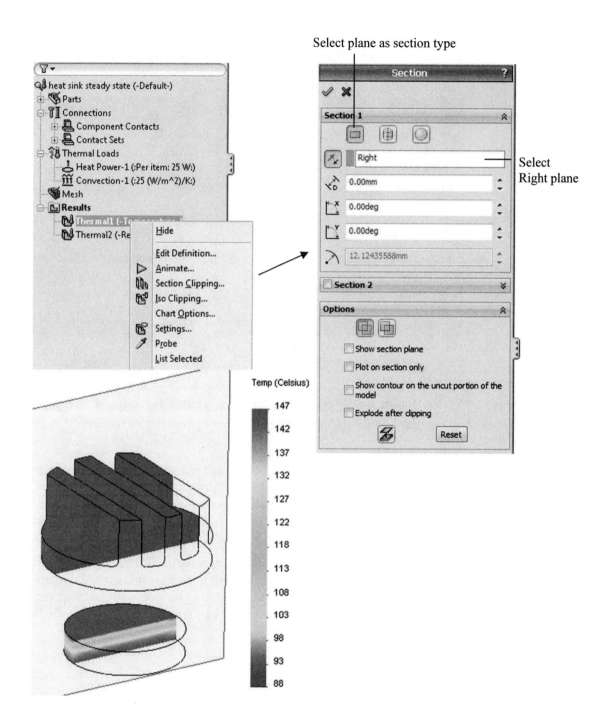

Figure 8-7: A section plot of the temperature distribution in the assembly using an exploded view.

The cutting plane is aligned with the Right reference plane. The position of the cutting plane can be modified in a way similar to modifying a SolidWorks section view. Experiment with Options in the Section window.

Now, construct a plot of heat flux shown as a vector plot. Follow the steps described in chapter 7 to create a heat flux vector plot. In addition to using a vector plot, use the exploded view to produce a heat flux plot similar to the one shown in Figure 8-8.

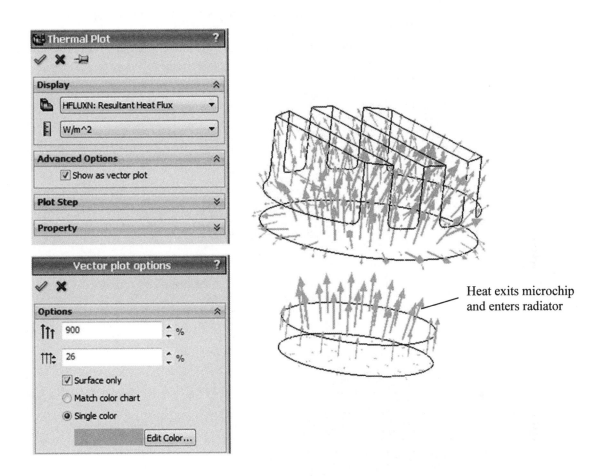

Figure 8-8: Vector plot of heat flux in the assembly using exploded view.

Notice that arrows "coming out" of the microchip visually represent where heat leaves the microchip. Vectors are tangent to faces where no convection coefficients have been defined.

Some irregularities in vector display are attributed to irregularities in the mesh. Try repeating the analysis with a more refined mesh.

This completes the steady state thermal analysis of the HEAT SINK assembly. We now proceed with a transient thermal analysis. Copy the study *heat sink steady state* into a new study named *heat sink transient*. Right-click the study *heat sink transient* folder and select **Properties** to open the window shown in Figure 8-9.

Select **Transient** analysis (**Steady state** is the default option). Our objective is to monitor temperature changes every 360 seconds during the first 3600 seconds. Enter 3600 as the **Total time** and 360 as the **Time increment**.

Transient ———
Total time 3600s ———
Time increment 360s

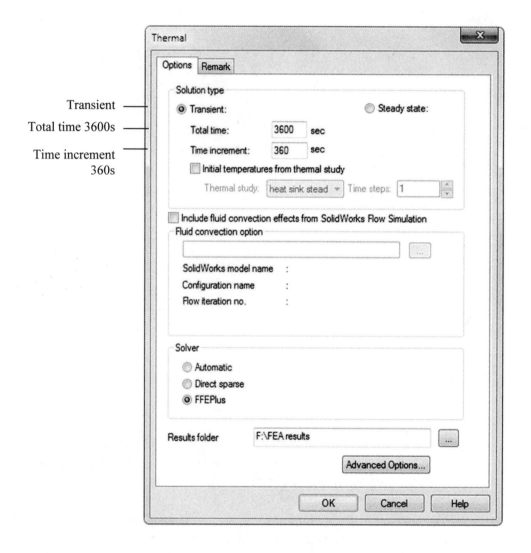

Figure 8-9: The **Transient** thermal analysis is specified in the thermal study **Options** tab.

Analysis will be carried on for 3600 seconds in 10 steps. Results will be reported every 360 seconds.

Transient thermal analysis requires that the initial temperature of the model be defined in addition to the already defined **Heat Power** and **Convection** coefficients which have been copied from the *heat sink steady state* study together with **Contact conditions** and the **Mesh**.

We assume that both components have the same initial temperature of 300K. Right-click the *Thermal Loads* folder in the *heat sink transient* study and select **Temperature** to open the window shown in Figure 8-10. Select **Initial Temperature** and enter 300K. From the fly-out menu select both assembly components.

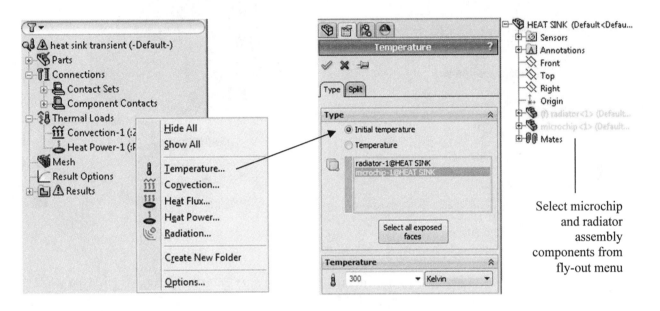

Select microchip and radiator assembly components from fly-out menu

Figure 8-10: Initial Temperature specified for both assembly components.

Assembly components can be selected from the SolidWorks fly-out menu.

Now run the analysis and display the temperature plot for step 10 (the last step) by right-clicking the plot icon, selecting **Edit Definition** and setting the **Plot Step** to 10 (Figure 8-11).

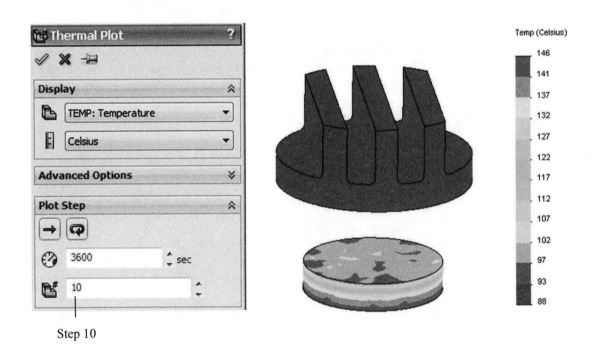

Step 10

Figure 8-11: Temperature distribution after 3600 seconds (step 10) from when the microchip was turned on.

Temperature results shown in degrees Celsius at the 10th time step.

Irregular fringes on the contacting faces seen in Figure 8-11 indicate the need for a more refined mesh. We use this coarse mesh to shorten the solution time of the transient analysis.

Since we have not specified heat power as function of time, it is assumed that the full power is turned on at time t=0, when the assembly is at an initial temperature of 300K. Figure 8-11 shows the temperature distribution after 3600 seconds. Notice that this result is very close to the result of steady state thermal analysis, meaning that after 3600 seconds, the temperature of assembly has almost stabilized.

To see the temperature history at selected locations of the model, proceed as follows: make sure the temperature plot is displaying the full model, and not just the section as in Fig 8-11. This can be done by right clicking the temperature plot, selecting **Section Clipping…** , and turning off **Clipping** under the **Options** menu. Next, right-click the temperature plot icon, and select **Probe** to probe temperature in the location shown in Figure 8-12.

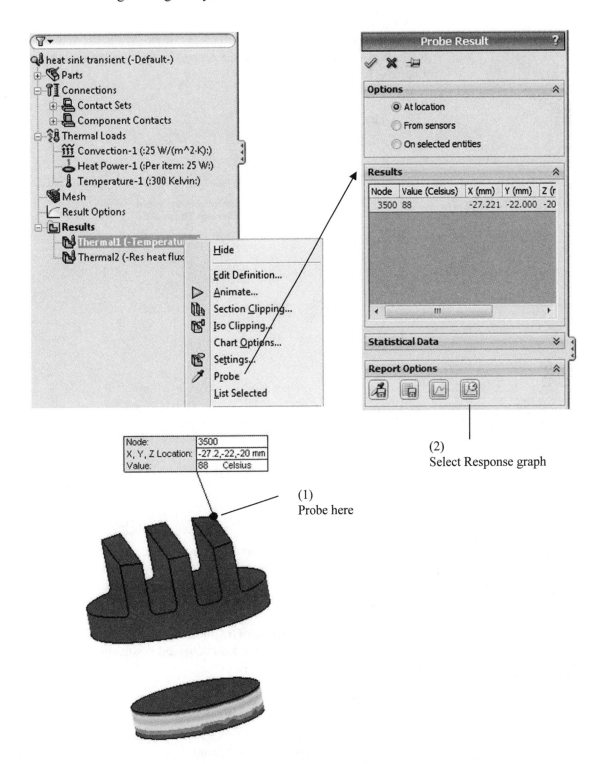

Figure 8-12: Temperature is probed in the indicated location.

Since the temperature of radiator is almost uniform, you may probe at any location on the radiator face. The response plot is shown in Figure 8-13.

Select **Response** in the **Probe Results** window (Figure 8-12) to display a graph showing the temperature at the probed location as a function of time (Figure 8-13).

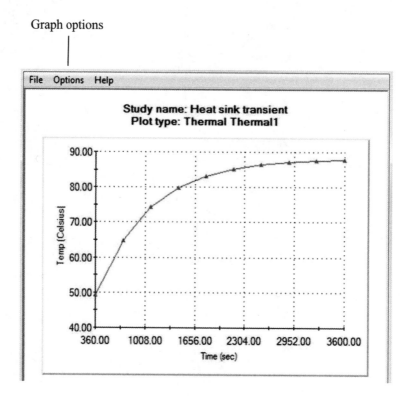

Figure 8-13: Temperature as a function of time in the probed location.

To produce a response graph (here temperature as a function of time), you may probe temperature from any of the 10 performed time steps. It does not have to be the last step. Experiment with different plot Options.

An examination of the **Response Graph** in Figure 8-13 proves that after 3600 seconds the probed location has almost achieved its steady state temperature.

To conclude the thermal analysis of the HEAT SINK assembly, we will study the effect of the thermal resistance layer. Switch to the exploded view and show any **Temperature** plot. Here we use the plot from the last step of the transient thermal analysis. Probe temperatures in corresponding locations on two contacting faces separated by the layer of thermal resistance and notice that a temperature gradient exists due to the presence of the thermal resistance layer (Figure 8-14). The temperature gradient is required to "push" heat through the layer of thermal resistance. Temperature time history in two locations corresponding to the microchip and radiator can be seen on the graph shown in Figure 8-14.

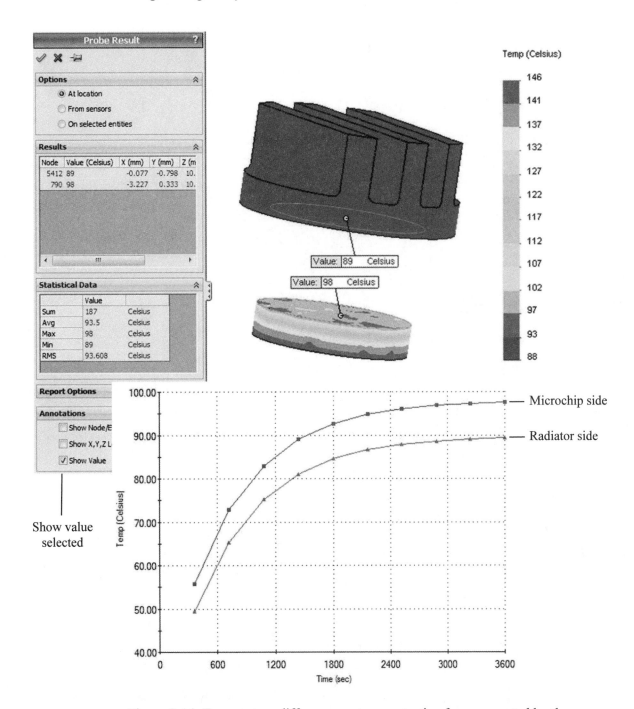

Figure 8-14: Temperature difference on two contacting faces separated by the layer of thermal resistance.

The presence of the thermal resistance layer creates a temperature gradient shown in the probed results and in the temperature time history graph. The step size is 360s, therefore graph starts at t=360s.

Only values are selected in annotations.

Notes:

9: Static analysis of a hanger

Topics covered

❑ Global and local Contact conditions

❑ Hierarchy of Contact conditions

Project description

In this exercise we introduce structural analysis of assemblies. To begin, we review different options available for defining the interactions between assembly components (we began exploring this topic in the previous exercise).

Open the HANGER assembly and create a Static study. Right-click **Global Contact** in the **Components Contact** folder to open the **Component Contact** window (Figure 9-1).

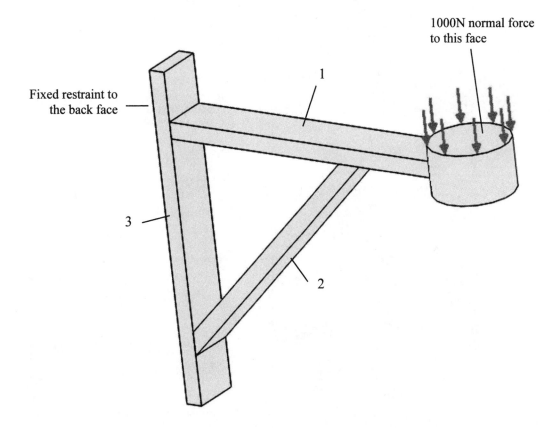

Figure 9-1: HANGER assembly consisting of three parts.

A 1000N load is applied to the round face; restraint is applied to the back face of the vertical component.

Right-click the *Connections* folder to invoke a pop-up menu that offers two types of contact: **Contact Set** and **Component Contact**. The same menu also offers different types of connectors that will be discussed in later chapters. Use the pop-up menu to open the **Contact Sets** window, then select **Component Contact** (Figure 9-2). Review options found in these two windows.

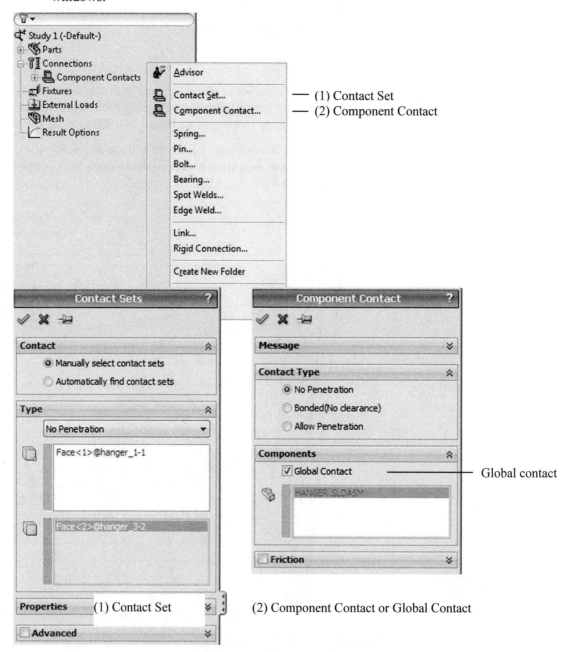

Figure 9-2: Types of contact offered in the Connections folder.

A Contact Set defines contact conditions between faces. Component Contact defines contact between selected assembly components. If Global Contact is selected then the contact condition specified in Component Contact applies to all assembly components.

The differences between **Component Contact** and **Contact Sets** are as follows:

❑ **Component Contact** - affects selected components (it may be only one component) or all components if **Global Contact** is selected.

❑ **Contact sets** - affects only two specified areas.

More detailed descriptions are given in the following tables:

COMPONENT CONTACT	
Option	**Description**
No penetration	The mesher will create compatible meshes on overlapping areas of touching faces. The nodes associated with the two parts on the common areas are coincident but different. The program creates a gap element connecting each two coincident nodes. This option is available for static, nonlinear, and thermal studies. For static studies, a gap element between two nodes prevents part interference but allows the two nodes to move away from each other.
Bonded	The mesher will bond common areas of the selected components at their interface with all other components. This option is available for structural (static, nonlinear, frequency, buckling) and thermal studies.
	This contact condition comes with two options: **Compatible mesh** and **Incompatible mesh** (not available for **Global Contact**) Using the **Compatible mesh** option, the two components are just meshed across the touching faces. Nodes located on touching faces are shared by elements on both sides. If a **Compatible mesh** causes meshing difficulties then an **Incompatible mesh** option can be used. Meshes on each face are then created independently but are automatically constrained to each other.
Allow penetration	The mesher will treat the selected components as disjointed from the rest of the assembly. This option is available for structural (static, frequency, buckling) and thermal studies. For static studies, the loads can cause interference between parts. Using this option can save solution time if the applied loads do not cause interference.

CONTACT SETS	
Option	**Description**
No penetration	Available for static, drop test and nonlinear studies only. This contact type prevents interference between source and target entities but allows gaps to form.
Bonded	The source and target entities are bonded. The entities may be touching or within a small distance from each other. The program gives a warning if the distance between bonded entities is larger than the average element size of the associated elements. Only source and target entities are required to define this contact type.
Allow Penetration	The selected faces are disjoined and can freely go through each other with no interaction.
Shrink fit	Valid for faces from two components which show interference. This interference is eliminated after solution.
Virtual wall	This contact type defines contact between the source entities and a virtual wall defined by a target plane. The target plane may be rigid or flexible. You can define friction between the source and the target plane.
Insulated	Available for thermal studies only. This option is similar to the Free option for structural studies. The program treats the source and target faces as disjointed and therefore prevents heat flow due to conduction through the source and target entities.
Thermal resistance	Specifies thermal resistance between source and target faces.

A **No penetration** contact set can be defined as a **Node to Node** or **Node to Surface** or **Surface to Surface** condition. We will now discuss the important differences between **Node to Node** and **Surface to Surface** conditions.

A **Node to Node** condition can be applied to faces that overlap. The faces do not have to be the same size, but do need to share some common area. **Node to Node** conditions can be specified between two:

❑   Flat faces

❑   Cylindrical faces of the same radius

❑   Spherical faces of the same radius

With these options, the mesh on both faces in the area where they overlap is created in such a manner that there is node to node correspondence (nodes are coincident) on both touching surfaces - hence the name **Node to Node**.

Surface contact may be specified between two faces of different shape and can only be specified as a local condition. Initially, faces can either touch or not touch, but are expected to come in contact once the load has been applied to the model. The **Surface to Surface** condition is more general, but less numerically efficient than the **Node to Surface** condition. Any contact could be defined as a **Surface to Surface** condition, but this would unnecessarily complicate the model.

The difference between **Node to Node** and **Surface to Surface** conditions is illustrated in Figure 9-3.

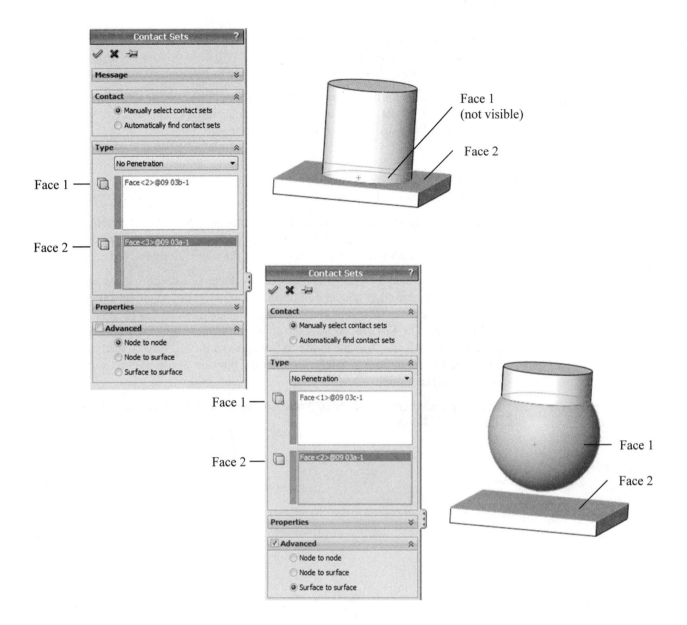

Figure 9-3: The contact between a flat end punch and a plate (top) is defined as a Node to Node contact. The contact between a spherical punch and a plate (bottom) is defined as Surface to surface contact. The model shown here is unrelated to the exercise in this chapter however is given for clarity.

Faces in Surface to Surface contact conditions don't have to touch initially, but they are expected to come in contact under the load.

Global Contact is by default set to **Bonded**. This can be overridden by contact conditions defined at the component or local (**Contact Set**) level. For example, using the default **Global** Contact conditions, we request that all faces be bonded. Next, we locally override this condition and define **Contact Set** for one or more pairs as **No penetration**. The hierarchy of **Global**, **Component**, and **Local** contact conditions is shown in Figure 9-4.

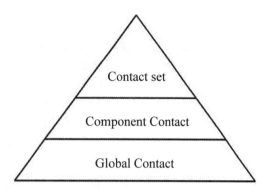

Figure 9-4: Hierarchy of Contact conditions.

Contact Set overrides Component Contact, Component Contact overrides Global Contact.

To access **Contact Set** and **Component Contact** you may right-click either the *Connections* folder or the *Component Contacts* folder (Figure 9-5).

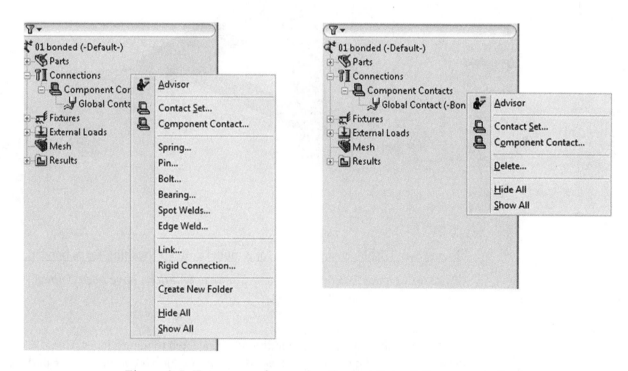

Figure 9-5: Two ways of accessing Contact Set and Components Contact.

Right-clicking on the Connections folder invokes a menu that contains Contact Set and Component Contact as well as Connectors (left). Right-clicking on the Component Contacts invokes a smaller menu with Contact Set and Component Contact (right).

Contact conditions are a very important part of FEA modeling. Please spend enough time reviewing the contact conditions options.

Procedure

Having reviewed contact conditions we may now continue with the analysis of the HANGER. Notice that the HANGER assembly model is adequate for analysis of displacements. However, due to stress singularities in the sharp re-entrant edges, it is not suitable for analysis of stresses in these edges.

The assembly HANGER, material (AISI 304) is assigned to all assembly components. Create study *01 bonded* and apply loads and restraints as shown in Figure 9-1.

If you do not modify the contact conditions, then by default all touching faces are bonded because the **Global Contact** is set to **Bonded**. In this case, the assembly will behave as one part. A sample result is shown in Figure 9-6.

Global Contact: Bonded —

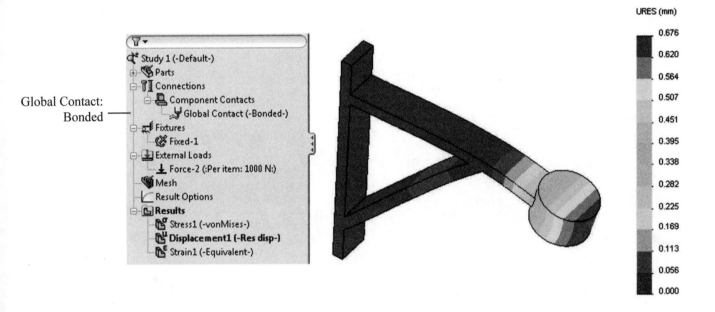

Figure 9-6: Displacement results for a model with all touching faces bonded.

Since no Contact Sets or Component Contact conditions have been defined, the assembly behaves as one part.

Now, we modify the contact conditions on selected touching faces. Copy study *01 bonded* into study *02 free*. We leave the global conditions as **Bonded**, but locally we override them by defining a local **Contact Set**. One of the three pairs of touching faces (Figure 9-7) will be defined using the **Allow Penetration** option, meaning that there is no interaction between the faces. These faces will be able to either come apart or penetrate each other with no consequences.

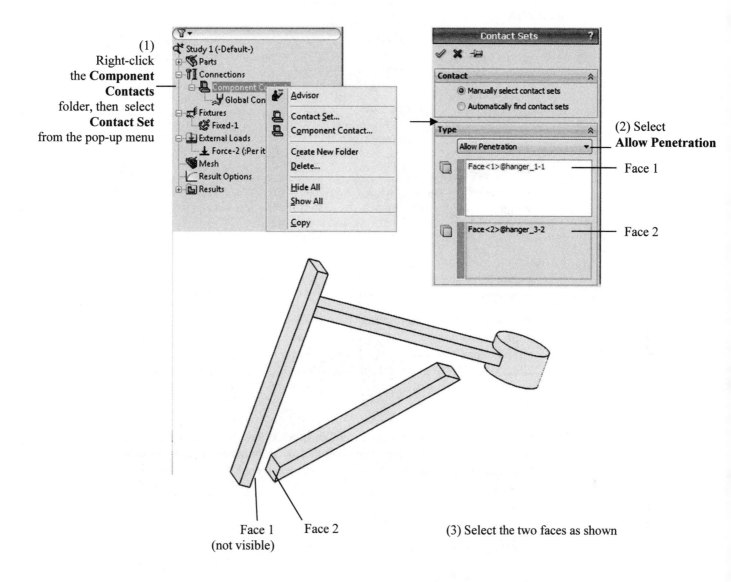

(1)
Right-click
the **Component**
Contacts
folder, then select
Contact Set
from the pop-up menu

(2) Select
Allow Penetration

Face 1

Face 2

Face 1   Face 2
(not visible)

(3) Select the two faces as shown

Figure 9-7: Touching Faces: **Allow Penetration**. When faces are defined as **Allow Penetration**, there is no interaction between them.

An exploded view of the HANGER makes it easier to define a local Contact Set.

Once a **Contact Set** has been defined, an icon is placed in the *Connectors* folder, as shown in Figure 9-8.

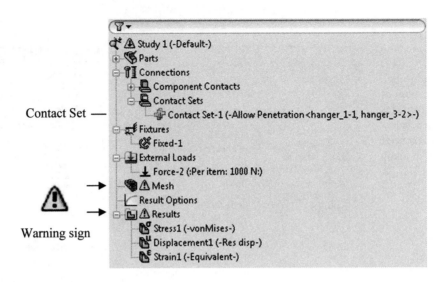

Contact Set

Warning sign

Figure 9-8: Figure 9-8: Any change in Connections invalidates the mesh and requires remeshing.

Remeshing deletes the previous results. This exclamation mark beside the mesh folder indicates that the model needs to be remeshed. In this case, a new mesh is required because previously bonded faces must be disconnected. The same symbol also indicates that Results copied from study 01 bonded are invalid.

The lack of interference between faces in a Contact Set locally defined as **Allow Penetration,** is best demonstrated by showing the deformed results, which are displacement plots with colors deselected (Figure 9-9).

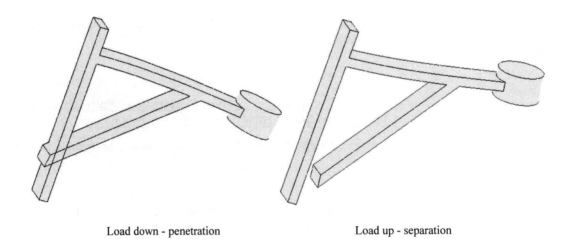

Load down - penetration   Load up - separation

Figure 9-9: Displacement results in a pair defined as **Allow Penetration.**

The plot on the left shows results for a load directed downwards and the plot on the right has the load direction reversed.

Copy study *02 free* to *03 no penetration* and change the local contact conditions between the faces shown in Figure 9-7 from **Allow Penetration** to **No penetration** using the **Node to node** or **Node to surface** option. Remesh the model, and run the solution again. Notice that the solution now requires much more time to run because the contact constraints must be resolved (Figure 9-10). **No penetration** contact conditions represent nonlinear problems and require an iterative solution procedure. This takes significantly longer to complete than the linear solutions of studies *01 bonded* and *02 free*.

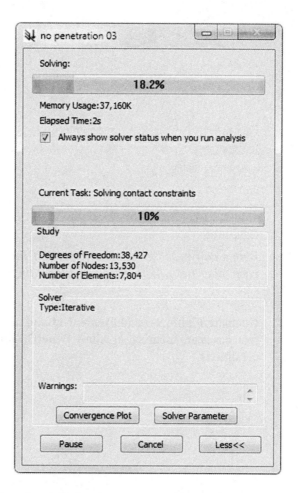

Figure 9-10: Iterative solution progress window for the HANGER assembly using a **No Penetration** condition.

The display of the solution status window can be toggled between more and less detail by selecting More >> and Less <<.

The displacement results, displayed in Figure 9-11, show that the two faces defined as **No Penetration** now slide when a downward load is applied (left) and separate when the load is applied upward (right).

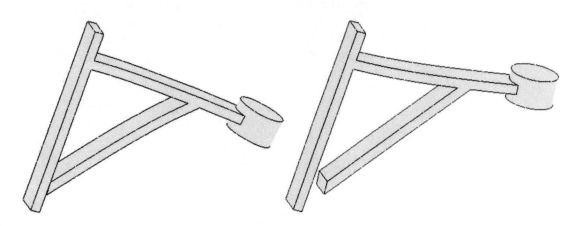

Load down - sliding   Load up - separation

Figure 9-11: Displacement results for the model with a No Penetration contact condition.

With a downward force, the two faces defined as No penetration slide against each other (left). With an upward force they separate (right).

Compare Figure 9-9 and Figure 9-11 and notice that the shapes in the upward load cases are identical in **Allow Penetration** and **No Penetration** contact conditions.

Closer examination of the displacement results for the sliding faces (Figure 9-12) shows that the sliding faces partially separate.

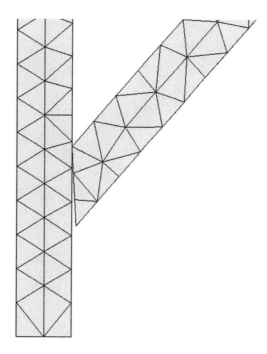

Figure 9-12: Partial separation of the sliding faces.

Only a portion of face 2 contacts face 1. The mesh in the contact area is too coarse to allow for the analysis of contact stresses.

While the mesh is adequate for the analysis of displacements, the mesh is not sufficiently refined for the analysis of the contact stresses that develop between the two sliding faces.

Also notice the sharp re-entrant edges in the model. The presence of sharp re-entrant edges, combined with a coarse mesh makes this model good enough for displacement analysis, but not for stress analysis.

Notes:

10: Thermal stress analysis of a bi- metal loop

Topics covered

- ❑ Thermal deformation and thermal stress analysis
- ❑ Eliminating rigid body motions
- ❑ Saving model in deformed shape

Project description

The temperature of the entire loop shown in Figure 10-1, increases uniformly from an initial 298K to 400K. We need to find the deformation induced by this increase in temperature.

Procedure

Open the LOOP assembly and notice that it consists of the same part twice. Therefore, material properties must be assigned in the **Simulation** study since two different material properties cannot be assigned to the same part in **SolidWorks**. Create a **Static** study and assign material properties as shown in Figure 10-1.

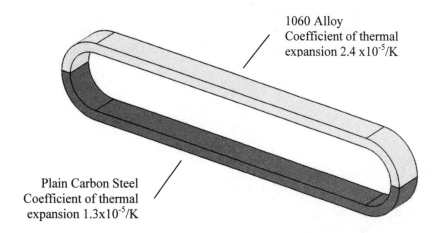

1060 Alloy
Coefficient of thermal
expansion 2.4×10^{-5}/K

Plain Carbon Steel
Coefficient of thermal
expansion 1.3×10^{-5}/K

Figure 10-1: Loop consisting of bonded steel and aluminum parts.

When temperature is increased, the loop will deform because of the different thermal expansion coefficients of steel and aluminum.

The assignment of material properties to assembly components is shown in Figure 10-2.

Material assignments ———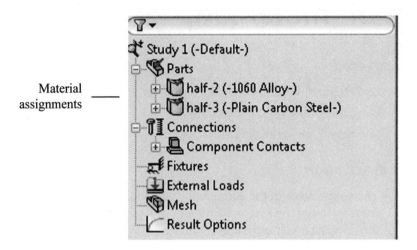

Figure 10-2: Material properties applied in Simulation study.

Since two different material properties could not have been assigned to the same SolidWorks part, the assignment of material properties must be done in a Simulation study.

To account for thermal effects we define the study as **Static,** and in the **Properties** of this study, under **Flow/Thermal Effects** make sure that the option **Input temperature** is selected (Figure 10-3).

Input temperature

Reference temperature

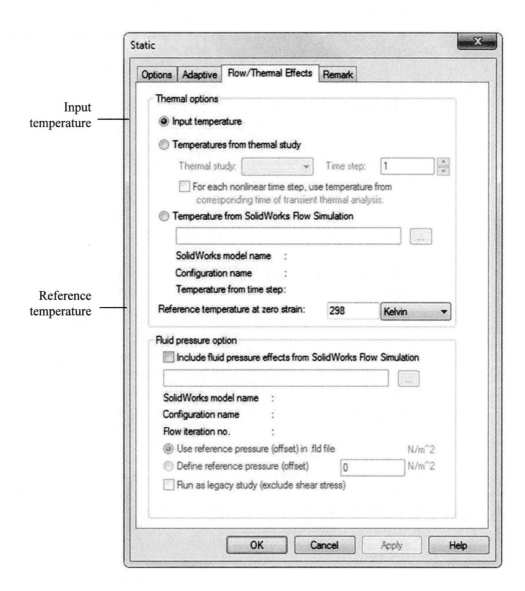

Figure 10-3: The Flow/Thermal Effects tab in the Static study properties window. We instruct the solver to account for the effect of an Input temperature and define the reference temperature at zero strain as 298K.

Input temperature is the default selection.

Before proceeding, let's take this opportunity to review all thermal options available in the study window.

Thermal Option	Definition
Input temperature	Use if prescribed temperatures will be defined in the *Load/Restraint* folder of the study to calculate thermal stresses. This is our case.
Temperature from thermal study	Use if temperature results are available from a previously conducted thermal study.
Temperature from SolidWorks Flow Simulation	Use if temperature results are available from a previously conducted **SolidWorks** Flow Simulation.

An important part of this exercise is the issue of restraints. Restraints should eliminate rigid body motions but should allow the model to deform freely. To accomplish that, we do not apply any restraints at all and use the solver option **"Use soft springs to stabilize model"** (Figure 10-4). This applies a very low stiffness to all nodes in the model in all directions thus eliminating rigid body motions.

Notice that in the absence of restraints, there is no reference point from where to measure displacements.

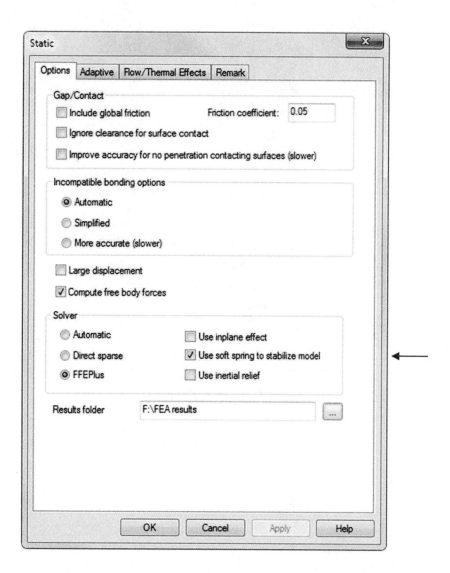

Figure 10-4: The solver option Use soft springs to stabilize the model applies an artificial stiffness to all nodes in the model.

To apply a temperature load, right-click the *External Loads* folder and select **Temperature**. This will open the **Temperature** window. From the fly-out menu, select both assembly components and enter a temperature of 500K. This means that assembly temperature will be increased by 202K from the initial 298K (Figure 10-5).

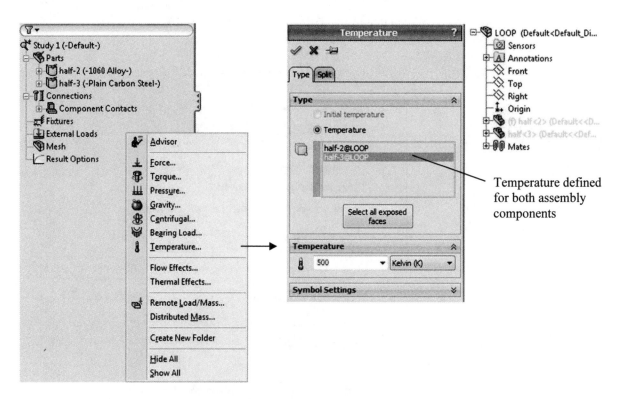

Figure 10-5: A temperature of 500K is applied to both assembly components, which are most conveniently selected from the SolidWorks fly-out menu.

Select both components from the fly-out menu.

Mesh the model with a default element size and run the study.

Displacement results are shown in Figure 10-6.

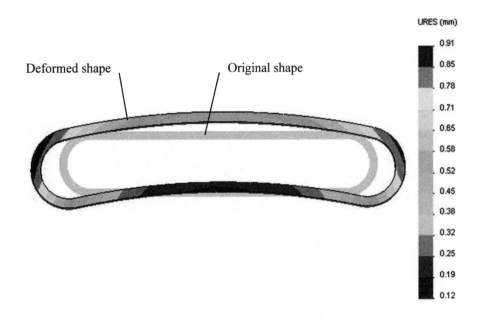

Figure 10-6: Displacement results for the bi-metal beam.

Due to the different thermal expansion ratios of steel and aluminum, thermal strains develop and bend the loop. The scale of deformation shown is 45:1.

Even though numeric values of displacement are reported, the absence of restraints make the interpretation of results difficult because there is no fixed reference system to measure the displacements from.

The deformation caused by thermal stress can be assessed by saving the model in the deformed shape (Figure 10-7). The deformed model can then be measured using **SolidWorks** tools.

To save the model in the deformed state, follow the steps explained in Figure 10-7.

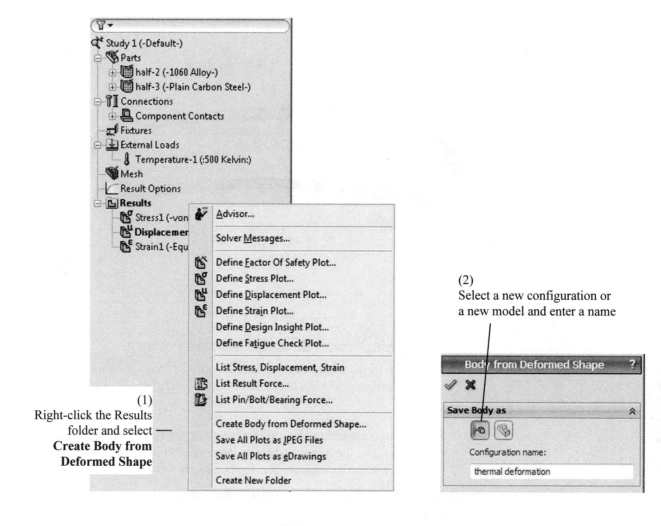

Figure 10-7: Saving a model in the deformed shape.

Here, we save the deformed model in a new configuration called thermal deformation. In the new configuration there is only one part composed of two imported features. The two original parts are suppressed.

Von Mises stress results are shown in Figure 10-8. Because of the different materials, stresses should not be averaged across the boundary separating these two components.

Do not select this option ——

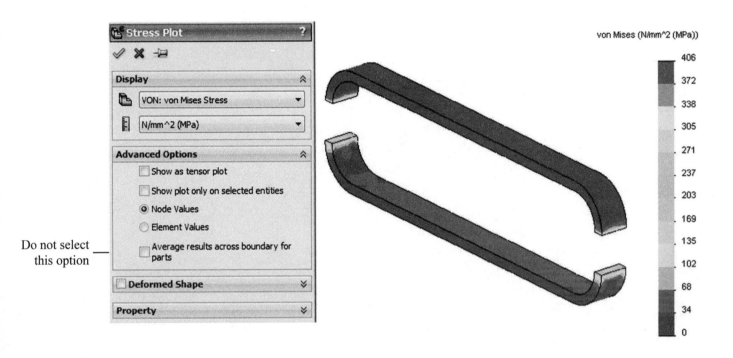

Figure 10-8: Von Mises stress results for the bi-metal assembly. Make sure that the option "Average results across boundary for parts" is not checked.

Exploded view is used.

Notice the unavoidable stress singularities along the connections between different materials. Stress singularities are present because of the rapid change in the material properties across the touching faces.

Because of stress singularities along the edges of the touching faces, the maximum stress strongly depends on the mesh size. You are encouraged to repeat the analysis with different mesh densities to see this effect.

Notes:

11: Buckling analysis of I-beam

Topics covered

❑ Buckling analysis
❑ Buckling load safety factor
❑ Stress safety factor

Project description

A curved I beam is compressed with a 2500N load, as shown in Figure 11-1. Our goal is to calculate the factor of safety related to the yield stress and the factor of safety related to buckling. We wish to find out what is the deciding mode of failure: yielding or buckling?

Procedure

Open the part file I BEAM. The beam material is AISI 304 steel with a yield strength of 207MPa.

Fixed restraint
to end face

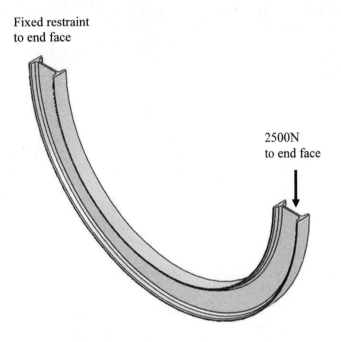

2500N
to end face

Figure 11-1: The I-beam assembly model.

A curved I-beam is loaded by a 2500N force uniformly distributed over the end face. A fixed restraint is applied to the opposite end face.

Before we run a buckling analysis, let us first obtain the results of a static analysis based on the load and restraint shown in Figure 11-1. The I-beam is defined in **SolidWorks** as a structural member and by default, is meshed with beam elements (see chapter 17). We wish to use solid elements instead; therefore we must instruct **Simulation** to treat the I-beam as a solid. Create a static study *01 static* and follow the steps indicated in Figure 11-2 to convert the **Simulation** model to solid geometry.

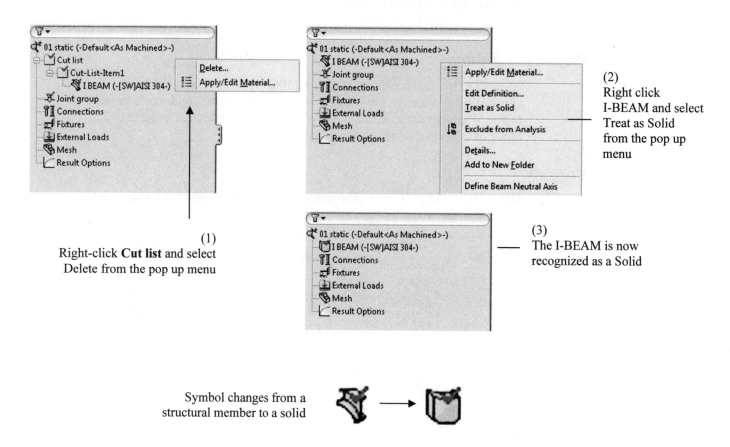

(1)
Right-click **Cut list** and select
Delete from the pop up menu

(2)
Right click
I-BEAM and select
Treat as Solid
from the pop up
menu

(3)
The I-BEAM is now
recognized as a Solid

Symbol changes from a
structural member to a solid

Figure 11-2: Follow these steps to convert the structural member to solid geometry.

Notice the change of symbol from a structural member to a solid.

Apply restraints and load as shown in Figure 11-1, mesh the model using a **Standard Mesh** with 8mm element size. These setting produce poor element shape in the fillets (too high of a turn angle). We accept this mesh because those poorly shaped elements will be far from the highest stresses. You may want to repeat the analysis with a more refined mesh to see that mesh refinement highlights the unavoidable singularities at the supports but does not significantly affects stress levels in the I beam flanges.

Run the solution and review the stress results shown in Figure 11-3.

The results of the static analysis show the maximum von Mises stress is 118MPa, which is below the yield strength of 207MPa.

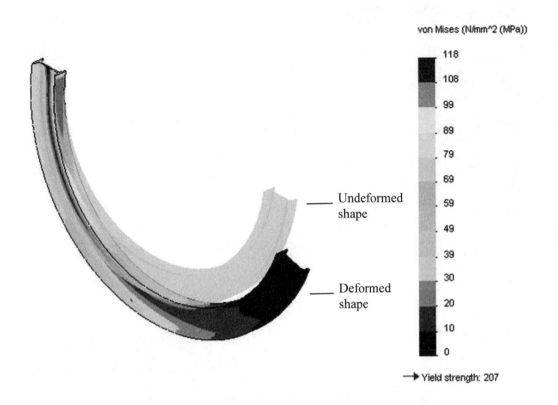

Figure 11-3: Von Mises stress results showed in a deformed shape.

The plot shows the undeformed shape superimposed on the stress plot. Notice that the deformation takes place in-plane.

Based on the results shown in Figure 11-3, the factor of safety to yield is:

$$FOS_{yield} = \frac{yield\ strength}{\max von\ Mises\ stress} = \frac{207MPa}{118MPa} = 1.75,$$

meaning that the beam's material is below yield. Therefore, based on the results of the static analysis, the structure is safe.

As is always the case with slender members, the factor of safety related to material yield strength may not be sufficient to describe the structure's safety. This is because of the possible occurrence of buckling. We need to calculate the factor of safety related to buckling, which requires performing a buckling analysis. Define a buckling study as shown in Figure 11-4.

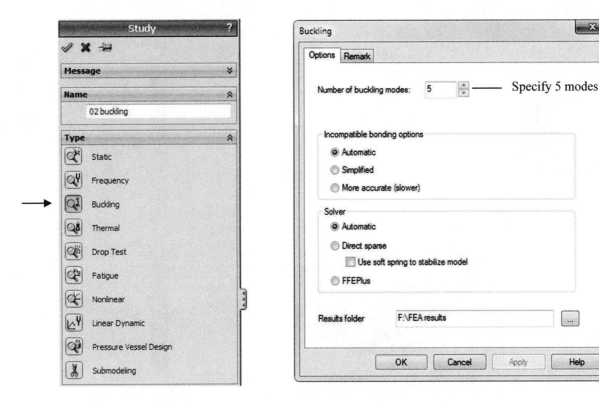

Figure 11-4: Definition of a buckling study and the Buckling study properties window.

Defining a buckling study requires specifying the number of desired buckling modes. Here we ask for five buckling modes.

When defining a buckling study, we need to decide how many buckling modes should be calculated. This is a close analogy to the number of modes in a frequency analysis. In most practical cases, the first buckling mode determines the safety of the analyzed structure. The reason why we specify five modes and not just one will become clear once the results are analyzed.

Convert the structural member to solid geometry, copy the loads, restraints and mesh from the static study to the buckling study and run the analysis.

Once the buckling analysis has been completed, right-click the *Results* folder to review the list of **Buckling Load Factors** (BLFs). The BLFs correspond to the five calculated buckling modes.

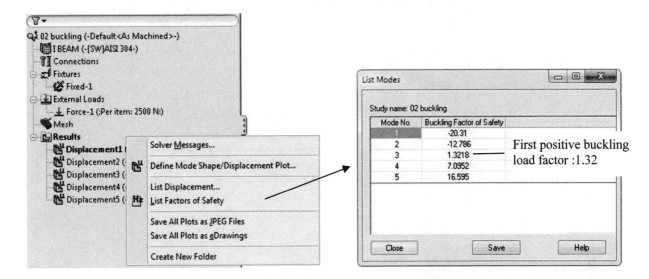

Figure 11-5: Summary of Buckling Load Factors (BLF) corresponding to five calculated buckling modes.

We calculated five buckling modes to introduce the concept of negative BLFs. If only one BLF is requested, Simulation reports the first positive BLF.

The BLF is a number by which the applied load has to be multiplied in order for buckling to take place for a given buckling mode. If the BLF is negative the load direction must be reversed. The list in Figure 11-5 shows two negative BLFs. The third BLF is therefore the first real BLF=1.32.

The buckling load can now be calculated as follows:

$$BLF = \frac{Buckling\ Load}{Applied\ Load} = 1.32$$

Buckling Load = Applied Load x *BLF* = 2500N x 1.32 = 3300N

The BLF is lower than the factor of safety related to yielding, meaning that the I-BEAM will buckle before it yields. Our conclusion is that buckling is the deciding mode of failure. Also notice that high stresses affect the beam only locally, while buckling is global. The onset of yielding does not yet mean a structural failure, while buckling does.

We will now review a displacement plot to study the shape of the first positive buckling mode.

Even though displacement results can be shown in color, they do not provide any useful information. In a buckling analysis, the magnitude of the displacement is meaningless, just like in a frequency analysis. The **Mode Shape** plot is shown in Figure 11-6. **Show colors** is deselected to eliminate confusing information on the magnitude of displacement. "Name view orientation" *mv*1 is used and text is added to **Plot Details**.

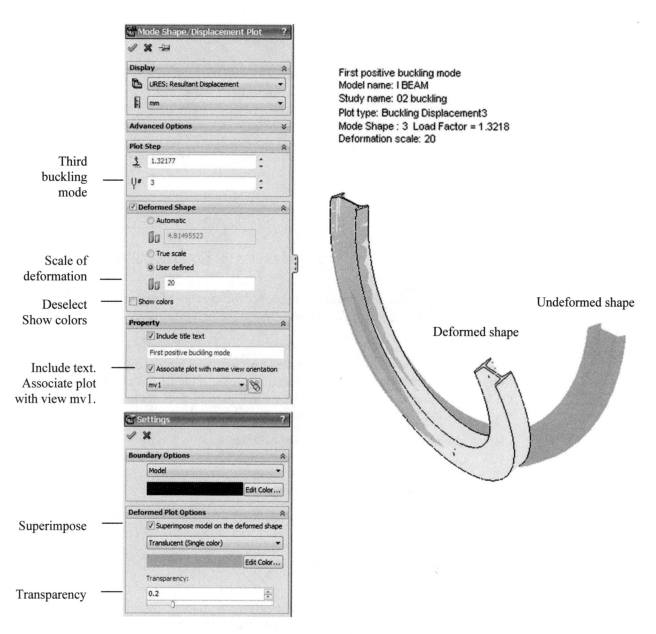

Third buckling mode

Scale of deformation

Deselect Show colors

Include text. Associate plot with view mv1.

Superimpose

Transparency

Undeformed shape

Deformed shape

First positive buckling mode
Model name: I BEAM
Study name: 02 buckling
Plot type: Buckling Displacement3
Mode Shape : 3 Load Factor = 1.3218
Deformation scale: 20

Figure 11-6: The deformation plot provides visual feedback on the shape of the buckled structure.

This plot shows the buckled shape along with the undeformed model.

Figure 11-7 presents an important comparison of the deformed shapes obtained from the static and buckling analyses.

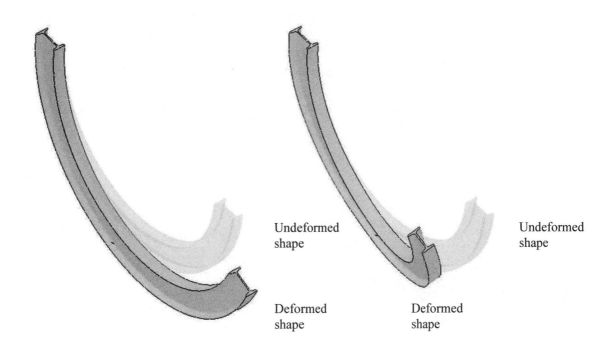

Undeformed shape

Undeformed shape

Deformed shape

Deformed shape

Static deformation

Deformation in the first buckling mode

Figure 11-7: A comparison of deformed shapes found in the static and buckling analyses.

The model deforms in-plane in the static analysis. The same model deforms out of plane in the buckling analysis.

A side-by-side comparison of the deformed shapes from the static and buckling analyses shown in Figure 11-7 reveals a very important difference in the nature of these deformed shapes. The static analysis predicts in plane bending for which the I-beam is well designed. The buckling mode plot shows that the I-beam will twist. An I-beam is poorly designed to resist torque and in fact, the low torsional stiffness of the I-beam is what makes buckling the deciding mode of failure.

Also the out of plane deformation may be counterintuitive making it easy to forget that the I-beam will fail in buckling rather than in yielding.

It should also be noted that the calculated value of the buckling load is non-conservative. It does not account for the always-present imperfections in real world geometry, materials, loads, and supports. Also, it does not account for the fact that the meshed model is stiffer than the corresponding model before meshing. With this in mind, the real buckling load may be significantly lower than the calculated 3300N.

As opposed to an I-beam which is designed to take bending but not torsion, a tube would be suitable for both types of loads. Therefore, you may wish to run a similar analysis on a curved tube to see what will be the deciding mode of failure.

12: Static analysis of a bracket using adaptive solution methods

Topics covered

- ❑ h-adaptive solution method
- ❑ p-adaptive solution method
- ❑ Comparison between h-elements and p-elements

Project description

A bracket shown in Figure 12-1 is supported along the backside. A 10000N load is uniformly distributed over the face surrounding the hole as shown in Figure 12-1. We need to find the location and magnitude of the maximum von Mises stress. Open the part BRACKET with material AISI 304 already assigned.

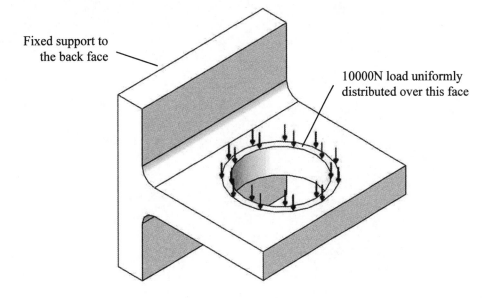

Fixed support to the back face

10000N load uniformly distributed over this face

Figure 12-1: Hollow cantilever bracket under a bending load.

Due to the symmetry of the BRACKET geometry, loads, and supports, we could simplify the geometry by cutting it in half along the plane of symmetry, but decide against it because the work involved would not save much time overall.

We use this simple problem to introduce two new solution methods: the **h-adaptive** and the **p-adaptive** solution methods. Both are available only for **Static** studies using solid elements.

We start with a description of the **h-adaptive** solution method. On several previous occasions, we performed mesh refinements to investigate the effect of mesh density on results. We also added mesh controls to analyze stresses more accurately in "difficult" locations. In this chapter we demonstrate that the **h-adaptive** solution method automates the mesh refinement process and to some extent, relieves users from having to make meshing decisions such as selecting element size and applying mesh controls.

Figure 12-2 shows the properties of an **h-adaptive** study. **Target accuracy**, **Accuracy bias** and **Maximum number of loops** control the iterative process of mesh refinement.

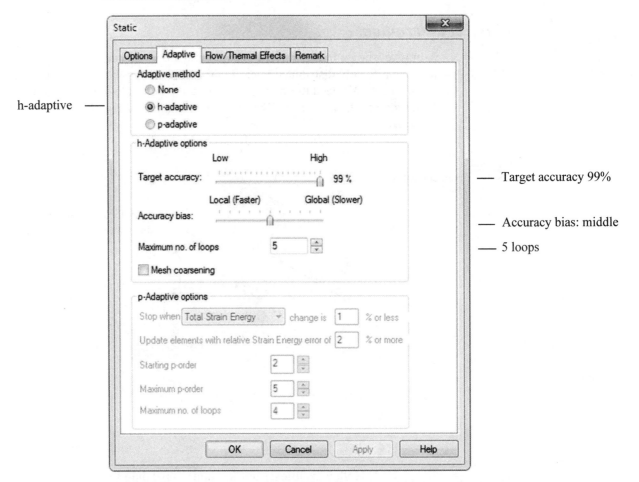

Figure 12-2: The Adaptive tab in the Static study properties window with the h-adaptive solution method selected.

The selection "h-adaptive" made in the Adaptive tab in the Static study properties window (selectable by right clicking the Static study and selecting Properties...), activates the use of the h-adaptive solution method. For the h-adaptive solution presented in this chapter, we use the settings as shown in this illustration.

The h-adaptive solution options are explained in the table below.

Setting	Definition
Target accuracy	Sets the accuracy level for the strain energy norm. This is NOT the stress accuracy level. However, a high level of accuracy indicates more accurate stress results.
Accuracy bias	You can move the slider towards Local to instruct the program to concentrate on getting accurate peak stress results using a fewer number of elements. You can also move the slider towards Global to instruct the program to concentrate on getting overall accurate results.
Maximum no. of loops	Sets the maximum number of loops allowed when you run the study. The maximum possible number of loops is five.
Mesh coarsening	Check this option to allow the program to coarsen the mesh in regions with low error during the adaptive loops. The number of elements in consecutive loops may increase or decrease depending on the model and the initial mesh. If this option is not checked, the program does not change the mesh in regions with low errors.

The **h-adaptive** solution method is called "adaptive" because mesh refinement is "adapted" to the stress pattern and the mesh is refined only where it is necessary to produce results satisfying accuracy requirements specified in the **Study** properties. h-elements retain their order; they cannot be upgraded to a higher order.

Now review the **p-adaptive** solution method. If you recall, in chapter 1 we mentioned that **SolidWorks Simulation** can use either first order elements (called draft quality), or second order elements (called high quality). Furthermore, recall that first order elements model a linear (or first order) displacement distribution and constant stress distribution, while second order elements model a parabolic (second order) displacement distribution and linear stress distribution. We now have to amend the above statements.

Aside from first and second order elements, **SolidWorks Simulation** can also work with elements of "floating" order which can change order during the iterative solution process. The highest available order is five. These elements of "floating" order are called p-elements and are available when the **p-adaptive** option is selected as the solution method in the **Study** properties window under the **Adaptive** tab (Figure 12-3). This option is available only for static studies using solid elements.

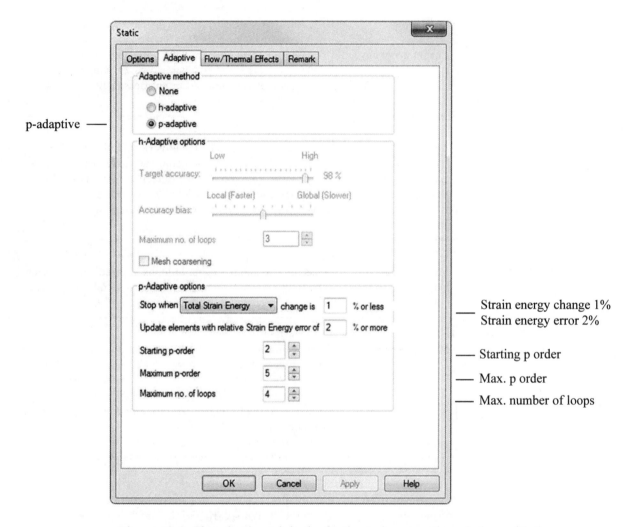

Figure 12-3: The adaptive tab in the Static study properties window with the p-adaptive solution method selected.

The selection "p-adaptive" made in the Adaptive tab in the Static study properties window activates the use of the p-adaptive solution method.

The p-adaptive solution options are shown in Figure 12-3 and explained in the table below:

Setting	Definition
Stop when	Iterations (looping) increase element order until the change in Total Strain Energy (or other measures like RMS resultant displacement or RMS von Mises stress) between the two consecutive iterations is less than the specified value (default is 1%) shown in the p-adaptive options area. If this requirement is not satisfied, then looping will stop when the elements reach the fifth order; this will be the fourth loop.
Update elements with relative Strain Energy error of ...	This setting controls which elements are upgraded during the iterative solution. By default, elements with relative Strain Energy error of 2% or more are updated.
Starting p-order	The initial order of elements. Usually the starting p-order is set to 2, which means that all elements are defined to start as second order elements.
Maximum p-order	The actual highest order to be used in p-adaptive solution. The highest order available in **SolidWorks Simulation** is the fifth order.
Maximum no. of loops	Sets the maximum number of iterations (loops) allowed when the p-adaptive study is run. The maximum possible number of loops is four.

Let us pause for a moment and explain some terminology. Refer to Figure 2-16 which explains that h denotes the characteristic element size. While the mesh is refined during the convergence process, the characteristic element size h becomes smaller. Therefore the mesh refinement process that we conducted in chapters 2 and 3 is called the h-convergence process, and the elements used in this process are called h-elements. An h-adaptive solution is an iterative solution where the h-element mesh is automatically refined in several iterations.

When p-elements are used, the iterative process does not involve mesh refinement. While the mesh remains unchanged, the element order changes from second all the way to fifth order elements. The iterations may also stop sooner if the convergence criterion (here the change in **Total Strain Energy**) is satisfied before the fifth order is reached.

The order of any element is defined by the order of polynomial functions that describe the displacements in the element. Because the polynomial order experiences changes in the p-adaptive solution, the process of consecutive element order upgrade is called a p-convergence process (p stands for polynomial), and the upgradeable elements used in this process are called p-elements.

Not all p-elements are upgraded during the solution process. Which elements are updated depends on the selection made in the field **Update elements with relative Strain Energy error of ___ % or more**. Here we set it to 2%, meaning that only those elements that do not satisfy the above criterion will be upgraded (investigate other criteria as well). Therefore we say that the element upgrading is "adaptive", or driven by the results of consecutive iterations.

The p-adaptive solution process is analogous to the process of mesh refinement, which also continues until the change in the selected result is no longer significant.

Procedure

We will solve the same problem in five different ways:

1. Using one mesh of h elements

2. Using one mesh of h elements with mesh controls added

3. Using the h-adaptive solution method

4. Using the p-adaptive solution method with default **p-adaptive** solution settings

5. Using the p-adaptive solution method with modified **p-adaptive** solution settings

First, solve the model using second order solid tetrahedral h-elements using the default element size. Name the study *standard*. Von Mises stress results with superimposed mesh are shown in Figure 12-4.

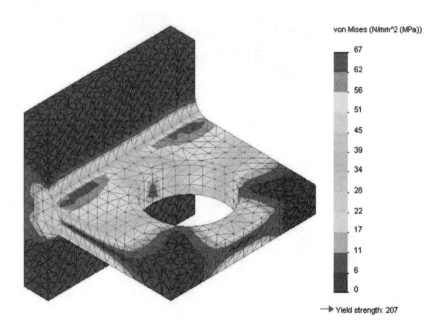

Figure 12-4: Von Mises stress results obtained in a standard study.

The maximum von Mises stress is 67MPa.

Now, repeat the analysis using a mesh with default mesh controls applied to both fillets (top and bottom). A default mesh control produces elements the size of one half of the default global element size. Name the study *standard with mesh controls*. Von Mises stress results produced by this study are shown in Figure 12-5.

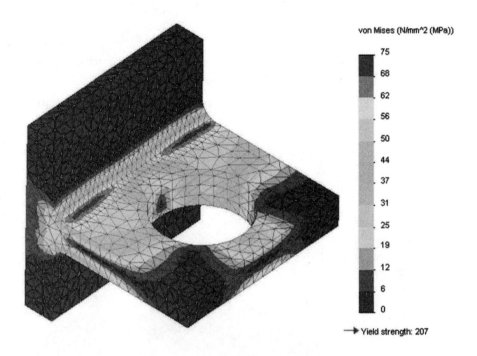

Figure 12-5: Von Mises stress results obtained in study *standard with mesh controls.*

The maximum von Mises stress is 75MPa. Notice that the decision of adding mesh controls was made based on results from the previous study.

Now, create a new study *h adaptive* identical to *standard* study (the one without the mesh control) except in the study properties window under the **Adaptive** tab, select **h-adaptive**. Use the settings shown in Figure 12-2: **Target accuracy 99%**, no **Accuracy bias** (slider in the middle), **Maximum no. of loops 5.** Do not use any mesh controls.

As we have previously mentioned, the finite element mesh is refined during the h-adaptive solution. The results are reported for the mesh from the last performed iteration (the most refined one). Run the solution of the *h-adaptive* study and display the results as shown in Figure 12-6.

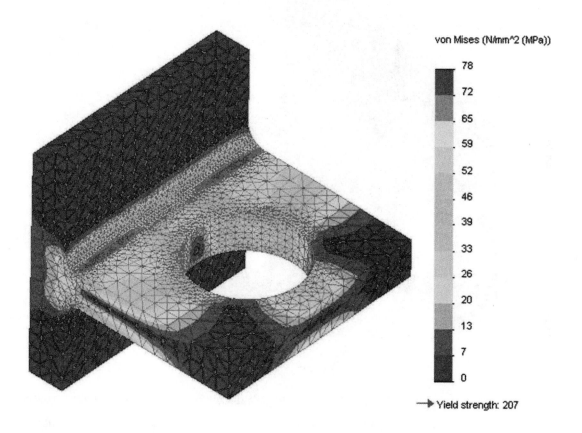

Figure 12-6: Von Mises stress results obtained with an h-adaptive solution.

Notice that the mesh has been automatically refined as compared to the initial mesh visible in Figure 12-4. The maximum von Mises stress is 78MPa.

Now, create a study called *p adaptive 01*. In the study window under the **Adaptive** tab, select **p-adaptive**. Use all defaults for a p-adaptive study definition as shown in Figure 12-3. Restraints and Loads can be copied from any of the two previous studies.

Considering that the p-adaptive solution will be used, we can manage with a mesh without bias (no controls need to be applied). Therefore, copy the mesh from the *standard* study. Using higher order elements, which is equivalent to refinement of an h-element mesh, our mesh without bias will still deliver results with acceptable accuracy.

Having solved the study with p-elements, the stress plot produced is shown in Figure 12-7.

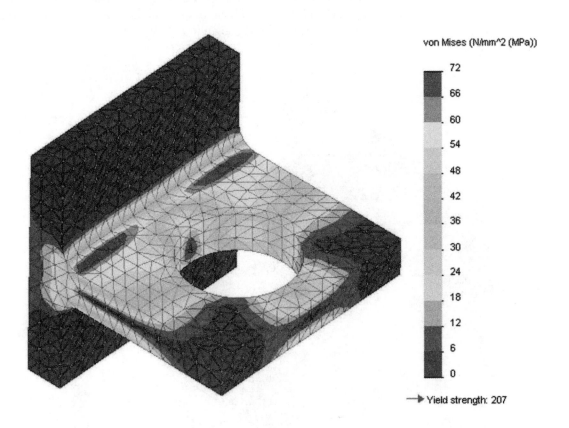

Figure 12-7: Von Mises stress results obtained using the p-adaptive method.

The mesh is identical to the mesh visible in Figure 12-4. The maximum von Mises stress is 72 MPa.

To illustrate the iterative nature of **h-adaptive** and **p-adaptive** solutions, create convergence graphs which are available for both types of adaptive solutions.

To create a convergence graph, right-click the *Results* folder and select **Define Adaptive Convergence Graph**. For both adaptive studies select **Maximum von Mises Stress** in the **Convergence Graph** window (Figure 12-8). Later try experimenting with other **Convergence Graph** options.

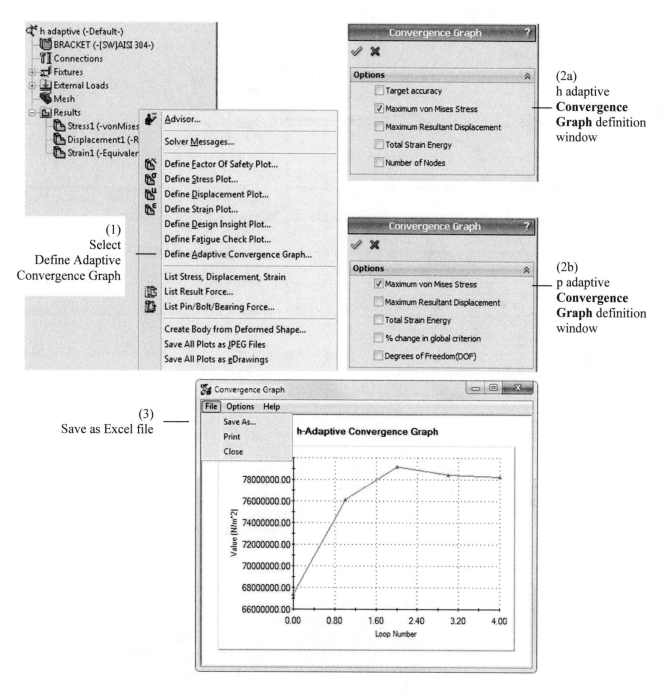

Figure 12-8: Defining a convergence graph for h-adaptive or p-adaptive solution methods.

Automatically created graphs can be modified using Graph Options or saved as a .csv file and formatted in Excel. Here we use the second method. The graph window has been modified to fit this page.

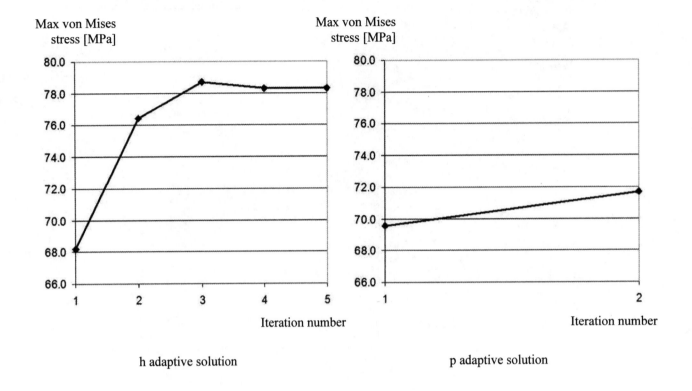

Figure 12-9: Convergence graphs of maximum von Mises stress results obtained in the adaptive solutions.

The h-adaptive convergence graph shows that five iterations were performed during the h-adaptive solutions. The p-adaptive graph shows that only two iterations were performed during p-adaptive solutions.

The maximum number of iterations in the h-adaptive process is five and as Figure 12-9 indicates, all five iterations were performed because we used a very demanding 99% **Target accuracy** specified in the settings of the h-adaptive study. **Target accuracy** indirectly controls the number of iterations performed during the **h-adaptive** solution. Try experimenting with a less demanding **Target accuracy** to observe that the solution will stop without using up all available iterations.

The maximum number of iterations in a p-adaptive study is four. Figure 12-9 shows that only two were performed, so the iterative solution must have stopped due to the convergence requirements being satisfied before all available iterations were used.

Create the last study and call it *p-adaptive 02* (you may copy study *p adaptive 01*). Define much more demanding convergence requirements to force the solver into using all available iterations and reaching the highest available element order (Figure 12-10).

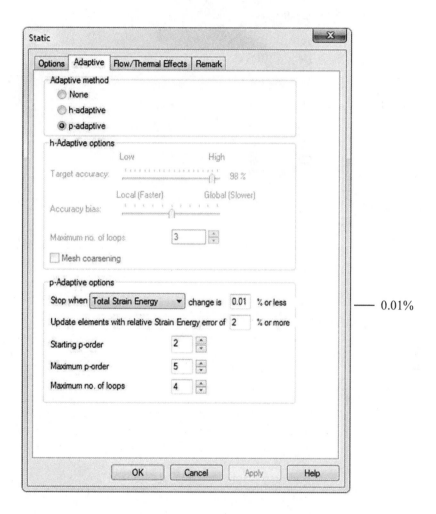

Figure 12-10: p-adaptive solution settings for study *p-adaptive 02.*

A very demanding convergence requirement forces the solver to go up to the highest available p order (fifth order) and hence to perform the maximum possible number of iterations (fourth iteration).

Von Mises stress results of study *p adaptive 02* are shown in Figure 12-11.

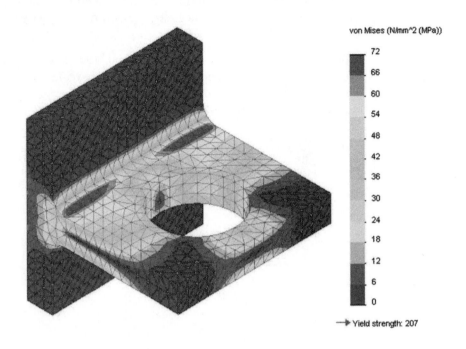

Figure 12-11: Von Mises stress results of study *p-adaptive 02.*

The maximum von Mises stress is 72MPa.

Convergence of von Mises stress results obtained in the *p adaptive 02* study is shown in Figure 12-12.

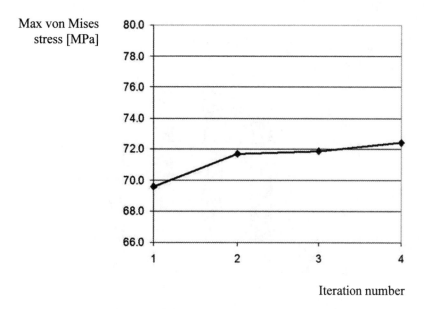

Figure 12-12: Convergence of von Mises stress results obtained in the *p-adaptive 02* study.

The p-adaptive convergence graph shows that four iterations were performed.

When the maximum number of iterations is performed as shown in Figure 12-12, we get no feedback as to whether the solution stopped because the specified accuracy in study properties was achieved, or because the maximum allowed number of iterations was reached. In the h-adaptive solution the maximum number of iterations is 5 whereas in the p-adaptive solution, the maximum number of iterations is 4 and coincides with the highest available element order 5.

A summary of results obtained in all studies is shown in Figure 12-13. These graphs were prepared outside of **SolidWorks Simulation** based on data exported from the **SolidWorks Simulation** graphs.

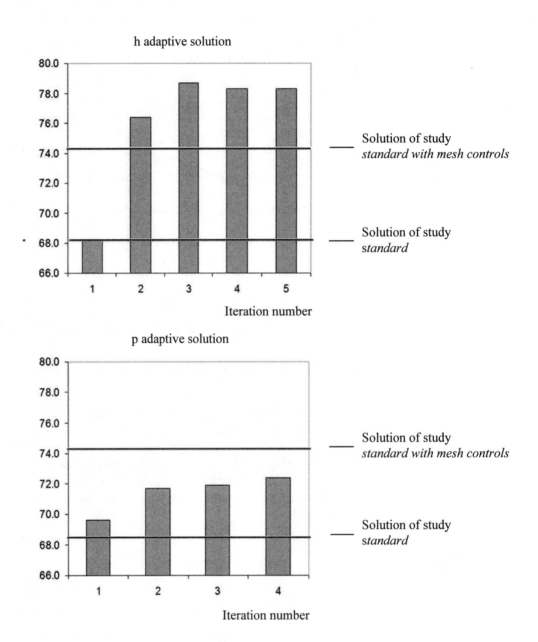

Figure 12-13: Summary of all results.

Top: *The results of the two non-adaptive studies shown with horizontal lines, and the results of the h-adaptive study repeated from Figure 12-9 shown with vertical bars.*

Bottom: *The results of the two non-adaptive studies shown with horizontal lines, and the results of the p-adaptive study shown with vertical bars repeated from Figure 12-12.*

Examine the bottom graph in Figure 12-13 and notice that the first two iterations are the results of study *p-adaptive 01*. All four iterations 1,2,3,4 are the results of study *p-adaptive 02*. The difference between studies *p-adaptive 01* and *p-adaptive 02* is that in study *p-adaptive 02,* two more iterations were performed because of the more demanding accuracy requirements.

You are encouraged to repeat both h and p convergence studies using an initially more refined mesh and different convergence criteria.

Which one of the three solution methods is preferred? The "regular" method using h-elements (here studies *standard* and *standard with mesh controls*), the h-adaptive solution (*h adaptive* study), or the p-adaptive solution (*p adaptive 01* and *p adaptive 02* studies)?

Experience indicates that second order h-elements offer the best combination of accuracy and computational simplicity. For this reason, the **SolidWorks Simulation** automesher is tuned to create h-element meshes. This makes h-elements preferable over p-elements. Also, a **p-adaptive** solution is much more computationally intensive than a standard or adaptive h-element solution. For these reasons, the **p-adaptive** solution should be reserved for special cases where solution accuracy must be known according to the settings available in the p-adaptive study.

This leaves us with the choice between standard and **h-adaptive** solution methods. The h-adaptive solution is more computationally demanding and more time-consuming than the standard solution. At the same time, it offers a very important advantage: it relieves users from the need to exercise judgment over meshing choices. In a standard solution, the user must decide if a default mesh is acceptable and how it should be modified by specifying mesh controls and/or global refinement. The **h-adaptive** solution automatically takes care of refining the mesh (both globally and locally).

With increasing computational power and the decreasing cost of computer hardware, the **h-adaptive** solution is becoming the preferred solution method in **SolidWorks Simulation**.

Both **h-adaptive** and **p-adaptive** methods are great learning tools, leading to a better understanding of element order, the convergence process, and discretization error. For this reason, readers are encouraged to repeat some, if not all of the previous exercises using both of the adaptive solution methods.

Notes:

13: Drop test

Topics covered

- ❑ Drop test analysis
- ❑ Stress wave propagation
- ❑ Direct time integration solution

Project description

A ceramic porcelain part RING is dropped from a height of 500mm and lands on a flat and horizontal rigid floor (Figure 13-1). We will simulate the impact using a **Drop Test** analysis.

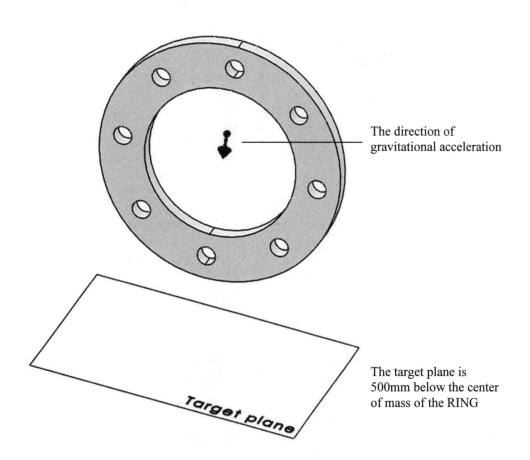

The direction of gravitational acceleration

The target plane is 500mm below the center of mass of the RING

Figure 13-1: The RING dropping on a rigid floor.

The direction of gravitational acceleration is normal to the target plane.

Procedure

Open the part called RING. It has ceramic porcelain material properties already assigned. Notice the split lines added to the RING geometry.

Create a **Drop Test** study named *drop*. **SolidWorks Simulation** creates two folders in the **Drop Test** study: *Setup* and *Result Options* (Figure 13-2).

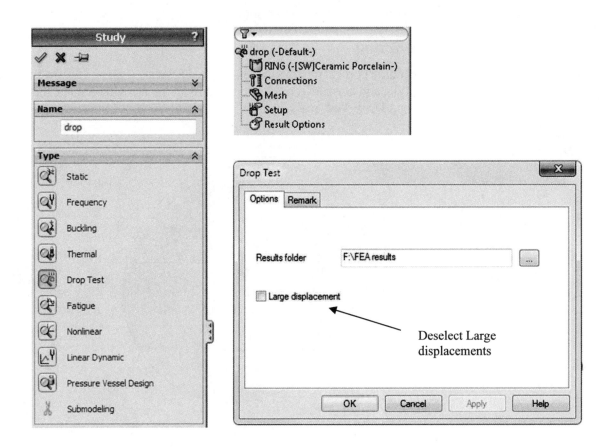

Figure 13-2: Drop Test study definition (left), Drop Test study window with *Setup* and *Result Options* (top right) and Drop test properties window (bottom right).

Displacement in the model will not be large and to speed up the solution process, you may deselect the Large displacements option in the study properties.

Right-click the *Setup* folder and select **Define/Edit** to open the **Drop Test Setup** window. Select **Drop height** and **From centroid** and enter 500mm as the drop height. From the fly-out **SolidWorks** menu (not shown in Figure 13-3), select the **Top Plane** to define the line of action of gravitational acceleration as normal to the **Top Plane**. Enter the magnitude of gravitational acceleration as 9.81m/s^2. Finally, select **Normal to gravity** as **Target**

Orientation. After completing the exercise, try experimenting with a different **Target Orientation** using the **Parallel to Ref. Plane** option in the **Drop Test Setup** window (Figure 13-3).

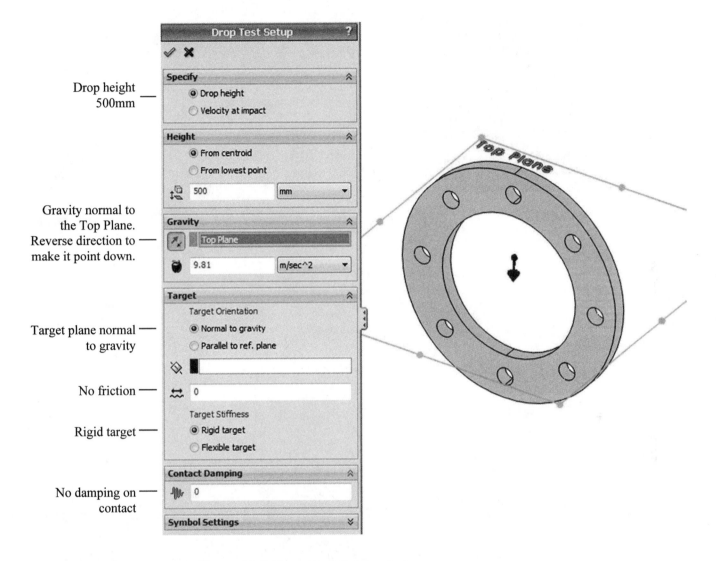

Drop height 500mm

Gravity normal to the Top Plane. Reverse direction to make it point down.

Target plane normal to gravity

No friction

Rigid target

No damping on contact

Figure 13-3: **Drop Test Setup** window.

RING landing perfectly square on a rigid floor may not be a realistic scenario but allows for an illustrative review of a Drop Test.

Having defined all the required entries in the **Drop Test Setup** window, we now need to define sensors under the **Sensor** folder. This is done in **SolidWorks Feature Manager**, as shown in Figure 13-4.

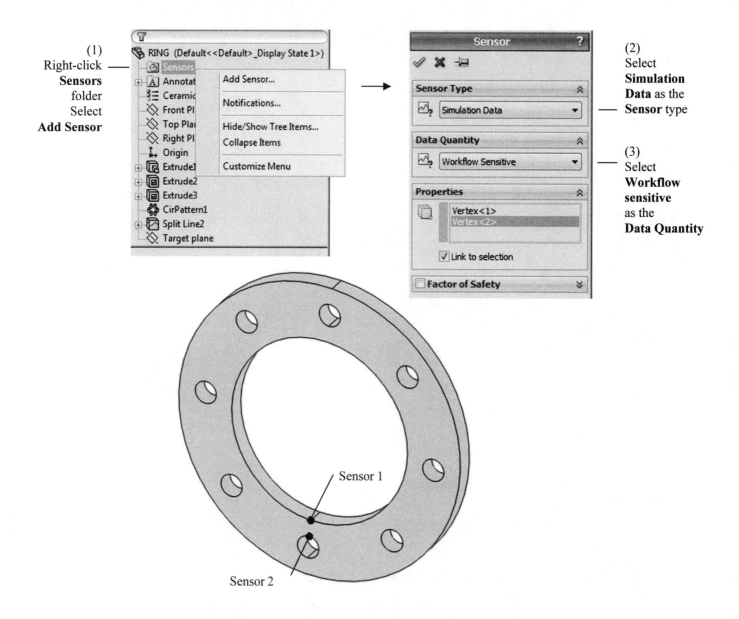

(1)
Right-click
Sensors
folder
Select
Add Sensor

(2)
Select
Simulation Data as the **Sensor** type

(3)
Select
Workflow sensitive as the **Data Quantity**

Sensor 1

Sensor 2

Figure 13-4: Simulation Data sensors defined in two locations.

Locations of the sensors used in the Results Options. Sensors are placed on vertices created by split lines in the SolidWorks model.

224

Referring to Figure 13-4, sensors are defined where the highest P1 stresses are to be expected. Notice that the maximum principal stress relates to the failure of porcelain, which is a brittle material. Von Mises stress is not applicable as a failure criterion for brittle material.

Right-click the *Result Options* folder to open the **Result Options** window.

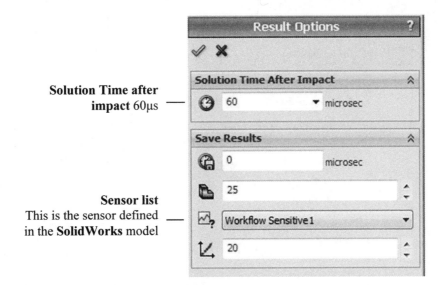

Figure 13-5: Result Options window.

To monitor what occurs to the ring during the first 60 microseconds after first impact, enter 60 as the **Solution time after impact**. See **SolidWorks Simulation** help for more information.

In the **Save Results** area of the **Result Options** window, accept the default 0 (microseconds) meaning that results will be saved immediately after the first impact. Also, accept the default 25 for the **No. of plots**. This means that the solution time is divided into twenty five intervals and full results (available as plots) are saved only for these intervals.

Notice that full results are saved for the 25 plots spaced out evenly over a 60 microseconds time period.

Since the impact time is very short, it is measured in microseconds. The maximum displacement or stress may occur during the first impact, or later when the model is rebounding. A sufficiently long solution time needs to be specified to capture maximum displacement and stress results.

Mesh the model with the default element size and run the solution. Upon completion of the solution, **SolidWorks Simulation** creates the following result folders: *Stress, Displacement and Strain*. To view a time history graph, right-click the *Results* folder and select **Define Time History Plot** (Figure 13-6).

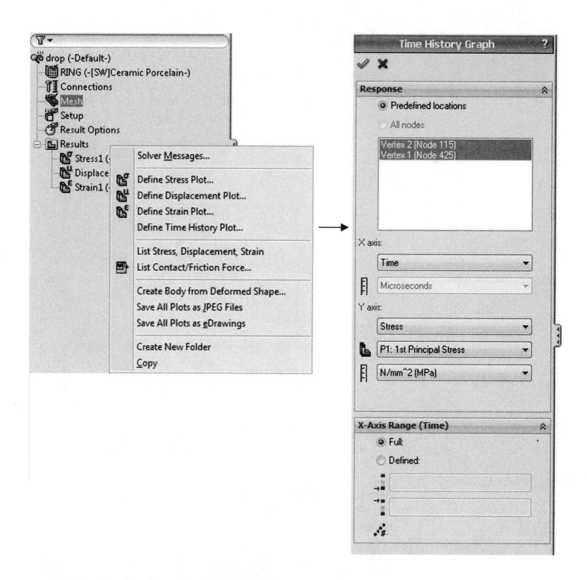

Figure 13-6: Define Time History Graph creates graphs of stress, displacement, velocity and acceleration as functions of time.

Graphs are created for locations defined by sensors; see Figure 13-7.

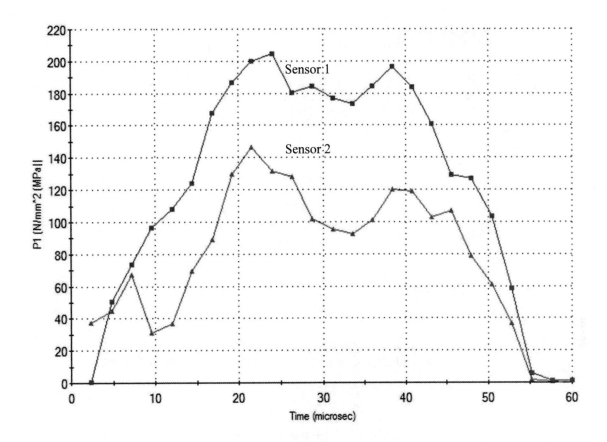

Figure 13-7: Time history graphs for sensor 1 and sensor 2 indicates that the highest P1 stress happens for sensor 1 at time 24µs.

Based on the review of the **Time History Graph**, we find that the highest P1 stress occurs at a time of 24 µs (move the cursor over the plot to find this time value). Therefore, we can create a P1 stress plot that approximately corresponds to this time point (Figure 13-8).

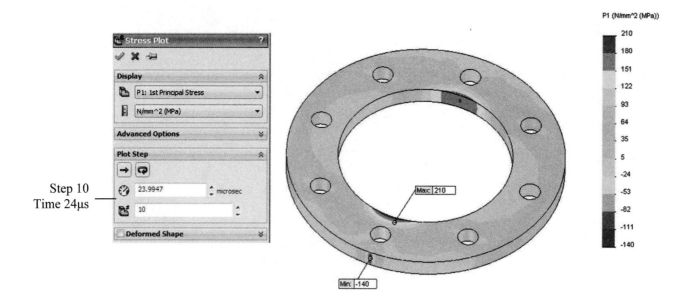

Step 10
Time 24μs

Figure 13-8: P1 stress plot for time step 24μs showing the maximum P1 stress. This is found based on temporal data from the graphs in Figure 13-7.

Location of maximum and minimum P1 stress is shown.

Will the ring break? The **Drop Test** analysis does not directly provide pass/fail results. It is best used to compare the severity of impact for different drop scenarios.

The maximum principal stress calculated is 209 MPa and compared to the ultimate strength of ceramic porcelain; which is 172 MPa, indications are that damage to the ring is likely.

To see the ring bouncing off the floor as well as the stress wave propagating in the model, repeat the study using a longer solution time and animate the stress plot. If a long enough solution time is used for the analysis you will see the ring bouncing off the floor more than once.

The **Drop Test** is an analysis intended to model the dynamic impact force of very short durations, since this is when damage is most likely to occur. The **Drop Test** analysis takes into consideration inertial effects but not damping. The **Drop Test** analysis uses a numerically intensive but stable direct (explicit) time integration method.

14: Selected nonlinear problems

Topics covered

- ❑ Large displacement analysis
- ❑ Analysis with shell elements
- ❑ Membrane effects
- ❑ Following and non-following load
- ❑ Nonlinear material analysis
- ❑ Residual stress

In all previous exercises we assumed that the model stiffness did not change significantly when the model deformed due to the applied load. Consequently the stiffness only needed to be calculated once, before any load had been applied. Since this stiffness adequately described model behavior during the entire loading process, the model stiffness did not have to be updated and the load could be applied in one single step. The only time we departed from these assumptions was in the analysis of the contact problem.

We will now discuss a few problems where the stiffness changes globally rather than locally, as was the case in the contact problem.

If a change of stiffness during the process of load application is caused by a change in model geometry, the problem may be solved with the **Large displacement** option selected in a **Static** study. Other types of nonlinear behavior require a **Nonlinear** study (Figure 14-1).

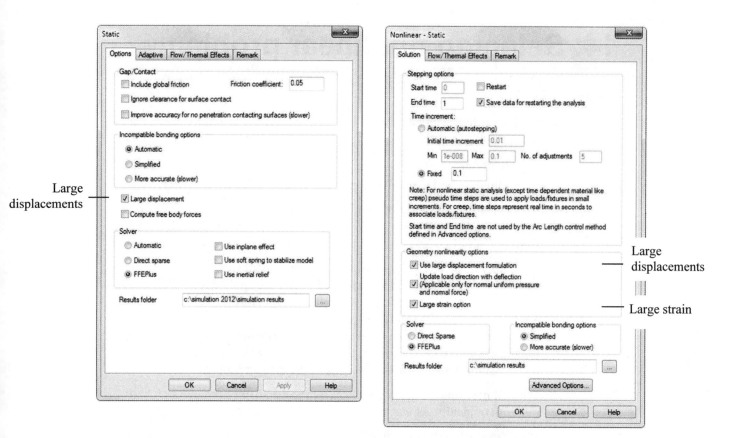

Static study   Nonlinear study

Figure 14-1: Nonlinear analysis option in Simulation studies: Static study (left), Nonlinear study (right).

The above options do not describe all nonlinear analysis capabilities of either study. Contact analysis is available in both Static and Nonlinear if Contact Sets are defined. Nonlinear material is available in a Nonlinear study.

Nonlinear problems caused by a change of model geometry can be solved either in a **Static** study with the **Large displacement** option selected, or in a **Nonlinear** study. All nonlinear problems may be solved in a **Nonlinear** study, which is available in **SolidWorks Simulation Premium**.

Some limitations apply to a nonlinear geometry analysis conducted in a Static study. You may always select the **Large displacement** option in a **Static** study, whether it is necessary or not. However, this significantly increases solution time.

There is a common misconception that nonlinear analysis is the analysis of nonlinear material only. Remember that material nonlinearity is just one of the many types of nonlinear behavior, some of which will be reviewed in this chapter.

Open model NL002 and review the **SolidWorks** Feature Manager. Notice that an offset surface has been inserted in the middle of the beam thickness and solid bodies have been deleted. Therefore, the model contains only surface geometry. **Simulation** will recognize it and will mesh the model with shell elements.

Create two **Static** studies: *linear* and *nonlinear*. Check the **Large displacement** option in the properties of the *nonlinear* study. This is the only difference between these two studies.

When a study is created using a model with surfaces only, we need to define shell thickness. Notice that this was not required in chapter 4 where a sheet metal model was analyzed. This was because shell thickness was taken from solid model geometry. Right-click the shell folder and select **Edit Definition** from the pop-up menu. In the **Shell Definition** window, select **Thin** as the shell element type and enter 2mm for the shell thickness, accept 0 as the shell offset (Figure 14-2). Material properties are transferred automatically from the **SolidWorks** model.

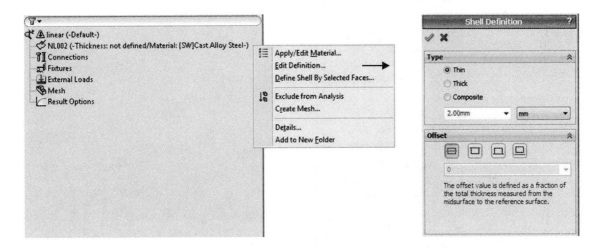

Figure 14-2: Shell Definition window.

Thin shell and thick shell models respectively, have a constant and parabolic transverse shear stress distribution across their thickness. Refer to Simulation help for information on Composite shells.

Apply a 10N force to the edge of the last hole in the direction normal to the **Top** plane, and a **Fixed** restraint to the edge of the opposite (wide) end (Figure 14-3).

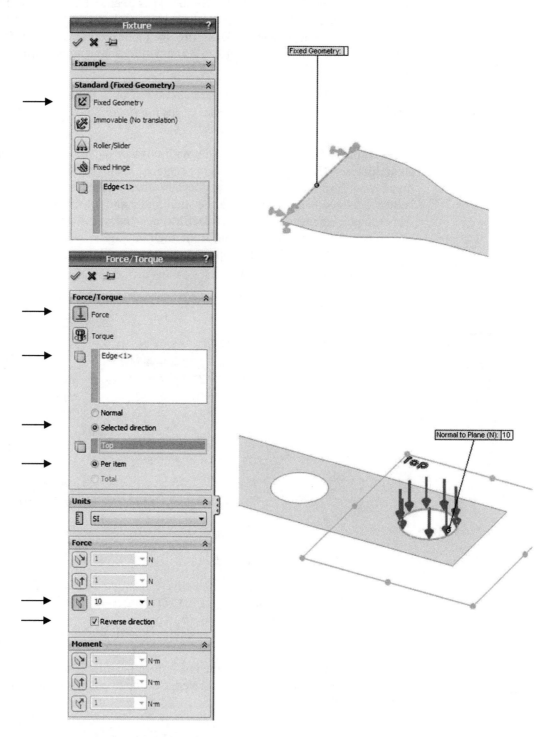

Figure 14-3: Restraints (top) and load (bottom) definition, arrows indicate the required selection.

Notice that the Fixture window offers the choice "Immovable" which is due to the shell elements being analyzed. In our case, defining the restraint as Immovable would result in a hinge.

Now mesh the model with shell elements using the default element size and notice the shell element orientation. (Figure 14-4).

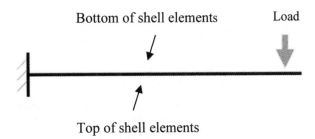

Figure 14-4: The shell mesh orientation is such that the bottoms of shell elements are on the load side.

The mesh is orange on the side where the load is applied. As you remember in chapter 4, the bottoms of shell elements are by default marked with the color specified in study Options. The default color is orange.

Solve the study named *linear* and notice that the solution of this study without the **Large displacement** option, displays a warning message (Figure 14-5) that must be acknowledged to complete the solution process.

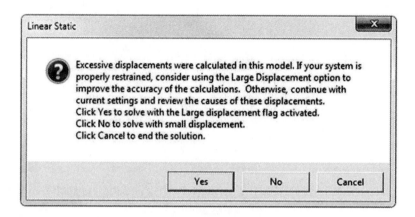

Figure 14-5: A warning message displayed by the solver if large displacements are detected and the Large Displacement option is not checked.

To obtain a linear solution select No. The above message is displayed if the maximum resultant displacement is larger than the default element size. Depending on the problem, it may be correct to ignore it.

Next solve the study *nonlinear* with the **Large displacement** option selected. Solving with the **Large displacement** option is a nonlinear solution, which progresses in iterations. The load is increased in automatically determined steps while the model stiffness is updated according to the progressing displacement (Figure 14-6).

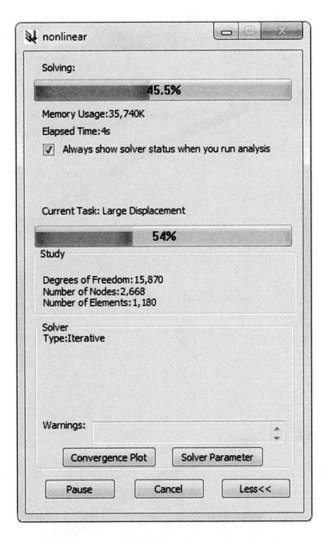

Figure 14-6: The nonlinear solution (with the Large Displacement option) progresses in iterations while the load gradually increases and the stiffness is updated.

Due to the iterative nature of the Large Displacement solution, the solution time is much longer in comparison to the corresponding linear solution.

Create displacement plots obtained from the linear and nonlinear solutions (Figure 14-7). Use a 1:1 scale of deformation for both plots.

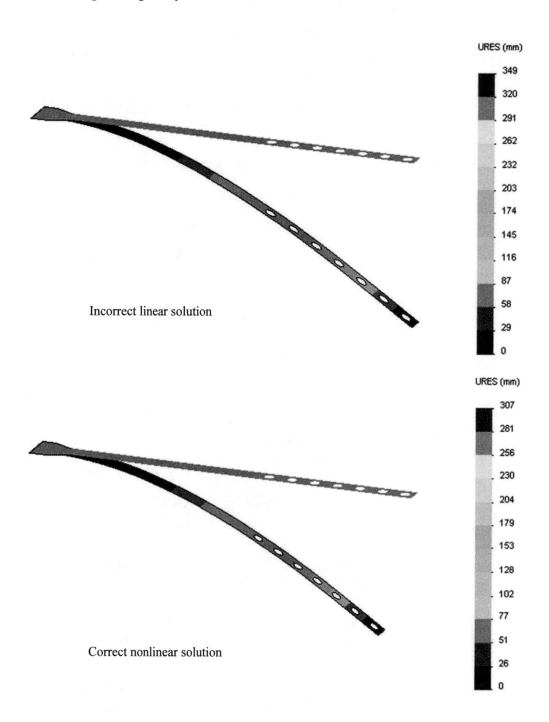

Figure 14-7: Incorrect linear solution (top) and correct nonlinear solution (bottom) obtained with the Large displacement option .

The undeformed model is superimposed on both plots. Notice that the linear solution produces an incorrect pattern of deformation. This is seen by following the tip of the beam which travels along a straight line through deformation (the beam appears to be stretching out).

Now create two stress plots based on the nonlinear solution using a 1:1 scale of deformation. Create a von Mises stress plot for the bottoms of shell elements and for the tops of shell elements.

Von Mises stress on **Bottom** of shell elements. This is the tensile side of the beam.

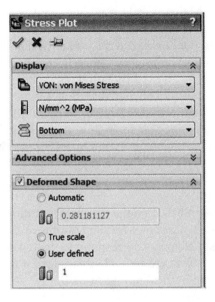

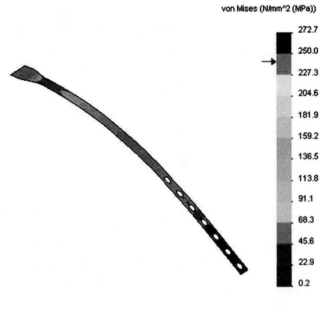

Von Mises stress on **Top** of shell elements. This is the compressive side of the beam

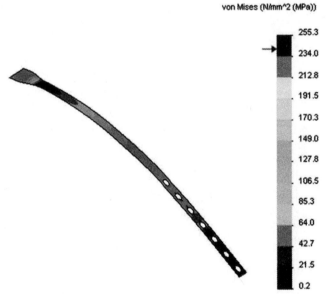

Figure 14-8: Von Mises stress results for element Bottoms (top illustration) and element Tops (bottom illustration).

Both plots show similar stress magnitudes because von Mises stress is always a positive, scalar value. Tensile and compressive stresses equally contribute to von Mises stress.

Examine the plots in Figure 14-8 to notice that the maximum von Mises stress on the bottom side (tensile side) is 273MPa, and that the maximum von Mises stress on the top side (compressive side) is 255MPa. Both values are above yield. Even though we ran a nonlinear analysis, the only source of nonlinear behavior is the large displacement. Material yield is not modeled. **SolidWorks Simulation Professional** can model nonlinear behavior due to **Large displacement** but not due to nonlinear material and even this is performed with limitations; the load is "ramped up" linearly (there is no other option) and local strain must remain small even though it may add up to large model displacements. Also, the load cannot change direction during the process of load application. To account for other sources of nonlinear behavior (e.g. material yielding) and to be able to apply a load with a time history, we need a **Nonlinear** study available in **SolidWorks Simulation Premium**.

Now create two more stress plots also based on the nonlinear solution using a 1:1 scale of deformation. Create a P1 stress plot for the bottoms of shell elements. Since the bottoms of shell elements correspond to the top side of the beam, this plot shows tensile stress. Next create a P3 stress plot for the tops of shell elements. These results are summarized in Figure 14-9.

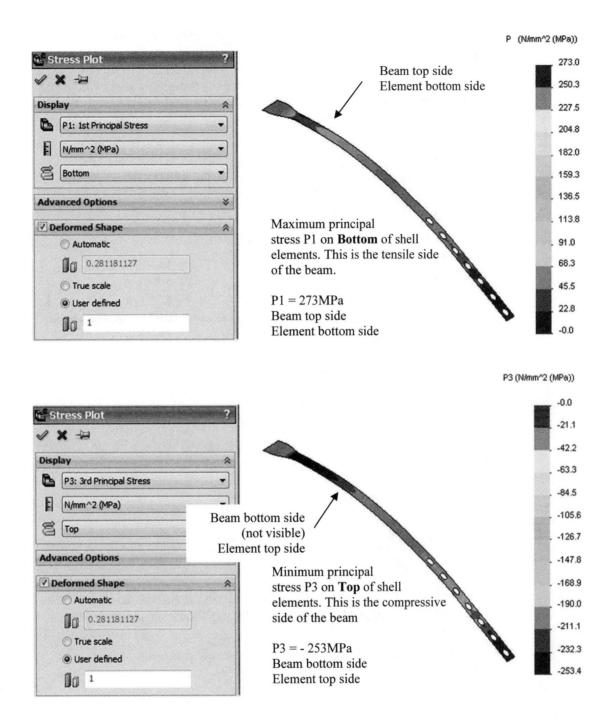

Figure 14-9: P1 stress results for element Bottoms (top illustration) and P3 stress results for element Tops (bottom illustration).

Figure 14-9 clearly illustrates the shell element capability to model bending. The highest P1 stress (tensile) is found on the bottom side of elements and the numerically lowest P3 stress (compressive) is found on the top side of elements, both are in the same location along the beam. The above discussion is of course applicable to both linear and nonlinear analyses.

The load in example NL002 was a non-following load; it retained its original direction and did not follow the deforming structure. A following load requires a **Nonlinear** study and will be used in the SPRING example later in this chapter. The difference between following and non-following load is explained in Figure 14-10.

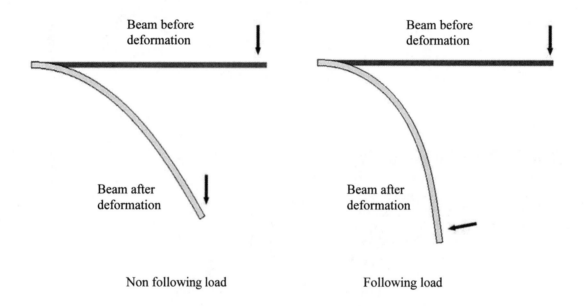

Non following load   Following load

Figure 14-10: A non-following load retains its original direction. A following load follows the deforming model retaining its original orientation relative to the model.

A following load is not available in a Static study; it is available in a Nonlinear study.

The next example introduces the analysis of large displacements combined with a contact problem, illustrated by the plastic part CLIP (Figure 14-11).

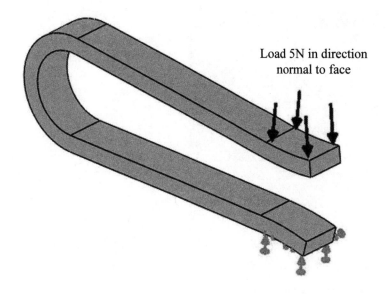

Load 5N in direction normal to face

Fixed restraint

Figure 14-11: The CLIP model complete with load and restraint.

Two surfaces, defined in a contact pair, will experience large displacement (even though not quite as large as in the NL002 example) before contacting each other. Therefore, the **Large displacement** option must be selected in the properties of the **Static** study. There are two sources of nonlinear behavior we have to account for: large displacement and contact.

Define a local contact set between the two surfaces likely to come in contact as **No penetration** (Figure 14-12). Notice that we say "likely" because this depends on the load magnitude.

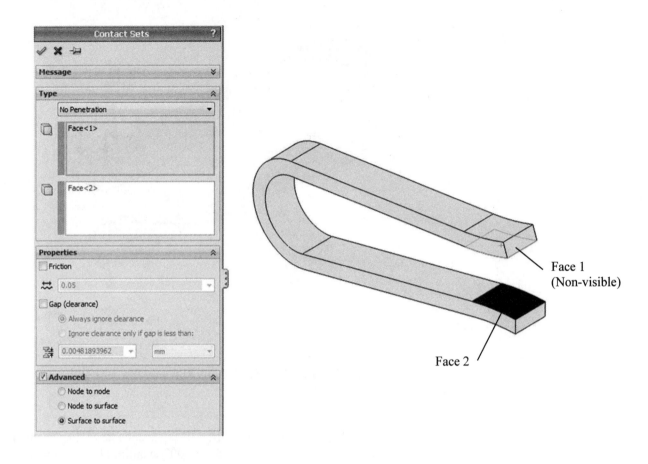

Figure 14-12: Definition of the Contact Set. Surface to surface contact is required when faces are not initially touching but may come in contact under the applied load.

Split lines in the SolidWorks model define small faces that may come in contact. The smaller size of the contacting faces shortens the solution time.

Mesh the assembly with the default element size, and then obtain two solutions: the first one without the **Large displacement** option, and the second one with the **Large displacement** option selected. Compare the displacement results obtained from these two studies (Figure 14-13).

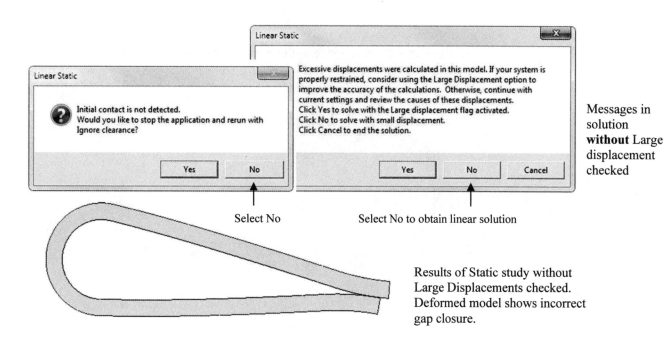

Messages in solution **without** Large displacement checked

Select No

Select No to obtain linear solution

Results of Static study without Large Displacements checked. Deformed model shows incorrect gap closure.

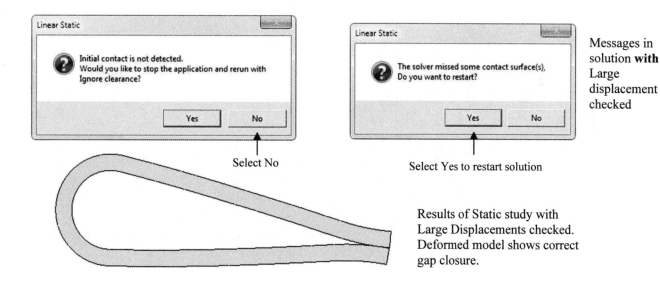

Messages in solution **with** Large displacement checked

Select No

Select Yes to restart solution

Results of Static study with Large Displacements checked. Deformed model shows correct gap closure.

Figure 14-13: Incorrect displacement results produced without **Large displacement** option (top) and correct displacement results produced with the **Large displacement** option selected (bottom). The Gap did not close properly in the solution executed without the Large displacement option.

Also shown are solver messages that need to be acknowledged in each solution. The solver messages may depend on the type of solver used, here both solution were obtained with the iterative solver FFEPlus.

Notice that the element size in the contact area is much too large to produce meaningful contact stress results (Figure 14-14).

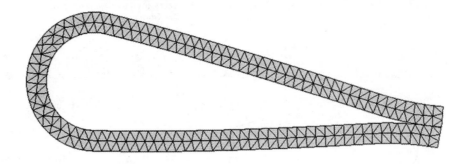

Figure 14-14: The large element size in the contact area does not allow a meaningful analysis of contact stresses.

The deformed shape can be saved as another configuration in the same model or as another part (recall chapter 11). To save the deformed shape as a different model, follow the steps in Figure 14-15.

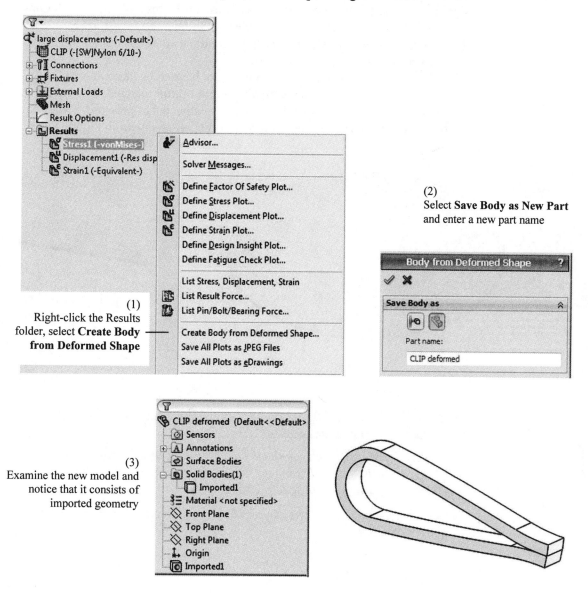

(1)
Right-click the Results folder, select **Create Body from Deformed Shape**

(2)
Select **Save Body as New Part** and enter a new part name

(3)
Examine the new model and notice that it consists of imported geometry

Figure 14-15: A model can be saved in the deformed configuration.

Examine the new SolidWorks part model.

To complete the exercise, review the stress results and notice that a more refined mesh would be required for detailed stress analysis.

The two previous exercises (NL002 and CLIP) required the **Large displacement** option because displacements were indeed large. However, there may exist problems where displacements are small, but they significantly change the model stiffness. These problems still require solutions with the **Large displacement** option selected. In fact, the term **Large displacement** may be misleading because it implies that this option should only be used if displacements are large.

We will demonstrate that displacements do not have to be large in order to require a solution with the **Large displacement** option selected. Open the model ROUND PLATE, which is a thin plate subjected to pressure. Switch to configuration *02 section* of the **SolidWorks** model, as shown in Figure 14-16.

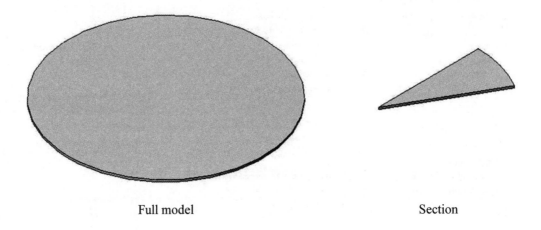

Full model   Section

Figure 14-16: The full ROUND PLATE model (left) and a section obtained by switching to configuration *02 section.*

Since there is axial symmetry in the geometry, loads, and restraints, an arbitrary slice with applied symmetry boundary conditions correctly represents the plate's response to pressure.

Symmetry boundary conditions are required to enforce flatness of radial faces in the section model.

Create a static study and apply **Symmetry** restraints to both radial faces created by the cut. Next, apply a **Fixed Geometry** restraint to the cylindrical face on the plate circumference and a pressure of 0.3MPa to the top face (Figure 14-17).

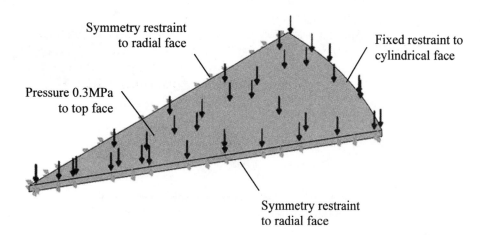

Symmetry restraint
to radial face

Fixed restraint to
cylindrical face

Pressure 0.3MPa
to top face

Symmetry restraint
to radial face

Figure 14-17: Load and restraints applied to the ROUND PLATE model.

The pressure is applied to the entire top face. The name "Symmetry" may be confusing here. It is used just to enforce flatness of the radial faces while the model deforms.

Mesh with the default element size and obtain two solutions: without and with the **Large displacement** option and compare the displacement results (Figure 14-18).

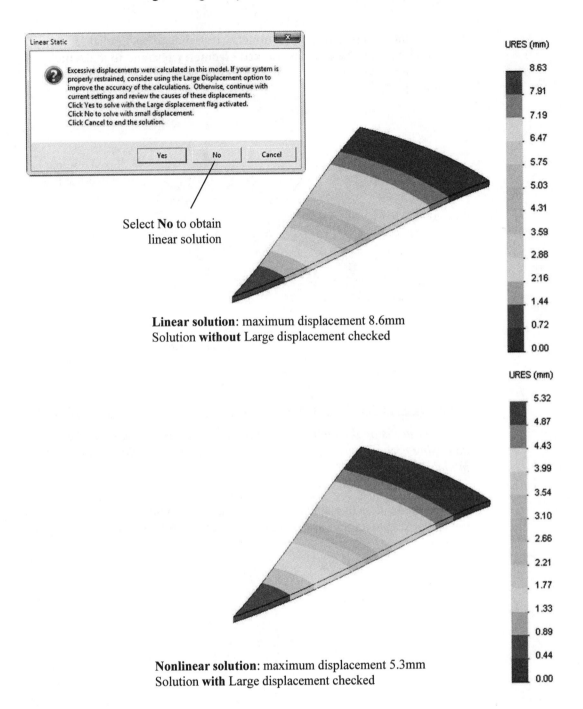

Linear solution: maximum displacement 8.6mm
Solution **without** Large displacement checked

Nonlinear solution: maximum displacement 5.3mm
Solution **with** Large displacement checked

Figure 14-18: Displacement results obtained without the Large displacement option (linear solution, top) and displacement results obtained with the Large displacement option (nonlinear solution, bottom). The nonlinear model deforms less than the linear model meaning that the nonlinear model is stiffer.

The message "Excessive displacements were calculated…" is displayed by the linear solver when the maximum resultant displacement exceeds the default element size. The decision whether to change to the Large displacement formulation is left up to the user.

A flat plate under pressure is a classic case where the assumption of small displacements leads to erroneous results. The analysis requires the use of the **Large displacement** option even though displacements are small in comparison to the size of the model.

The need to use the **Large displacement** option is due to the change of shape (from flat to curved) altering the mechanism resisting the load; a deformed plate is able to resist pressure with membrane (tensile) stress additionally to the original bending stress (Figure 14-19).

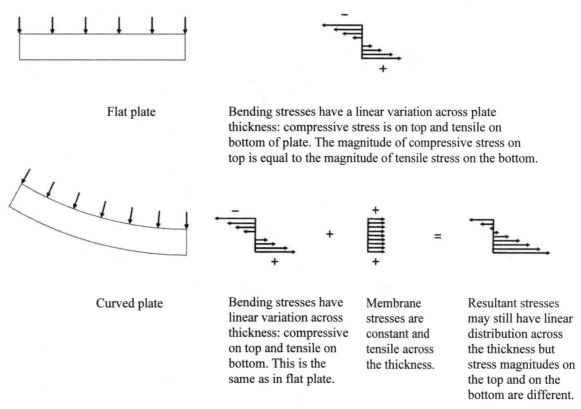

Flat plate

Bending stresses have a linear variation across plate thickness: compressive stress is on top and tensile on bottom of plate. The magnitude of compressive stress on top is equal to the magnitude of tensile stress on the bottom.

Curved plate

Bending stresses have linear variation across thickness: compressive on top and tensile on bottom. This is the same as in flat plate.

Membrane stresses are constant and tensile across the thickness.

Resultant stresses may still have linear distribution across the thickness but stress magnitudes on the top and on the bottom are different.

Figure 14-19: Load resisting mechanism in an undeformed plate (top) and in a deformed plate (bottom).

The stress distribution across the plate thickness does not have to be necessarily linear.

To account for the change of plate stiffness that takes place due to deformation (even though the deformation is small), the stiffness must be updated during the deformation process. This is only possible if a nonlinear analysis is executed. The linear analysis only takes into account the initial bending stiffness, which is the reason why the linear model is softer than the corresponding nonlinear model.

We will illustrate the same problem with one more example, similar to LINK described in chapter 5. Open the model LINK02 and notice that the material properties of ABS have been assigned to this model. Due to this material's low stiffness, the model will experience large deformation which will make it easy to show the difference between the correct nonlinear (**Large displacement**) solution and incorrect linear solution. Apply a 300N load to the top face and hinge restraints to the "eyes" (Figure 14-20).

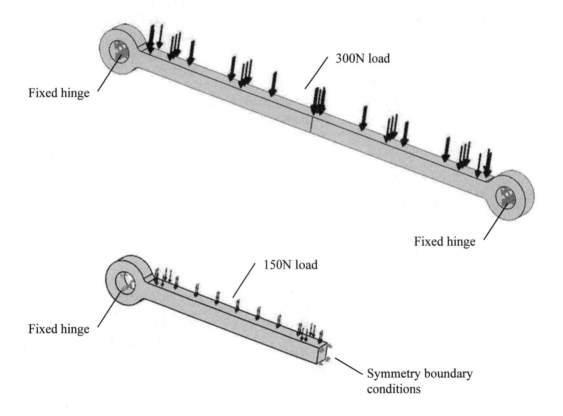

Figure 14-20: Loads and restraints on LINK02 model.

The analysis can be conducted either on the full model or on the half model with symmetry boundary conditions and half of the load. Select the desired model configuration.

Obtain linear and nonlinear solutions and compare von Mises stress results from both solutions (as shown in Figure 14-21).

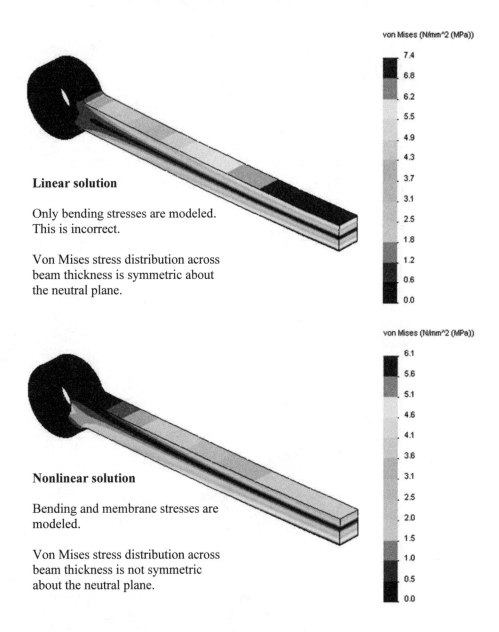

Linear solution

Only bending stresses are modeled. This is incorrect.

Von Mises stress distribution across beam thickness is symmetric about the neutral plane.

Nonlinear solution

Bending and membrane stresses are modeled.

Von Mises stress distribution across beam thickness is not symmetric about the neutral plane.

Figure 14-21: Von Mises stress results for the same problem treated as linear (top) and nonlinear (bottom).

Top: *the absence of membrane (tensile) stresses in the linear solution is illustrated by the symmetric distribution of von Mises stresses in the section stress plot.*

Bottom: *the von Mises section plot obtained in the nonlinear (large displacement) solution shows a non-symmetric distribution of stress proving the presence of membrane (tensile) stresses.*

Another way to demonstrate the presence of membrane stress is to examine a graph of the SX stress distribution across the height of the link. To create a plot of SX stresses, follow the steps in Figure 14-22a and Figure 22b.

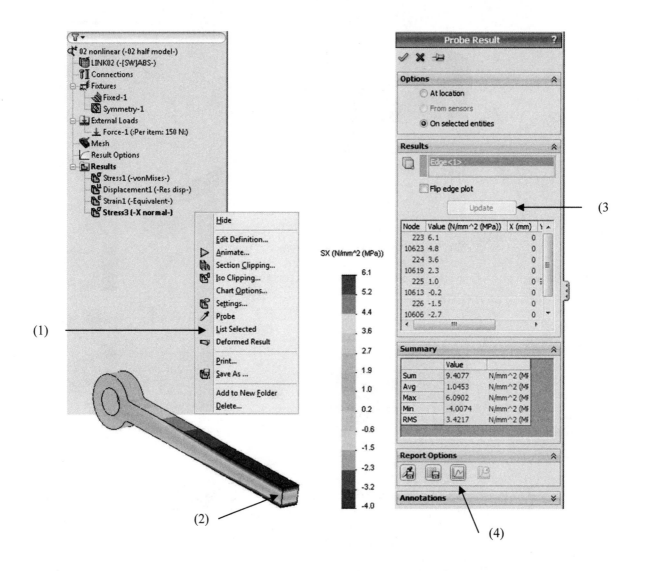

Figure 14-22a: Distribution of SX stress component across the thickness can be graphed by following the steps explained in this Figure.

(1) Right-click SX stress plot and select List Selected.

(2) Select the vertical edge (or split line if you are using the full model). This opens the Probe Result window.

(3) In the Probe Results window click Update and Graph (4) to produce a graph of the SX stress distribution along the entity selected in (2).

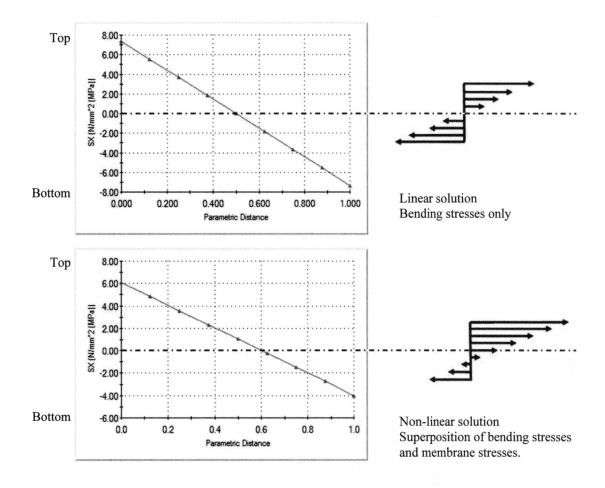

Linear solution
Bending stresses only

Non-linear solution
Superposition of bending stresses
and membrane stresses.

Figure 14-22b: **Top**: distribution of SX stress across the thickness in the linear model. **Bottom**: distribution of SX stress across the thickness in the nonlinear model.

Refer back to Figure 14-19 for an explanation of the differences between linear and nonlinear solutions.

The difference between a linear and nonlinear solution is schematically shown in Figure 14-23.

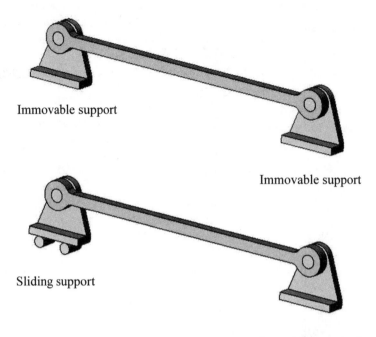

Immovable support

Immovable support

Sliding support

Immovable support

Figure 14-23: The nonlinear solution correctly models displacements and stresses in a hinge supported link where the distance between hinges cannot change (top). The linear solution can only model the configurations where one of the hinges is floating (bottom).

A linear model cannot distinguish between the two configurations shown in Figure 14-22.

The nonlinear solution correctly models displacements and stresses in a hinge supported link as shown at the top of Figure 14-22. The linear solution cannot model membrane stresses that develop during the deformation, so this link is modeled as if one of the hinges had a floating support (symbolically shown in Figure 14-22 as rollers). Notice that horizontal displacements are not modeled in a linear solution, even if the floating support is modeled. All nonlinear problems presented in this chapter owe their nonlinearity to changes in geometry and contact taking place during the loading process. They can be solved using a **Static** study with the **Large displacement** option selected. Now we present a problem where nonlinear behavior is caused by nonlinear material. This example requires **SolidWorks Simulation Premium**.

Open part file BRACKET NL, which is almost identical to the model analyzed in chapter 13. The differences are that the assigned material is aluminum 1060 Alloy, there is an added cut along the plane of symmetry to work with one half of the model, and split faces exist in the area where we detected stress concentrations in chapter 13. Use the *02 half model* configuration. Since an h-adaptive solution is not available in a **Nonlinear** study, we draw on our past experience with the model and use these split faces to define mesh controls.

Open a **Nonlinear** study with the **Static** option and define its properties as shown in Figure 14-24.

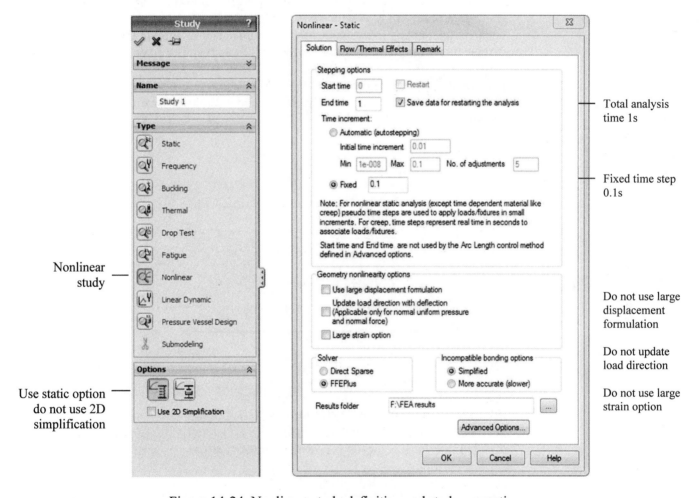

Figure 14-24: Nonlinear study definition and study properties.

Make selections as shown above. We do not expect large displacements so load direction does not need to be updated during the load application process, and a fixed time step can be used. We also do not expect large strain magnitudes, therefore the Large strain option should not be selected. Nonlinear material is the only source of nonlinear behavior in this model.

Following the selections shown in Figure 14-24, the load application will take 1s. Considering the fixed time step of 0.1s, the load will be applied in 10 steps. It is important to remember that in our case of static analysis, time is only used to define the shape of the load history curve. The same results are obtained if the analysis time is 1s and the time steps are 0.1s or if the analysis takes 1000s and a time step of 100s. To differentiate it from "real" time used in a dynamic analysis, the time used to defined the load history curve is called "pseudo time". The BRACKET NL can be also solved with automatic time stepping.

The ability to control the load time history is an important difference between a **Static** study executed with the **Large displacement** option and a **Nonlinear** study. In a **Static** study executed with **Large displacement**, a load can only be increased linearly in automatically determined steps. Without the **Large displacement** option, a load in a **Static** study is applied just in one step.

Now we define a nonlinear material. We use the simplest type of nonlinear material called the elastic-perfectly plastic model. Its stress-strain curve is shown in Figure 14-25.

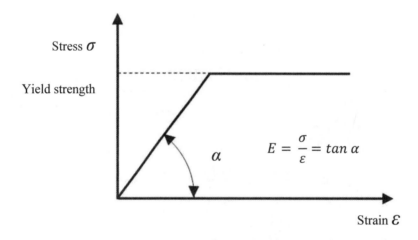

Figure 14-25: Stress-strain curve of an elastic-perfectly plastic material.

According to an elastic-perfectly plastic material model, stress is proportional to strain until the stress magnitude reaches yield strength. After that, stress becomes constant, regardless of the magnitude of strain.

The modulus of elasticity of material in the linear elastic range is E = tan α. When stress reaches the yield strength, the modulus of elasticity of the material becomes zero. This is the plastic range.

To define an elastic-perfectly plastic material model, we need to know the material modulus of elasticity describing its behavior in the elastic range and the magnitude of the yield strength. We also need to decide how to determine if yield strength has been reached. In this example we compare von Mises stress to yield strength. Once von Mises stress reaches yield strength, the material modulus of elasticity becomes zero. In **SolidWorks Simulation** this material is called **Plasticity – von Mises**.

Edit the material properties of the 1060 alloy assigned in the **SolidWorks** model and change it to **Plasticity – von Mises** (Figure 14-26).

(1)
Right-click
Solid folder,
Select
Apply/Edit
Material

(3)
Select Plasticity von Mises
as material Model Type

(2)
Select 1060 Alloy
in SolidWorks
Materials Aluminum
Alloys

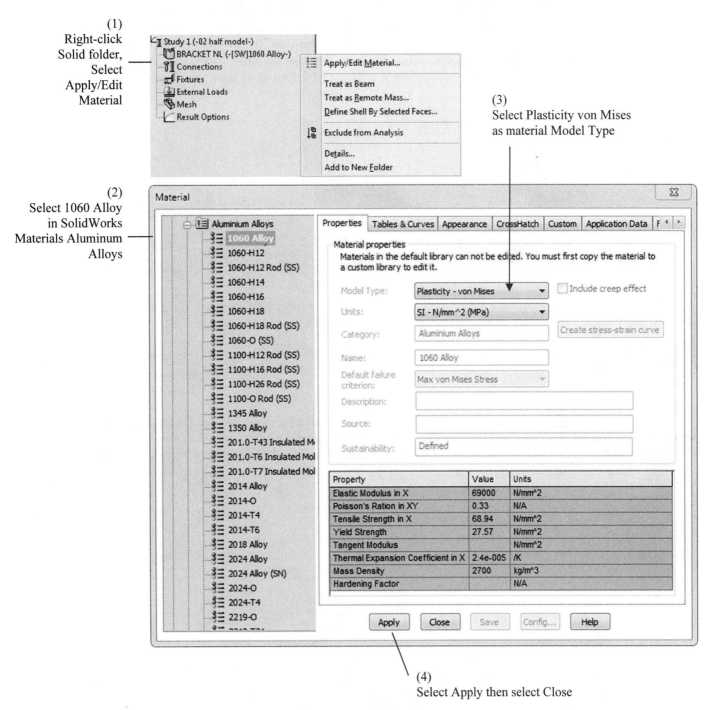

(4)
Select Apply then select Close

Figure 14-26: Plasticity – von Mises material definition. Follow the above steps to define a custom material.

Yield strength of 27.57MPa is the highest von Mises stress that the model will see.

Define a **Fixed** restraint on the back side and a **Symmetry** restraint to the faces created by the symmetry cut. The total load on the model is 5000N (see chapter 13. Here, remember to apply only 2500N because we are working with one half of the model geometry. The load application requires definition of the load time history. We want to "ramp-up" the load to the maximum value to see the maximum stresses, then we will drop it back down to zero to examine the residual stresses. The load definition is shown in Figure 14-27.

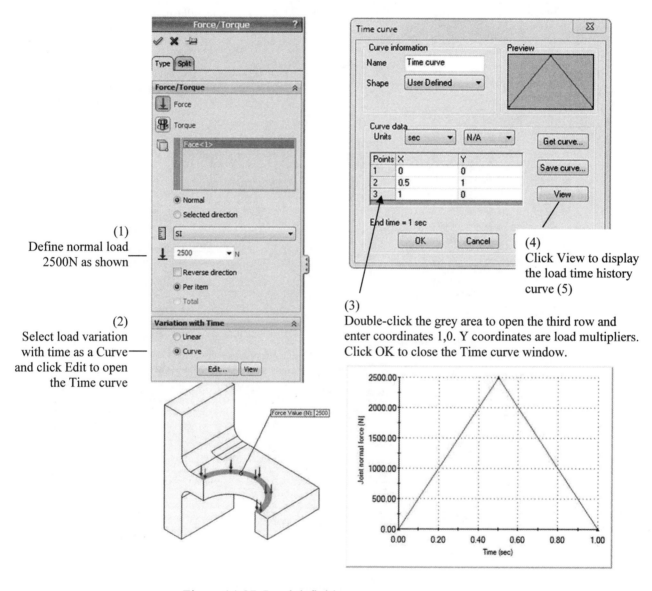

(1)
Define normal load 2500N as shown

(2)
Select load variation with time as a Curve and click Edit to open the Time curve

(3)
Double-click the grey area to open the third row and enter coordinates 1,0. Y coordinates are load multipliers. Click OK to close the Time curve window.

(4)
Click View to display the load time history curve (5)

Figure 14-27: Load definition.

Load definition includes load time history. The maximum load 2500N takes place at time t=0.5s. At t=1s, the load is back to zero.

In the **SolidWorks** Feature Manager, define a **Sensor** in the location indicated in Figure 14-28. Return to the **Simulation** study, right click the *Result Options* folder to open the **Results Option** window. Select **For all solutions steps**, and specify **Response Plots** as **Workflow Sensitive**. This links the **Result Options** to the Sensor (Figure 14-28).

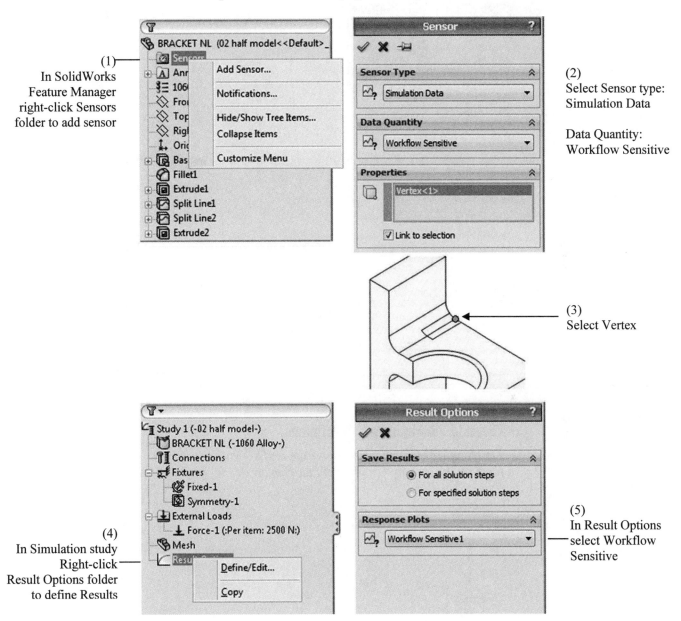

(1)
In SolidWorks Feature Manager right-click Sensors folder to add sensor

(2)
Select Sensor type: Simulation Data

Data Quantity: Workflow Sensitive

(3)
Select Vertex

(4)
In Simulation study Right-click Result Options folder to define Results

(5)
In Result Options select Workflow Sensitive

Figure 14-28: Sensor definition (1), (2), (3) and Results Options definition (bottom).

In step (3), select the vertex where high stresses are expected.

Apply mesh controls as shown in Figure 14-29. Defining these mesh controls requires knowledge of where stress concentrations are located. We investigated this in Chapter 13.

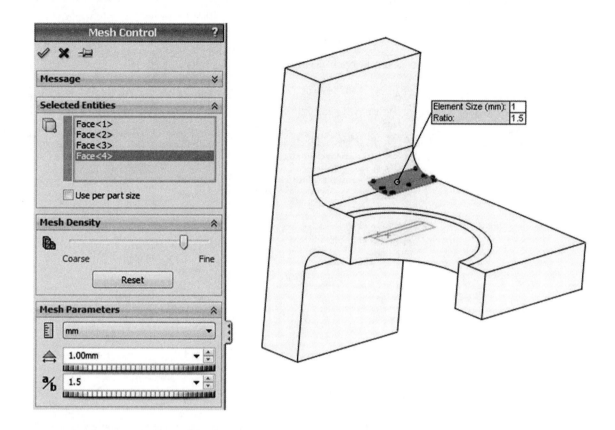

Figure 14-29: Mesh controls definition.

Mesh controls (element size 1mm) applied to two faces on the top and two faces on the bottom. Use the default element size to mesh the rest of the model.

Execute the solution of the nonlinear study and observe the solution progress in the Solver window. Be prepared for a solution time much longer than a typical linear analysis. The nonlinear solver window is shown in Figure 14-30.

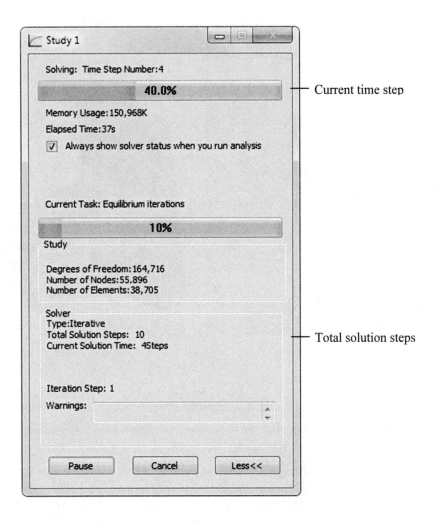

Figure 14-30: Nonlinear solver window.

The above nonlinear solver window shows the solution progress for time step 4 of 10.

Von Mises stress results for the maximum load (time step 5) are shown in Figure 14-31.

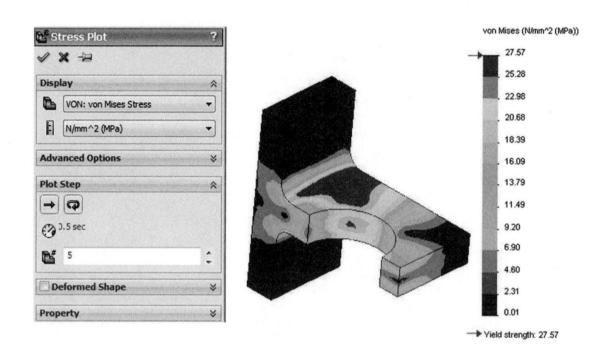

Figure 14-31: Von Mises stresses under the maximum load, time step 5.

Notice that the maximum von Mises stress magnitude is 27.57MPa, which is the yield stress of the elastic-perfectly plastic material we used in the analysis.

Yielding occurs in the portions of the model where stress reaches the maximum magnitude. The large size of the yield zone indicates that the mesh controls were not necessary to produce these results.

Von Mises stress results for zero load (time step 10) are shown in Figure 14-32. These are residual stresses after completing the load cycle.

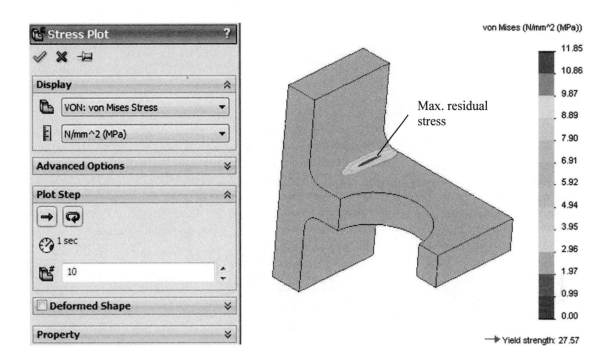

Figure 14-32: Residual von Mises stresses after the load has been removed at time step 10.

Residual stresses reach 11.8MPa in the area that experienced plastic deformation (yield). The small size of the high stress zone indicates that the mesh controls were necessary to produce these results.

Follow the steps in Figure 14-33 to display the maximum von Mises stress as a function of the time step number.

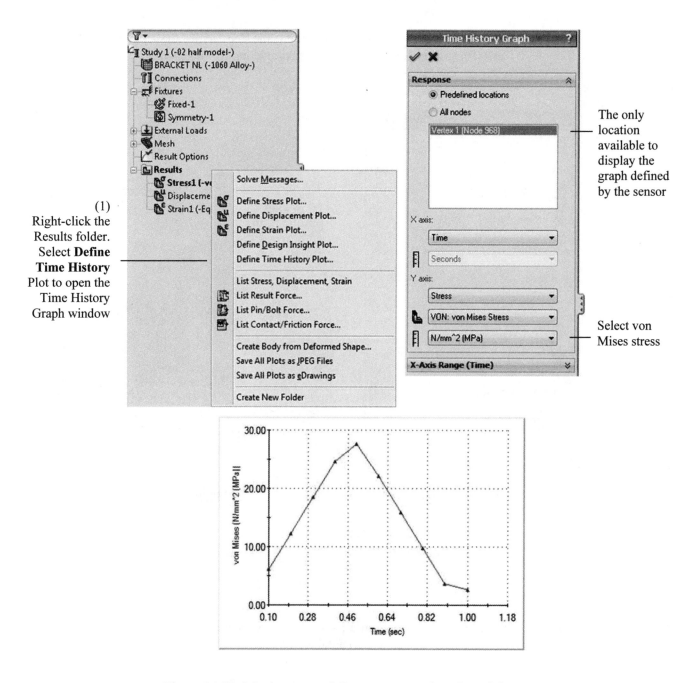

(1)
Right-click the
Results folder.
Select **Define
Time History**
Plot to open the
Time History
Graph window

The only
location
available to
display the
graph defined
by the sensor

Select von
Mises stress

Figure 14-33: Maximum von Mises stress as a function of time.

The maximum stress is 27.57MPa, which is the yield strength.

Try running the same analysis with 20 time steps to see a more detailed graph,
especially a "dip" in stress between step 9 and 10.

To continue with the theme of elastic-perfectly plastic materials, open the model SPRING, and create a nonlinear study. Apply loads and restraints as shown in Figure 14-34.

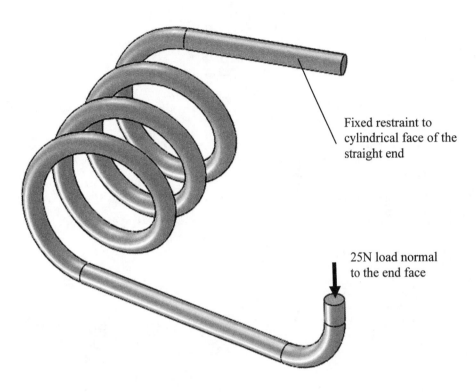

Fixed restraint to cylindrical face of the straight end

25N load normal to the end face

Figure 14-34: Restraint and load of SPRING model.

Use Linear variation with Time in the load definition. Linear variation means that the load is a linear function of time.

To model a load that remains normal to the face while the SPRING deforms, select the **Update load direction with deflection** option in the study properties.

The model has material properties of stainless steel assigned. Modify them to make it into an elastic-perfectly plastic material with a yield strength of 620MPa (Figure 14-35).

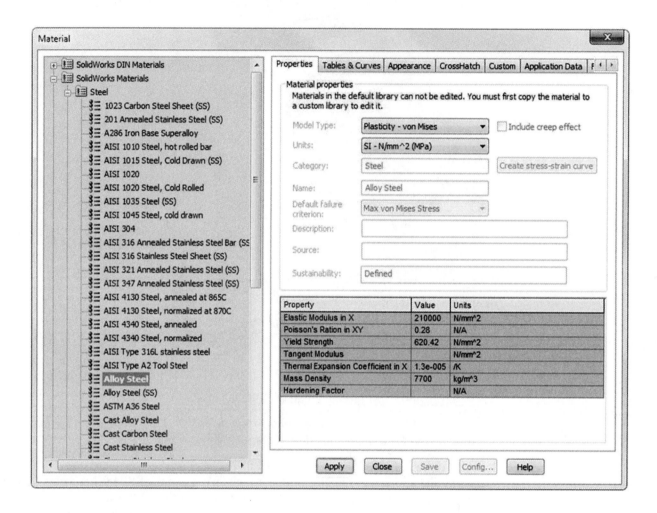

Figure 14-35: Elastic-perfectly plastic material definition in the SPRING model.

The materials yield strength is 620MPa.

Notice that the material's yield strength shows both in the linear and nonlinear material definitions. In case of a linear material, the yield strength is used only for results interpretation such as making a plot of the factor of safety to yield. Stress results are not affected in any way by the yield strength value. In a nonlinear material definition, yield strength plays a crucial role. In the case of the Plasticity-von Mises material model, once von Mises stress reaches the yielding value, the modulus of elasticity is changed to zero in that location.

Mesh the model with a **Curvature Based** mesh, with a maximum element size of 0.75mm. In study properties select the option **Use large displacement formulation** and **Update load direction with deflection** in the study properties window (Figure 14-36). This option defines a following load, one that changes direction to follow the deforming model during the loading process.

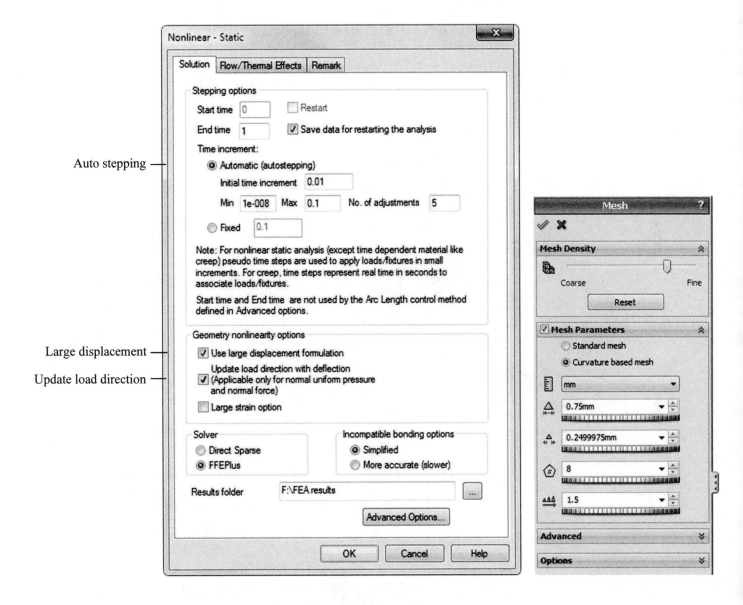

Figure 14-36: Study properties and Mesh parameters.

When Automatic time steps are used, the load increment is selected automatically by the solver.

The Large displacement formulation and Update load direction with deflection are selected (left). Use a 0.75mm maximum element size with a Curvature based mesh (right).

Notice that we don't select the **Large strain** option. Once the solution becomes available we will examine if the small strain assumption has been correct.

Run the nonlinear solution and be prepared for a long solution time. Review the displacement results and notice the large displacement that the model has experienced under the load (Figure 14-37). Next, review the von Mises Stress and examine the portions of the model that reached yield strength (Figure 14-38). Finally, review the equivalent strain (Figure 14-39). Display all plots for the last performed time step (this is step 13). Because the load has a Linear Variation with time, the last step has the highest load magnitude.

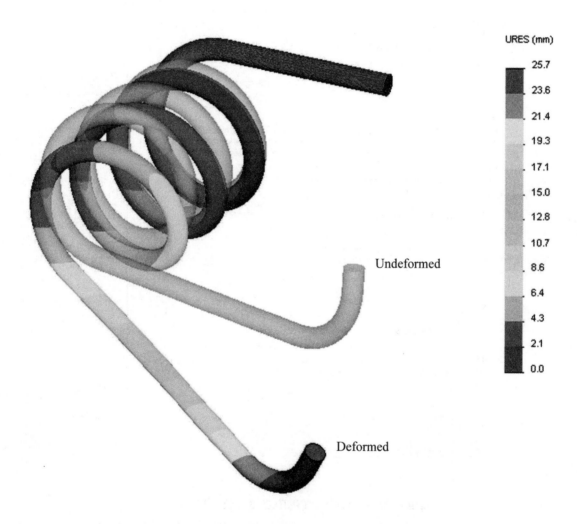

Figure 14-37: The displacement results plot in 1:1 scale of deformation shows that the model has experienced a large displacement under the applied load.

The undeformed model is superimposed on the deformed plot.

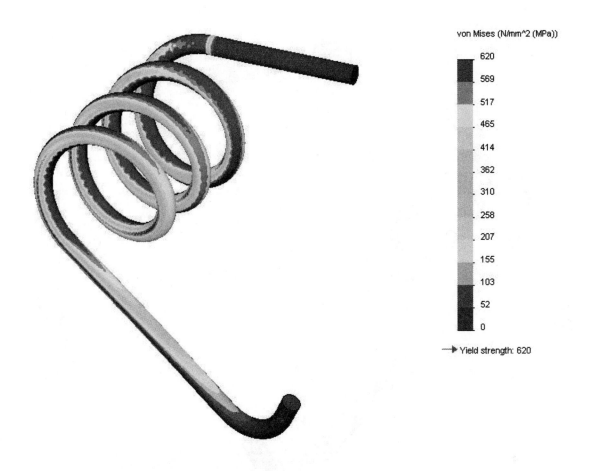

von Mises (N/mm^2 (MPa))

620
569
517
465
414
362
310
258
207
155
103
52
0

→ Yield strength: 620

Figure 14-38: A von Mises stress plot shows that large portions of the model have yielded.

The model shows large areas with stress equal to the yield strength of 620MPa.

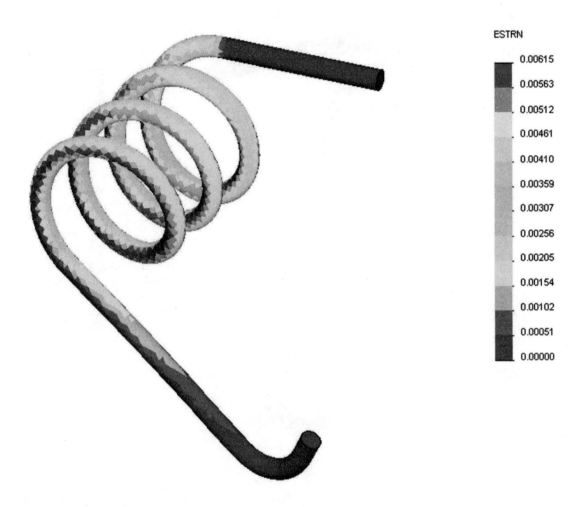

ESTRN

0.00615
0.00563
0.00512
0.00461
0.00410
0.00359
0.00307
0.00256
0.00205
0.00154
0.00102
0.00051
0.00000

Figure 14-39: Equivalent strain plot.

The highest strain is 0.6%. This justifies not selecting the Large strain option in study properties.

You may want to experiment with the model by increasing the load until the solution crashes, meaning that the entire spring cross section has yielded and it is no longer capable of resisting the applied load.

15: Mixed meshing problem

Topics covered

❑ Using solid and shell elements in the same mesh

❑ Mixed mesh compatibility

❑ Manual and automatic finding of contact sets

While in previous exercises we used different types of meshes such as solid and shell meshes, they have never been used together in the same model. This exercise introduces the use of different mesh types within the same model.

Open the part model WHEEL. Notice that the "bulky" hub and rim are connected by thin spokes. Since the spokes are thin, meshing them with solid elements would require a large number of small solid elements. Therefore, to reduce the problem size, the hub and rim will be meshed with solid elements and the spokes with shell elements. To accomplish this, the model geometry must be prepared in **SolidWorks**. Start the exercise by examining the features of the WHEEL assembly, shown in Figure 15-1.

Figure 15-1: Spokes are represented by surfaces.

In preparation for analysis, mid-surfaces have been placed in the middle of each spoke thickness and bodies defining spokes have been deleted. The model has two solid bodies: hub (small ring) and rim (large ring) and three surface bodies modeling spokes.

Create a **Frequency** study and notice that the parts folder contains two types of icons: **Solids** and **Shells**. Since surfaces do not contain information on thickness we must define this parameter. Select all surfaces in the *wheel* folder, right-click, and select **Edit Definition** to open the **Shell definition** window. Use a **Thin** shell formulation and enter 2mm as the shell thickness, which is analogous to the thickness of the spokes (Figure 15-2).

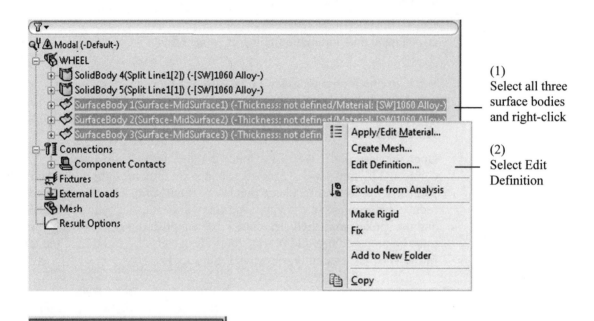

(1)
Select all three
surface bodies
and right-click

(2)
Select Edit
Definition

(3)
Enter shell
thickness
2mm

Leave offset
at 0

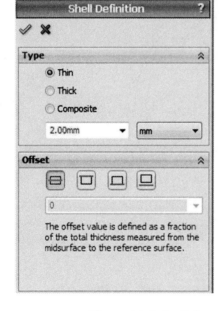

Figure 15-2: Defining shell thickness of spokes: 2mm.

Offset equal 0 means that shell thickness is symmetric about the surface.
Selected surface bodies are indicated by numbers.

Mesh the model with a default mesh and examine the incompatible shell and solid element meshes shown in Figure 15-3.

Nodes are misaligned along the connection between shells and solids

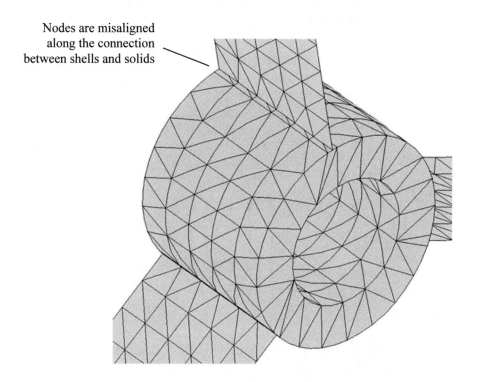

Figure 15-3: Mixed mesh: rim and hub are meshed with solid elements. Spokes are meshed with shell elements. The shell element mesh is not correctly connected to the solid element mesh.

Nodes along lines connecting shells to solids are misaligned. This applies to all six locations in the model. No mesh controls have been used to prepare this illustration.

The lack of correct connectivity between shell and solid element mesh causes discontinuity of displacement between the solid and shell mesh. This is called mesh incompatibility. Mesh incompatibility shown in Figure 15-3 must be eliminated by defining contact conditions that will force compatibility between both types of elements.

Therefore, a very important part of this exercise is the definition of contact conditions. In a mixed mesh study, all global and component contact conditions are ignored and we must ensure connectivity between solid bodies to be meshed with solid elements and surface bodies to be meshed with shell elements by defining contact sets. Define **Contact sets** manually (Figure 15-4) or automatically (Figure 15-5).

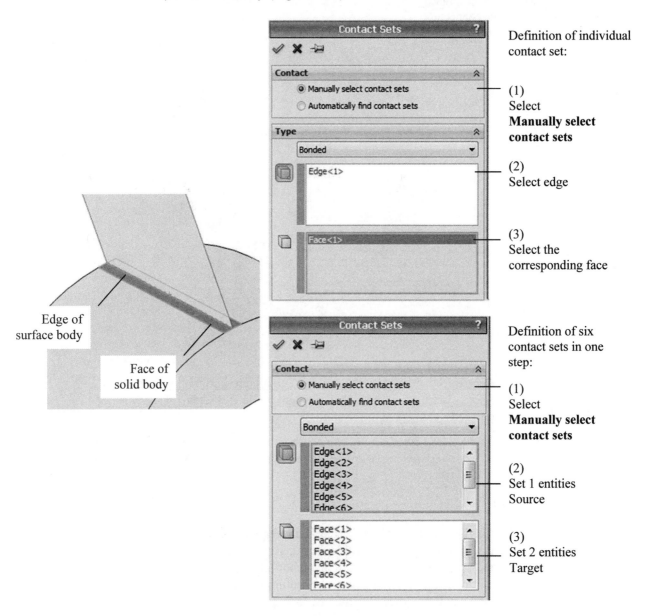

Figure 15-4: Manual definition of contact set.

A contact set is defined between an edge of the surface and a face of the solid (top). This definition has to be repeated six times for all six locations.

Alternatively, rather than opening the Contact Sets window six times, you may select all edges as source entities and all surfacees as target entities (bottom).

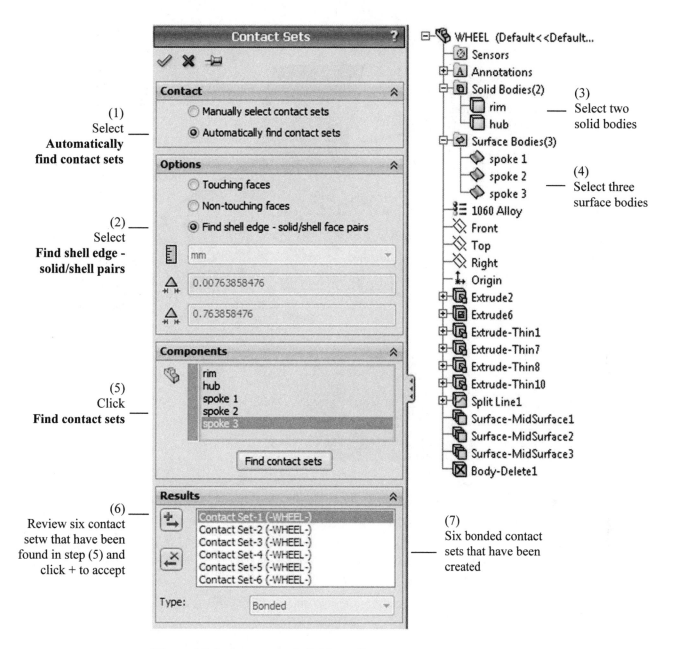

Figure 15-5: Automatic definition of contact sets.

Follow the above steps to create contact set automatically. Solid bodies and Surface bodies have been re-named in SolidWorks Feature Manager to give them meaningful names.

When bonding a shell edge to a solid or shell target face, the software rigidly bonds each node of the edge to the nearest element's face on the target. The stiffness of the connection depends on the element size near the interface. The element size on the target face should be equal to the thickness of the shell. This is the reason for the split faces where the spokes connect to the rim and hub. Define a mesh control size of 2mm for these split faces and mesh the model with the 5mm element size. The mixed mesh is shown in Figure 15-6.

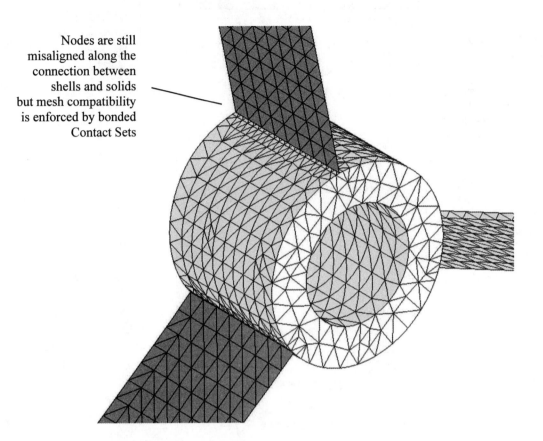

Nodes are still
misaligned along the
connection between
shells and solids
but mesh compatibility
is enforced by bonded
Contact Sets

**Figure 15-6: Mixed mesh: rim and hub are meshed with solid elements.
Spokes are meshed with shell elements.**

*Notice again that the shell element mesh and the solid element do not share
nodes. The spokes would be disconnected from the rim if not for the contact
set that enforces connection.*

*The large element size of solid and shell elements is acceptable in a frequency
analysis.*

Before solving, apply a **Fixed** restraint to the hole in the hub.

The shapes of the first two modes of vibration are shown in Figure 15-7.

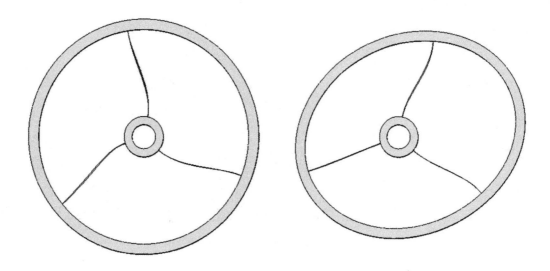

Mode 1: 25Hz   Mode 2: 265Hz

Figure 15-7: Deformation pattern corresponding to the first two modes of vibration.

Notice that mode 1 and mode 2 are in-plane modes meaning that vibrations takes place in the plane of the wheel.

Recall that it is recommended to deselect colors when presenting results of frequency (modal) analysis.

As you might have noticed, a model suitable for mixed meshing requires careful preparation of geometry in **SolidWorks** and definition of contact conditions in **Simulation**. But once the model is ready for analysis, it is easy to analyze the effect of different spoke thickness. This would not require any geometry modification, only a change in the **Shell Definition** and a change in the **Mesh Control** size.

Notes:

16: Analysis of a weldment using beam elements

Topics covered

- ❑ Different levels of idealization implemented in finite elements
- ❑ Preparation of a SolidWorks model for analysis with beam elements
- ❑ Beam elements and truss elements
- ❑ Analysis of results using beam elements
- ❑ Limitations of analysis with beam elements

Project description

Open the ROPS model showing a Roll-Over Protective Structure (ROPS) used to protect an operator of heavy equipment in the case of roll-over. The model consists of eight hollow square tubes 3" x 2" x 0.25" (Figure 16-1). All tubes are created in **SolidWorks** as structural members.

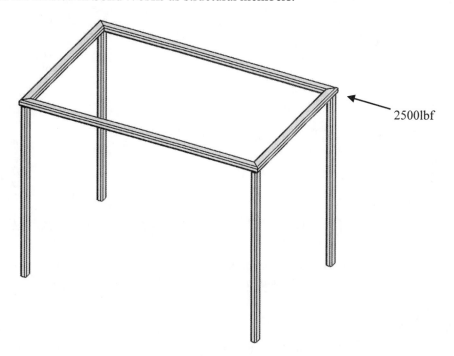

2500lbf

Figure 16-1: A ROPS cage is loaded in one corner with a horizontal load of 2500lbf.

All legs are restrained at the lower end faces.

We need to find the displacements and stresses of this structure under a load of 2500lbf as shown in Figure 16-1 with all four legs restrained.

The tube cross section and details of corner treatment and trims are shown in Figure 16-2.

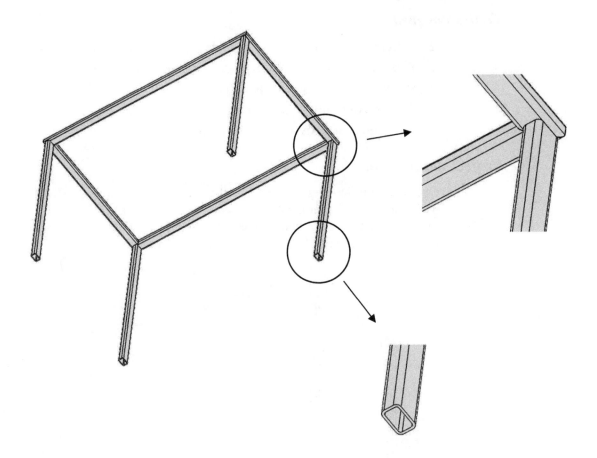

Figure 16-2: A detail of the corner; all tubes are 3″x2″x0.25″ with a 0.5″ radius.

Corner treatments and trims are applied in the SolidWorks model using Weldment tools. The weld bead is not modeled.

Due to thin walls and complicated geometry in the corners, this model is not suitable for meshing with solid or shell elements. Even if we were ready to accept long meshing and solution times, the stress results in the corners would be useless because of numerous sharp re-entrant edges causing stress singularities.

To avoid these problems, the model can be meshed and analyzed with beam elements. Before we proceed with analysis, we need to explain what beam elements are and how they compare to solid and shell elements.

The differences between solid, shell and beam elements are summarized in the following table.

Element type	Idealizations made to geometry intended to be meshed with this element	Assumptions on stress distribution in the element
Solid	No idealization required; solid elements are created by meshing 3D solid geometry.	No assumptions on stress distribution need to be made in any direction
Shell	Surfaces must be created; shell elements are created by meshing surfaces. Thickness is not present in the geometry and must be entered as a numerical value in the shell element definition.	Assumptions on stress distribution across thickness are made. In-plane stresses are assumed to be distributed linearly across the thickness. Transverse shear stresses are either assumed to have uniform distribution across element thickness (thin shell formulation), or to have parabolic distribution (thick shell formulation).
Beam	Curves must be created; beam elements are created by meshing curves. Curves represent beam geometry mathematically and do not physically model the cross section. In CAD terminology this is called wire frame geometry.	Assumptions about the stress distribution must be made in two directions perpendicular to the curve. These assumptions are the same as in beam theory: bending stresses are distributed linearly in both directions, and both axial and shear stresses are constant.

In summary, solid elements are a natural choice for meshing models with approximately the same size in all three dimensions, shells are the natural choice to mesh models such as sheet metal, and beams are the natural choice to mesh structural members.

Beam cross section geometry is only used to define beam element properties such as the area and second moments of inertia of the beam cross-section. It does not become part of the finite element model.

The information about beam cross sections is retrieved from the **SolidWorks** model which must be created as a **Weldment**. It is important to understand that the solid geometry of a **Weldment** is not meshed when beam elements are used. What is meshed is the underlying wire frame geometry (Figure 16-3).

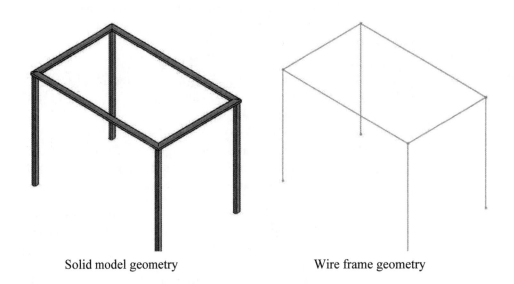

Solid model geometry   Wire frame geometry

Figure 16-3: Solid model and the underlying wire frame geometry.

Solid geometry is used only to define beam cross sections. Beam elements are created by meshing curves. You can think of beam elements as lines with assigned beam cross section properties.

Corner treatments and trims have no relevance in beam element models. Before creating the study, change to configuration *02 no end treatment* where trims are suppressed (Figure 16-4).

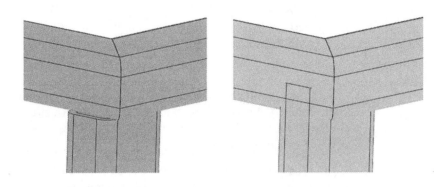

Trim applied (*01 complete weldment*)   No trim (*02 no end treatment*)

Figure 16-4: Corner treatment and trims have no relevance in beam element models. Both geometries will produce the same finite element model when meshed with beam elements.

End treatments may be suppressed.

Procedure

Having examined the ROPS part, move to **SolidWorks Simulation** and create a **Static** study. Simulation recognizes the weldment geometry and anticipates that we intend to use beam elements. It creates a **Solid Body** for each structural member present in the geometry and places them in folders corresponding to **Cut-Lists** present in the **SolidWork**s model (Figure 16-5).

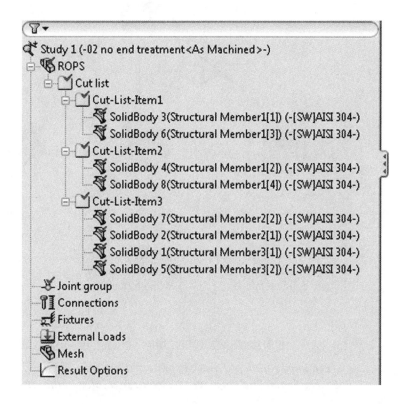

Figure 16-5: Study definition with beam elements (numbering of Solid Bodies may differ).

By default, the structural member is meshed with beam elements. You may change it by right-clicking and selecting Treat as Solid.

*Material can be imported from the SolidWorks model or defined in **SolidWorks Simulation** individually to each or all beams. Here, the material was imported from the **SolidWorks** model.*

Recall Figure 4-2 which shows icons denoting geometry intended for Solid and Shell meshing. We may now append one more: Beam geometry (Figure 16-6).

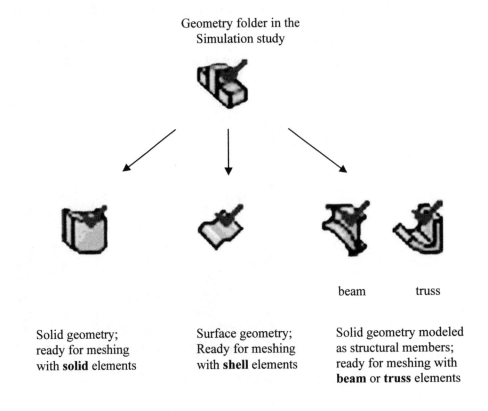

Geometry folder in the
Simulation study

beam   truss

Solid geometry;
ready for meshing
with **solid** elements

Surface geometry;
Ready for meshing
with **shell** elements

Solid geometry modeled
as structural members;
ready for meshing with
beam or **truss** elements

Figure 16-6: A geometry folder may contain all three types of geometries.

*Check marks indicate that the material has been defined. The difference
between beam and truss will be explained later in this chapter.*

In many cases the automatic designation of geometry to one of three geometry types can be changed. **Beams** may be replaced by **Solids** and **Surfaces,** and sheet metal parts may be replaced by **Solids**. This is accomplished by right-clicking the geometry folder component and selecting the appropriate choice from the pop-up menu.

In this exercise we accept the default assignment of all parts to **Beam** elements. As Figure 16-5 indicates, the geometry folder holds eight bodies and they are all intended for meshing with beam elements.

The next step is the definition of connectivity between the soon to be created beam elements.

Right-click the *Joint Group* folder and select **Edit** from the pop-up menu to open the **Edit Joints** window which shows automatically created joints. If necessary, these automatically created joints may be edited in this window,

Accept the default selection **All** beams and click **Calculate** to create joints automatically (Figure 16-7).

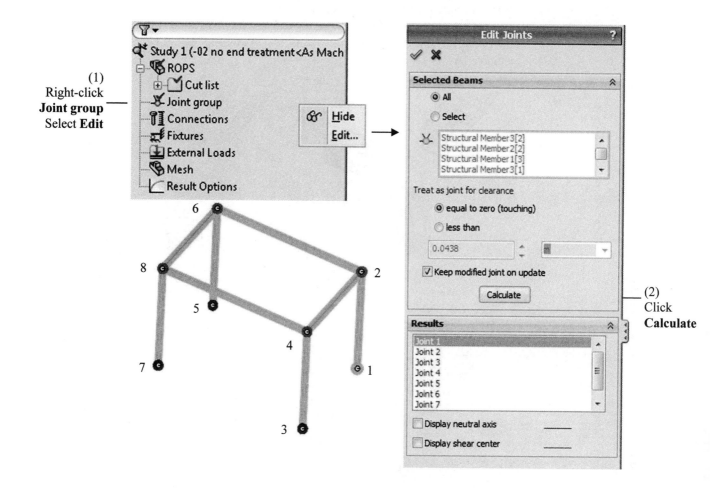

Figure 16-7: Joints are automatically created between beams. Numbers indicate joint position.

No action is required in our case. Working with a simplified geometry (no end treatments) facilitated automatic joint creation.

Joints (or beam ends) are connected to each other only if they are contained within the pinball diameter which can be changed in the **Edit joints** window. It is recommended that beam ends intended to be connected are made coincident. Non coincident beam ends can still be connected if they fall inside the pinball diameter, but this may result in a "patch-up" beam element mesh (Figure 16-8).

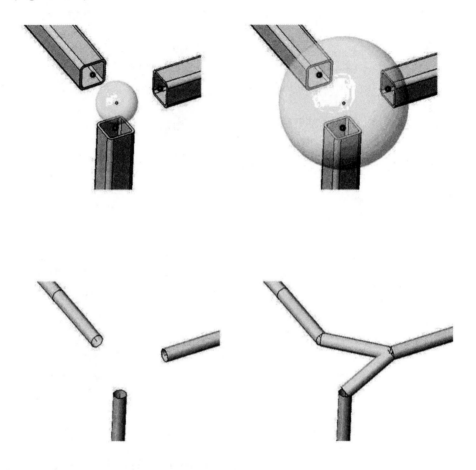

Imaginary pin ball does not contain joints.
Beam element mesh is disconnected

Imaginary pin ball contains joints.
Beam element mesh is connected

Figure 16-8: Joints (beam ends) are connected only if they are contained within the imaginary pinball not visible in the model display. Beam elements are shown as thin tubes.

Beam elements are graphically depicted as round tubes even though the beam elements are in fact just lines. The tube diameter is always the same, regardless of the actual cross-section size, shape and orientation.

Disjoined structural members can be connected if their ends fall within the volume of the pinball (Figure 16-8 top right). However, the beam element mesh (Figure 16-8 bottom right) will then contain automatically created connecting elements. This may create unpredictable results.

Apply fixed restraints to all four joints at the free ends (at the bottom) of the vertical members (Figure 16-9).

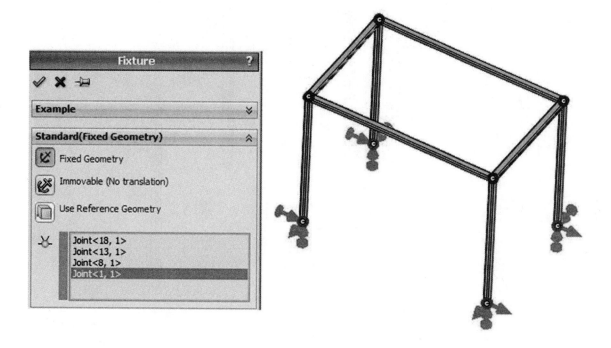

Figure 16-9: Fixed restraints applied to the free ends of vertical members.

Notice that beam elements have six degrees of freedom per node and therefore, can distinguish between Fixed and Immovable restraints. Here, we need to apply a Fixed restraint.

Apply a 2500 lbf load to the corner as shown in Figure 16-10.

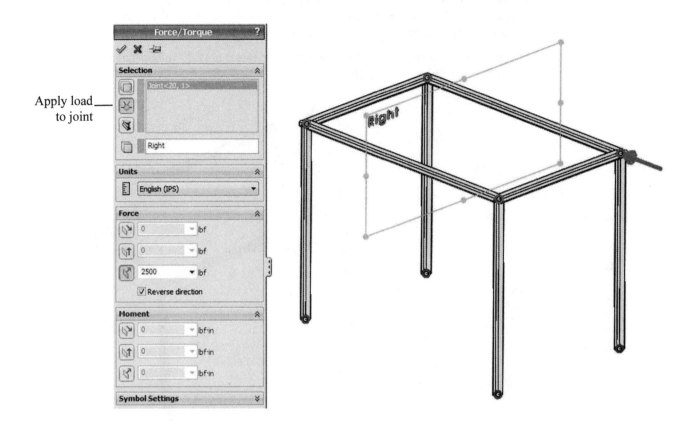

Apply load to joint

Figure 16-10: Force load applied to the corner joint.

Notice that beam elements have six degrees of freedom per node and therefore can be loaded with a force load as well as with a moment load. Here we apply force load only.

Now create the beam element mesh, noticing that there are no user controlled mesh parameters. The beam element mesh is shown in Figure 16-11.

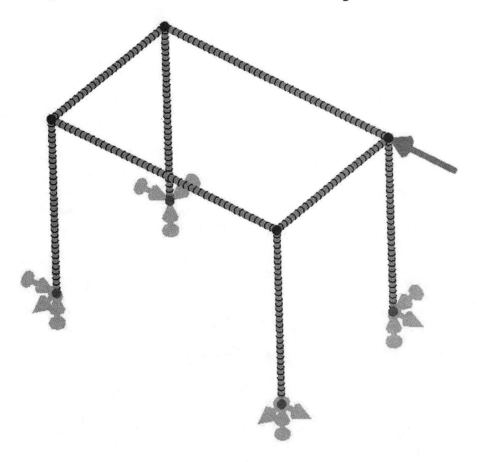

Figure 16-11: A beam element mesh is created from curves (here straight lines) used in the SolidWorks model to define Structural Members.

A beam element is a line with cross-section properties taken from the Structural Member cross section geometry. This is schematically illustrated in Figure 1-8. A beam element mesh is schematically shown as round tubes. The size of the tube shown does not depend on the actual size of the beam cross section.

Also shown are the load and restraints.

Run the solution and create a displacement plot (Figure 16-12) as well as a stress plot (Figure 16-13).

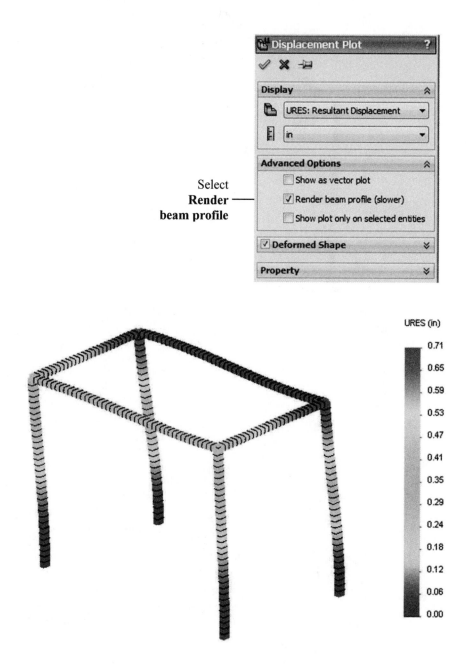

Figure 16-12: Resultant displacement results of ROPS model.

The maximum displacement is 0.71". Notice that the actual beam profile may be shown in result plots by selecting Render beam profile in plot setting. This applies also to stress results.

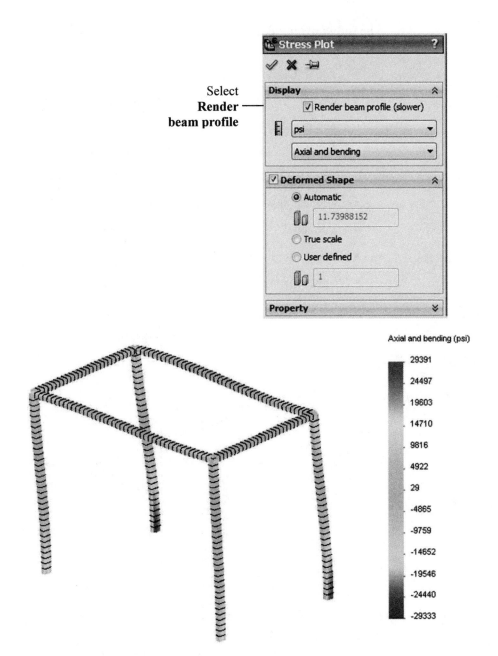

Figure 16-13: A stress plot of the "Axial and bending" stresses.

The maximum stress is 29690psi. Compared with the material yield strength of 90000psi, this indicates that the structure is below yield.

Notice that the **Axial and bending** stress is NOT von Mises stress. To understand what it is, we need to review all stress result options available for beam elements.

The software provides the following options for viewing stresses (refer to Figure 16-14):

- Axial: Uniform axial stress = P/A

- Bending in local direction 1: Bending stresses due to moment M1 about axis DIR1.

- Bending in local direction 2: Bending stress due to moment M2 about axis DIR2

- Highest axial and bending

- Torsional

- Shear stress in DIR1

- Shear stress in DIR2

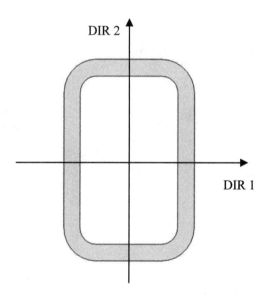

Figure 16-14: Positions of axis DIR1 and axis DIR2 for the beam cross section used in this exercise.

Axis DIR 1 and axis DIR 2 cross the centroid of the cross section.

Stress plots are different depending on the selection made in display settings. If **Render beam profile** is selected, then the stress distribution on the beam profile is shown. If **Render beam profile** is not selected, then only the upper bounds of bending stress components can be shown (Figure 16-15).

Beam profile is shown;
Axial and bending stress plot
is available

Beam profile is not shown; Upper
bound axial and bending stress plot
is available

<u>Figure 16-15: Stress results are different depending on how the beam profile
is shown.</u>

*If a beam profile is not shown (right,) then only the upper bounds of axial and
bending stress components can be presented.*

The **Axial and bending** stress is calculated by combining axial stress and
bending stresses due to moments M1 and M2. This is the default selection in
the **Stress Plot** window.

Simulation offers ample ways of analyzing beam element results such as a
Beam Diagrams (Figure 16-16).

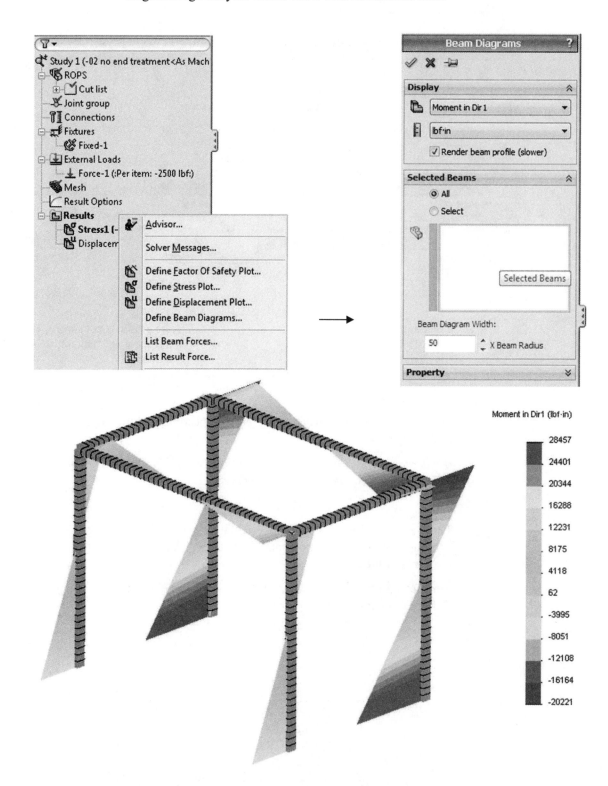

Figure 16-16: Bending moments in DIR1, bending takes place about the DIR1 axis shown in Figure 16-14.

Notice that the beam directions are defined relative to beam not to the reference system. Repeat this exercise with Immovable restraints and observe a very different Beam Diagram plot; there will be no moment at the supports.

Using the pop-up menu shown in Figure 16-16 you may also review beam forces by selecting **List Beam Forces** to display the window shown in Figure 16-17.

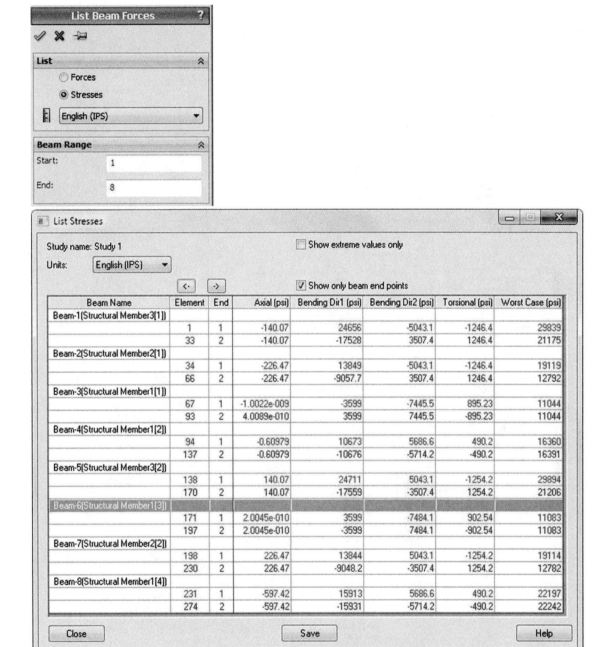

Figure 16-17: List Forces window offers tools to review force and stress components in the beams.

When Show only beam end points is selected, numbers are color coded (red and blue) and match the colors of beam elements that are displayed along with this window. The beam elements (not shown here) also show the orientation of DIR1 and DIR2.

The beam orientation, useful in interpretation of results can be shown by selecting **Show Beam direction** in the **Apply/Edit Beam** window (Figure 16-18).

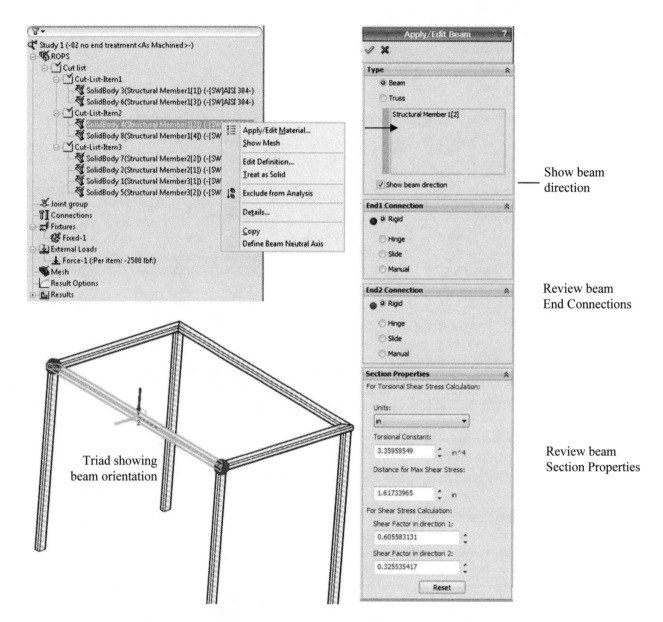

Figure 16-18: Apply/Edit Beam window offers ample tools to review beam orientation and Section Properties.

Right-click the selected structural member and select Edit Definition from the pop-up menu to open the Apply/Edit Beam window. Select Show beam direction. For easier selection, the Cut List may be deleted from the geometry folder in a Simulation study. Beam ends are color coded to show End1 and End2. A triad shows the beam orientation. Connectivity and section properties can be modified.

For a better understanding of beam elements we will review another example shown in Figure 16-19. Open the part TRUSS.

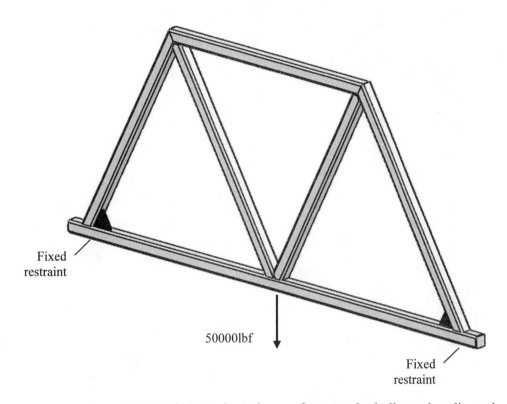

Figure 16-19: The truss is made out of rectangular hollow tubes dimensioned 3" x 3" x 0.25" with 0.5" radius. Restraints and load are also shown.

This SolidWorks model includes gussets and end caps which won't be included in the finite element mesh.

Gussets and end caps cannot be meshed with beam elements so we need to inform the automesher to ignore them. Also, trims applied to structural members may interfere with the definition of joints in the beam element mesh.

There are two ways to proceed: we can remove them from the analysis after the study has been created, or we can use a model configuration where gussets, end caps and end treatments are suppressed. We will proceed this way and use model configuration *02 simplified*.

Create a **Static** study and delete *Cut List* from the *TRUSS* folder. Next, right-click the *Joint Group* folder select **Edit**, and verify that seven joints have been correctly calculated (Figure 16-20).

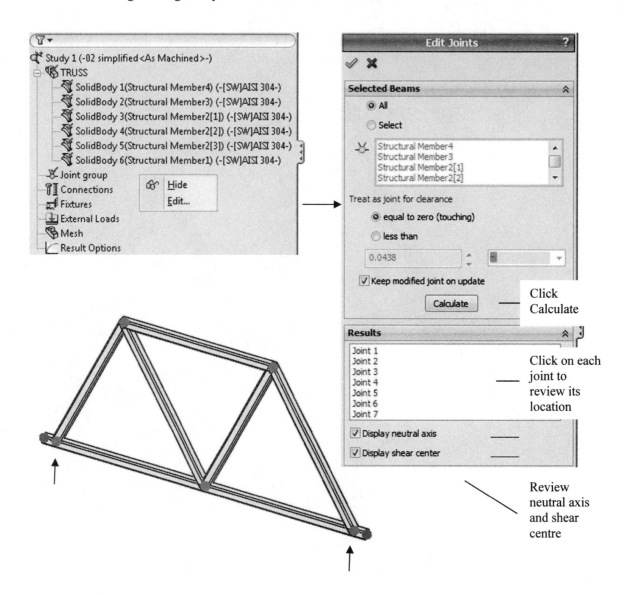

Figure 16-20: Seven joints (including two beam ends) were calculated.

Restraints will be applied to joints indicated with arrows.

Apply restraints and a load to the joints as shown in Figure 16-21.

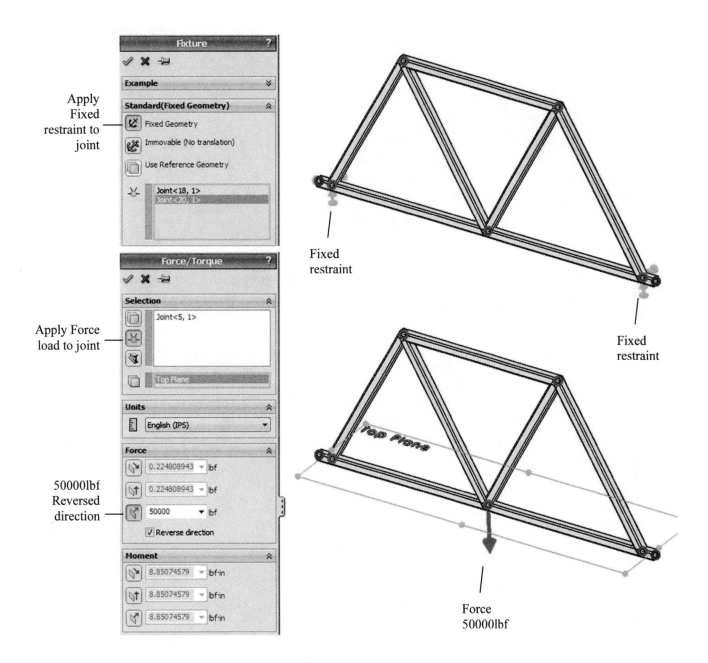

Figure 16-21: Restraints and load applied to joints.

No moment load is applied.

Mesh and solve the model and review the displacement and stress results.

Now copy the completed study *Study1* into *Study 2*. In *Study 2* delete *Cut List*, and select all structural members in the *TRUSS* folder and right-click to open a pop-up menu. Select **Edit definition** to open the **Apply/Edit beam** window. Select **Truss** in the **Apply/Edit beam** window (Figure 16-22).

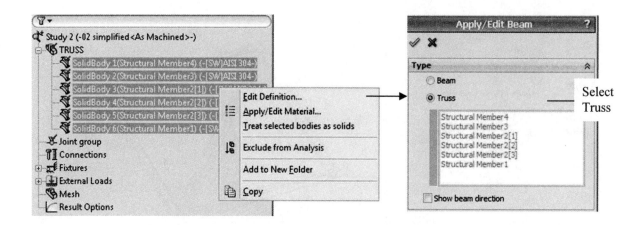

Figure 16-22: All beams are now defined as trusses.

This can be done for all beams or individually for selected beams.

This redefines connectivity between beams from rigid to pin joints. While beams can be loaded with any combination of forces and moments, trusses can be only loaded with axial force. Trusses behave as a tension/compression springs and are meshed with only one element. See Figure 16-23 for a comparison between beam and truss element meshes.

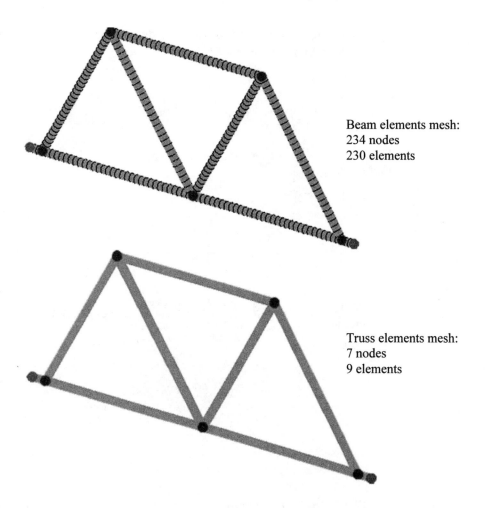

Beam elements mesh:
234 nodes
230 elements

Truss elements mesh:
7 nodes
9 elements

Figure 16-23: Finite element mesh in model with beam elements (top) and with truss elements (bottom).

There are nine elements in the model meshed with truss elements They behave as if they were pin jointed and can be loaded only with axial loads.

An attempt to run a truss element model displays an error message shown at the top of Figure 16-24.

Direct Sparse solver message

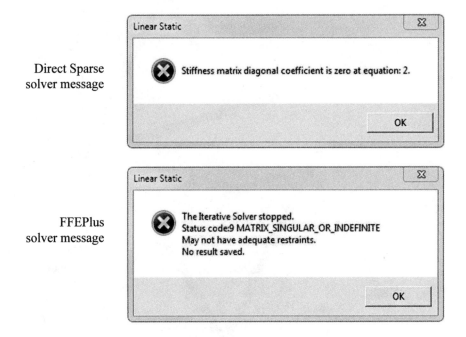

FFEPlus solver message

Figure 16-24: An attempt to run model meshed with truss elements brings up an error message which differs with the solver used but in either case is caused by Rigid Body Motions present in the model.

The solver is selected in study Properties.

The supports are insufficient and allow rigid body motion of the model because truss elements have only three degrees of freedom (translations in three directions) and cannot accept any restraints on rotations. Therefore, the entire model can spin about the line passing through the supports. The short ends can freely rotate about the joint where the restraint is defined. To eliminate these rigid body motions we need to execute a solution with the **Use soft springs to stabilize model** option checked.

Obtain the solution of study with truss elements and compare the displacement and stress results between the two studies (Figure 16-25).

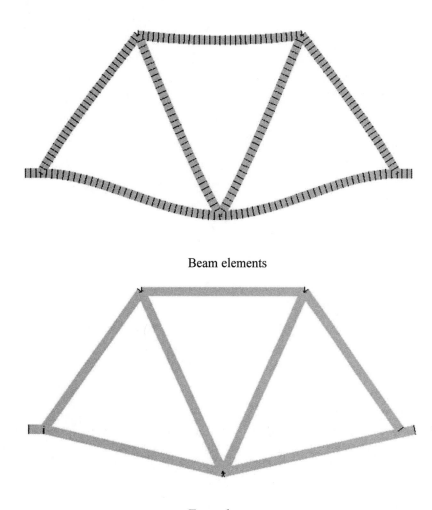

Beam elements

Truss elements

Figure 16-25: The deformation pattern of the model with beam elements (top) and truss elements (bottom).

The scale of deformation is the same for both models. Beam profiles are not rendered in these illustrations. Notice that the short ends in both models do not experience any displacements.

Bending of structural members observed in the beam element model proves that beam elements are rigidly connected to each other and transmit bending moments. Conversely, truss elements are connected by pin joints; they cannot transmit bending. Deformation of truss elements can only take the form of stretching and compressing, and therefore deformed truss elements remain straight. Remember that buckling is not modeled in either of these static studies.

Notes:

17: Review of 2D problems

Topics covered

- Classification of finite elements
- 2D axi-symmetric element
- 2D plane stress element
- 2D plane strain element

Recall Figure 1-10 that lists basic elements used in **SolidWorks Simulation**: solids, shells and beams which represent different levels of idealization possible in 3D space. Solids were introduced in chapter 2, shells in chapter 4 and beams in chapter 16. In this chapter we introduce two dimensional (2D) elements but before proceeding we will summarize once again properties of the elements we are already familiar with.

Solid elements

Solid elements mesh volumes and therefore all three dimensions are fully represented. Notice that the volume is called "solid" in CAD terminology. This "solid" should not be confused with the term "solid" in FEA which corresponds to solid elements.

The displacement field in a solid element is three dimensional (3D). No assumptions on the displacement field or stress distribution in any direction are made.

Nodal displacements have three components: translation in the x, y, and z directions. Loads and restraints can be applied in these three directions. Nodes of solid elements have three degrees of freedom.

Shell elements

Shell elements mesh surfaces that have one dimension (thickness) collapsed. Thickness is assumed to be small in comparison to other dimensions. Shell elements model displacement and stress fields in two in-plane directions. The stress distribution across the missing dimension (thickness) is assumed to have a linear distribution.

Nodal displacements have six components: translation in the x, y, and z directions, and rotation about the x, y, and z directions. Loads and restraints can be applied in each of these six directions. Nodes of shell elements have six degrees of freedom.

Beam elements

Beam elements mesh curves (wireframe) as they have two dimensions collapsed. It is assumed that the beam cross section is small in comparison with the length. Beam elements model displacements and stresses in one (in-line) direction. Stress in the two missing dimensions must be assumed. These assumptions are based on beam theory.

Nodal displacements have six components: translation in the x, y, and z directions, and rotation about the x, y, and z directions. Nodes of beam elements have six degrees of freedom. Loads and restraints can be applied in these six directions.

Solid, shell and beam elements all belong to the class of 3D elements. In this chapter we introduce **two dimensional elements**. Consider an axi-symmetric model with axi-symmetric loads and restraints as shown in Figure 17-1. Notice that due to the axial symmetry of the geometry, loads and restraints, all points located on any radial cross section perform displacements only in two directions: radial and axial translation. There is no translation in the circumferential direction and there are no rotations.

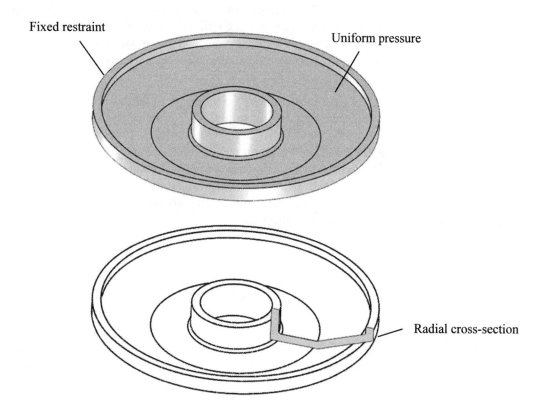

Figure 17-1: Axi-symmetric model (top) and radial cross section (bottom). Displacements in the model are fully described by radial and axial translations of points on any radial cross section.

Loads and restraint shown are examples of an axi-symmetric load and restraint.

If displacements, and consequently strains and stresses are fully defined by two displacement components: translation in radial and axial directions, then the analysis of any axi-symmetric model can be simplified to the analysis of displacements and stresses of one radial cross section meshed with elements that have only two degrees of freedom per node. These elements are called 2D axi-symmetric elements.

We will demonstrate the use of axi-symmetric elements on part file END CAP. The material is 6/10 Nylon with a yield strength 139MPa.

For a better understanding of the differences between 3D solid elements and 2D axi-symmetric elements, we will solve the model first with 3D solids and then with 2D axi-symmetric elements. Additionally, we will study nonlinear effects using both modeling approaches. Notice the similarities between this problem and the ROUND PLATE from chapter 15.

The END CAP model offers a wide range of modeling choices. Analysis can be conducted using the full solid CAD geometry or as using a section shown in Figure 17-2. It can also be represented by shell geometry either as a whole model or a section. Finally it can be represented by a radial cross section meshed with 2D axi-symmetric elements. In this exercise we will first analyze a section meshed with solid elements, and then a radial cross section meshed with 2D axi-symmetric elements. In both cases we will perform linear and nonlinear geometry analyses.

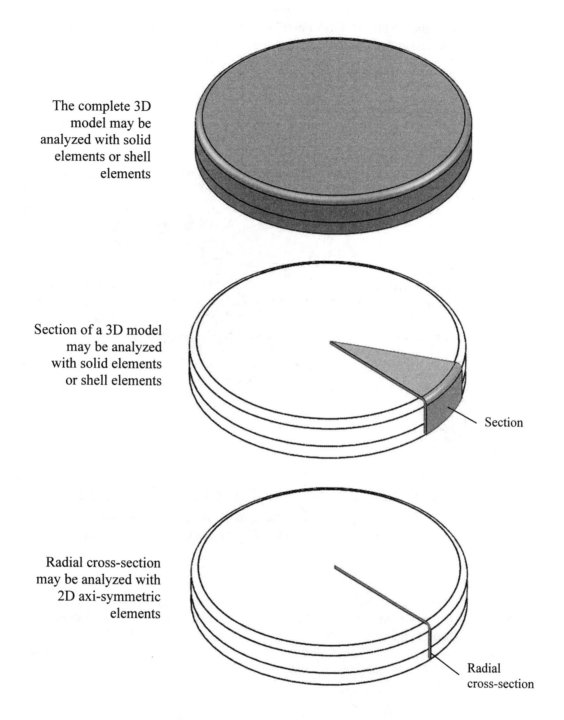

The complete 3D model may be analyzed with solid elements or shell elements

Section of a 3D model may be analyzed with solid elements or shell elements

Section

Radial cross-section may be analyzed with 2D axi-symmetric elements

Radial cross-section

Figure 17-2: Modeling choices in the END CAP.

The END CAP model may be analyzed without modifications (top), as a solid or shell section (middle), or as a radial cross-section (bottom).

Open the END CAP model in *02 section* configuration and apply the loads, restraints and symmetry boundary conditions as shown in Figure 17-3.

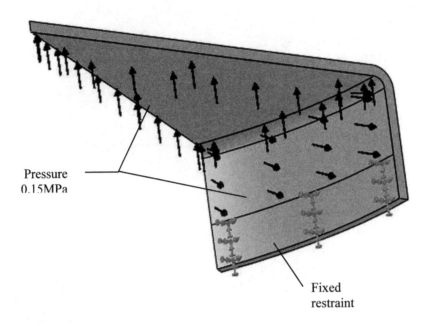

Pressure
0.15MPa

Fixed
restraint

Figure 17-3: Pressure load and fixed restraints applied to the section.

Don't forget to apply symmetry boundary conditions to radial cross sections. The symbols of symmetry boundary conditions are not shown in this illustration.

Use a mesh with the default element size and obtain results without the **Large Displacement** option checked (study *01 3D linear*) and with the **Large Displacement** option checked (study *02 3D nonlinear*). Results are summarized in Figures 17-4 and 17-5. Notice the long solution time required to obtain the nonlinear solution.

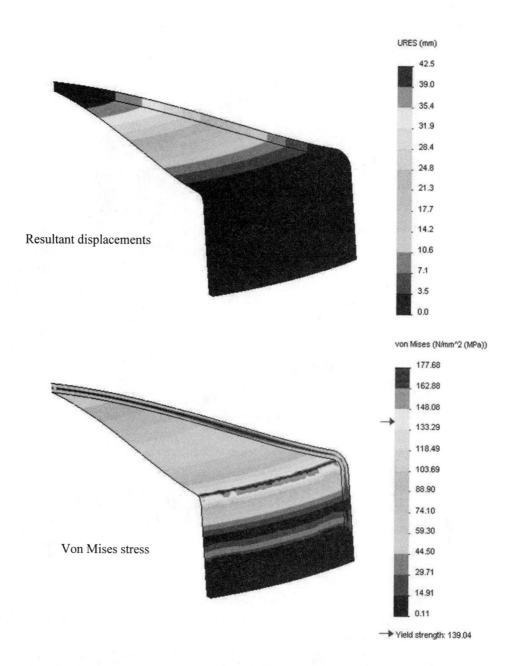

Resultant displacements

Von Mises stress

Figure 17-4: Displacement (top) and von Mises stress (bottom) results of the linear study.

Notice that stress concentrations are "spotty" and attracted to nodes. This is an indication that a more refined mesh should have been used. The same applies to results of the nonlinear study in Figure 17-5.

Notice that linear analysis reports the maximum von Mises stress above yield.

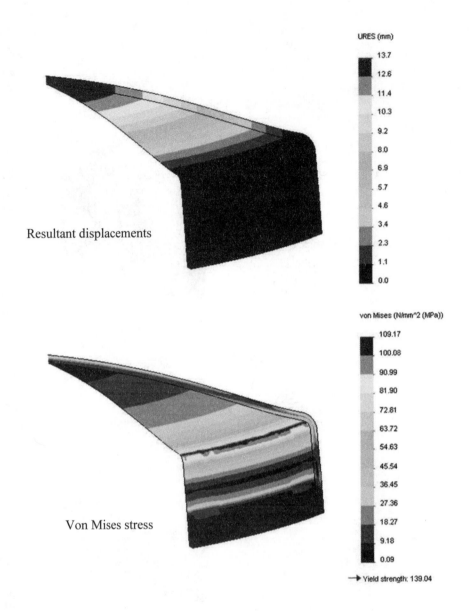

Figure 17-5: Displacement (top) and von Mises stress (bottom) results of the nonlinear study.

The maximum von Mises stress is below yield in the model solved with large displacements.

The nonlinear analysis reports much lower displacements, and the stress is below yield. This indicates the importance of modeling nonlinear effects. As indicated in Figure 17-4, a more refined mesh should be used where stress concentrations have been found. However, using a more refined mesh for a nonlinear analysis would produce very long solution times, even if the simplified section model is used.

This is where the advantages of a 2D representation become obvious. With 2D axi-symmetric elements, we will be able to obtain a solution using a refined mesh in less time than that required for the solution with 3D solid elements. Of course, 2D elements can also be used for linear analysis.

Switch to the *01 full* configuration and create a **Nonlinear** study called *03 2D nonlinear*. In the study definition window, select **Use 2D simplification**, then select **Axi-symmetric** to define a study using 2D axi-symmetric elements (Figure 17-6).

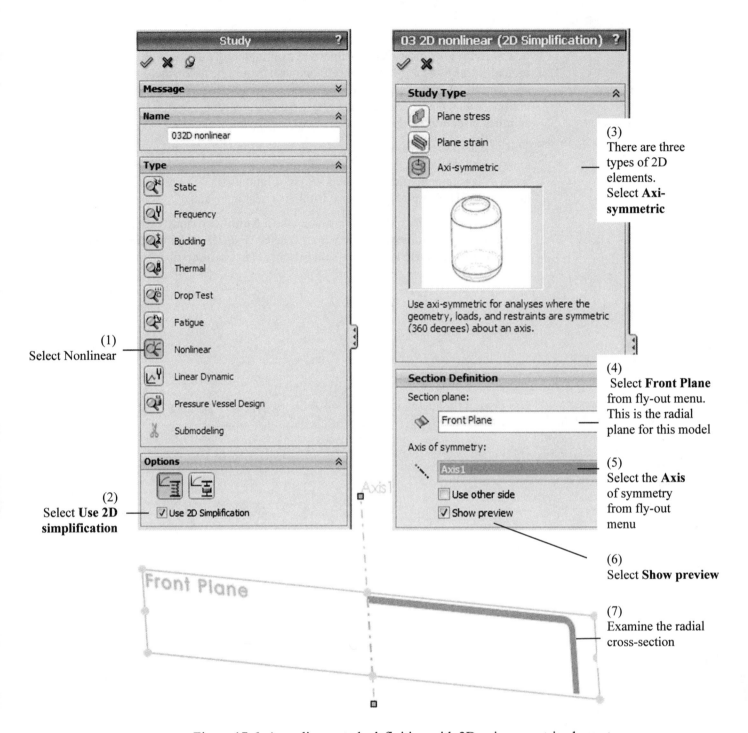

Figure 17-6: A nonlinear study definition with 2D axi-symmetric elements.

The model is represented by a radial cross-section. The fly-out menu is used for the selection of the plane and axis and is not shown in this illustration.

Having created the cross section that will be meshed with 2D axi-symmetric elements, go to the **SolidWorks Feature Manager** and define a sensor as shown in Figure 17-7.

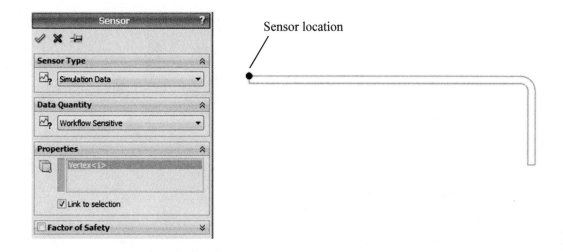

Figure 17-7: Sensor definition in the model indented for meshing with 2D axi-symmetric elements.

The sensor is located in the middle of the top face.

Apply the restraint and pressure load as shown in Figure 17-8.

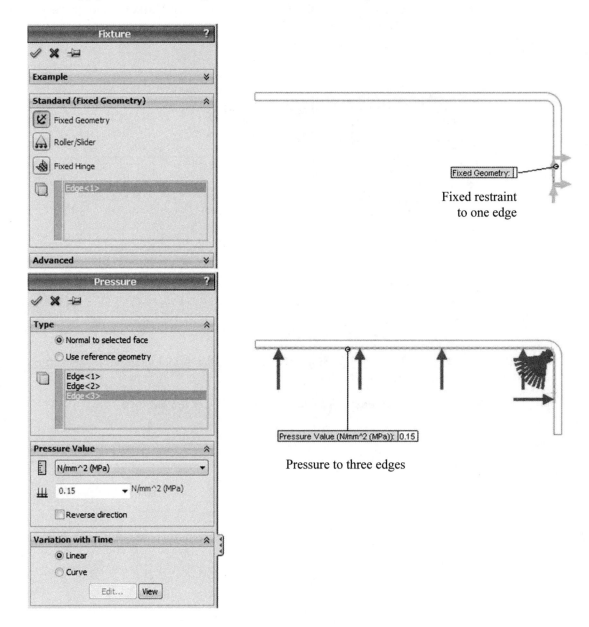

Figure 17-8: The restraint (top) and pressure load (bottom) defined in the 2D axi-symmetric model.

The restraint and pressure load are applied to edges of the 2D model that correspond to faces of the 3D model (refer to Figure 17-3).

Apply a **mesh control** of 0.1mm and element ratio 1.1 to the arc corresponding to the round face where stress concentrations were found in the 3D model. Mesh the model using the default element size and a **Curvature based mesh** (Figure 17-9).

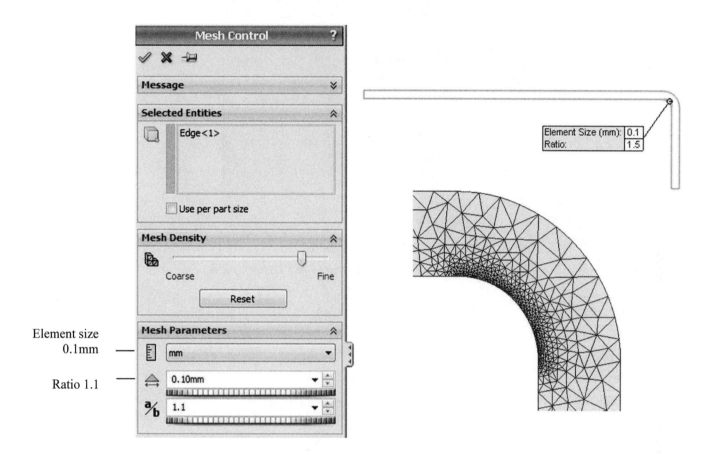

Element size
0.1mm

Ratio 1.1

Figure 17-9: Mesh control applied to the arc where stress concentrations need to be modeled precisely.

Mesh controls produce a very fine mesh around the bend.

317

Right-click *Results Option*, select edit and set it up as shown in Figure 17-10.

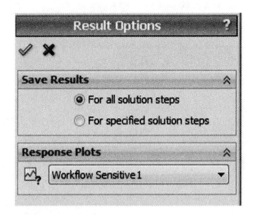

Figure 17-10: Results Options definition.

This definition is required to construct Time History plots.

Obtain a nonlinear solution with the settings shown in Figure 17-11.

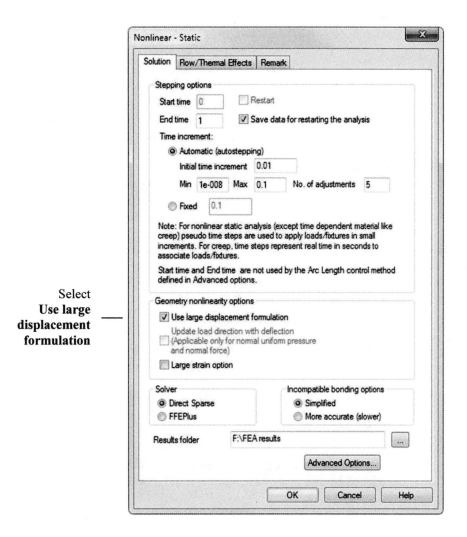

<u>Figure 17-11: Nonlinear study settings.</u>

Select Use large displacement formulation. The only source of nonlinear behavior in this model is the changing shape. This is geometric nonlinearity.

Review the displacement and stress results as shown in Figure 17-12 and Figure 17-13.

Figure 17-12: Displacement results from the 2D axi-symmetric model.

Plot is shown in normal view along with undeformed shape shown.

The maximum resultant displacement of 13.8mm is very close to the result produced by analysis of the nonlinear 3D model.

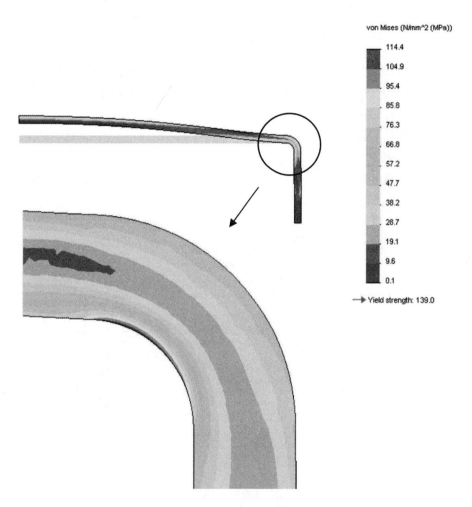

Figure 17-13: Von Mises stress results from the 2D axi-symmetric model.

A refined mesh allows for accurate stress modeling. The 2D model produces these results in a fraction of the time required to solve the 3D model with a similar mesh density.

The maximum von Mises stress reported by the 2D model is 114MPa as compared to 109MPa reported by 3D model. The difference is not caused by different model dimensionality but by a more refined mesh. This mesh refinement is much easier to solve in a nonlinear 2D model and would be much more time intensive in a nonlinear 3D model.

To investigate the importance of nonlinear effects, complete this exercise by making a displacement time history plot using the previously defined sensor. Follow steps indicated in Figure 17-14.

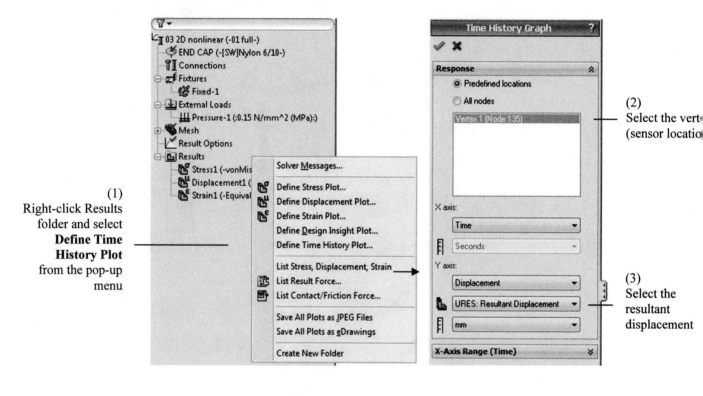

(1)
Right-click Results folder and select **Define Time History Plot** from the pop-up menu

(2)
Select the vert (sensor locatio

(3)
Select the resultant displacement

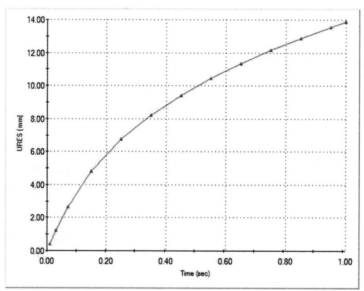

Figure 17-14: Displacement time history.

The plot clearly shows stiffening of the model as deformation progresses. The same plot could have been produced using the 3D model, but solution times would be much longer.

As shown in the menu in Figure 17-6, there are other types of 2D elements. Here is the summary:

2D plane stress elements are intended for thin models restrained and loaded in plane. A constant stress distribution across the thickness is assumed.

2D plane strain elements are intended for thick models restrained and loaded in plane. Constant strain across the thickness is assumed.

2D axi-symmetric elements are intended for axially symmetric models with axis symmetric restraints and loads.

We will now introduce 2D plane stress elements. Open HOLLOW PLATE 2D which is identical to the model in chapter 2 except that it has material properties assigned.

Follow the steps in Figure 17-15 to create a study with a 2D plane stress model. Follow the steps in Figure 17-16 to apply restraints and loads.

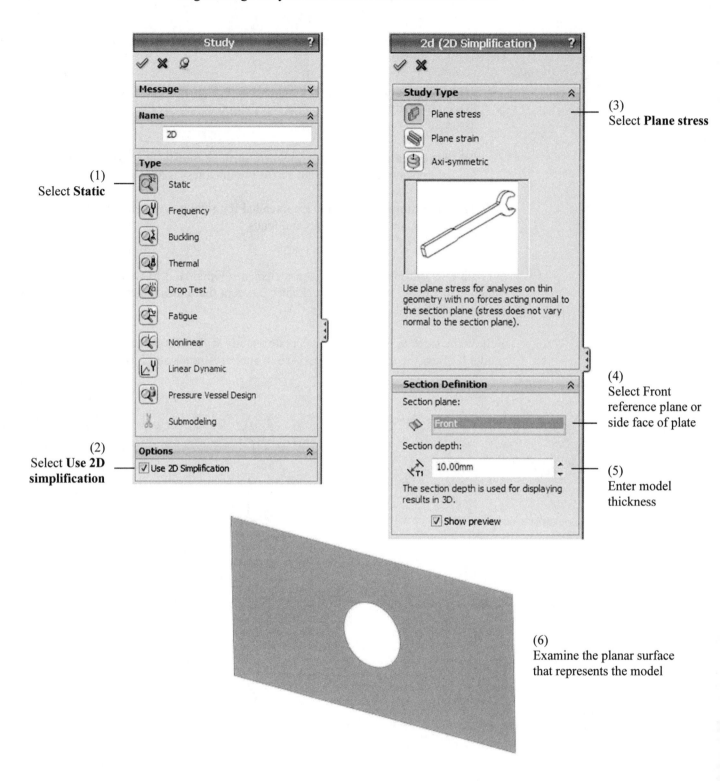

(1)
Select **Static**

(2)
Select **Use 2D simplification**

(3)
Select **Plane stress**

(4)
Select Front reference plane or side face of plate

(5)
Enter model thickness

(6)
Examine the planar surface that represents the model

Figure 17-15: Static study definition with 2D plane stress elements.

The model is represented by a planar surface.

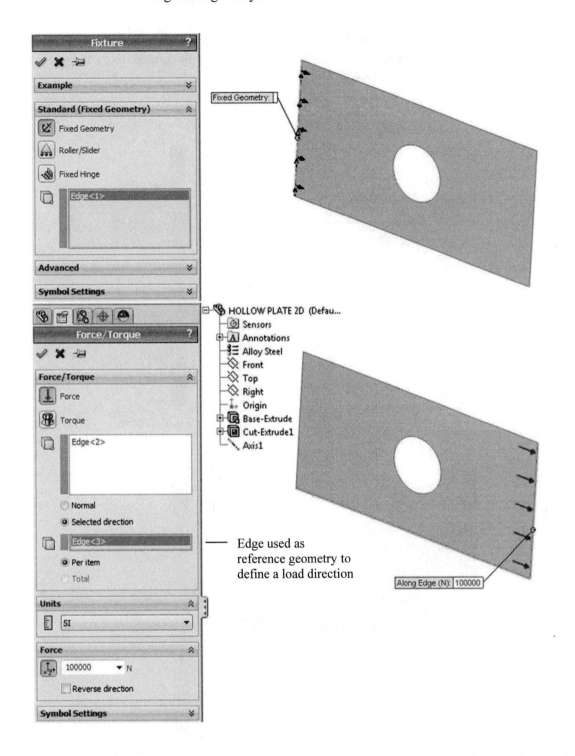

Figure 17-16: Restraint (top) and tensile load (bottom) defined in the 2D plane stress model.

The restraint and load are applied to the edges of the 2D model that correspond to the faces of the 3D model (refer to chapter 2).

Mesh the model with the default element size. Solve and compare displacements and stress results (Figure 17-17) to those obtained with the 3D solid model in chapter 2.

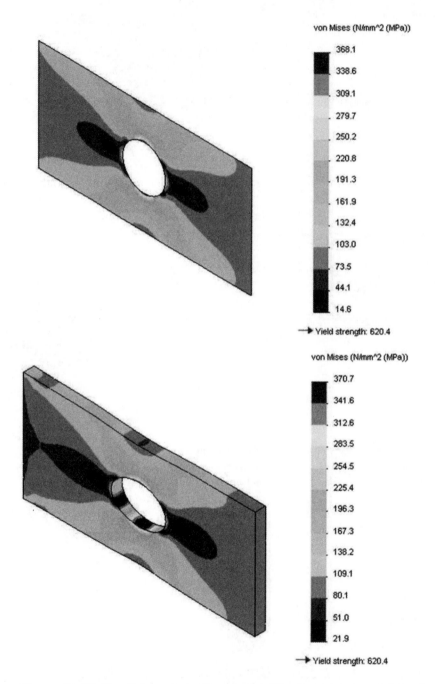

Figure 17-17: Von Mises stress plots in the 2D plane stress model (top) and the 3D model (bottom) show practically the same results.

The problem can be represented by 2D plane stress model because of low plate thickness.

The HOLLOW PLATE 2D model does not really show any advantages of using 2D simplification. These advantages are clear only if the problem requires an iterative solution as in previous example or highly refined meshes as is the case with the next example.

Open L BRACKET 2D which is a planar surface similar in shape (but not in thickness) to the model studied in chapter 3. Our objective is to demonstrate that stresses around a corner with a small radius do not diverge but converge to a finite value. To do that we will have to conduct an h-convergence process working with a highly refined mesh that will be facilitated by using the **2D simplification**.

Create a static study *2D 01* using the **2D Simplification** and select **Plane stress**. Select the model surface for the **Section plane** and enter 1mm for the **Section Depth**. Notice that the two planes (surfaces) exist in the plane folder.

Apply restraints and load as shown in Figure 17-18.

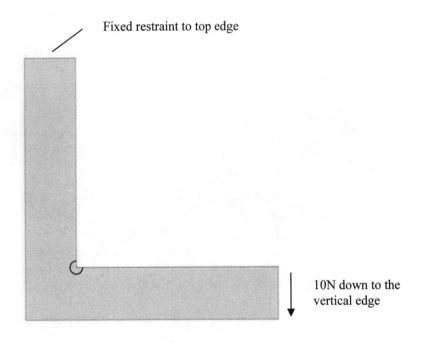

Fixed restraint to top edge

10N down to the vertical edge

Figure 17-18: Restraint and load applied to the 2D plane stress model.

Restraints and loads must be all in-plane to be compatible with this 2D model.

Obtain a solution with the default curvature based mesh, and then proceed with three more studies with different mesh controls applied to the surface area around the radius (Figure 17-19).

Study *2D 01*; no mesh control   Study *2D 02*; mesh control 0.25mm

Study *2D 03*; mesh control 0.10mm   Study *2D 04*; mesh control 0.05mm

Figure 17-19: Meshed used in four studies.

Mesh control is applied to the Surface body 2 shown in Figure 17-17. Notice the poorly shaped elements (high aspect ratio) in the study with no mesh controls.

Results are summarized in a graph shown in Figure 17-20.

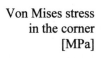

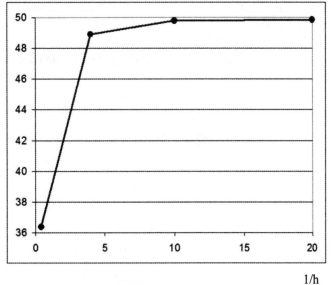

1/h

Figure 17-20: Converged maximum von Mises stress results in four studies as a function of mesh refinement 1/h.

h is the element size as defined by the mesh control.

Results indicate that convergence does take place. To fully appreciate the advantages of the **2D Simplification** you may want to repeat this analysis using solid elements and observe the much longer solution times.

Notice that the 2D model would not be suitable for analysis of buckling which may be the dominant mode of failure in such a thin plate. Construct and analyze a buckling study on an equivalent 3D model.

To introduce 2D plane strain elements, we will perform an analysis of contact stress between two plates in the assembly model named CONTACT. The model consists of two identical plates ready to touch each other on the curved faces and connected by a U-shape clamp (Figure 17-21). The material for all parts is Alloy Steel; it has already been assigned to all parts. Our objective is to study contact stress on two cylindrical faces when the model is loaded with 15000N compressive load.

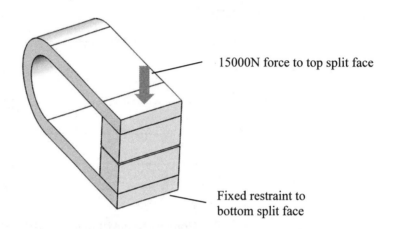

Figure 17-21: Load and restraint in the CONTACT model.

Notice the small gap between top and bottom plates.

Treating this as a 2D plane strain problem we assume constant strain along the thickness, therefore all models shown in Figure 17-22 will give the same results.

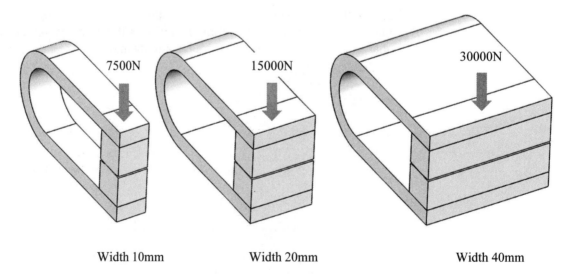

Figure 17-22: All the models will give the same results when treated as 2D plane strain problems.

Notice that load per unit of width is the same in the above three models: 750N/mm.

Follow steps in Figure 17-23 to create a study with 2D plane strain model. Follow the steps in Figure 17-24 to apply restraints and loads.

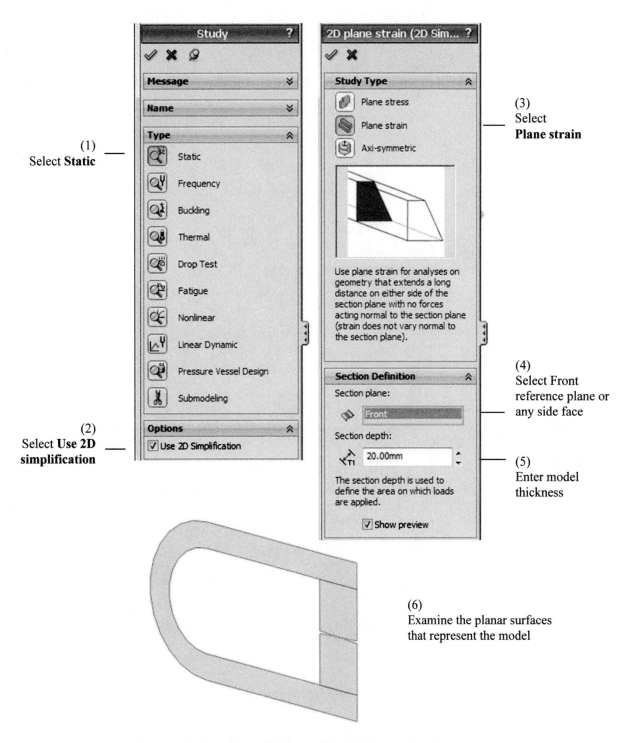

(1) Select **Static**

(2) Select **Use 2D simplification**

(3) Select **Plane strain**

(4) Select Front reference plane or any side face

(5) Enter model thickness

(6) Examine the planar surfaces that represent the model

Figure 17-23: Static study definition with 2D plane strain elements.

The model is represented by planar surfaces.

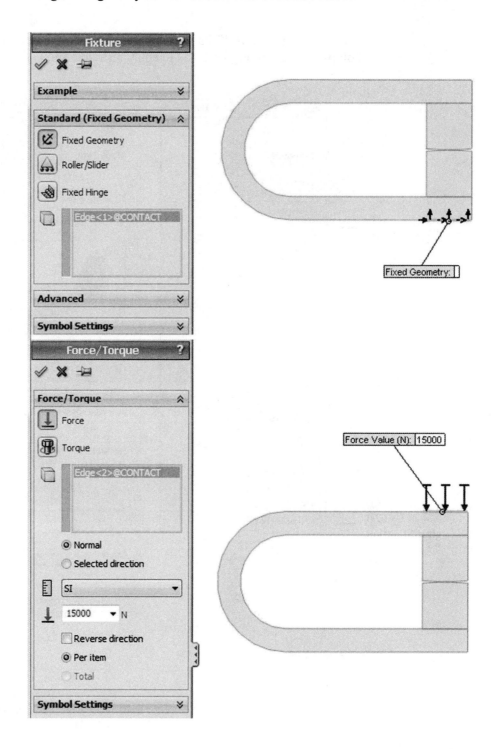

Figure 17-24: Restraint (top) and load (bottom) defined in the 2D plane strain model.

The restraint and load are applied to the edges of the 2D model that correspond to the faces of the 3D model.

Define a **Contact Set** between the two cylindrical faces as shown in Figure 17-25.

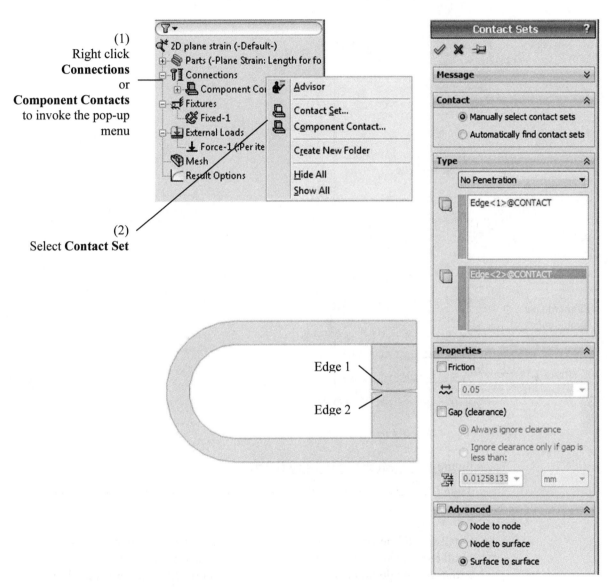

(1)
Right click
Connections
or
Component Contacts
to invoke the pop-up
menu

(2)
Select **Contact Set**

(3)
Select
two edges

Edge 1

Edge 2

Figure 17-25: Contact Set definition.

Gap (clearance) is not selected meaning that the gap will be closed during the solution. A surface to surface type contact must be selected always when faces are not touching initially but may come into contact after the load is applied.

We are now ready to mesh the model. Adequate mesh density in the contact area is of paramount importance in any contact stress analysis. It is the responsibility of the user to make sure that there are enough elements in the contact area to properly model the distribution of contact stresses. In this exercise we use a default global element size and apply mesh controls 0.05mm to contacting edges as shown in Figure 17-26.

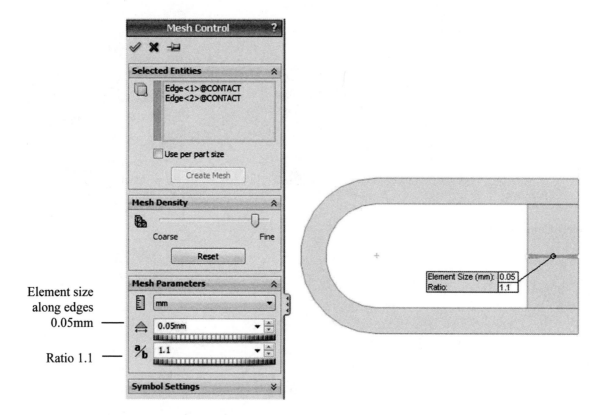

Element size along edges 0.05mm

Ratio 1.1

Figure 17-26: Mesh Control size is 0.05mm.

Mesh Control is defined on the cylindrical edges where contact will take place.

Small size of the contact area that will develop under the load necessitates small element size. Solving this as a 3D problem would results in a model with a very large number of elements. This, combined with iterative solution always required for any contact problem which by its nature is non-linear, would result in a very long solution time. 2D representation reduces the numerical complexity of the problem very significantly.

Run the solution and answer No to question about initial contact posed by the solver (Figure 17-27).

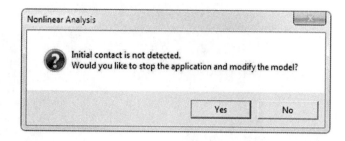

Figure 17-27: No initial contact is intentional, therefore answer No.

In most contact problems contacting faces (or edges) already touch each other before load has been applied but in this problem we have a gap.

Von Mises stress results are shown in Figure 17-28.

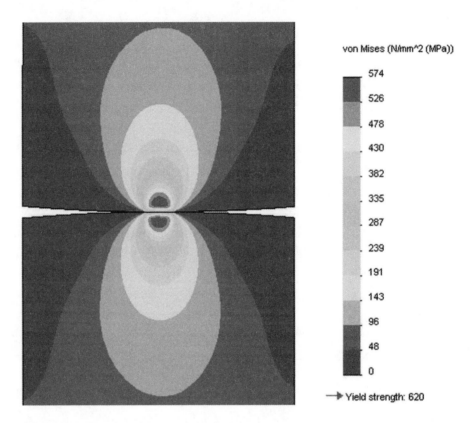

Figure 17-28: Von Mises stress results with in the contact area. The maximum von Mises stress is 574MPa.

Von Mises stress is close to yield.

The **Factor of Safety** (FOS) plot based on the **Maximum Shear Stress** is shown in Figure 17-29. The **Factor of Safety** plot based on the **Maximum von Mises Stress** is shown in Figure 17-30. Notice that the **Maximum Shear Stress** criterion gives the FOS = 1 while the **Maximum von Mises Stress**, being less conservative, gives the FOS = 1.1.

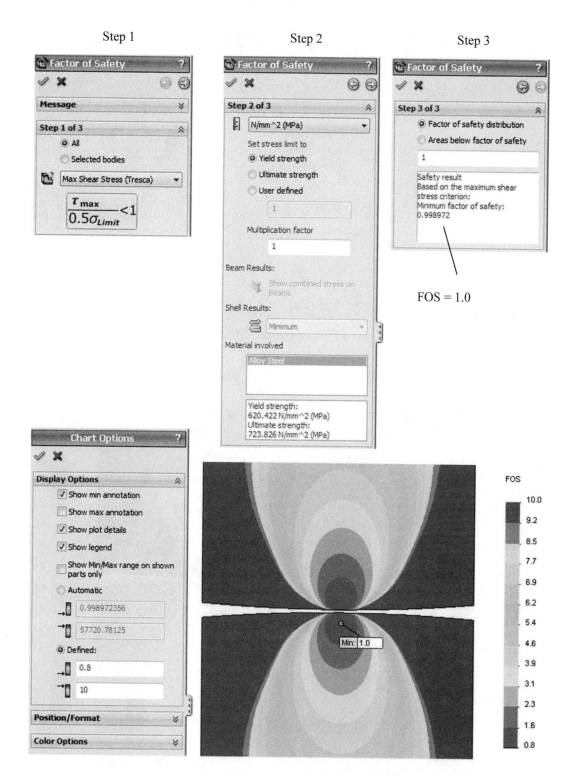

Figure 17-29: Factor of safety based on the Maximum Shear Stress.

A factor of safety plot is created in three steps. The range of the factor of safety 0-10 is defined in Chart Options. Notice that stress distribution closely matches the location of maximum shear stress in the Hertz contact problem.

Step 1   Step 2   Step 3

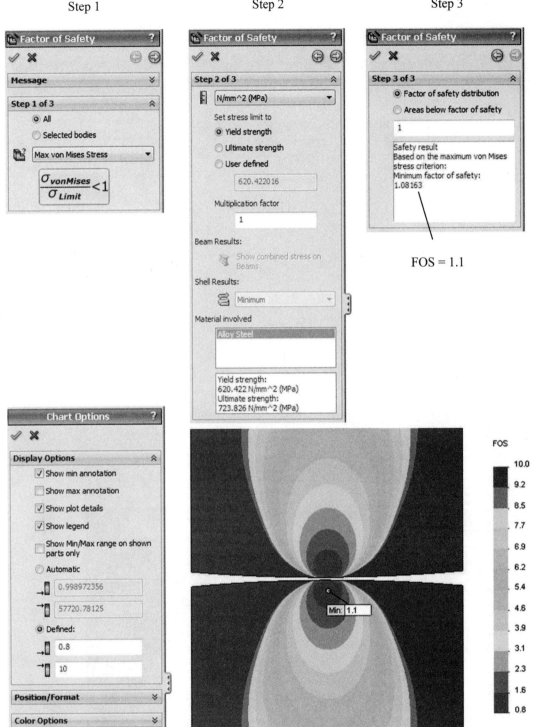

Figure 17-30: Factor of safety based on the Maximum von Mises Stress.

A factor of safety plot is created in three steps. The range of the factor of safety 0-10 is defined in Chart Options.

Figure 17-31 presents a summary of the elements available in **Simulation**. This figure expands the information first presented in Figure 4-2, then again in Figure 16-6.

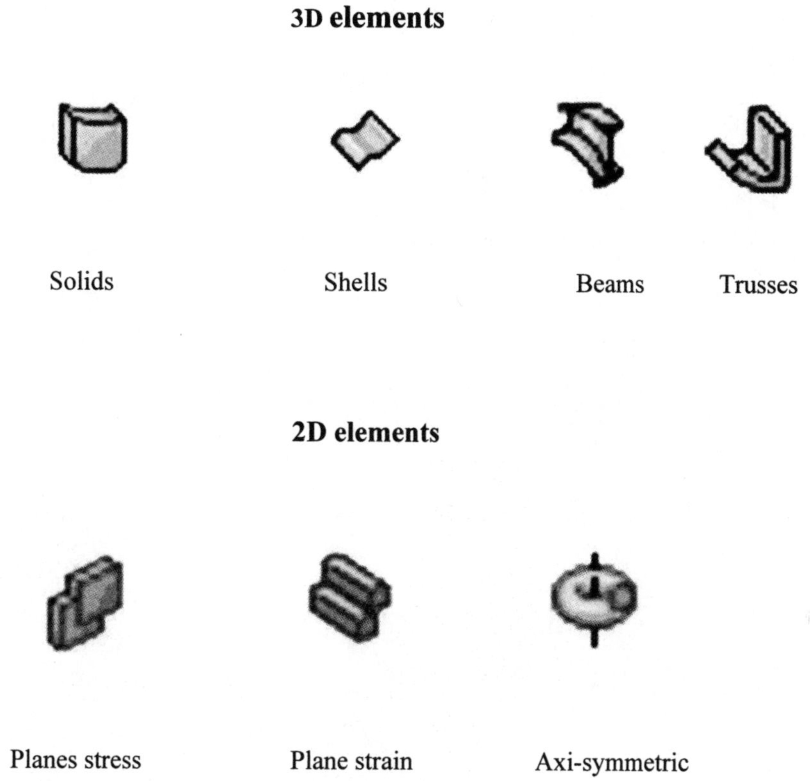

3D elements

Solids	Shells	Beams	Trusses

2D elements

Planes stress	Plane strain	Axi-symmetric

Figure 17-31: Summary of elements and their icons in SolidWorks Simulation.

See chapter 17 for an explanation of differences between beams and trusses which both belong to the class of beam elements.

Notes:

18: Vibration Analysis - Modal Time History and Harmonic

Topics covered

- ❏ Modal Time History analysis (Time Response)
- ❏ Harmonic analysis (Frequency Response)
- ❏ Modal Superposition Method
- ❏ Damping

What is dynamic analysis?

In preparation for the dynamic analysis exercises, we need to clarify an important terminology issue. The term "Dynamic Analysis" applies to an analysis of unrestrained or partially restrained bodies (mechanisms) as well as to restrained bodies such as structures. "Dynamic Analysis" within the scope of FEA deals only with the vibration of deformable bodies about the position of equilibrium. A more appropriate term to use would be "Vibration Analysis" but the term "Dynamic Analysis" is well entrenched in the FEA literature. We will use the term understanding that Dynamic Analysis within FEA really means vibration analysis of structures.

All types of analyses that we have discussed so far have assumed that the load is not a function of time. We will now lift this restriction to introduce two common types of dynamic analyses: **Modal Time History** and **Harmonic,** which are available in **SolidWorks Simulation Premium. Modal Time History** is also known as a Time Response analysis. **Harmonic** analysis is also known as a Frequency Response analysis or as a Steady State Harmonic Response analysis. **Modal Time History** and **Harmonic analyses** both belong to the category of linear analyses.

Modal superposition method

The review of dynamic analyses needs to be preceded by a description of the modal superposition method on which both Time Response and Frequency Response analyses are most often based. The modal superposition method represents a dynamic response of a vibrating structure by using the superposition of responses that characterize a single Degree Of Freedom (1DOF) system. The natural frequencies of these 1DOF systems correspond to the natural frequencies of the analyzed structure. The number of DOF contributing to a dynamic response is equal to the number of modes calculated by a pre-requisite modal (frequency) analysis. How many modes should then be calculated to represent dynamic responses using the modal superposition method? The first few modes are the most important, but the exact number of required modes is not known prior to analysis. One should use a convergence process to demonstrate that increasing the number of modes past a certain number no longer significantly affects results.

The modal superposition method is not always a prerequisite for dynamic analysis. Other methods like the Direct Integration method do not require modal analysis. **SolidWorks Simulation** uses the Direct Integration method in the **Drop test** study.

Modal Time History (Time Response) analysis

In a **Modal Time History** analysis, the applied load is an explicit function of time, mass and damping properties all of which are taken into consideration and the vibration equation appears in its full form:

$$[M]\ddot{d} + [C]\dot{d} + [K]d = F(t)$$

Where:

[M]	is mass matrix
[C]	is damping matrix
[K]	is stiffness matrix
F(t)	is vector of nodal loads, this vector is a function of
d	is an unknown vector of nodal displacements

A Time Response analysis requires the definition of a damping coefficient which is most often expressed as a percentage of critical damping. Readers are referred to (1) as listed in Chapter 24 for selected numerical values of damping coefficients.

A Time Response analysis is used to model events of a short duration. A typical example would be an analysis of a structure's vibrations due to an impact load or acceleration applied to the base (called base excitation). Results of the Time Response analysis will capture both the response during the time when the load is applied, as well as the free vibration after the load has been removed.

Harmonic (Frequency Response) analysis

Harmonic analysis assumes that the load is a function of frequency rather than being directly dependent on time as is the case of a Time Response analysis.

$$[M]\ddot{d} + [C]\dot{d} + [K]d = F sin(\omega t)$$

A Frequency Response analysis models a structure's response to forced excitation or base excitation (excitation applied to the support) that is a sinusoidal function of time. It is assumed that the excitation frequency changes very slowly, hence the alternative name **Steady State Harmonic Response** is often used for this type of analysis. A Frequency Response analysis also uses the modal superposition method and requires that damping be defined, usually as a percentage of critical damping.

A typical application of a **Frequency Response** analysis is a simulation of a shaker table, which will be demonstrated later in this chapter.

Both examples presented in this chapter feature discrete systems where mass and stiffness are separated. These examples are intuitive and have simple analytical solutions that can be found in any introductory textbook on vibration analysis, for example (2) listed in Chapter 24. **SolidWorks Simulation** is of course capable of the vibrational analysis of distributed systems, which is presented in Chapter 20.

Single Degree of Freedom Oscillator (1DOF)

To introduce **Modal Time History** and **Harmonic** analyses as implemented in **SolidWorks Simulation**, a very simple model is used to illustrate the physics of vibration. Open the assembly model 1DOF shown in Figure 18-1.

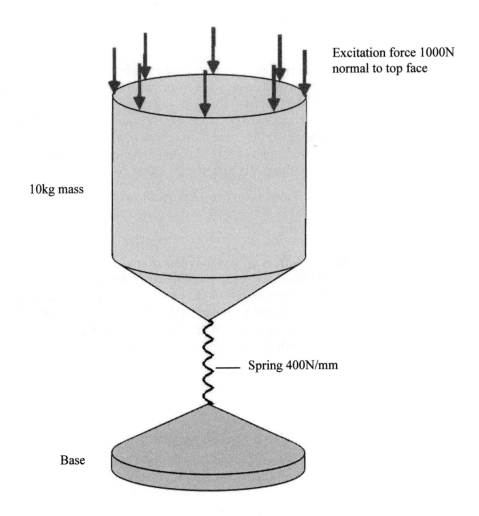

Figure 18-1: One degree of freedom oscillator.

Verify that the mass of the cylinder is 10kg. The spring connector connects to the vertices of the two cones.

To investigate the vibration of the 1DOF model, we start with a **Frequency** analysis. Create a **Frequency** study called *Modal*. In order to make the 1DOF assembly model behave as a Single Degree of Freedom oscillator, apply a **Spring Connector** and **Restraint** as shown in Figure 18-2 and 18-3.

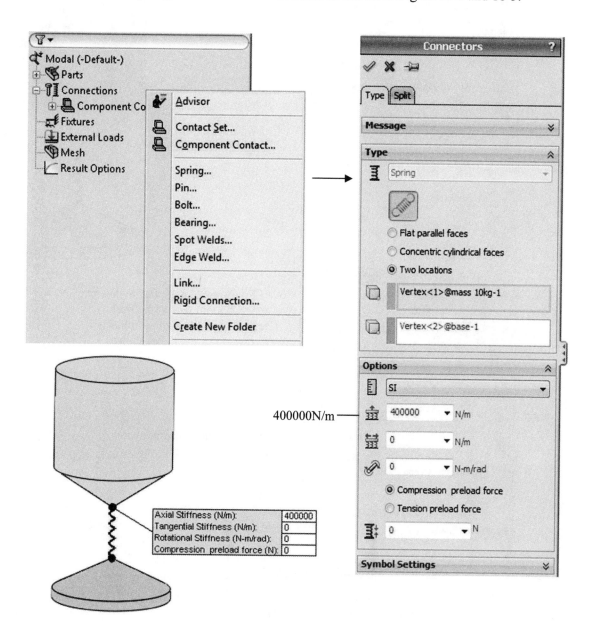

Figure 18-2: Spring connector definition.

Right-click the Connections folder, select Spring to open the Connectors window. Define a Spring Connector between the vertices of the two components.

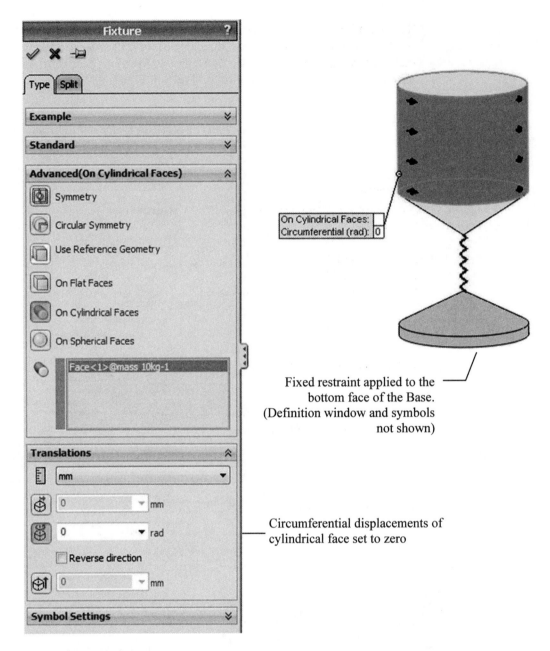

Figure 18-3: Restraints definition.

Define restraints in the circumferential direction on the cylindrical face to prevent the mass from rotating. This way the 10kg mass can only move up and down.

Define a **Fixed** restraint to the bottom face of the base as shown in Figure 18-3. Mesh the model with the default mesh size. Run the *Modal* study and verify that the first natural frequency is 33Hz (Figure 18-4).

List Modes			

Study name: Modal

Mode No.	Frequency(Rad/sec)	Frequency(Hertz)	Period(Seconds)
1	210.03	33.427	0.029916
2	42524	6768	0.00014776
3	42975	6839.7	0.00014621
4	58264	9273	0.00010784
5	85883	13669	7.316e-005

Figure 18-4: Resonant frequency results for the *Modal* study.

Recall from the theory of vibration that the natural frequency, ω, of a Single Degree of Freedom Oscillator is:

$$\omega = \sqrt{\frac{k}{m}} = \sqrt{\frac{400000}{10}} = 200 \; rad/s$$

To express the same in Hz:

$$f = \frac{\omega}{2\pi} = \frac{200}{2\pi} = 31.8 \; cycles/s$$

Vibration period T:

$$T = 1/f$$

SolidWorks Simulation results closely match analytical results. Notice that the higher mode results shown in Figure 18-4 correspond to the deformation of the cylinder, not the spring, and therefore are not related to the Single Degree of Freedom oscillations.

Now, create a **Modal Time History** study called *Time Response* as shown in Figure 18-5.

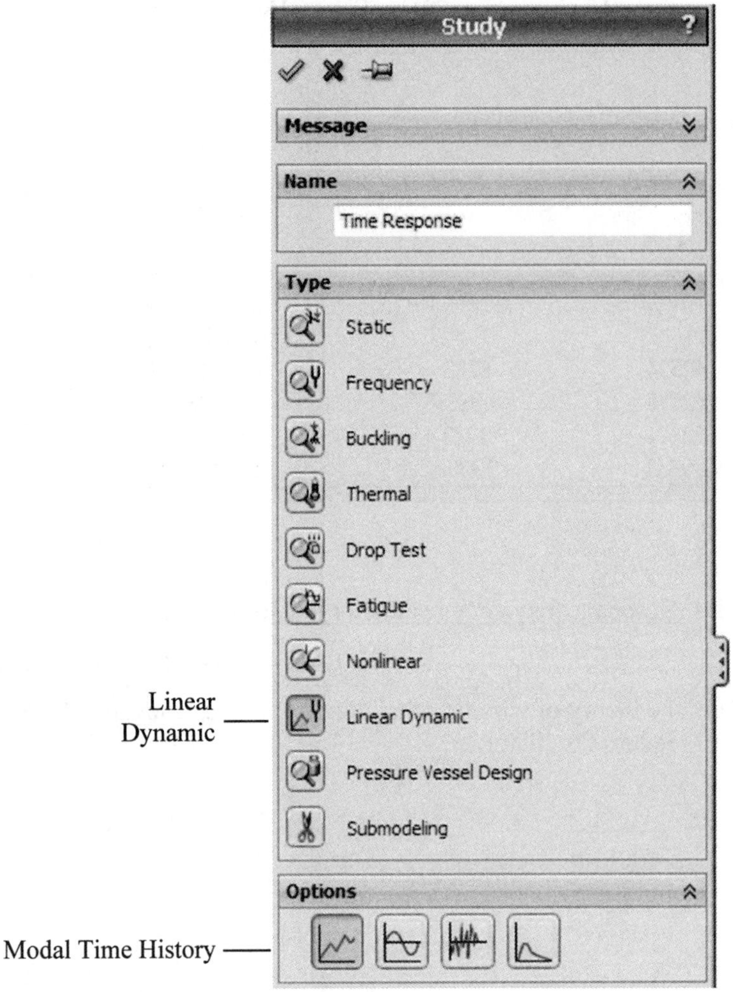

Linear Dynamic

Modal Time History

Figure 18-5: Defining a Modal Time History study.

A Modal Time History study is created by selecting a Linear Dynamic study with the Modal Time History option.

You can copy restraints (one at a time) from the modal study, but the **Spring Connector** must be defined in **Modal Time History** since its definition has an option to include damping. Damping can also be defined as modal damping and not explicitly in the spring connector. Modal damping specifies damping as a fraction of critical damping. Oscillations no longer occur when the damping value is critical or above critical. The critical damping in Single Degree of Freedom oscillator is:

$$c_{cr} = 2\sqrt{km} = 4000 \frac{Ns}{m}$$

To define damping as 5% of critical damping we can either enter 200 in the **Spring-Damper Connector** window, or as 0.05 in the **Global Damping** window (Figure 18-6).

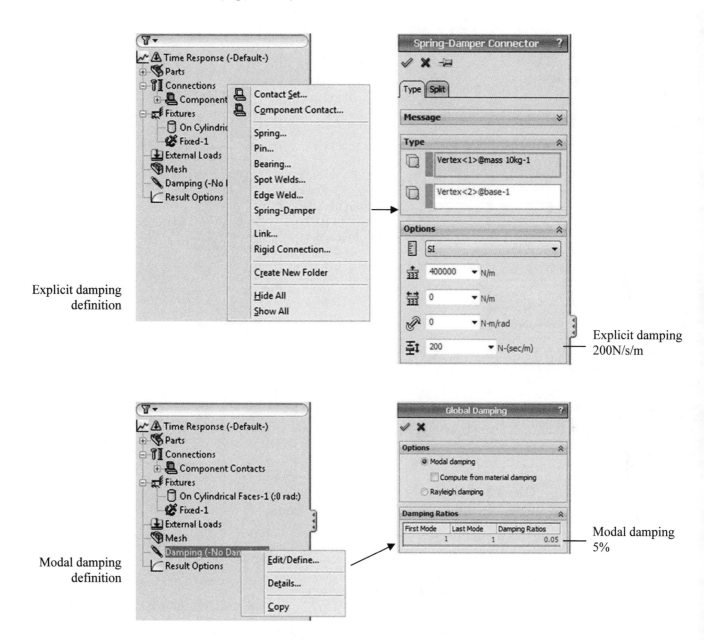

Explicit damping definition

Explicit damping 200N/s/m

Modal damping definition

Modal damping 5%

Figure 18-6: Damping can be defined explicitly (top) or as a fraction of critical damping (bottom). The entries in both windows define the same damping. In this example we use an explicit damping definition.

Modal damping makes it possible to define damping individually for each mode. Since we base this analysis on one mode only, we define damping for this single mode.

Dynamic analysis requires a load defined as a function of time. To apply a 1000N force as shown in Figure 18-1 and define its time history, follow the steps explained in Figure 18-7.

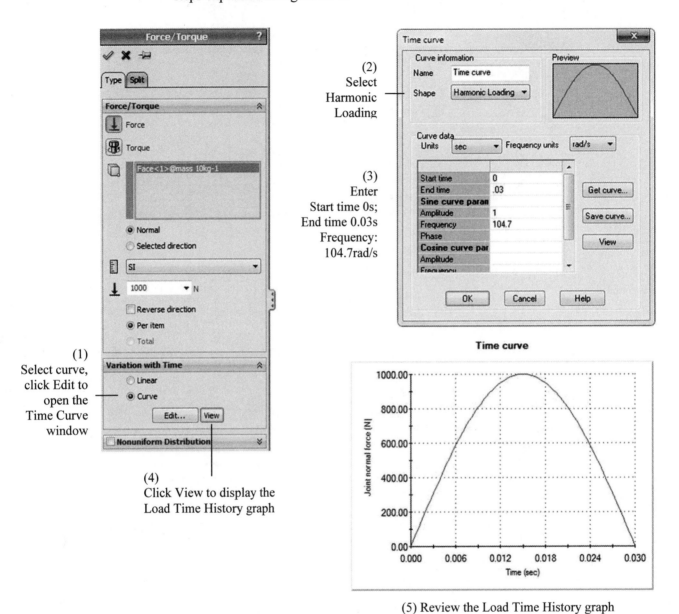

(5) Review the Load Time History graph

Figure 18-7: Defining load as a function of time. The force takes 0.015s to reach the maximum of 1000N, then another 0.015s to drop back to zero.

Select Variation with Time as Curve (1), and click Edit to open the Time curve definition window. Define the shape as harmonic loading (2) and enter values as shown (3). Click View (4) to examine the Load time history curve (5).

Notice that neither the entry in the **Force** window or the values defining the **Time curve** defines the load time history on their own. The corresponding values are multiplied to calculate force magnitude as a function of time.

Define the properties of the *Time Response* study as shown in Figure 18-8.

Frequency
Options tab

Dynamic
Options tab

Remark
tab

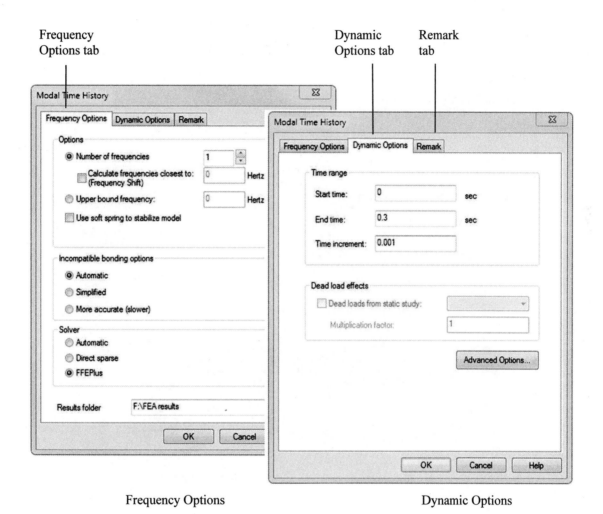

Frequency Options

Dynamic Options

<u>Figure 18-8: Frequency Options definition window and Dynamic Options definition window.</u>

Take this opportunity to look at the Remark tab, as this is where notes about the study can be made.

In the **Frequency Options**, define the **Number of frequencies** as 1. This is because our objective is to analyze the Single Degree of Freedom oscillator which only has one natural frequency. In the **Dynamic Options** define **End time** as 0.3s and **Time increment** as 0.001s. This way, the dynamic response will be analyzed during the first 0.3s counting from the beginning of force application. The dynamic response will be evaluated every 0.001s in 300 time steps.

Notice that the duration of the load is 0.03s (Figure 18-7), while the duration of analysis is 0.3s (Figure 18-8).

Define a **Sensor** as shown in Figure 18-9.

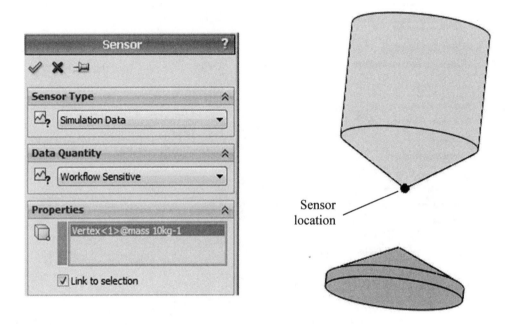

Figure 18-9: Sensor definition.

Define a sensor in the SolidWorks Feature Manager. Select the point where the spring is attached.

Right-click the *Results Options* folder to define the **Results Options,** as shown in Figure 18-10.

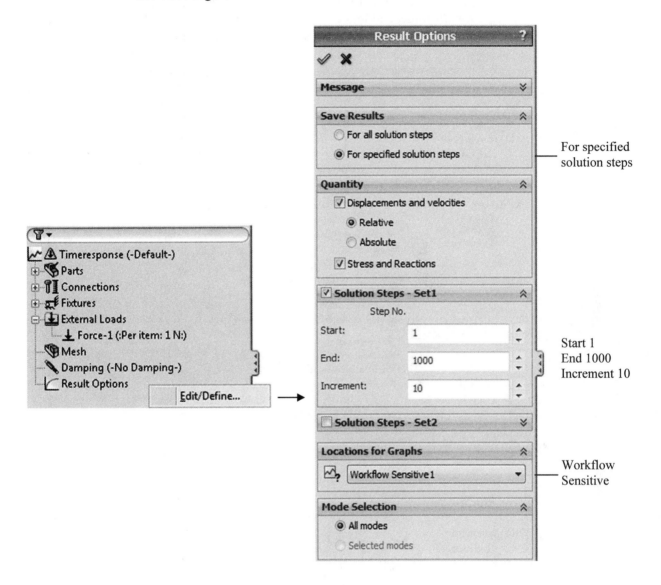

Figure 18-10: Results Options definition.

Make the indicated selections in preparation for graphing results. Results will be plotted for every tenth step.

Mesh with a coarse mesh (element size 40mm) because accurate modeling of the elastic properties of the cylinder and base is irrelevant in this exercise. The vibration of a single degree of freedom oscillator is related to spring stiffness and mass of the cylinder. Element size has no effect on spring and cylinder stiffness.

Run the *Time Response* study observing that each solution stage is completed in 300 steps as specified in the study properties (Figure 18-8). Right-click the *Results* folder and follow the steps illustrated in Figure 18-11 to create a graph showing displacement in the sensor location as a function of time.

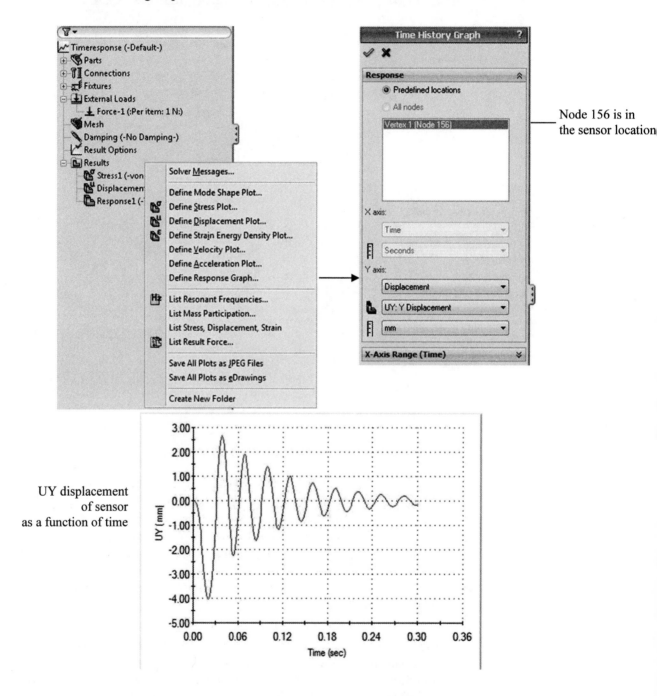

UY displacement of sensor as a function of time

Figure 18-11: Displacement of the 10kg mass for the first 0.3s after load application.

Notice that after 0.03s, the load becomes zero and the 1DOF performs free damped oscillations.

Since **Modal Time History** requires results of a **Frequency** analysis, a **Frequency** analysis is always run prior to a **Modal Time History**. Within **Modal Time History**, you may select to run only the **Frequency** analysis (Figure 18-12). Other ways of transferring results from **Frequency** analysis to **Dynamic** analysis are discussed in chapter 20.

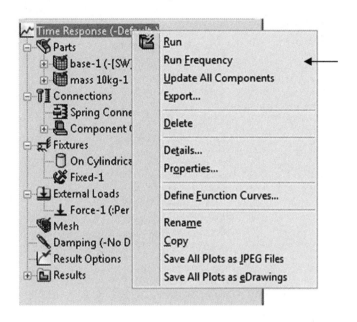

Figure 18-12: The pop-up menu invoked by right-clicking the Time Response study folder.

The Modal Time History study gives an option to run just the Frequency study without subsequent dynamic analysis.

Since a **Frequency** analysis is always run prior to a **Modal Time History** analysis, **Modal Time History** results include the same results that are available in a **Frequency** study. To verify this, define a mode shape plot or review the list of modal frequencies. Notice that you will see only one frequency as specified in the **Modal Time History** properties (Figure 18-8).

In continuation of the 1DOF analysis, create a **Harmonic** study called *Frequency response* (Figure 18-13).

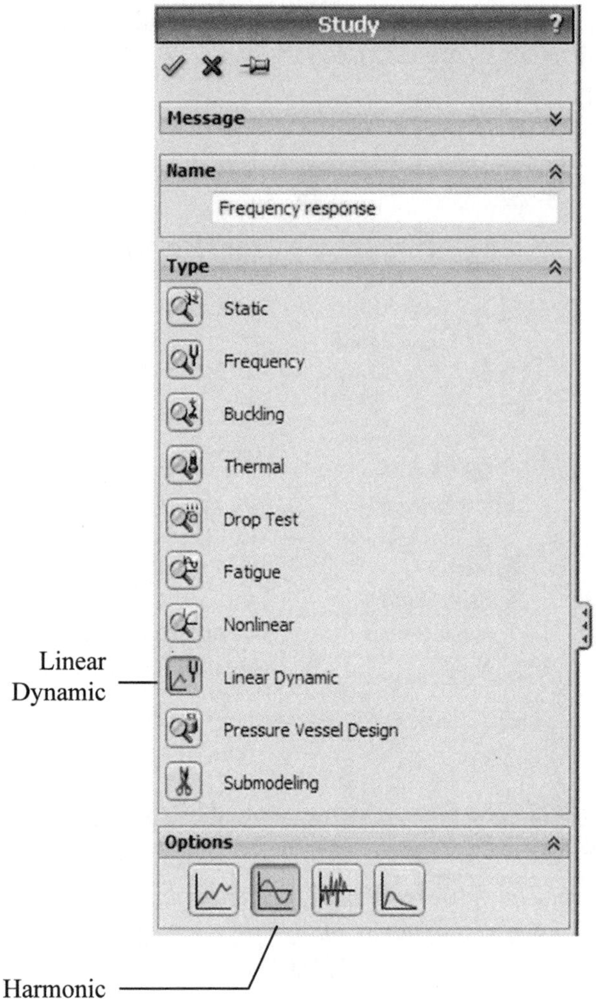

Figure 18-13: Defining a Harmonic study.

A harmonic study is created by selecting a Linear Dynamic study with the Harmonic option.

We will investigate the dynamic response of a 1DOF system under an oscillating force with a 1000N magnitude, applied in the same way as in previous study. The frequency of oscillation will change from 0Hz to 100Hz. The excitation force is a function of frequency. We assume that the magnitude of the force remains constant while the frequency of oscillations increases from 0Hz to 100Hz.

$$F = 1000sin(2\pi ft)$$

$$0 \le f \le 100$$

Define the *Frequency response* study properties as shown in Figure 18-14.

Frequency
Options tab

Harmonic
Options tab

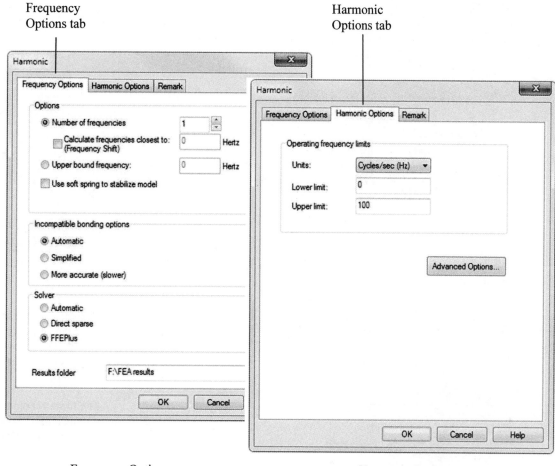

Frequency Options   Harmonic Options

Figure 18-14: Properties of study *Frequency Response 01.*

The left window defines the number of frequencies as 1 because the analyzed system only has one degree of freedom. The right window defines the range of oscillation frequency from 0 to 100Hz.

In a **Harmonic** analysis, the excitation load is a function of frequency defined for this analysis as shown in Figure 18-15.

Define identical restraints as in the *Time Response* study. To define the spring connector, damping and load, follow the steps explained in Figure 18-15.

In the **Harmonic** study, damping must be defined as **Global Damping**. Refer to Figure 18-15 and define it as 5% of critical damping.

Define default Result Options the same as in the previous *Time Response* study.

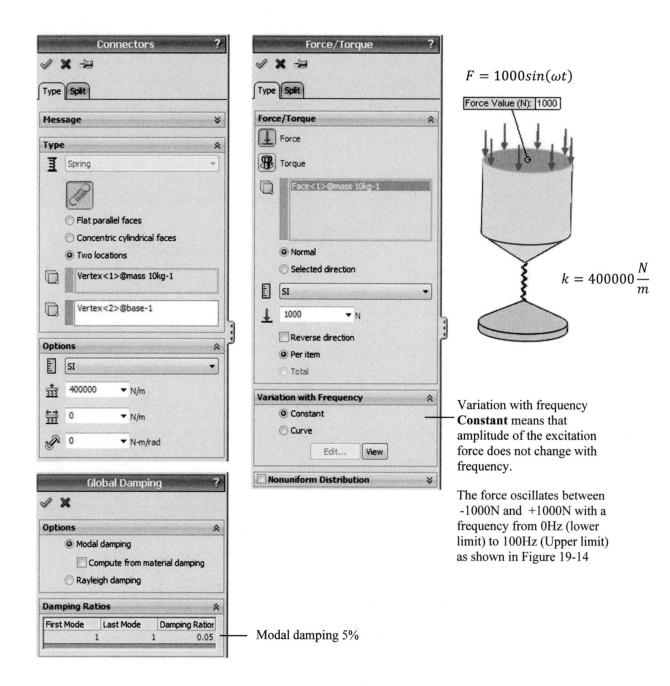

Figure 18-15: Definition of a spring connector, global damping, and load in the *Frequency response* study.

Notice that the Spring-Damper Connector in the Harmonic study does not include a definition of damping. Damping must be defined as global damping.

Copy restraints from the *Time Response* study, define **Result Options** as explained in Figure 18-10. Run the study and define a **Response Graph** for the UY displacement component (Figure 18-16). The **Response Graph** shows the amplitude of vibration as a function of the excitation frequency.

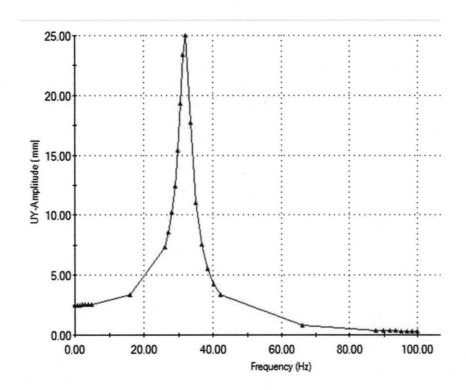

Figure 18-16: **Response Graph** showing the amplitude of vibration as a function of the excitation frequency.

Notice that the amplitude at zero frequency is the static displacement of the spring under a 1000N force. The maximum amplitude corresponds to the excitation frequency very close to the natural frequency of the 1DOF model.

The sharp peak in amplitude magnitude visible in Figure 18-16 is the *1DOF* response under an excitation frequency equal to the natural frequency of the system (this is labeled resonance). The amplitude of vibration in resonance is controlled only by damping. To demonstrate the relationship between the amplitude of vibration in resonance and damping, copy study *Frequency response* into a new study and decrease the **Global Damping** to 0.02. Run the solution and observe the much higher resonant amplitude. Repeat this exercise with the **Global Damping** equal to 0.1.

The graph in Figure 18-17 presents a summary of results for modal damping, ζ = 0.02, 0.05, 0.10. The graph has been created in Excel using data exported from **SolidWorks Simulation** graphs.

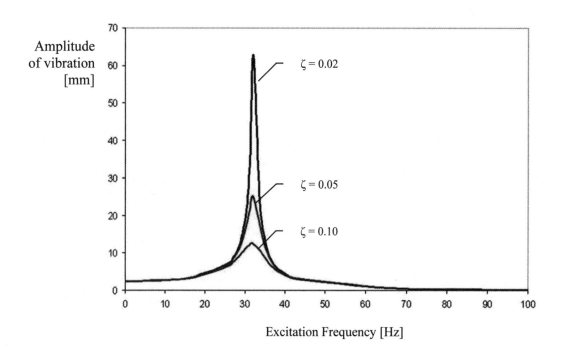

Figure 18-17: Amplitude of vibration as a function of the excitation frequency for different modal damping ratios.

Notice that damping strongly affects the amplitude for excitation frequencies close to the resonant frequency. It has no effect for excitation frequencies much lower or much higher than the resonant frequency.

Notice that the amplitude of vibration is measured from the neutral position, not between negative and positive peaks.

Now open the assembly model *2DOF* and create a **Linear Dynamic** study with the **Harmonic** option called *Shaker table.* Verify that the mass of the cylinders are 100kg and 150kg.

Define **Restraints** and **Spring Connectors** as shown in Figure 18-18. Remember that **Spring Connectors** in a **Dynamic** study with the **Harmonic** option does not have explicit damping. Mesh with element size 50mm and run the **Run Frequency** solution to verify that the system has two natural frequencies related to the deformation of the springs: 2.5Hz and 5.4Hz. These values may vary slightly depending on the solver used (FFEPlus or Direct Sparse).

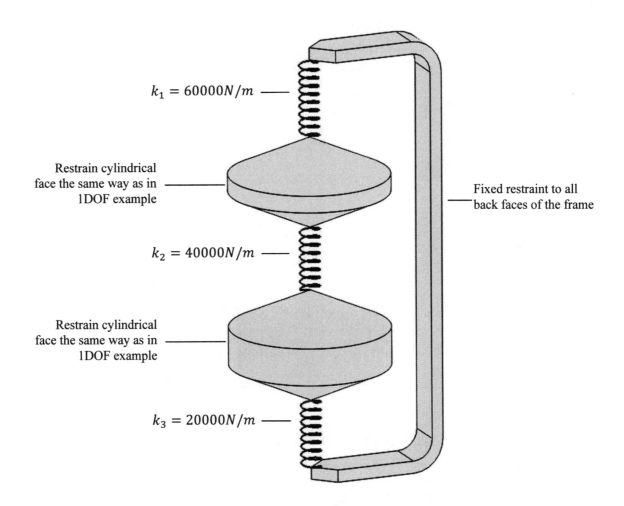

$k_1 = 60000N/m$ ——

Restrain cylindrical face the same way as in 1DOF example ——

Fixed restraint to all back faces of the frame

$k_2 = 40000N/m$ ——

Restrain cylindrical face the same way as in 1DOF example ——

$k_3 = 20000N/m$ ——

Figure 18-18: Fixed restraints and Spring Connectors definition in the 2DOF model.

Restrain the cylindrical faces of both masses the same way as in the 1DOF example. The masses should only have the ability to move in the axial direction. Restrain all back faces of the frame to make it practically rigid. You may restraint the front faces too.

This example introduces a different way of loading the model called **Base Excitation**. The concept is presented in Figure 18-19.

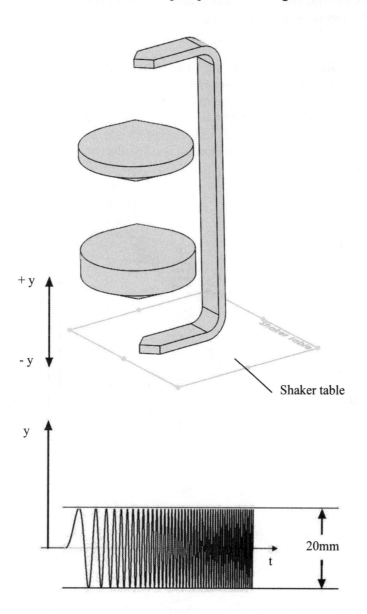

Figure 18-19: Concept of base excitation.

The model sits on a shaker table which oscillates up and down with an amplitude of 10mm; the distance between extreme up and extreme down position is 20mm. In some textbooks 10mm would be called the half amplitude. Shaker table is illustrated here by a reference plane.

To define a base excitation, right-click the **Uniform Base Excitation** icon in the *External Loads* folder. This opens the **Uniform Base Excitation** window. Define it as shown in Figure 18-20.

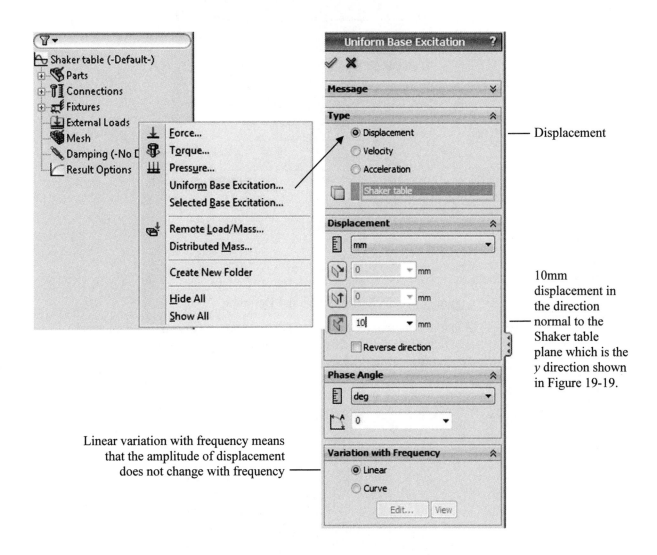

Figure 18-20: Defining base excitation in the Uniform Base Excitation window.

Base Excitation in the specified direction (here the direction of movement of masses) is applied to all restraints present in the model. Due to restraints on all outside faces, the frame moves "up and down" practically as a rigid body. Linear variation with frequency means the displacement does not change with frequency.

The frequency of oscillation changes from 0Hz to 10Hz as defined in Figure 18-22. We use displacement excitation as defined in Figure 18-20 because it is more intuitive than velocity or acceleration excitation. However, acceleration excitation is the most commonly used in vibration analysis and testing.

Specify a modal damping of 0.05 (Figure 18-21).

Figure 18-21: Definition of Modal Damping.

A modal damping of 0.05 (5% of critical damping) is defined for modes 1 and 2 in this analysis. The Last mode (number 15) shown here has no relevance in this analysis which is based on two modes only, as shown in Figure 18-22. Defining the first mode as 1 and the last mode as 2 would have the same effect.

Define study properties as shown in Figure 18-22.

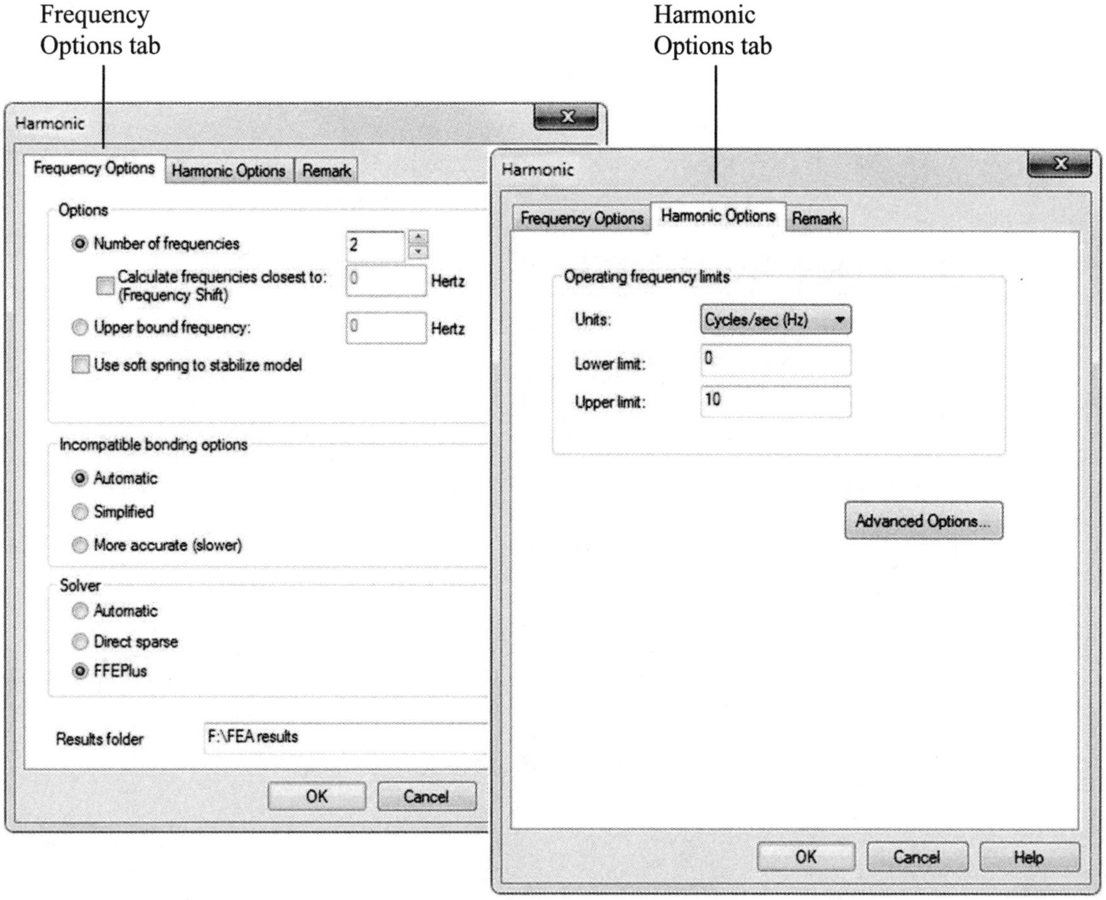

Frequency
Options tab

Harmonic
Options tab

Frequency Options

Harmonic Options

Figure 18-22: Properties of the frequency response study.

The Frequency Options tab (left) specifies that two frequencies will be included in the dynamic response. The Harmonic Options tab (right) specifies that excitation frequency will be changed from 0Hz to 10Hz.

Define **Sensors** at the two points shown in Figure 18-23, to be included in the detailed results.

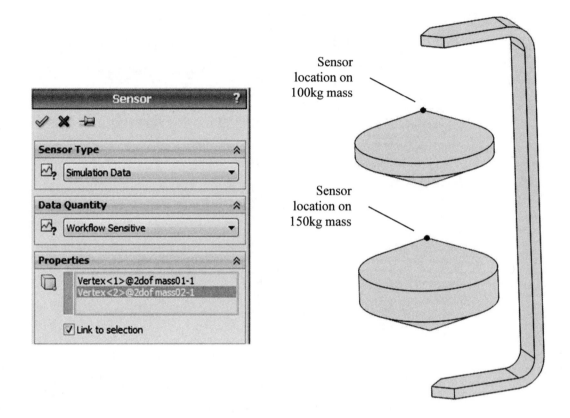

Figure 18-23: Definition of Sensors.

Select vertices on the tops of each mass where Spring Connectors are attached. Spring Connectors are not shown in this illustration.

Define the **Result Options** as shown in Figure 18-24.

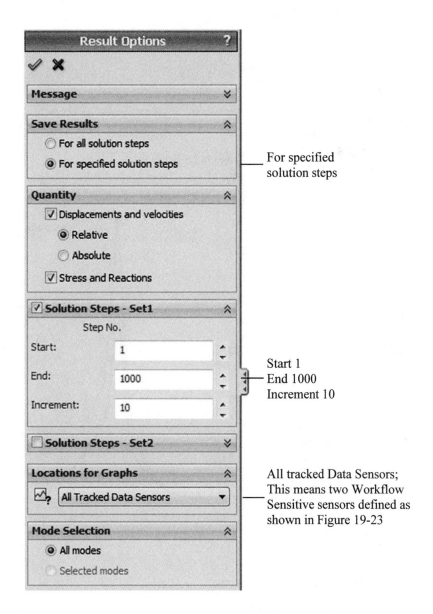

For specified solution steps

Start 1
End 1000
Increment 10

All tracked Data Sensors;
This means two Workflow
Sensitive sensors defined as
shown in Figure 19-23

Figure 18-24 Result Options definition.

Make the indicated selections in preparation for graphing results.

Run the *Shaker table* study and create a response graph following the steps shown in Figure 18-10, select both vertices and display the graph shown in Figure 18-25.

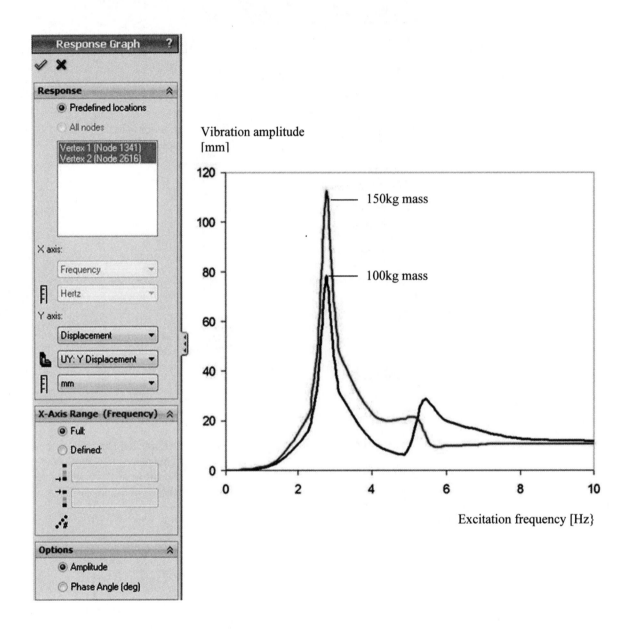

Figure 18-25: The amplitude of vibration of the two masses as a function of excitation frequency.

You can also create graphs individually for each mass. The actual node numbering shown in Response Graph window changes with the mesh density used in the study. The above graph was formatted in Excel.

The response graph in Figure 18-25 clearly shows that there are two peaks of amplitude response which correspond to the natural (resonant) frequencies of the model.

Repeat this exercise for different values of Modal Damping to study the effect of damping on the vibration amplitudes of the two masses.

Notice again that all examples studied in this chapter represent discrete systems where stiffness and mass are separated. Coarse meshes are used because we do not have to model elastic properties of the masses – they are considered as rigid bodies in our one and two degrees of freedom systems. Any stress analysis would have been meaningless.

All modeling techniques presented here can be extended to real life parts and assemblies which are distributed systems. Proper meshes must then be created to model elastic properties of these models. This will be illustrated with a random vibration analysis in the next chapter.

Notes:

19: Analysis of random vibration

Topics covered

- ❑ Random vibration
- ❑ Power Spectral Density
- ❑ RMS results
- ❑ PSD results
- ❑ Modal excitation

Random vibration

Random vibrations are non-periodic. Knowing the history of random vibration, we can predict the probability of occurrence of acceleration, velocity and displacement magnitudes, but cannot predict the precise magnitude at a specific time instant.

Random vibration is composed of a continuous spectrum of frequencies. The huge amount of time history data makes it impractical to run a dynamic time analysis.

For most structural vibrations, the excitation such as force or base acceleration alternates about zero. Consequently, mean values characterizing the excitation as well as responses to that excitation such as displacement or stress are equal to zero. For this reason, results of a random vibration analysis are given in the form of Root Mean Square (RMS) values.

To explain the concept of an RMS value, refer to the graph in Figure 19-1 which shows the acceleration time history (acceleration as a function of time) of random vibration expressed in units of gravitational acceleration [G].

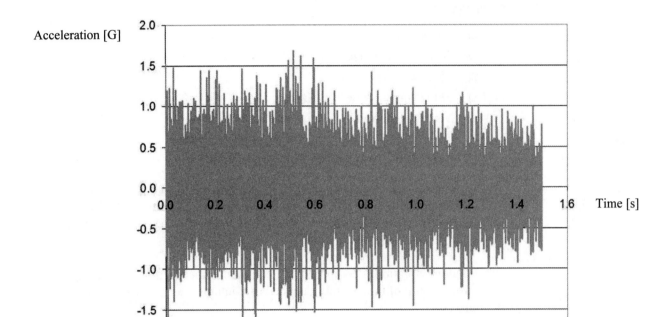

Figure 19-1: An example of acceleration time history data collected during 1.5s.

Considering the sampling rate of 5000 samples per second, this time history curve contains 7500 data samples.

The acceleration time history shown in Figure 19-1 has a zero mean value. However, if we multiply the function by itself, we obtain a function with a positive value. Its mean will no longer be zero and this squared function will be well suited to characterize the acceleration time history. This mean value of square acceleration time history is the mean square value and has units of $[G^2]$.

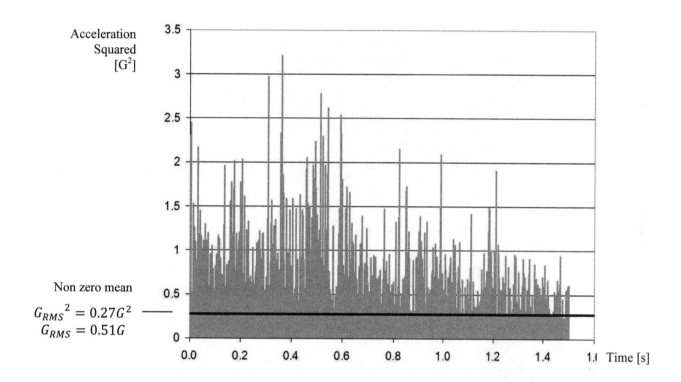

Figure 19-2: Squaring acceleration time history function (Figure 19-1) produces s function with s non-zero mean.

As shown in Figure 19-2, calculating the mean square value gives $G_{RMS}^2 = 0.27G$. The square root of the mean square value gives $G_{RMS} = 0.51G$.

The square root of the mean value is the root-mean-square (RMS) acceleration and has units of $[G]$. The same applies to RMS displacement, velocity, stress etc.

In random vibration, the magnitudes of acceleration, velocity, displacement etc. all follow a normal distribution. The RMS value corresponds to one standard deviation σ characterizing the normal distribution. To explain this, we refer again to Figure 19-2. The acceleration, as characterized by the given acceleration time history, has a 68% probability of remaining between -0.51G and +0.51G. Consequently, it has a 32% probability of being less than -0.51G or more than 0.51G.

Acceleration Power Spectral Density

Let's assume that the acceleration time history in Figure 19-1 is a stationary random process where probability numbers characterizing this process do not change with time. In this case, the acceleration time history can be used to calculate the Acceleration Power Spectral Density (PSD) curve (the variation of any property with respect to frequency is called "spectrum").

The overall G_{RMS}^2 of random vibrations shown in Figure 19-2 is $0.27G^2$. However, random vibrations are composed of a large number of frequencies. Let us say we wish to investigate G_{RMS}^2 individually for a number of frequencies in the range from 0 to 2000Hz. Therefore, we divide the 0-2000Hz range into 20 sections (bins), each 100Hz wide and calculate G_{RMS}^2 characterizing each section by filtering out all frequencies falling outside of the section (Figure 19-3).

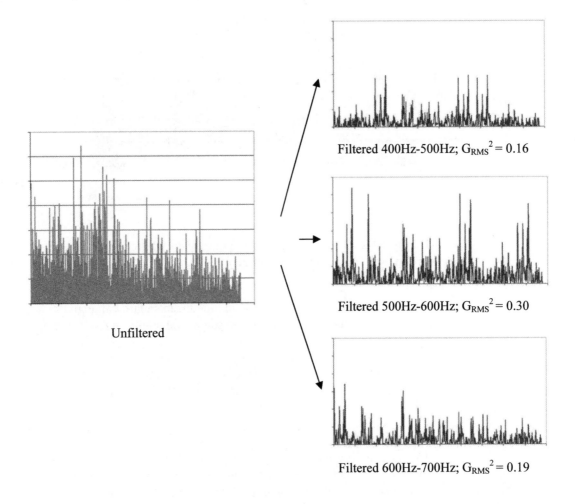

Filtered 400Hz-500Hz; $G_{RMS}^2 = 0.16$

Filtered 500Hz-600Hz; $G_{RMS}^2 = 0.30$

Unfiltered

Filtered 600Hz-700Hz; $G_{RMS}^2 = 0.19$

Figure 19-3: G_{RMS}^2 calculated individually for specified frequency ranges.

The graph on the left shows squared acceleration time history from Figure 19-2. Only three frequency ranges (sections) are illustrated here for brevity.

Having found G_{RMS}^2 values obtained for each frequency range, we can now calculate individual "densities" of G_{RMS}^2 in each section by dividing G_{RMS}^2 in each section by the width of the section. Results obtained for all sections may be plotted as a function of the frequency in the center of each section. This function is the Acceleration Power Spectral Density (Figure 19-4).

Band pass filter	Band center	G_{RMS}^2	Bandwidth	Acceleration PSD
	Hz	$(m/s^2)^2$	Hz	$(m/s^2)^2/Hz$
400Hz - 500Hz	450	0.16	100	0.0016
500Hz - 600Hz	550	0.30	100	0.0030
600Hz - 700Hz	650	0.19	100	0.0019

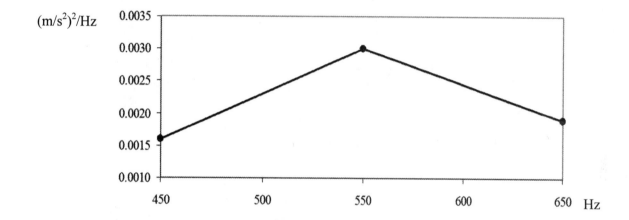

Figure 19-4: Constructing the Acceleration Power Spectral Density function (PSD).

Three points of the Acceleration PSD curve have been calculated by dividing G_{RMS}^2 in each section (each frequency range) by the width of the section.

The Acceleration Power Spectral Density (PSD) allows for a compression of data and is commonly used to characterize a random process. In particular, mechanical vibrations are commonly described by the Acceleration Power Spectral Density, which is easily generated by testing equipment. Design specifications and test results of an apparatus subjected to random vibration are typically given in the form Acceleration PSD.

Analysis of random vibration of a hard drive head

With the short introduction on random vibration complete, we can now begin a random vibration analysis of a hard drive head. Open part HD HEAD and create a **Frequency** study with properties shown in Figure 19-5. Call the study *Modal*.

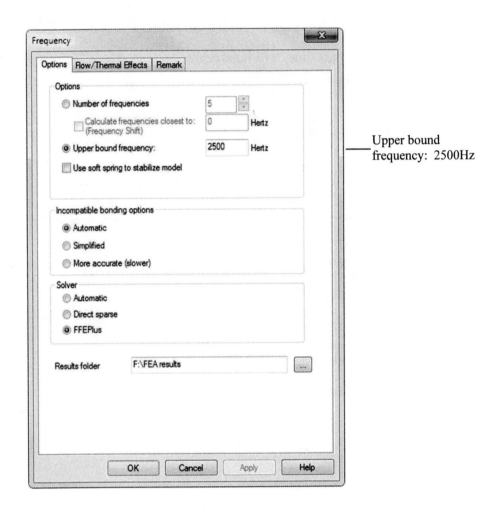

Upper bound frequency: 2500Hz

Figure 19-5: Properties of study Modal.

All frequencies in the range of 0-2500Hz will be calculated.

Apply restraints as shown in Figure 19-6.

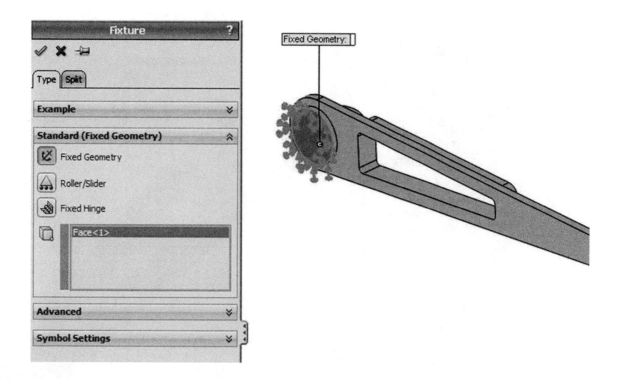

Figure 19-6: Restraints applied to a hard drive head model.

Apply a **Mesh Control** as shown in Figure 19-7 and mesh with the default element size.

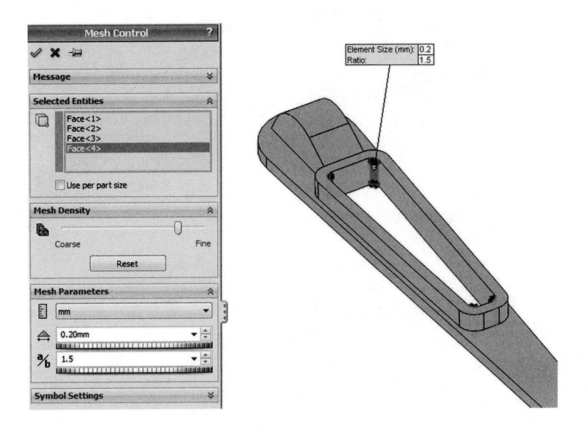

Figure 19-7: Mesh controls (0.20mm) applied to four round fillets.

Use the default global element size.

If displacement results were our only objective, the default mesh would be acceptable for both Frequency Analysis and subsequent Random Analysis. However, since in the next study we intend to analyze displacements and stresses, mesh controls are required to ensure correct element shape and size in the area of stress concentrations. Prior to this exercise, analyses were run without mesh controls to find where mesh controls are required.

Solve the *Modal* study and review the results shown in Figure 19-8. Notice that there are four modes of vibration within the requested range of frequencies 0 - 2500Hz

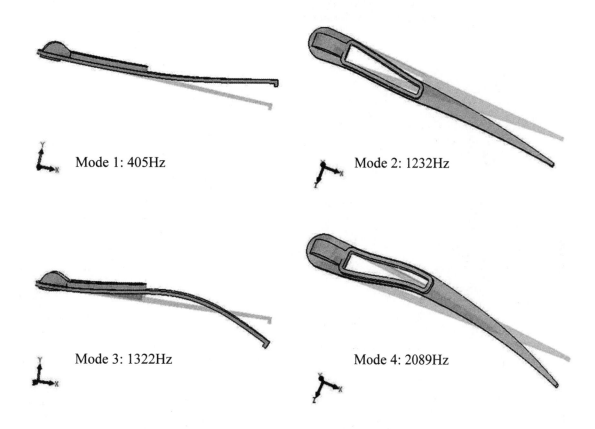

Mode 1: 405Hz

Mode 2: 1232Hz

Mode 3: 1322Hz

Mode 4: 2089Hz

Figure 19-8: Modes of vibration within the range of 0 – 2500Hz.

Vibration in mode 1 and 3 take place in the XY plane, vibrations in mode 2 and 4 take place in the XZ plane. The undeformed model is overlaid on the modal shape plots.

Proceeding to the analysis of Random Vibration, we could create a new **Dynamic** study independent from the completed **Frequency** study, this time with the **Random** option selected. However, a **Frequency** analysis would then have to be repeated within a **Dynamic Random** study. To avoid this repetition, we can copy the results of the **Frequency** study into a **Dynamic Random** study as shown in Figure 19-9.

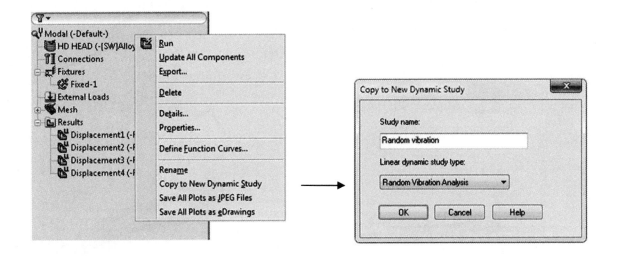

Figure 19-9: Results of a Frequency study can be copied to a new Dynamic study.

Right-click the Modal study folder and select Copy to New Dynamic Study. Select Random Vibration as the type of dynamic study. Name the study Random Vibration.

Copying the **Frequency** study into a **Dynamic Random** study also copies the mesh information and restraints.

The required properties of the **Random Vibration** study are shown in Figure 19-10.

Frequency
Options tab

Random Vibration
Options tab

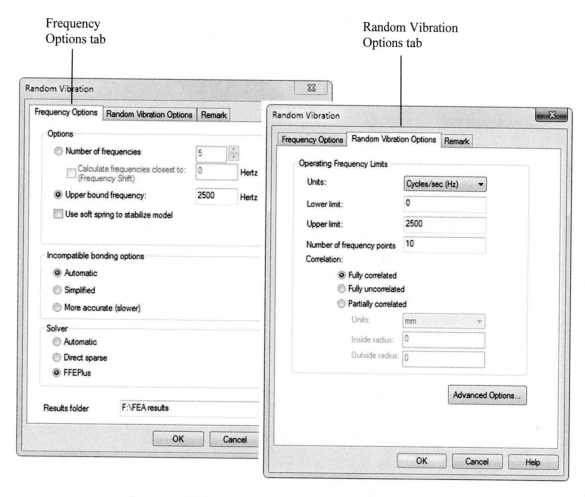

Frequency Options

Random Vibration Options

Figure 19-10: Properties of the Random Vibration study.

The Frequency Options specify all modes in the range of 0-2500Hz to be considered in the analysis of random vibrations.

In the Random Vibration options, specify the Upper limit as 2500Hz to investigate responses to Random Vibration in the frequency range from 0 to 2500Hz.

Define **Global Damping** as shown in Figure 19-11.

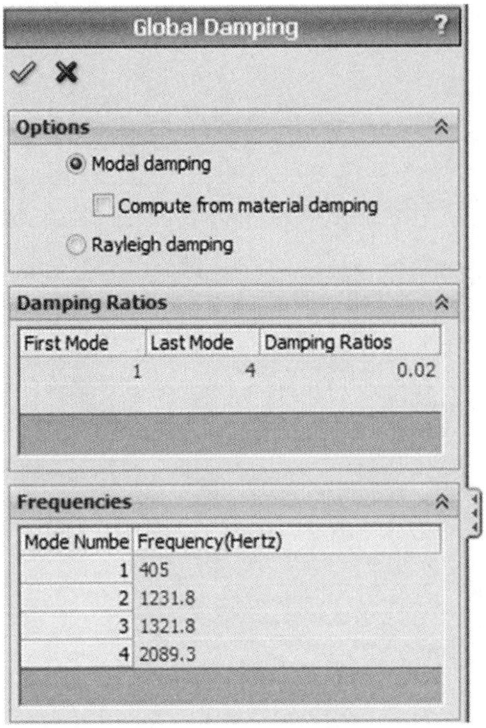

Figure 19-11: Global damping definition.

Global damping is defined as 2% of critical damping. The number of modes (4) corresponds to the number of modes in the frequency range 0-2500Hz, as is specified in Figure 19-10.

Assigning the same damping ratio to all modes represents a simplified and conservative approach. In most cases damping for higher modes will be higher than for lower modes.

The load on the hard drive head comes from random excitation of the base in the global Y direction. Follow Figure 19-12 to define the Acceleration PSD. This acceleration PSD has been obtained from testing.

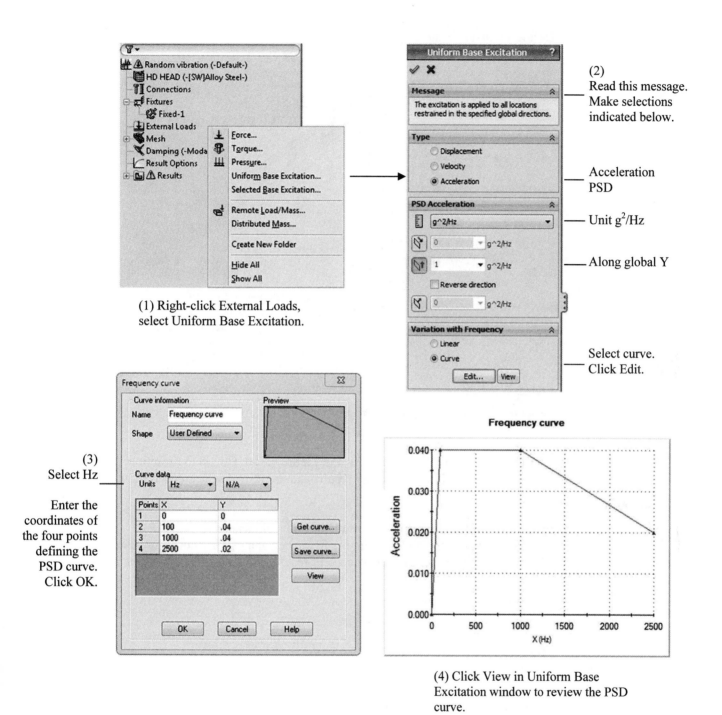

(1) Right-click External Loads, select Uniform Base Excitation.

(2) Read this message. Make selections indicated below.

Acceleration PSD

Unit g^2/Hz

Along global Y

Select curve. Click Edit.

(3) Select Hz

Enter the coordinates of the four points defining the PSD curve. Click OK.

(4) Click View in Uniform Base Excitation window to review the PSD curve.

Figure 19-12: Uniform Base Excitation defined as Acceleration PSD in the global Y direction acting on all restraints present in the model (here only one restraint is present).

Follow the above steps to create the PSD curve.

Define a **Sensor** as shown in Figure 19-13.

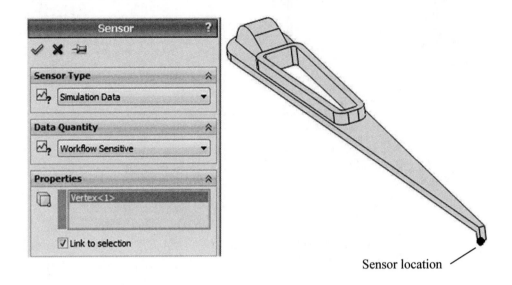

Figure 19-13: Sensor location.

Select the vertex at the tip of the head.

Define **Result Options** as was shown in Figure 18-10. Obtain the solution and analyze the RMS displacement results and the PSD displacement results.

In order to analyze the displacement results, new plots need to be created. The results in the copied plots from the frequency analysis are not valid since modal analysis does not give displacement results. Make a new displacement plot.

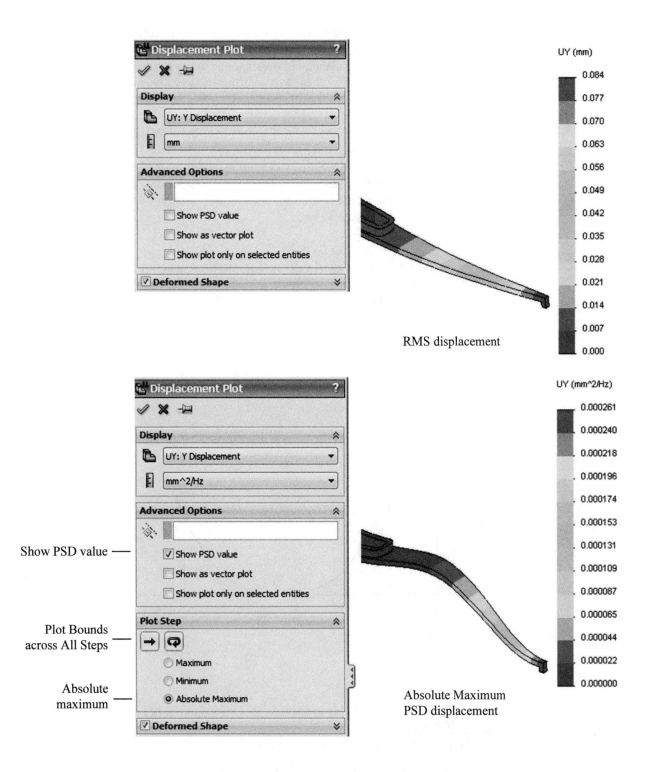

RMS displacement

Show PSD value

Plot Bounds
across All Steps

Absolute
maximum

Absolute Maximum
PSD displacement

Figure 19-14: RMS displacement results (top) and PSD displacement results (bottom) for the UY displacement component.

The maximum RMS displacement is 0.084mm. The maximum PSD displacement is 0.00026mm^2/Hz.

PSD displacements are displayed in units of mm²/Hz for the selected frequency, Minimum, Maximum or Absolute Maximum as used here. The Absolute Maximum of PSD displacement corresponds to the first mode frequency 405Hz. See Figure 19-17 for explanations of the PSD results.

It is important to understand the meaning of results in a Random Vibration analysis. The displacement results in Figure 19-14, top, are the RMS displacements. The maximum RMS displacement is 0.084mm meaning that the magnitude of displacement has a 68% probability of remaining under 0.084mm. The probability of the maximum displacement magnitude exceeding 0.084mm is of course 32%.

Remembering that the probability of a given displacement is defined by a normal distribution for which $\sigma = 0.084$mm. We can calculate the probability of displacement magnitude exceeding any defined value (Figure 19-15).

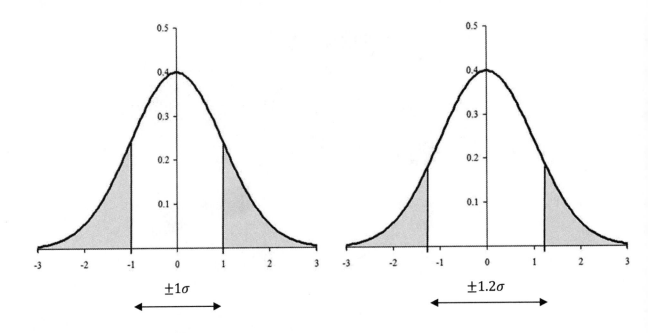

Figure 19-15: The total area under the normalized Gauss curve is 1. The probability of displacement magnitude exceeding ±σ (left) and ±1.2σ (right) is equal to the corresponding shaded areas.

The probability of the displacement magnitude exceeding 1*RMS displacement (here 0.084mm), is given by the area outside ± 1σ which is 32% (left).

The probability of displacement magnitude exceeding 1.2*RMS displacement (0.10mm) is given by the area outside ± 1.2σ which is 23% (right).

The same applies to all results of a Random Vibration analysis. The RMS P1 stress result is shown in Figure 19-16.

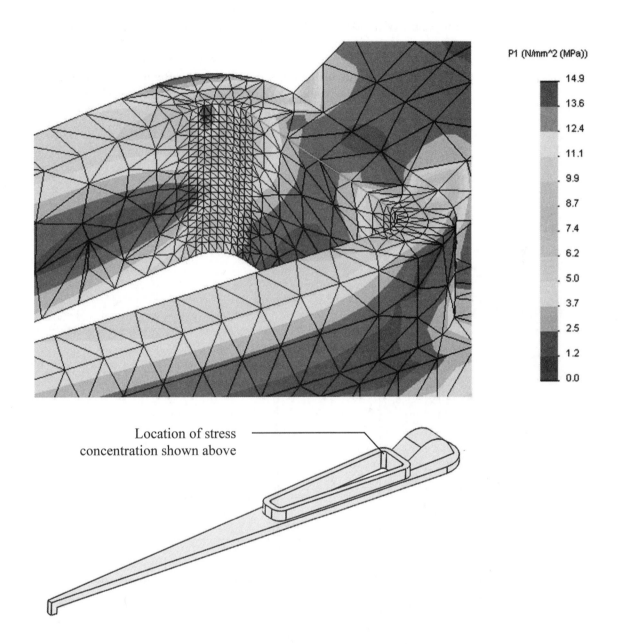

Figure 19-16: RMS P1 stress results.

The maximum P1 stress has a 68% probability of remaining below 15MPa.

Notice that stress singularities present in the model geometry (not in the detail) do not show as stress concentrations because of the large element size used for meshing.

Refer to Figure 19-16 and compare the size of elements to the size of the stress concentration. Even with mesh controls applied, the mesh is at best marginal to model stress concentrations. Repeat the analysis with a more aggressive mesh control.

The results of the **Dynamic Random** analysis presented as RMS values provide one result for the entire frequency range of excitation. All results (displacement, stresses etc.) can also be presented as PSD values (Figure 19-14 bottom), which are different for each excitation frequency. Examine the PSD options of displacements and stress result plots and notice that displacement results are given in mm^2/Hz, and stress results are given in MPa^2/Hz. These units are a consequence of the base excitation being defined as acceleration squared per frequency range, in our case G_{RMS}^2/Hz.

The most informative way to review PSD results is to graph them over the frequency range. Create a graph showing PSD displacement in the selected location shown in Figure 19-13. Define a Y Displacement **Response Graph** as shown in Figure 19-17.

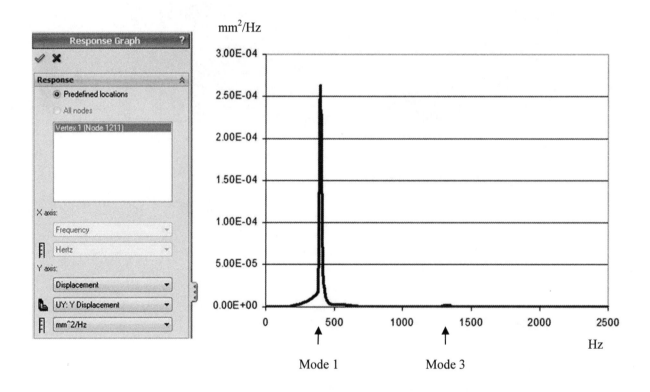

Figure 19-17: PSD displacement as a function of excitation frequency.

Mode 1 and mode 3 (barely visible) are excited. Verify that the area under the curve equals the RMS² displacement of the vertex where the sensor has been defined.

Upon examination of the graph in Figure 19-17, we find that the applied base acceleration excites mode 1 and mode 3 because these modes occur in the XY plane. Mode 2 and mode 4 occur in the XZ plane which is orthogonal to the direction of base acceleration and are therefore are not excited.

Repeat this exercise with a base excitation where the direction is not orthogonal to any global direction to see that all four modes will be excited.

Notes:

20: Miscellaneous topics

Topics covered

- Mesh quality
- Solvers and solver options
- Displaying the mesh in result plots
- Automatic reports
- E-drawings
- Non uniform loads
- Frequency analysis with pre-stress
- Shrink fit analysis
- Rigid connector
- Pin connector
- Bolt connector
- Remote load/mass
- Weld connector
- Bearing connector
- Circular symmetry
- Strongly nonlinear problem
- Submodeling
- Terminology issues in Finite Element Analysis

The analysis capabilities of **SolidWorks Simulation** go beyond those we have discussed so far. In this chapter we review a variety of topics that have not been addressed in previous exercises. All models discussed in this chapter come complete with partially or fully defined studies.

Mesh quality

The ideal shape of a tetrahedral element is a regular tetrahedron. The aspect ratio of a regular tetrahedron is assumed to be 1. Analogously, an equilateral triangle is the ideal shape for a shell element. During meshing, elements are mapped onto model geometry. This distorts the element shape. The aspect ratio becomes higher when the element departs further from its original shape (Figure 20-1). An aspect ratio that is too high causes element degeneration, which negatively affects the quality of results.

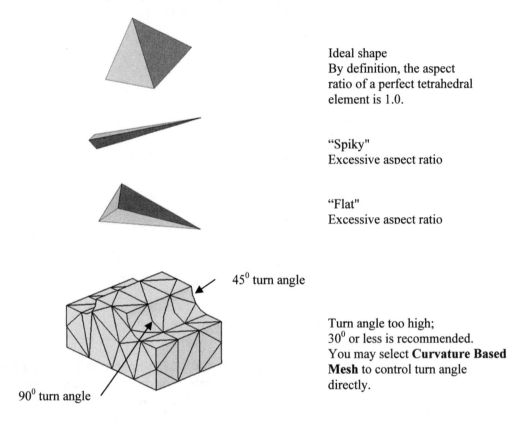

Ideal shape
By definition, the aspect ratio of a perfect tetrahedral element is 1.0.

"Spiky"
Excessive aspect ratio

"Flat"
Excessive aspect ratio

45^0 turn angle

90^0 turn angle

Turn angle too high; 30^0 or less is recommended. You may select **Curvature Based Mesh** to control turn angle directly.

Figure 20-1: Tetrahedral element shapes: ideal and after mapping.

A tetrahedral element with an ideal shape (top) has an aspect ratio of 1. "Spiky" and "flat" elements shown in this illustration (middle) have excessively high aspect ratios. "Concave" elements (bottom) have excessive turn angles.

While the automesher tries to create elements with aspect ratios close to 1, the nature of geometry sometimes makes it impossible to avoid high aspect ratios (Figure 20-2).

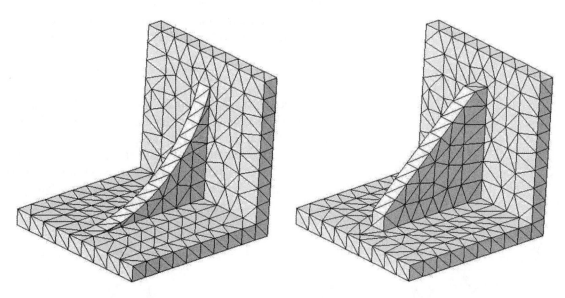

Bad design and bad mesh   Improved design and correct mesh

Figure 20-2: Mesh of a curved and a straight gusset.

Meshing a curved gusset creates highly distorted elements near the tangent edges (left).Notice that this is also a bad design. Simple modification shown on the right improves the design and improves meshing. In both cases, large elements are used for the clarity of illustration. In most cases a more refined mesh would be required. Stresses along the sharp re-entrant edges won't be valid, regardless of the element size.

Review mesh problems illustrated here using the assembly model GUSSET.

A failure diagnostic can be used to spot problem areas if meshing fails. To run a failure diagnostic, right-click the **Mesh** icon. This opens the associated pop-up window from which **Failure Diagnostic ...** is selectable.

By right-clicking the *Mesh* folder you can **Create Mesh plot** showing the mesh itself or mesh quality measures such as **Aspect Ratio** and **Jacobian**, explained in the table below, and shown in Figure 20-3.

Aspect ratio	The aspect ratio of an element is defined as the ratio between an element's longest edge and the shortest height normalized with respect to a perfect tetrahedron. The aspect ratio check assumes straight edges connecting the four corner nodes. It cannot differentiate between first order elements (straight edges) and second order elements which may have curved edges.
Jacobian	The Jacobian is a measure of the quality of second order elements. The Jacobian of an element, with all mid-side nodes located exactly at the middle of the straight edges, is 1.0. The Jacobian increases as the curvatures of the edges increases. The Jacobian at a point inside the element provides a measure of the degree of distortion of the element at that location. The software calculates the Jacobian at the selected number of points for each element.

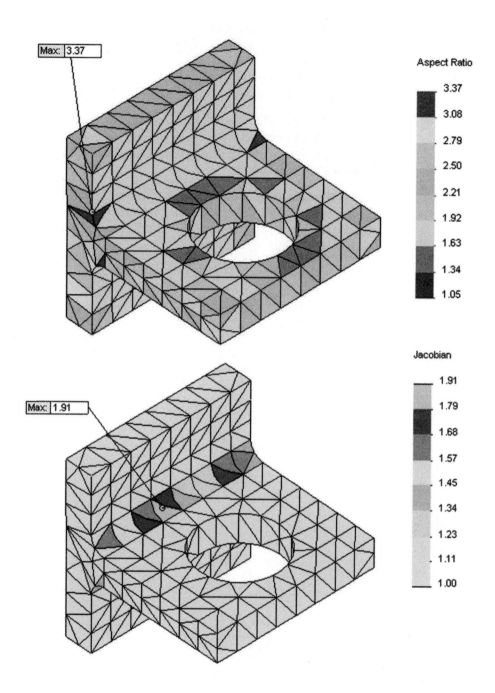

Figure 20-3: Aspect ratio plot (top) and Jacobian plot (bottom).

For clarity of illustrations a coarse mesh is used for these plots. Notice than only eight colors are used in the color chart. This was specified in Chart Options.

You may review plots in Figure 20-3 in the model MESH QUALITY 01.

Meshing difficult geometries may sometimes result in highly distorted elements without any warning. If mesh distortion is only local, then we can simply not look at the results (especially the stress results) produced by those degenerated elements. If distortion affects large portions of the mesh, then even global results cannot be trusted.

We have studied different methods to control the mesh size such as **Mesh Controls**, **Standard** and **Curvature Based** automeshers. Another way to control a mesh is to use the **Automatic Transition** option available in the **Standard** automesher.

With **Automatic transition**, the automesher applies mesh controls to small features (Figure 20-4). Do not use **Automatic transition** when meshing large models with many small features and details to avoid generating a very large number of elements.

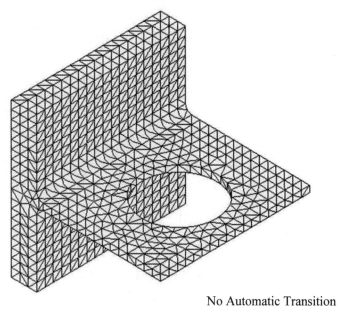

No Automatic Transition

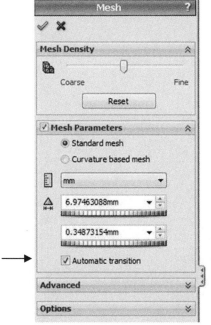

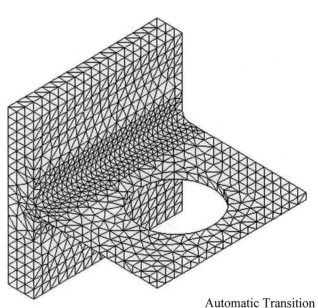

Automatic Transition

Figure 20-4: Mesh without Automatic Transition option (top) and mesh with Automatic Transition option (bottom).

Here, automatic transition has a similar effect to applying mesh controls to the fillets.

Review the effect of Automatic transition using the model MESH QUALITY 02.

Solvers and solvers options

In Finite Element Analysis, a problem is represented by a large set of linear algebraic equations that must be solved simultaneously. There are two classes of solution methods: direct and iterative.

Direct methods solve equations using exact numerical techniques, while iterative methods solve equations using approximate techniques. With an iterative method, a solution is approximated iteratively and the associated errors are evaluated. The iterations continue until the errors become acceptable. The **Direct Sparse** solver (usually slower) uses a direct solution technique, and the **FFEPlus** solver uses an iterative technique.

A solution can be run with three solver options (Figure 20-5).

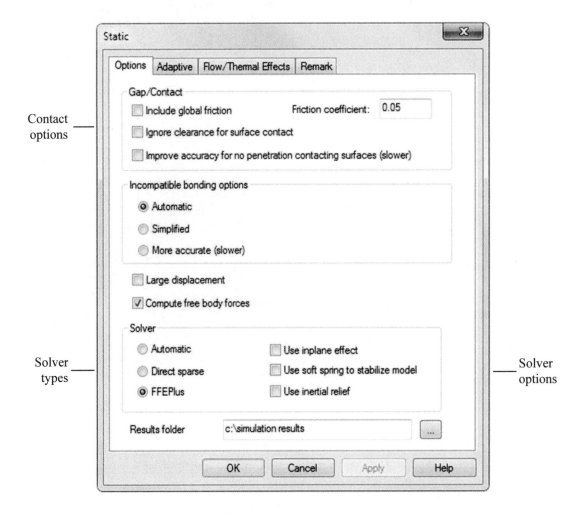

Figure 20-5: Different solvers and solver options are available in SolidWorks Simulation.

Both **Direct sparse** and **FFEPlus** solvers give comparable results if the required options are supported. It is generally recommended to use the **Automatic** option to select the solver automatically based on user specified solver options.

If a solver requires more memory than available, then disk space is used to store and retrieve temporary data. When this situation occurs, a message is displayed which states that the solution is going out of core and the solution progress slows down very significantly. Three solver options are available:

Option	Purpose
Use in plane effect	In a static analysis, use this option to account for changes in structural stiffness due to the effect of stress stiffening (when stresses are predominantly tensile) or stress softening (when stresses are predominantly compressive).
Use soft springs to stabilize model	Use this option primarily to locate problems with restraints that result in rigid body motion. If the solver runs without this option selected and reports that the model is insufficiently constrained (an error message appears), the problem can be re-run with this option selected (checked). Insufficient restraints can then be detected by animating the displacement results. We used soft springs to balance the model in a thermal stress analysis (chapter 7). An alternative to using this option is to run a frequency analysis, identify the modes with zero frequency (these correspond to rigid body modes), and animate them to determine in which direction the model is insufficiently constrained.
Use inertial relief	Use this option if a model is loaded with a balanced load, but no restraints. Due to numerical inaccuracies, the balanced load will report a non-zero resultant. This option can then be used to restore model equilibrium. This option is most often used to balance a model with loads imported from a Motion Simulation.

Several options are available when solving contact problems: **Include global friction, Ignore clearance for surface contact** and **Friction coefficient**. These options are defined in the study properties, as shown in the table below.

The five options are described below:

Option	Purpose
Include global friction	If selected, friction between contacted surfaces is considered.
Ignore clearance for surface contact	Use this option to ignore the initial clearance that may exist between surfaces in contact. The contacting surfaces start interacting immediately without first canceling out the gap.
Improve accuracy for no penetration contacting surfaces	This method produces continuous and more accurate stresses in regions with definitions of no penetration contact. The method is used when defining contact between faces to faces and faces to edges.
Large displacement	See Chapter 14.
Compute free body forces	Enables probing of forces and moments transmitted by nodes.

Three different options can be used for solving problems with bonded surfaces.

Option	Purpose
Automatic	If the default surface-to-surface bonding contact slows down the solution considerably, the solver switches to node-to-surface bonding automatically. The automatic option is available for static, frequency, buckling, and linear dynamic studies.
Simplified	The program overrides the default surface-based bonding contact and resumes to a node-based bonding contact. Check this option only in cases when you run into performance issues when solving models with extensive contact surfaces. For a 2D simplification analysis, if you check this option, the program applies a node to edge bonding contact.
More accurate	The program applies the default surface-based bonding contact, which results in a longer solution time than the node-based contact formulation. For a 2D simplification study, the solver applies an edge to edge bonding contact.

Displaying mesh in result plots

The default brightness of **Ambient** light, defined in the **SolidWorks Display Manager** in the **Lighting** folder, is usually too dark to display the mesh, especially a high-density mesh. A clear display of the mesh (Figure 20-6) requires increasing the brightness of ambient light. You will also notice that using models with light colors, disabling perspective, shading and other display effect makes it easier to work with **Simulation** models.

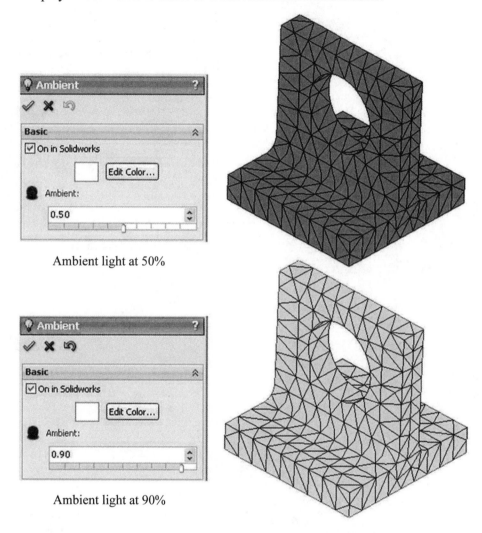

Ambient light at 50%

Ambient light at 90%

Figure 20-6: Mesh display in default ambient light (top) and adjusted ambient light (bottom).

A finite element mesh is displayed with ambient light brightness suitable for a CAD model (top), and with the brightness adjusted for displaying the mesh (bottom).

All models used in this book are lighter colors and use ambient light at around 90%. Notice the excessive turn angle in the rounded areas.

Automatic reports

SolidWorks Simulation provides automated report creation. After a solution finishes, select **Report** from the **Simulation** menu or from the **Simulation Command Manager** to define the report format and the items it will contain. The report is created in a few steps and contains all plots from the result folders (Figure 20-7).

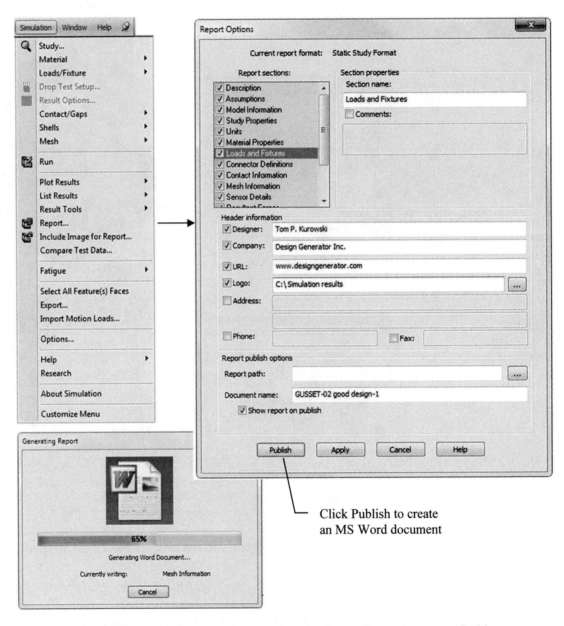

Click Publish to create an MS Word document

Figure 20-7: The Report is automatically created with the options specified in the Report Options windows.

A report in Word format is created individually for each study.

E-drawings

Each result plot can be saved in various graphic formats (Bitmap, JPEG, VRML, XGL, ZGL), as well as in the **SolidWorks** eDrawing format. To save a plot, first show it then right-click it and select **Save as**. Select the desired format from the pop-out menu.

Examine the eDrawing format which offers a very convenient 3D way of communicating FEA results to people who do not have **SolidWorks Simulation** or no **SolidWorks** at all (Figure 20-8).

Figure 20-8: Simulation results saved in eDrawing format can be viewed in 3D.

Review options offered by the eDrawing results viewer.

Non-uniform loads

We will illustrate the use of non-uniformly distributed loads with an example of hydrostatic pressure acting on the walls of a 1.95m deep tank, presented in the **SolidWorks** part file called NON UNIFORM LOAD. Notice that this model uses meters for the unit of length. The pressure magnitude expressed in $[N/m^2]$ follows the equation p = 10000x, with x being the distance from the top of tank (where the coordinate system *cs1* is located). The pressure definition requires selecting the coordinate system and the face where pressure is to be applied. The formula governing pressure distribution can then be entered, as shown in Figure 20-9.

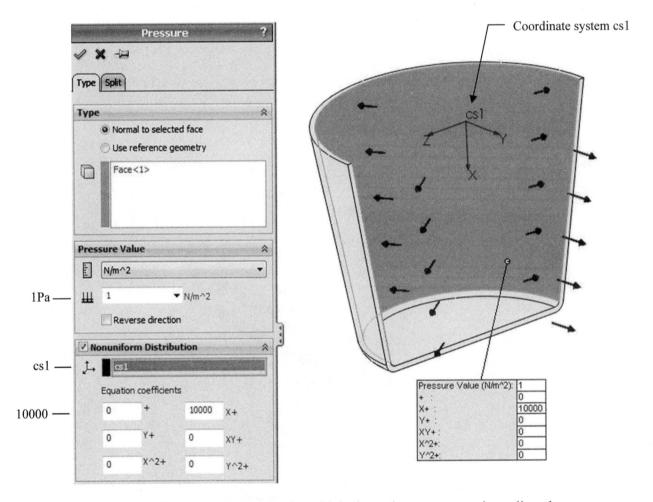

Figure 20-9: A water tank loaded with hydrostatic pressure requires a linearly distributed pressure.

This illustration uses a section view. Notice that the vector lengths correspond to pressure magnitudes that vary with the x axis of the cs1 coordinate system. This model uses meter as its units of length, and Pascals as its units of pressure. For clarity of illustration, arrows depicting pressure acting on the bottom face and round fillet arrows are not shown.

You may want to complete this exercise by applying a **Fixed** restraint to the bottom of the tank and a material of your choice. Notice that the tank geometry makes it suitable for meshing with shell elements.

Frequency analysis with pre-stress

A frequency analysis of rotating machinery most often must account for stress stiffening. Stress stiffening is the increase in stiffness due to tensile loads. We will illustrate this concept with the example of a helicopter blade. Since HELICOPTER ROTOR model has four identical blades, switch to the *02 section* configuration, which will work with geometry containing only one blade. The model comes with assigned material properties and two defined **SolidWorks Simulation** studies: *no preload* and *preload*.

A load definition is not required in a **Frequency** analysis. However if loads are defined, their effect will be considered. The **Direct sparse** solver is the only solver that accounts for the effect of loads in a **Frequency** analysis.

A centrifugal load is defined as shown in Figure 20-10. An axis or a cylindrical face is required as a reference to define a centrifugal load. Review the restraint, which is the same in both studies. Restraints may be represented as **Fixed** restraints applied to hub.

Cylindrical face of hub —

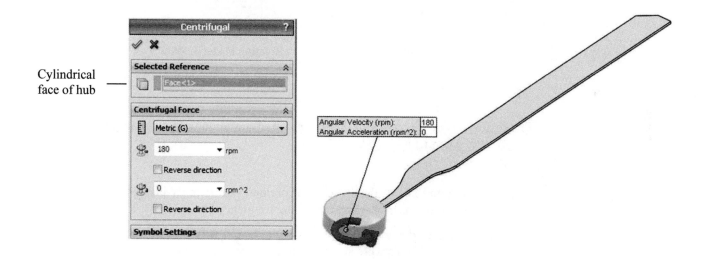

Figure 20-10: The **Centrifugal** load window with centrifugal force defined.

A centrifugal load resulting from an angular velocity of 180 RPM is applied to the model, simulating the effect of rotation about the axis of the cylindrical face. Angular acceleration can also be defined. Metric units are used to express the angular velocity in RPM.

Solve both studies and compare frequency results (Figure 20-11) with and without the pre-stress effect caused by a centrifugal force.

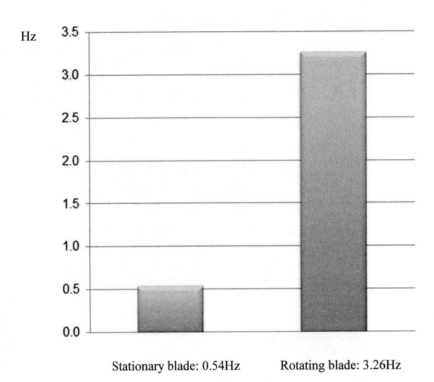

Stationary blade: 0.54Hz   Rotating blade: 3.26Hz

Figure 20-11: The frequency of the first mode of vibration with and without the effect of a centrifugal load.

As shown in Figure 20-11, the presence of preload significantly increases the first mode of vibration. In the first mode, the frequency increases by 2.4 times.

The opposite effect (decrease in the natural frequency) would be observed if, hypothetically, the blades were subjected to a compressive load.

For more practice, try conducting a frequency analysis of a beam under a compressive load. You may re-use the HELICOPTER ROTOR model. The higher the compressive load, the lower the first natural frequency. Higher frequencies follow the same pattern. The magnitude of the compressive load that causes the first natural frequency to drop to zero is the buckling load. This is where frequency and buckling analyses meet!

Shrink fit

Shrink fit is another type of **Contact** condition. We use it here to analyze stresses developed as a result of the interference (press fit) between two assembly components. Open the SHRINK FIT assembly. The definition of the shrink fit condition is shown in Figure 20-12. Review this model for definitions of restraints, supports and contact conditions.

Notice that the contact condition does not include friction, therefore the inside cylindrical face of the pressed-in component has been restrained in circumferential and axial directions to prevent rigid body motions.

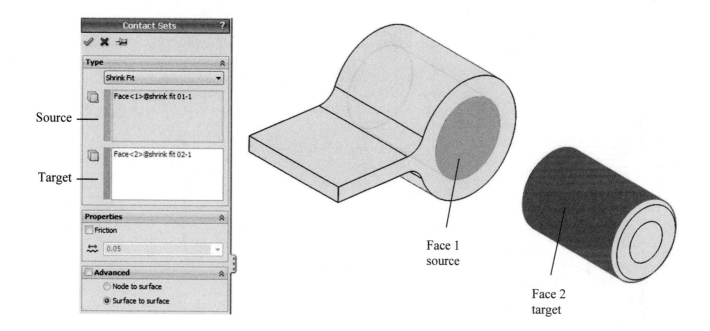

Figure 20-12: Cylindrical Face 2 has a larger diameter than cylindrical Face 1. Solving the model with a Shrink Fit contact condition eliminates this interference.

An exploded view should be used to select the interfering faces.

Apply a restraint to the "tail" of the housing and restrain the hole of the shaft as shown in Figure 20-13. This is necessary to eliminate rigid body motions of the shaft.

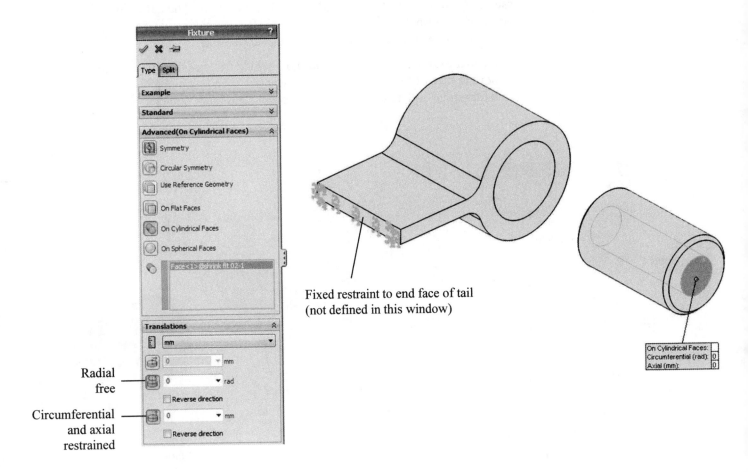

Fixed restraint to end face of tail
(not defined in this window)

Radial free

Circumferential and axial restrained

Figure 20-13: Restraints applied to the hole are required to eliminate rigid body motions.

A restraint is applied using an On Cylindrical Faces restraint.

The same could have been applied using Axis1 as the reference geometry.

Mesh the model with a 1mm element size using a **Curvature based mesh** and obtain the solution. Display the SX stress plot using Axis1 as reference geometry to convert SX stress into radial stress (Figure 20-14). When stresses SX, SY, and SZ are plotted using an axis as a reference, as in Figure 20-14, SX becomes radial stress, SY becomes circumferential stress and SZ becomes axial stress. The symbol in the lower right corner indicates that the results are presented in a local cylindrical coordinate system.

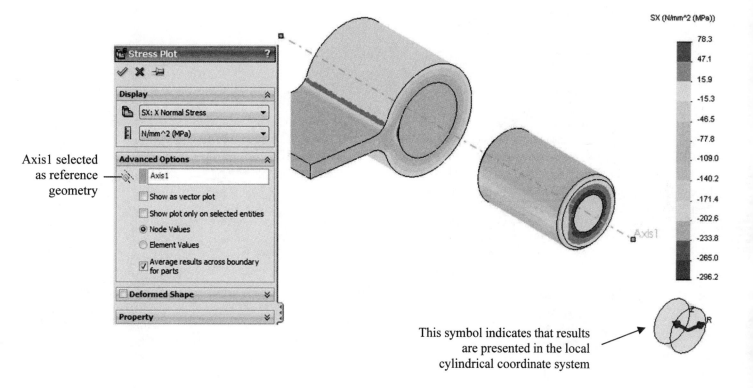

Figure 20-14: Radial stresses developed due to the shrink fit.

Notice that on contacting faces, the absolute magnitude of contact stress is the absolute magnitude of SX stress.

The highest contact stress is numerically the lowest stress: 296MPa.

Review the options in the **Stress Plot** window in Figure 20-14 and use the vector display option to visualize the radial direction of stress SX (Figure 20-15).

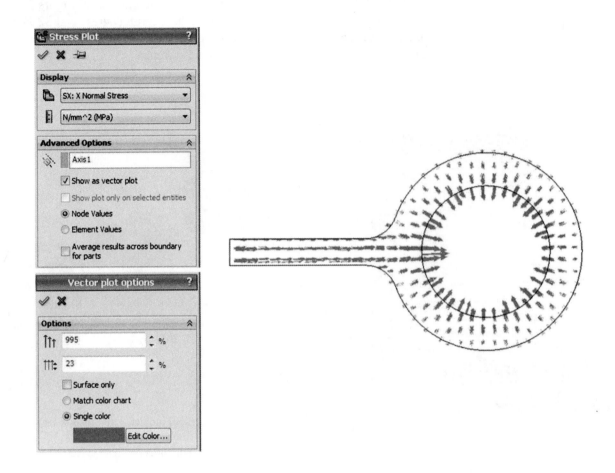

Figure 20-15: Radial stresses SX presented as vectors.

Use the Vector plot options window to adjust the vector plot.

Only the housing component is shown.

Return to the fringe plot, explode the view, and probe the radial stresses on both contacting faces approximately in the same location (Figure 20-16).

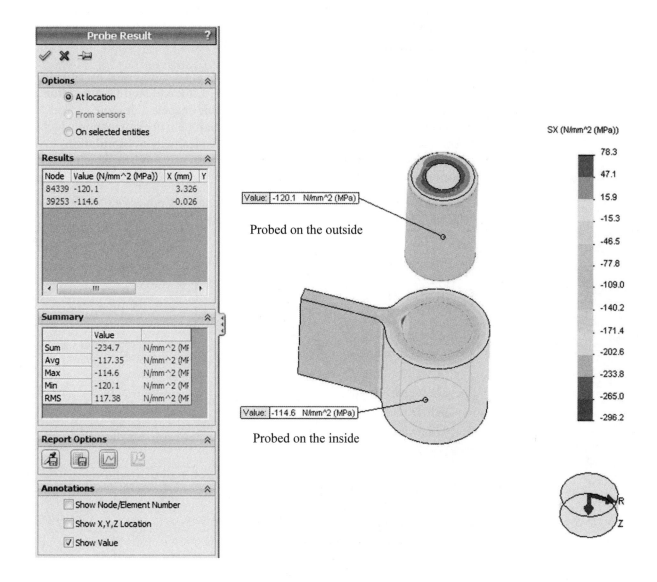

Figure 20-16: Radial stress SX on the face of the tube (top) equals the radial stress SX on the side of the hole (bottom).

Radial stresses correspond to contact pressure which is the same on both contacting faces due to the equilibrium conditions. In the housing, probing is done on the inner face, not visible in the view used in this illustration.

Connectors

A connector defines how an entity (vertex, edge, face) is connected to another entity or to the ground. Using connectors simplifies modeling because, in many cases, you can simulate the desired behavior without having to create the detailed geometry or define contact conditions.

SolidWorks Simulation offers several types of connectors listed as: **Spring, Pin, Bolt, Bearing, Spot Welds, Edge Welds, Link** and **Rigid Connection**. Selected connectors are briefly introduced in this chapter. For more information, refer to the **SolidWorks Simulation** help documentation which offers extensive explanations with examples. To learn about **Simulation** functionality (including connectors), you may also use **Advisor** which is located in the **SolidWorks** task pane.

A connector definition is called by right-clicking the *Connectors* folder and selecting the desired connector type (Figure 20-17).

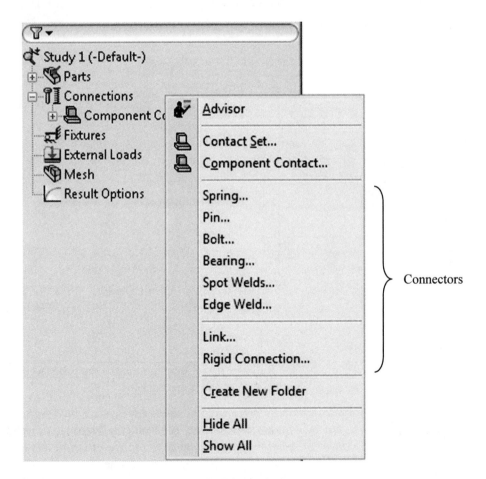

Figure 20-17: Connectors are called from the same pop-up menu as contact conditions.

Connectors available in **SolidWorks Simulation** 2013 are summarized in the table below.

TYPE OF CONNECTOR	FUNCTION
Spring	Connects a face of a component to a face of another component by defining total stiffness or stiffness per area. Both normal and shear stiffness can be specified. The two faces must be planar and parallel to each other. Springs are introduced in the common area of the projection of one of the faces onto the other. You can specify a compressive or tensile preload for the spring connector.
Pin	A pin connects cylindrical faces of two components. Two options are available: No Translation: specifies a pin that prevents relative axial translation between the two cylindrical faces. No Rotation: specifies a pin that prevents relative rotation between the two cylindrical faces. Additionally, axial and/or rotational pin stiffness can be defined.
Bolt	Defines a bolt connector between two components. The bolt connector accounts for bolt pre-load. Configurations with and without a nut are available.
Bearing	Simulates the interaction between a shaft and a housing through a bearing. You have to model the geometries for the shaft and the housing.
Spot weld	You can define spot welds to weld two solid faces or two shell faces. You should also define a No Penetration contact condition between the two faces for proper modeling.
Edge weld	The edge weld connector estimates the appropriate size of a weld needed to attach two metal components. The program calculates the appropriate weld size at each mesh node location along the weld seam.
Link	The Link connector ties any two locations in the model by a rigid bar that is hinged at both ends. The distance between the two locations remains unchanged during deformation. The link connector is available for static, buckling, and frequency studies.
Rigid Connection	Defines a rigid link between the selected faces. Faces connected by a rigid link do not translate or rotate in relation to each other.

Rigid Connection and Pin Connector

We will review the use of a **Rigid Connection** and a **Pin** in the assembly CRANE. This model comes with a defined **Rigid Connection** and three **Pin** connectors. The **Rigid** connector is shown in Figure 20-18.

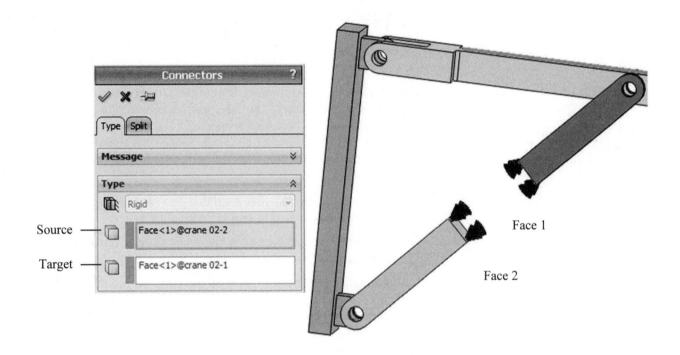

Figure 20-18: Rigid connector rigidly connects two faces.

The selection of the face as a source and as a target is arbitrary.

One of the **Pin** connectors is shown in Figure 20-19.

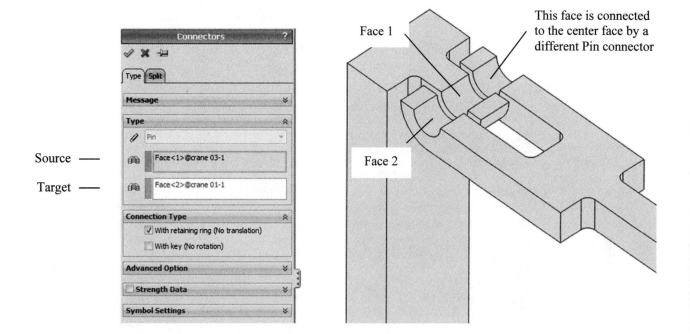

Source ——

Target ——

Figure 20-19: The Pin connector connects faces of two components.

In this model, each location requires two Connectors. Only one connector is shown in this illustration. A sectioned view is used to show the connected faces. You need to select the Strength Data box to perform a pass/no pass pin check.

Notice that the torsional stiffness of the **Pin** connector shown in Figure 20-19 is specified as 0 (this is the default value). This means that **Pin** connectors allow for rotation between the two components. All degrees of freedom on the selected faces are coupled (must be the same) except for circumferential translations, which are disjoined.

Practice using **Pin** connectors using the assembly STAND. Our objective is to find the first mode of vibration of the assembly. This model has little relevance to real life devices but offers a good opportunity to practice **Pin** connectors.

Notice that no **Global Contact** conditions exist in the study *Modal* (they have been deleted). In the absence of **Global Contact** conditions, all touching faces are treated as free, they are not bonded and penetration is allowed. Consequently, the four links are not bonded to the top or the bottom plate. They are connected to them by **Pin** Connectors.

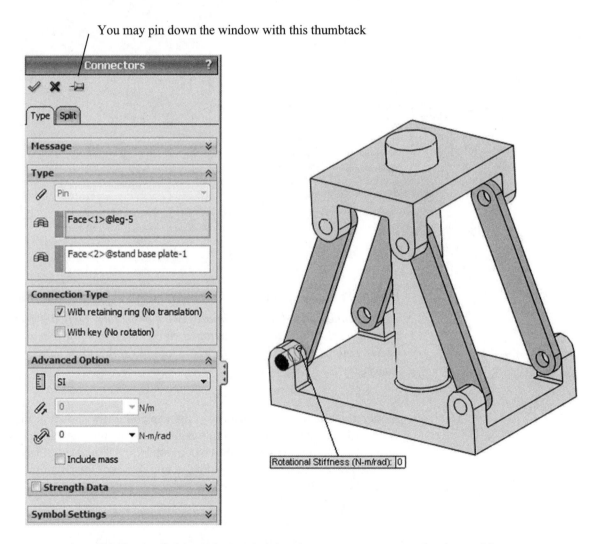

Figure 20-20: Definition of one of eight Pin connectors connecting legs with the top and bottom plate.

You may pin down the Connectors window to create a number of pins in one step. All connectors will then be placed in a separate folder. Notice that "pin" as in "Pin down the window" has nothing to do with "pin" as in the Pin connector.

The vertical shaft is connected by a **Pin** connector to the top plate. The important difference between this **Pin** connector and the previously discussed **Pin** connectors is explained in Figure 20-21.

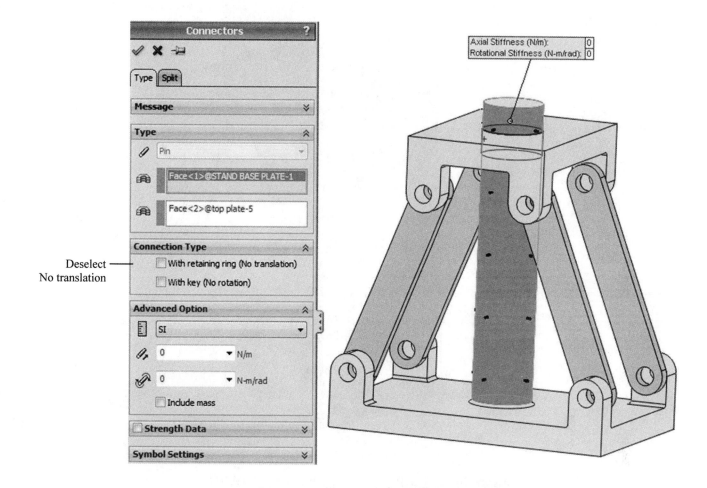

Figure 20-21: This Pin connector allows axial translation.

To allow axial translation, deselect "With retaining ring (No translation)" in the Connection Type definition.

Review the restraints of the model (bottom of the BASE PLATE is rigidly restrained), mesh with **Curvature based mesh** and default element size, then run a modal (Frequency) analysis. The first mode of vibration is shown in Figure 20-22.

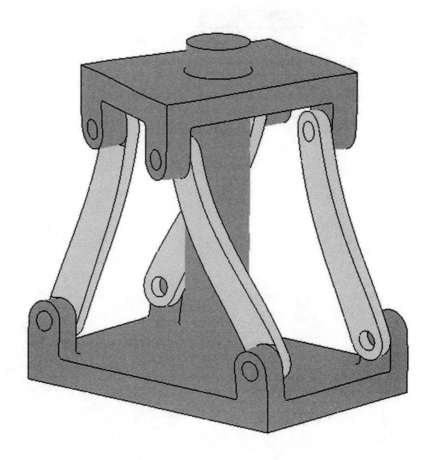

Figure 20-22: The first mode of vibration of STAND.

The frequency is 436Hz. Notice that this is an anti-symmetric, torsional mode.

Bolt connector

To review the **Bolt** connector; as well as, the load type called **Remote Load**, open the assembly PIPES in the *01 long* configuration and go to **Simulation** study *01 long*. The model comes with six bolt connectors already defined. Right-click one of the **Bolt Connector** icons and select **Edit Definition** to open the **Connectors** windows (Figure 20-23).

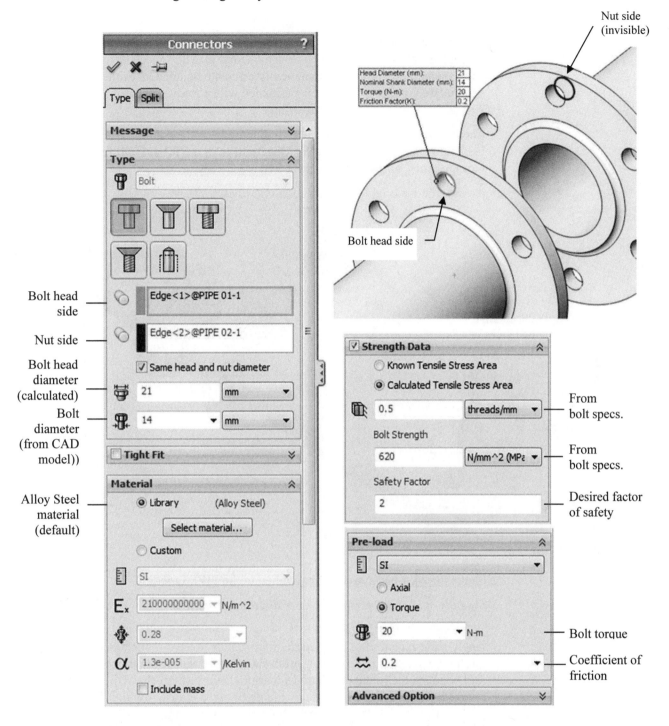

Figure 20-23: One of six bolt connectors in the PIPES assembly model. A no penetration contact condition must be defined between the touching faces of the two flanges. To transmit the shear force in the absence of friction between the flanges, a Tight Fit must be defined.

The pre-load definition indicates that each bolt is loaded with 20Nm of torque, the coefficient of friction is 0.2. Strength data is required only if bolt check is to be conducted.

419

Defining the **Bolt Connector** offers several options. In this example, we model the bolt with a nut. The bolt is made out of Alloy Steel, has a loose fit, and a diameter of 14mm. Automatically calculated diameters of the bolt head and nut are accepted. The bolt is preloaded with a torque of 20Nm. Review **Advanced Options** before proceeding.

There is one set of contacting faces in the model and a contact condition must be defined, so you may define **No Penetration** as a **Global Contact**, **Component Contact** or a **Contact Set**.

Review the loads and restraints shown in Figure 20-24.

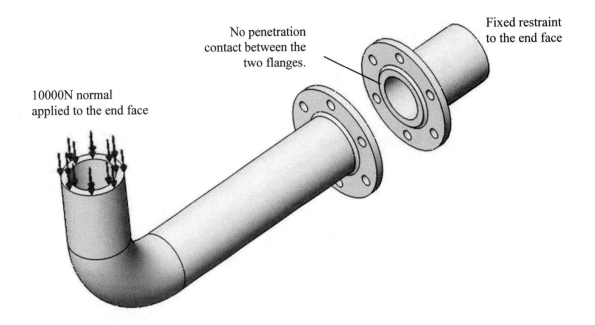

Figure 20-24: Load and restraint applied to the PIPES model.

Symbols of connectors and the restraint are not shown.

Apply a mesh control of 4mm to the four rounds present in the assembly and mesh the model with the default mesh size. Notice that while the mesh is refined along the rounds it is at best marginal everywhere else. Upon solution, review the bolt forces which are available by right-clicking on the *Results* folder and selecting **Define Pin/Bolt Check Force**. (Figure 20-25).

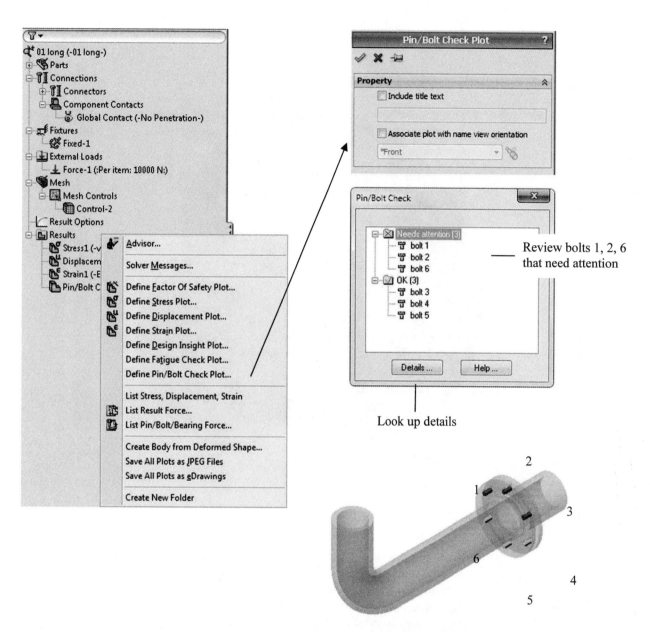

Figure 20-25: The pop-up menu activated by right-clicking the Results folder (left). The Pin/Bolt Check window (top right) where failed bolts are shown in red (bottom right).

Also investigate other result options shown in the pop-up menu on the left such as List Pin/Bolt/Bearing Force. This list may be also activated by clicking Details in Pin/Bolt Check window. The plot is accompanied by a small window listing passed and failed bolts (upper right).

Review von Mises stress results to notice that the mesh in the area of the stress concentration is insufficient (Figure 20-26). Maximum von Mises stress magnitude is more than double the yield strength proving that the PIPES are severely overloaded.

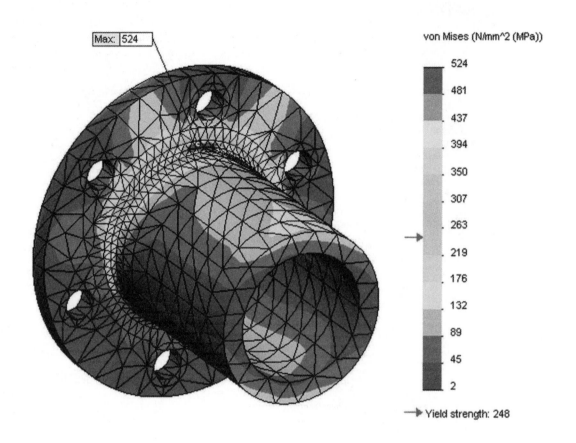

Figure 20-26: A review of stress concentrations indicates that the mesh should be refined. Only one assembly component is shown.

Stress concentrations that are attracted to nodes and are smaller than the element size indicates the need for mesh refinement. Notice that stresses are more than twice the yield strength, and if this does not disqualify the design right away, it certainly requires the analysis with a non-linear material to investigate the extent of the yield zone.

Remote load

Stay with the PIPES assembly model and switch to the *02 short* configuration and go to **Simulation** study *02 short*. We use this configuration to demonstrate a **Remote load.** When a **Remote load** is used, it allows us to reduce the model size by cutting the pipe and applying a load as if the eliminated portion of the model was still present (Figure 20-27).

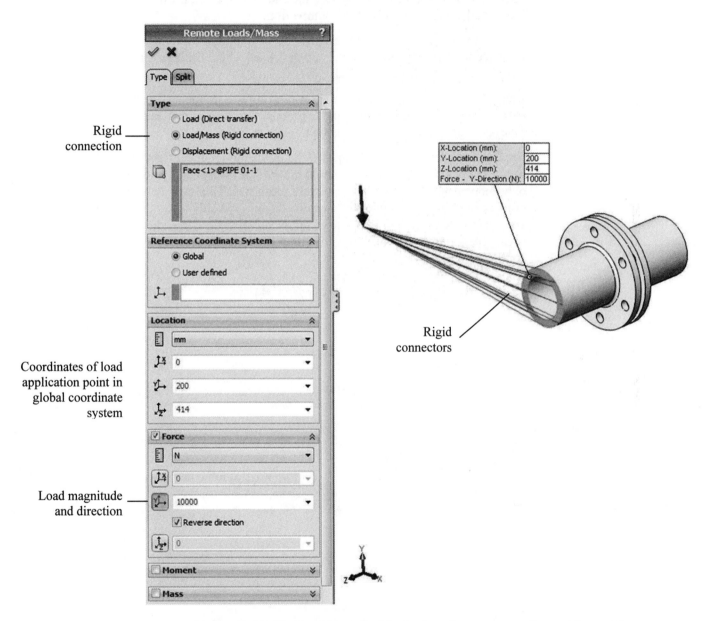

Figure 20-27: The load is applied in the location corresponding to Figure 20-24. The point of the load application is rigidly connected to the end face of the pipe in the 02 short configuration.

The load is transferred from the point of application to the face by means of rigid connectors.

There are two types of Remote Loads: **Direct Transfer** and **Rigid Connection**. The choice between these two types depends on the stiffness of the suppressed/eliminated component as compared to the rest of the model. For example a thin-walled tube would just transfer the load to the face of the link and therefore the **Direct transfer** option would have to be specified. A thick wall pipe as in our case, stiffens the end face of the short flange where it is attached, so we specify a **Rigid connection**.

Load/Mass (Rigid connection) can also be used to define a remote mass. The **Displacement (Rigid connection)** option is used when displacement boundary conditions are specified.

Remote load also offers a convenient way to apply a moment to a solid element model. Using **Remote load**, a moment load is automatically translated into an equivalent force load.

Apply a fixed restraint to the opposite end of the model in configuration *02 short*. Apply a mesh control of 4mm to the outside rounds on the loaded pipe only and mesh the model with the default mesh size. This way we will produce reasonably accurate stress results on one side only (the side with the applied mesh control), and also speed up the solution time in addition to the savings resulting from working with a simplified model (*02 short* configuration).

Von Mises stress results shown in Figure 20-28 are similar to the results produced by the analyzed full model (*01 long* configuration). Repeat this exercise with several more mesh refinements until the stress concentrations are modeled by 4 - 6 elements.

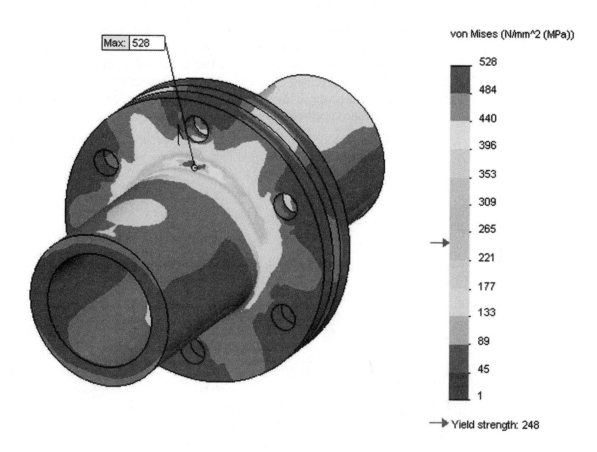

Figure 20-28: Von Mises stress results produced by the simplified *02 short* configuration model with a load applied remotely.

Mesh not shown.

Edge Weld connector

Open the assembly TUBE WELDMENT (Figure 20-29). The assembly consists of a square hollow tube modeled as a solid, endplates modeled as solids, and a hanger modeled as a surface. The hanger is connected to the tube by welds. We need to check if the welds are "strong enough".

We use an **Edge Weld** connector to connect the hanger to the tube and calculate the weld loads. **Edge Welds** model connections along a line where the weld would be located. Notice that the actual weld is not modeled and welds are represented by lines connecting the surface to the solid. Loads transmitted by those lines are calculated and these loads are then used to assess if the specified weld is adequate.

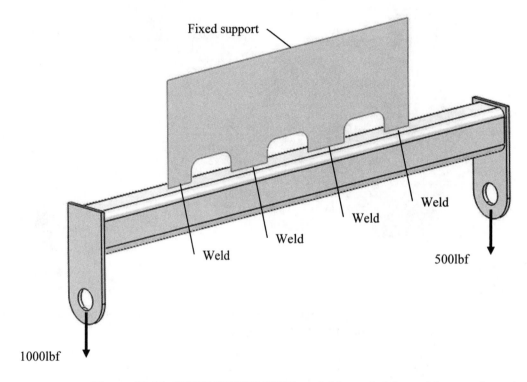

Figure 20-29: TUBE WELDMENT model intended for weld strength analysis.

The hanger thickness is 0.25", and the weld is a double sided 3/16" fillet weld. Loads are pointing down and are applied to split faces on the cylindrical surfaces of the holes. See Figure 20-30 for load details.

The load applied to the model is explained in Figure 20-30.

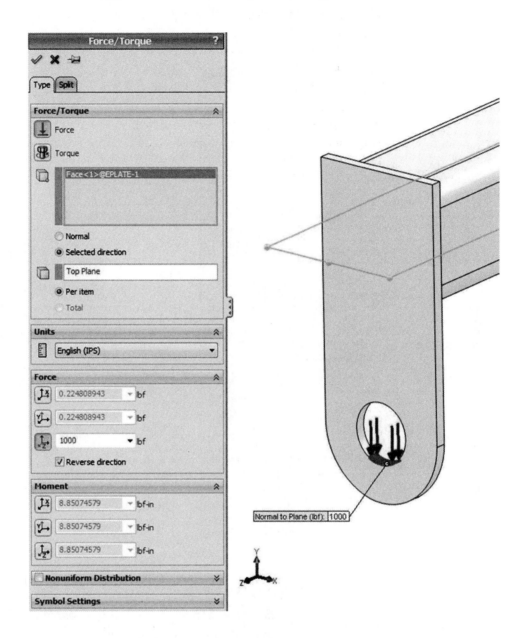

Figure 20-30: Force load applied to the left endplate.

Force is distributed uniformly over the split face. Alternatively you may apply a bearing load. Remember to apply 500lbf force to the other endplate.

Four **Edge Weld** connectors have to be defined in the model. Figure 20-31 shows the steps necessary to define them.

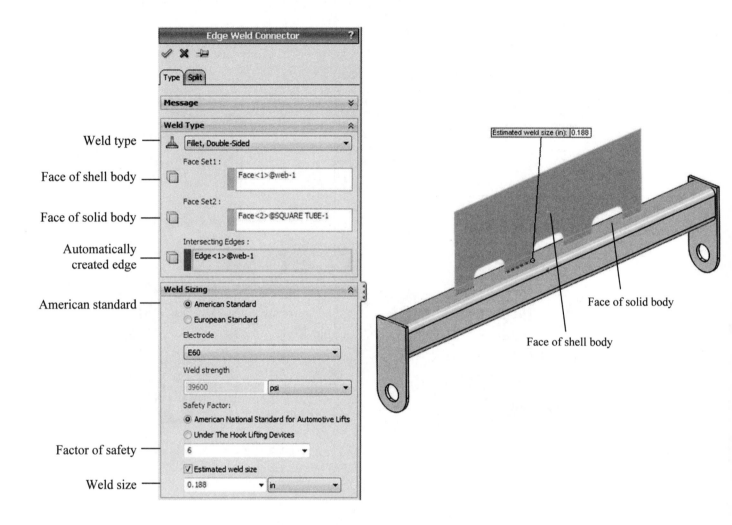

<u>Figure 20-31: Edge weld definition.</u>

The definition includes the weld type and size: it is a double sided fillet weld 0.188" in size. It also includes the electrode material type: E60 in this example. The above window creates all four weld connectors.

Run the analysis and display the **Weld Check Plot** following the steps shown in Figure 20-32.

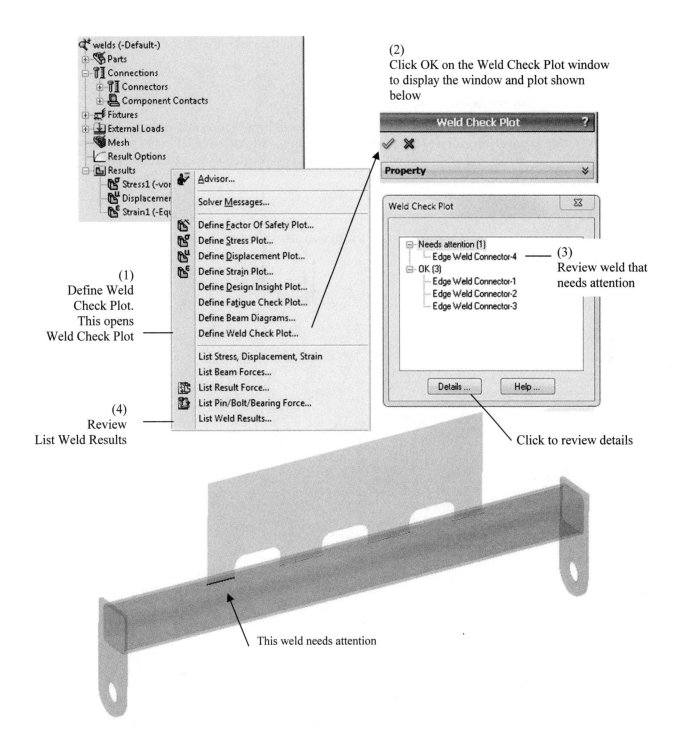

(2)
Click OK on the Weld Check Plot window to display the window and plot shown below

(1)
Define Weld Check Plot. This opens Weld Check Plot

(3)
Review weld that needs attention

(4)
Review List Weld Results

Click to review details

This weld needs attention

Figure 20-32: The Weld Check Plot windows indicates that a weld failed the check.

The plot is accompanied by a Weld Check Plot window listing passed and failed welds. Also review List Weld Results shown in step (4).

Complete the analysis of the TUBE WELDMENT by reviewing the von Mises stress results and comparing them to the yield strength of the assembly components.

Bearing connector

A bearing connector models support offered by a bearing and allows for angular rotation of the supported shaft. In the BEARING SUPPORT assembly model, a shaft loaded with a radial force is supported by two bearings (Figure 20-33).

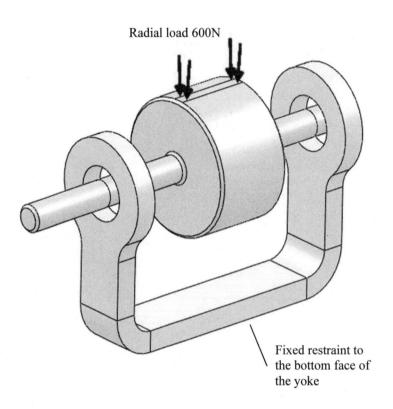

Figure 20-33: Shaft supported by two bearings.

Each bearing support is modeled by a Bearing connector. Notice that bearings are not modeled explicitly. The bearing connector connects the shaft to the bearing housings. Examine split lines on both ends of the shaft. Load is applied to the split face on the rotor, and restraint is applied to the bottom face of the yoke.

Notice that the yoke supporting the rotor has been created as a sheet metal part. By default, **Simulation** would mesh it with shell elements (Figure 20-34 left). To force meshing with solid elements, follow the steps explained in Figure 20-34. To avoid excessive turn angles refine the mesh globally.

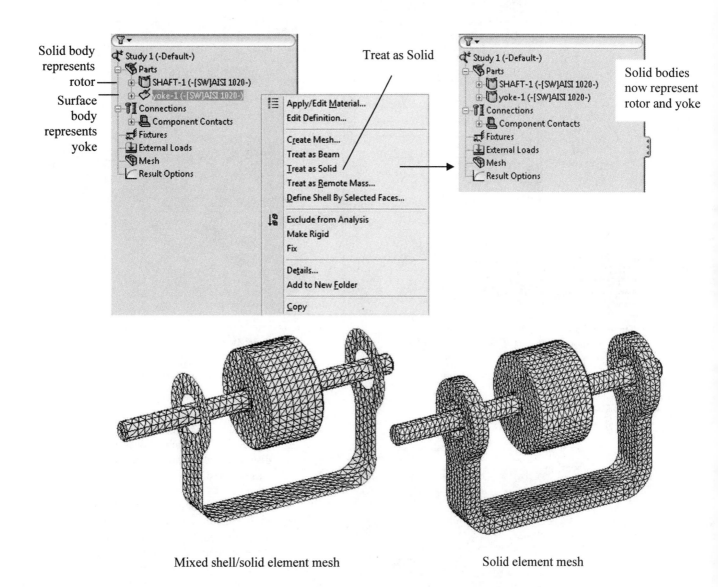

Mixed shell/solid element mesh

Solid element mesh

Figure 20-34: Converting the shell element mesh to a solid element mesh.

Open the Parts folder and right-click the yoke part. Select Treat as Solid from the pop-up menu.

The definition of **Bearing connectors** is shown in Figure 20-35.

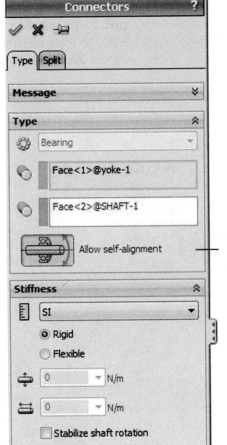

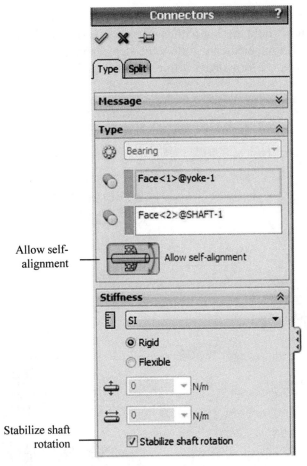

Allow self-alignment

Stabilize shaft rotation

Allow self-alignment

Left bearing connector

Right bearing connector

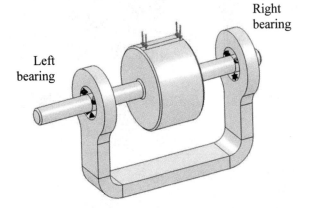

Left bearing

Right bearing

Note:
At the time this exercise was prepared "Allow self -alignment" was mistakenly disabled when "Stabilize shaft rotation" was selected.

As a work-around, don't use "Stabilize shaft rotation" and prevent rigid body motion by applying restraints in the circumferential direction to the cylindrical face where the load is applied. This method was used to prepare Figure 21-36 top.

Figure 20-35: Definition of Bearing connectors.

The "Stabilize shaft rotation" option is selected in the left bearing connector. Self-alignment is allowed on both sides.

The definition of the connectors on the left and right sides differ because we need to eliminate the rotation of the shaft about the z axis. This would result in a rigid body motion.

Both bearings are modeled as rigid. **Allow self-alignment** is selected meaning that the deflecting shaft can rotate about the center of the imaginary bearing.

Complete the analysis of the BEARING SUPPORT assembly by repeating the analysis with one **Bearing Connector** without **Allow self-alignment**.

Deformed shapes of the shafts are shown in Figure 2-36.

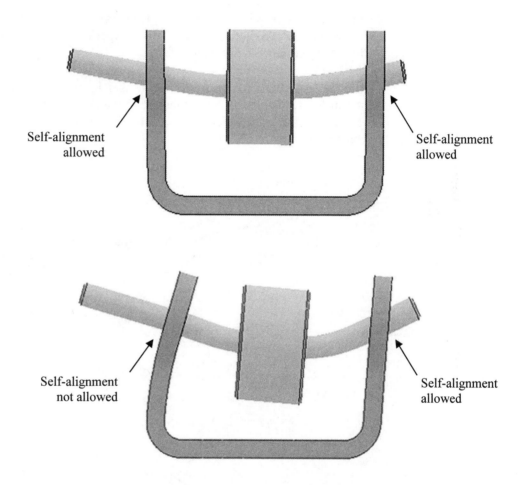

Figure 20-36: Deformed shapes of the shaft with supports defined as Bearing connectors.

Top: self-alignment is allowed on both sides. Bottom: self-alignment is allowed on the right side only. The scale of deformation was individually adjusted for each plot.

Circular symmetry

The use of **Circular symmetry** simplifies the analysis of a model with circular patterns around an axis by modeling only one representative segment. The geometry, restraints, and loading conditions must be the same for all other segments making up the model. This means that the geometry as well as the loads and restraints must be characterized by the same circular pattern. Typical examples of machine components suitable for analysis with circular symmetry include turbines, fans, flywheels, and motor rotors.

At the time this exercise was prepared, **Circular symmetry** restraint was not working properly. Skip this exercise if you experience problems with defining **Circular symmetry** to non-planar faces.

Open the part CIRCULAR and review the sketch called Circular symmetry cut. This sketch is used in the last feature of the Design Tree. Switch to the *02 section* configuration. Notice that this is a 1/7th section of the complete geometry (Figure 20-37).

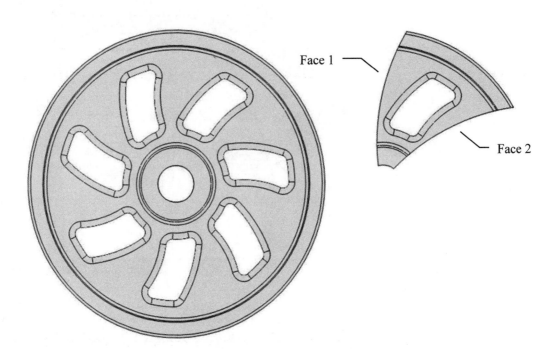

Figure 20-37: Complete model (left), and 1/7th section suitable for analysis with Circular symmetry (right).

The program enforces equal displacements at all corresponding locations on both faces. The faces where circular symmetry is enforced do not have to be of any particular shape. The only requirement is that the segment is a part of a repetitive geometry.

The definition of circular symmetry is explained in Figure 20-38.

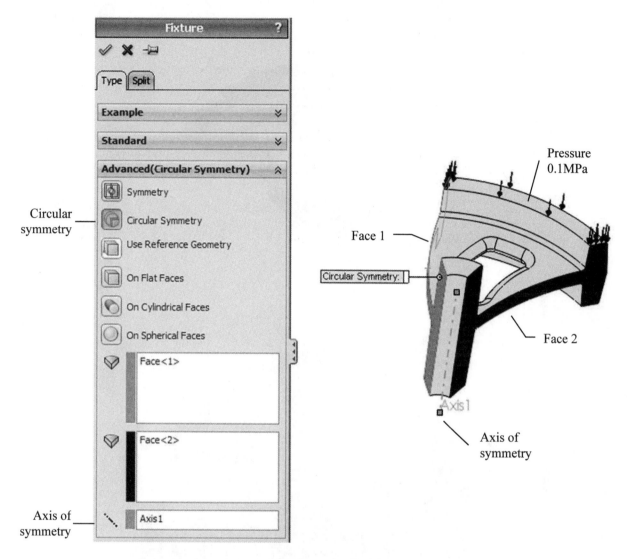

Figure 20-38: Definition of Circular Symmetry. Also shown is a pressure load.

The definition requires a reference axis which is aligned with the central hole.

Apply a **Fixed** restraint to the central hole. Apply a 0.1MPa **Pressure** to the rim. Mesh with the default size of a **Curvature based mesh** and run the model. Analyze the stress results and decide if the mesh needs refinement. Compare the results with those obtained using the model in configuration *01 full* (Figure 20-39).

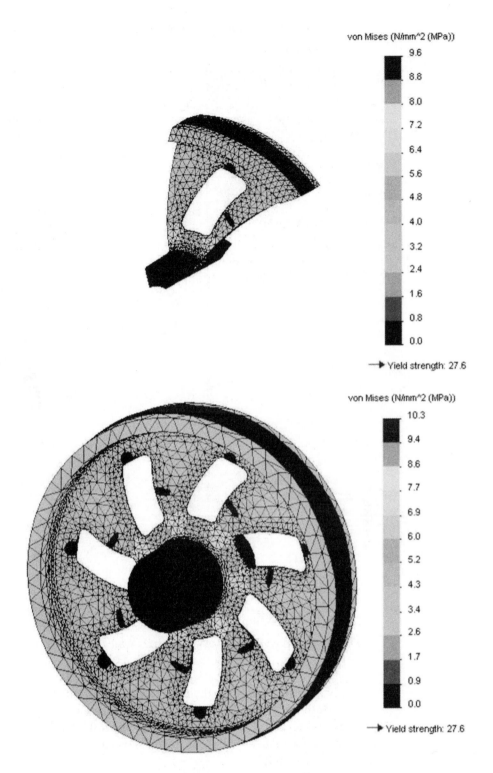

Figure 20-39: Von Mises stress results in the 1/7th section of the model (top) the full model (bottom).

The differences in results are caused by the different element sizes used for meshing. Compare the element size in the section model and the full model.

Strongly nonlinear problem

In the introduction, we said that not all **Simulation** capabilities such as nonlinear analysis will be covered. Indeed, nonlinear buckling analysis or large strain analysis have been left out from this introductory text. It is the author's belief that the topics presented in the book have provided the readers with an understanding of finite element tools and methods, as well, have prepared them to tackle those more complex problems. To give you a taste of things to come, we will review one more example which presents the unexplored capabilities of **Simulation**, in the analysis of strongly nonlinear problems.

Open the CLAMP assembly and review the material properties of the clamp made out of Nylon 6/10 and a tube which has custom material properties of a silicon-like material: $E = 1$MPa, $\varepsilon = 0.45$. This model is intended to analyze deformation of both components as the clamp moves over the tube from its initial to its final position (Figure 20-40).

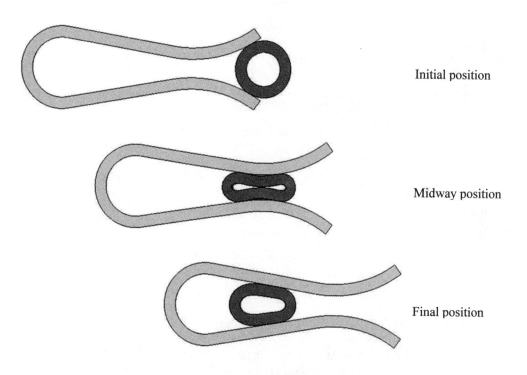

Initial position

Midway position

Final position

Figure 20-40: Clamp moves over the tube as it is pushed from its initial position, to its final position.

Go to study *01 NL*, review the restraints, and notice that the clamp restraint is defined as a prescribed displacement to the split face. This is what forces the clamp to move over the tube which has a **Fixed** restraint applied to the split face. There are no loads defined in the model. Also review the *Contact Set* to see which faces participate in contact.

The CLAMP assembly model has two types of geometric nonlinearities: large displacements and large strain. These strong nonlinearities cause significant numerical difficulties if the default solver settings are used. Review Figure 20-41 to see what solver setting lead to a successful solution. Notice that the material of both components is linear.

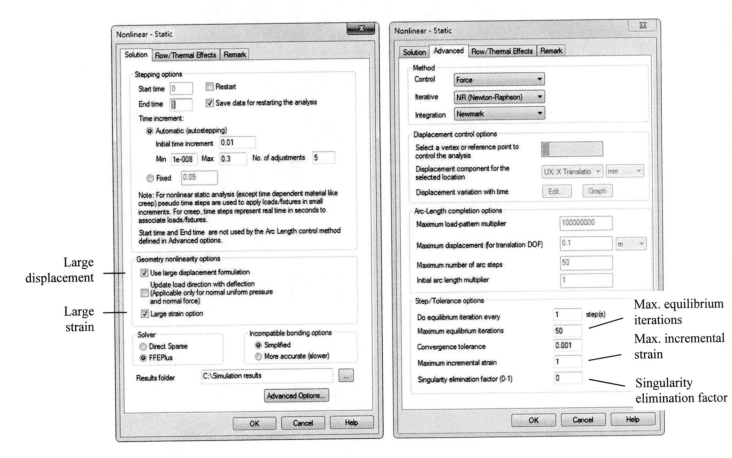

Figure 20-41: Strong nonlinearities in CLAMP require custom settings of Step/Tolerance options.

Often, these settings have to be adjusted following an unsuccessful solution.

Solve the model with the options shown in Figure 20-41, be prepared for a long solution time.

Figure 20-42 shows strain results for time step 0.41s which corresponds to the displacement of the CLAMP of 0.41*50mm = 20.5mm.

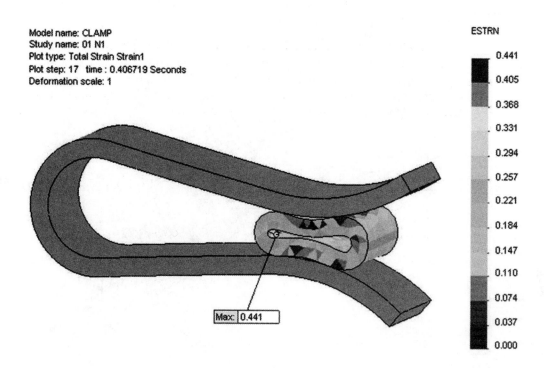

Model name: CLAMP
Study name: 01 N1
Plot type: Total Strain Strain1
Plot step: 17   time : 0.406719 Seconds
Deformation scale: 1

ESTRN

0.441
0.405
0.368
0.331
0.294
0.257
0.221
0.184
0.147
0.110
0.074
0.037
0.000

Max: 0.441

Figure 20-42: Strain results.

The maximum strain 44% is in the rubber tube, which is definitely a large strain.

The model with the mesh superimposed on the deformed shape is shown in Figure 20-43.

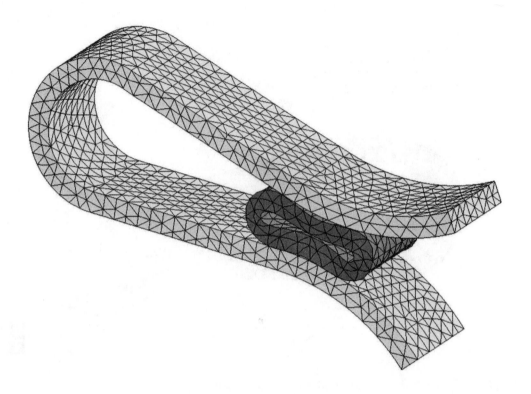

Figure 20-43: Deformed model in the position where the tube experiences its highest deformation.

Notice the "bulging out" of the tube due to a high Poisson's ratio of the tube material.

You may want to repeat the above analysis treating displacements and strain as small (see study *02 LIN*). Upon solution, review the displacement plot with a 1:1 scale of deformation to observe the incorrect solution.

A similar problem is presented in assembly CLAMP2013 shown in Figure 20-44.

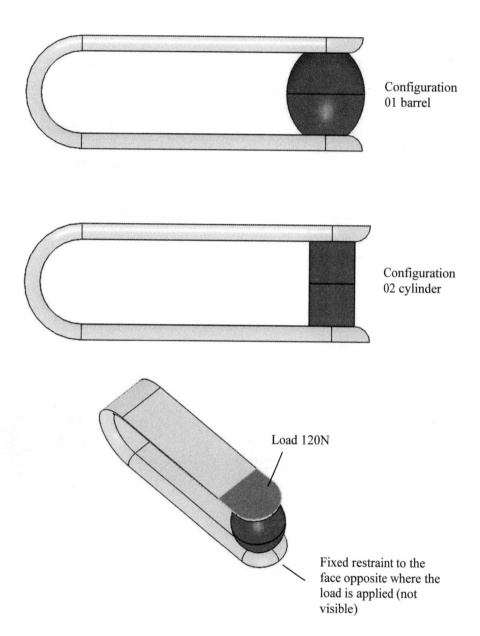

Configuration 01 barrel

Configuration 02 cylinder

Load 120N

Fixed restraint to the face opposite where the load is applied (not visible)

Figure 20-44: Rubber piece squeezed in a clamp.

Notice the initial curvature of the rubber piece in the 01 barrel configuration.

Make sure that the model is in *01 barrel* configuration and define a **Nonlinear** study called *01 barrel*. In the study properties select all geometry nonlinearity options:

Use large displacement formulation

Update load direction with deflection

Large strain option

Define all other settings as shown in Figure 20-41 including the use of default automatic time stepping. Use a linear load time curve.

Define one contact set between the upper portion of the rubber piece and the rounds of the upper arm of the clamp. Define the second contact set between the corresponding lower part of the rubber piece and the lower arm. You may review the contact definition because the model comes with study *01 barrel* defined. Define the load and restraint as shown in Figure 20-44 and mesh the assembly with an element size of 4mm with no mesh controls.

Simulation successfully completes the solution producing a deformed shape as shown in Figure 20-45.

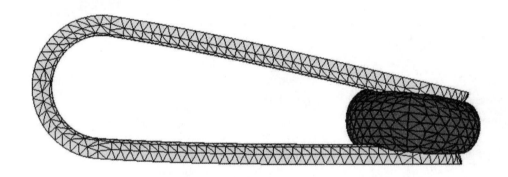

.

Figure 20-45: Deformed shape of the model in the *01 barrel* configuration.

Notice that the rubber piece contacts round portions of the clamp. This is why we needed contact conditions in this problem.

Switch to the *02 cylinder* configuration and set up a nonlinear study identical to the previous one. Expecting that rubber cylinder will "bulge out", define one contact set between the upper portion of rubber piece and the rounds of the upper arm of the clamp. Define the second contact set between corresponding lower part of the rubber piece and the lower arm. You may again review contact definitions because the model comes with study *02 cylinder* defined.

This time the solution terminates at step 10 producing an error message shown in Figure 20-46.

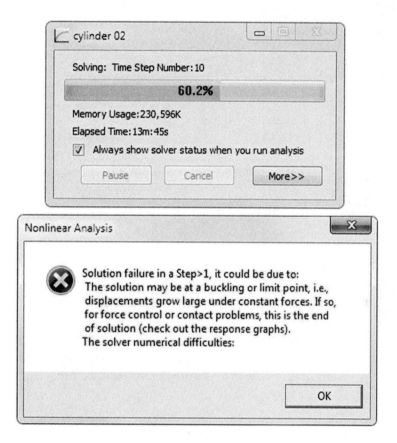

Figure 20-46: Error message produced in step 10 of the solution.

The last successfully completed load step was step 9.

The last successfully completed step was step 9, which corresponds to a solution time of 0.6s as can be read in the properties of the displacement plot (Figure 20-47). Since the load has a linear time history with a total time of 1s, the last successfully performed step corresponds to 60% of the maximum load which is 72N.

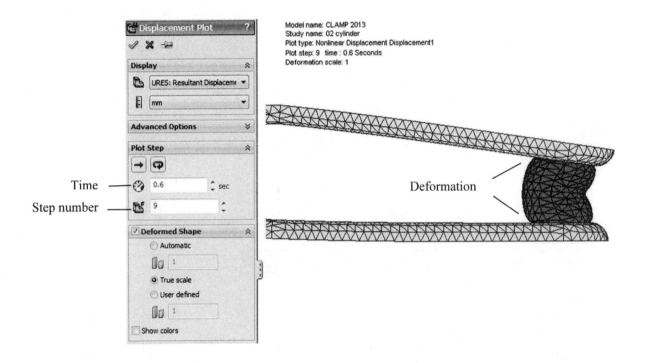

<u>Figure 20-47: Deformed shape under the load 72N.</u>

Notice severe deformation of the cylinder, especially in the area of contact with clamp. Zoom in to investigate the deformed shape of the elements.

The large strain in the rubber cylinder visible in Figure 20-47 led to severe deformation of elements and was the reason for solution failure in step 10.

Submodeling

Submodeling is a technique used when working with large models where the nature of analysis requires a highly refined mesh of a portion of the model, while the rest may be meshed with a much coarser mesh. **Submodeling** is particularly useful in nonlinear stress analysis where nonlinearity requires an iterative solution and a refined mesh must be used to model the expected stress patterns. We will demonstrate **Submodeling** using a fairly simple model named OUTRIGGER, which experiences yielding under the applied load. Review the OUTRIGGER assembly model and notice that it consists of three parts: a tube and two endplates. The tube itself consists of three solid bodies. Therefore, the model has a total of five bodies (Figure 20-48). The division of the tube into three solid bodies has been done to prepare the model for this **Submodeling** exercise.

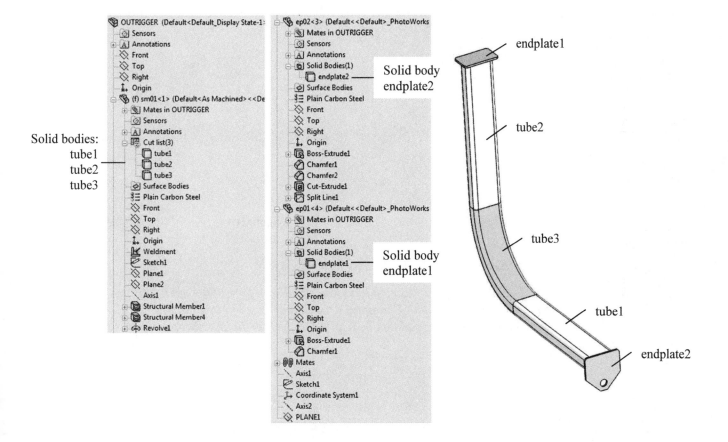

Figure 20-48: The model of OUTRIGGER composed of five solid bodies.

The Feature Manager Design Tree is split to fit this page. CoordinateSystem1 will be used to apply a bearing load, PLANE1 will be used to create a section view when analyzing stress results.

The load and restraint are shown in Figure 20-49.

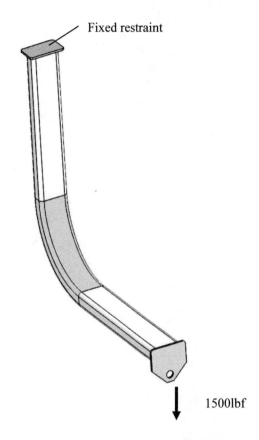

Figure 20-49: Load and restraint on OUTRIGGER.

The load is applied as a bearing load to a small split face in the hole. This is to review this type of load. Endplates are not the focus of attention in this analysis; therefore the load can be applied to the hole in just about any way.

Create and run the **Static** study *01 full model* using a default mesh size. Review von Mises stress results as shown in Figure 20-50 and notice that the stress exceeds the yield strength of Plain Carbon Steel, which is 32ksi. Also notice that high stress is confined to the curved potion of the tube which is modeled by solid body *tube3*. Finally, notice that the irregular pattern of fringes in the stress plot indicates the need of mesh refinement. Examine the displacement results (not shown here) to find that the displacements are not large.

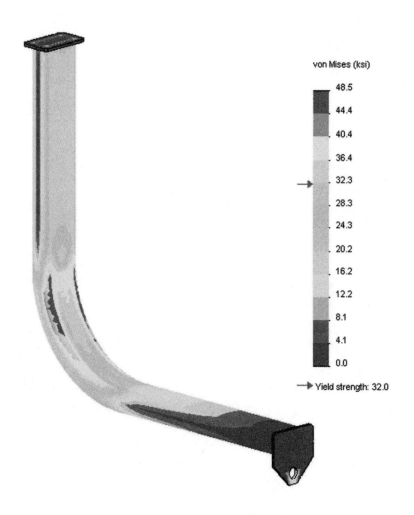

Figure 20-50: Von Mises stress results produced by a linear analysis.

The load is applied as a bearing load to a small split face in the hole. This is to review this type of load.

The results of the **Static** analysis can be treated only as preliminary; they indicate need for a nonlinear material analysis and that the mesh should be more refined in the curved portion of tube.

In preparation for **Submodeling**, create and run the **Nonlinear** study *02 full model* where the only source of nonlinear behavior is the nonlinear material; use the **Plasticity-von Mises** option (Figure 20-51).

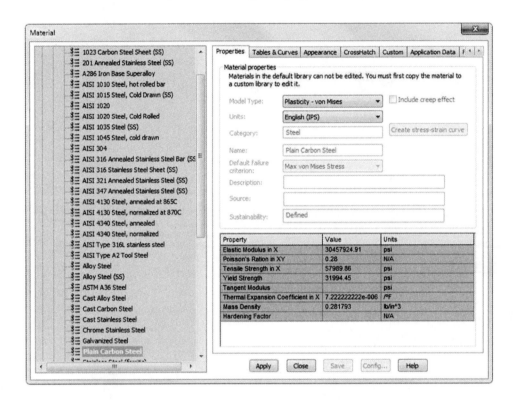

Figure 20-51: Nonlinear material definition in 02 full model study.

A nonlinear material is applied to all bodies in the model. For numerical efficiency it could be applied only to tube3 (the curved portion) while the rest of the model could use a linear material.

The full model that provides displacement boundary conditions for the submodel has to model stiffness correctly, not stresses, and this requires a less refined mesh. Use the default element size to mesh the full model.

Obtain a solution with the default mesh size and review the stress results as shown in Figure 20-52.

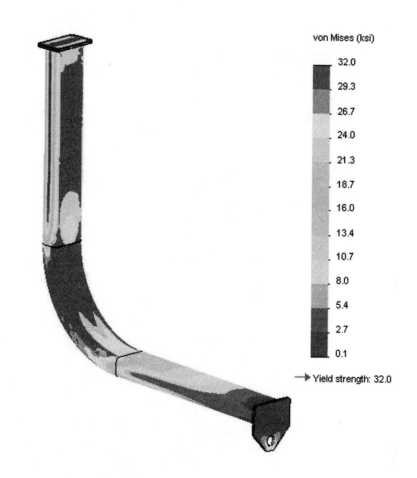

<u>Figure 20-52: Von Mises stress results produced by a nonlinear analysis.</u>

The zone where material yielded is still confined to the curved potion of tube modeled as body tube3.

As Figure 20-52 indicates, highly stressed areas are larger as compared to the results of the linear analysis (Figure 20-50), but this does not make the default mesh size used in the analysis acceptable. This is especially true if we want to study how far into the tube thickness the material yields. For this purpose at least two layers of elements are needed and an aggressive mesh refinement is required.

We could refine the mesh either globally (less efficient) or locally (more efficient) but expecting the need for a number of runs, we use **Submodeling**, where *tube3* is isolated from the model and the results of the nonlinear study *02 NL full model* are used only to provide displacement boundary conditions applied to this isolated model of *tube3*.

To create a **Submodeling** study based on the *02 NL full model* study, follow the steps shown in Figure 20-53.

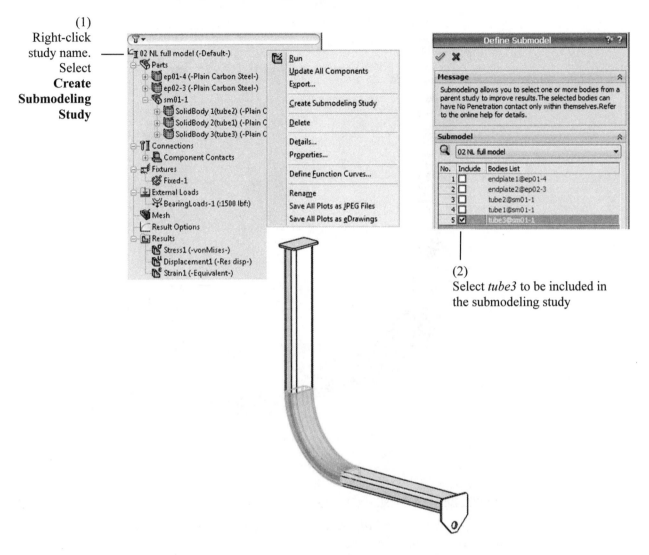

(1)
Right-click study name. Select **Create Submodeling Study**

(2)
Select *tube3* to be included in the submodeling study

Figure 20-53: Creating Submodeling study.

Every Submodeling study is based on a parent study (here, the 02 NL full model study).

The parent study for the **Submodeling** study is **Nonlinear**; therefore the **Submodeling** study is also **Nonlinear**.

Creating a **Submodeling** study adds a new configuration to the **SolidWorks** model; the study name is created automatically (Figure 20-54).

New configuration

Displacement boundary conditions from results of parent study

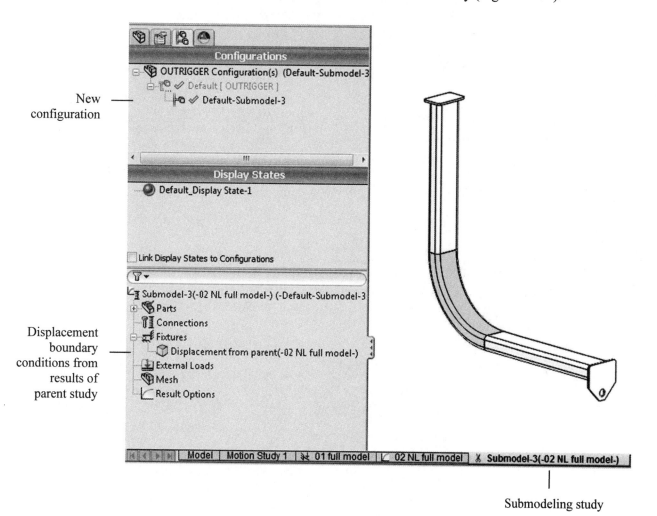

Submodeling study

Figure 20-54: Creating a Submodeling study.

The Submodeling study here is named Submodel-3(02 NL full model).

When a **Submodeling** study is created, **Simulation** displays messages shown in Figure 20-55.

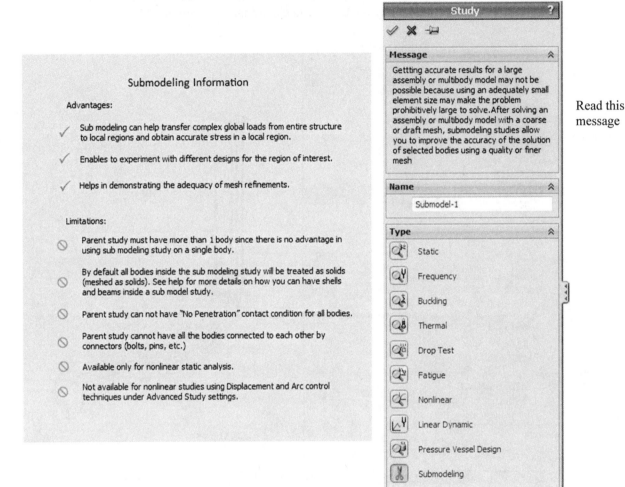

Figure 20-55: Messages related to the Submodeling study.

Information on the left is displayed during the creation of a Submodeling study.

A Submodeling study cannot be created in the Study window. Selecting Submodeling from the study window only displays a message (right).

The submodel is now ready for meshing; mesh it with an element size of 3mm to create two layers of elements across the tube wall thickness (Figure 20-56).

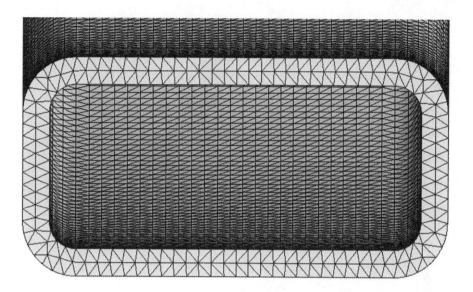

Figure 20-56: Detail of fine mesh showing two layers of solid elements across wall thickness.

Using this small element size to mesh the parent model would mean a very long solution time.

Run the **Nonlinear Submodeling** study where the only source of nonlinear behavior is nonlinear material and *tube3* is isolated from the full model and subjected to displacement boundary conditions. Von Mises stress results are shown in Figure 20-57.

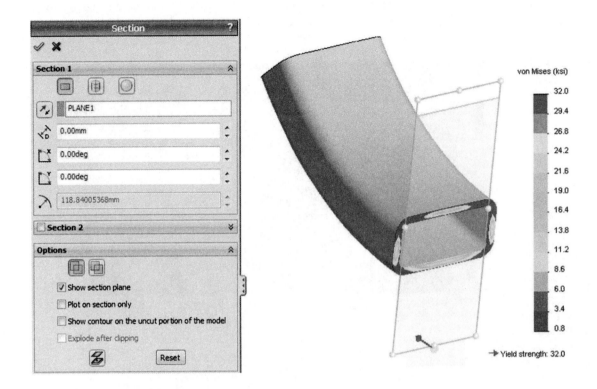

Figure 20-57: Von Mises stress results of the Submodel presented using a section view.

PLANE1 is selected as the cutting plane.

Examine the results as shown in Figure 20-57 and notice that all four round edges and the wall on the inside of the tube experienced yielding. Therefore, the OUTRIGGER is close to structural collapse.

You may now study the effect of different mesh sizes on the results without having to re-run the full model. This can be done by duplicating the **Submodeling** study.

Terminology issues in Finite Element Analysis

Finite Element Analysis (FEA), or Finite Element Method as mathematicians call it, is one of many numerical techniques of solving partial differential equations that describe, among others, the structural and thermal problems presented in this book. FEA has seen rapid development during the last few decades and it has displaced other numerical techniques into niche applications assuming a dominant position in the market of engineering analysis tools. Still, FEA is a relatively new engineering tool that has evolved from being an exclusive tool for highly trained analysts, to the present day where it has become an everyday tool of design engineers. Deeply rooted in mathematics and developed, often independently by competitive commercial firms, FEA shows discrepancies in the development of terminology, which has not yet been unified across the industry.

Users of different FEA programs may use different terminology for similar problems or use the same term describing different things. Constraints, restraints, supports and fixtures may all mean the same for some people while others will understand them differently. Many FEA users will argue that loads and boundary conditions are different entities; while other will say that loads are just one type of boundary condition because they are applied to the boundary of a model (loads external to the model are in fact boundary conditions, volume loads are not). Make sure you understand what is meant by each term you use and do not be afraid to ask exactly what is meant when an element "locks" or what a "nonconforming hexahedral element" is when you hear such a term. Many of those terms come from legacy sources and have long lost their relevance in modern programs such as **SolidWorks Simulation**.

While volumes could and in fact should be written about FEA terminology, here we will only review terminology issues that apply to names of analysis types used by **SolidWorks Simulation**. As you know, the following studies are available: **Static, Frequency, Buckling, Thermal, Drop test, Fatigue, Nonlinear, Linear Dynamic** and **Pressure Vessel Design**. Don't take each name literally as a short description of the analysis capabilities of each study. Instead treat them just as labels, here is why:

Static

This can be a linear static analysis or a nonlinear static analysis. However, a nonlinear analysis is limited to large displacements and/or contact. In a nonlinear analysis conducted under a **Static** study, the user has no control over the load time history which must be linear ("ramping-up" the load at a uniform pace). Nonlinear material is not available.

Frequency

A common name for this type of analysis is modal analysis as you find in every textbook on vibration analysis. Modal analysis finds natural frequencies and the associated shapes of vibration. A combination of frequency and shape is called a mode of vibration. Modal analysis does not find displacements, strains, or stresses.

Buckling

This is a linear buckling analysis which finds buckling load factors and the associated buckling shapes. The name "Eigenvalue based buckling analysis" is sometimes used. Linear buckling analysis does not say how far a structure will buckle or if it will survive buckling. To solve these questions, you must use a nonlinear buckling analysis which is available in **Simulation** under **Nonlinear** analysis.

Thermal

A thermal analysis can be executed as a **Steady State thermal** analysis or a **Transient Thermal** analysis and is utilized to find temperatures, temperature gradients, and heat flux. Notice that thermal stresses are not calculated in a thermal analysis; they are calculated in a **Static** or **Nonlinear** analysis using the temperature results from a **Thermal** analysis.

Drop Test

This is a specialized type of analysis intended for analysis of collision between two bodies. This is a dynamic analysis based on the direct integration method, which is stable but very time consuming.

Fatigue

A fatigue analysis uses results of a Static analysis to calculate fatigue life under periodic loads.

Nonlinear

A **Nonlinear** analysis will do everything that a **Static** analysis can do and much more, but at a higher computational cost. All types of nonlinear behaviors can be analyzed including nonlinear buckling and nonlinear materials. **Simulation** features an extensive library of nonlinear materials available in a **Nonlinear** study. Beware of the common misconception that a **Nonlinear** analysis is used only for nonlinear materials. In this book we have presented many examples where other types of nonlinear behaviors were present. Additionally, a **Nonlinear** analysis can be executed as static or dynamic. And so it is more general than a **Linear Dynamic** analysis.

Linear Dynamic

This should really be called "Linear Vibration" analysis. Remember that FEA is a tool of structural analysis and as such, deals with elastic bodies. Any motion of elastic bodies can only take the form of vibration about the position of equilibrium. Linear Dynamic (Vibration) analysis is based on the Modal Superposition method and this makes it very numerically efficient, but less general than Nonlinear Dynamic (Vibration) analysis. **Linear Dynamic** analysis has four sub-categories in **Simulation: Modal Time History, Harmonic, Random Vibration Analysis, and Response Spectrum Analysis**.

Modal Time History

Vibration analysis textbooks call this a Time Response analysis (the term Dynamic Time is also used). This analysis is intended for problems where the load is an explicit function of time.

Harmonic

Vibration analysis textbooks often call this Frequency response (the terms Steady State Harmonic analysis and Dynamic Frequency analysis are also used). This analysis is intended for problems where load is a function of frequency which in turn is a function of time. It is assumed that frequency changes very slowly (if at all), hence the alternative name: Steady State Harmonic analysis.

Random Vibration Analysis

Here, loads are given as a Power Spectral Density (PSD) of displacements, velocities or accelerations. Results such as RMS and PSD displacements, velocities and accelerations are calculated only in probabilistic terms.

Response Spectrum Analysis

This analysis is intended for excitation loads of longer duration that are non-stationary and therefore, cannot be presented as PSD. Instead, the excitation is presented as a Response Spectrum which is useful to analyze events such as earthquakes.

Pressure Vessel Design

This analysis offers a convenient way of superposing results of different Static studies as required in the analysis of pressure vessels for compliance with safety codes. Notice that a Pressure Vessel Design study can be used to analyze superposed results of anything, not just pressure vessels.

Notes:

21: Implementation of FEA into the design process

Topics covered

- ❑ Verification and Validation of FEA results
- ❑ FEA driven design process
- ❑ FEA project management
- ❑ FEA project checkpoints
- ❑ FEA reports

VERIFICATION AND VALIDATION OF FEA RESULTS

Tools of Computer Aided Engineering (CAE) are now widely used to make design decisions. The reliance on CAE tools such as Finite Element Analysis (FEA) to make design decisions brings about the issue of how relevant results from FEA models are to real life design problems. To make sure that correct decisions are made, FEA results must be verified and validated. The terms "verification" and "validation" are often used interchangeably in casual conversations.

In FEA, verification and validation pertain to different steps in the FEA modeling process. We will define and differentiate these terms while describing FEA modeling steps. We will repeat and expand the discussion found in Chapter 1.

Step 1: Creation of the mathematical model

Every FEA project starts with the creation of the mathematical model. The mathematical model needs information on the geometry of the part or assembly that we analyze, material properties, as well as loads and restraints assigned to that geometry. The definition of the type of analysis along with its simplifying assumptions (for example nonlinear static analysis, linear buckling analysis or transient thermal analysis) completes the creation of the mathematical model (Figure 21-1).

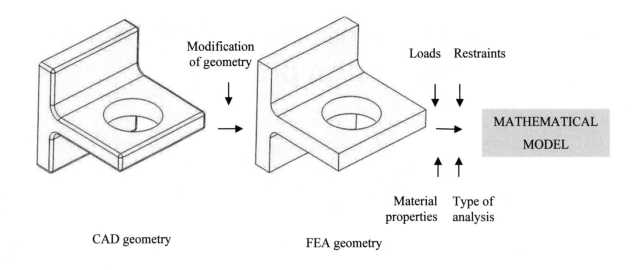

CAD geometry   FEA geometry

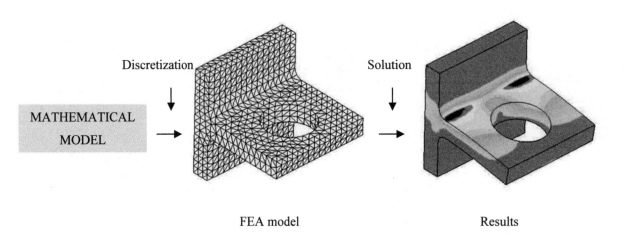

FEA model   Results

Figure 21-1: Steps in a FEA project.

This is a repetition of Figure 1-2 and Figure 1-3.

All components of a mathematical model definition bring with them inherent simplifying assumptions which affect the results. A correctly formulated mathematical model captures aspects of the real object that are important in analysis. For example, analysis of a compliant link under a static load requires nonlinear formulation due to expected large displacements. Analysis of a cooling process requires transient thermal analysis and a drop test calls for nonlinear dynamic analysis.

Very serious errors result if the mathematical model does not capture the physics of the analyzed phenomenon. For example, if we neglect the large displacements and use a linear rather than nonlinear analysis to calculate beam displacement, we produce nonsensical results as shown in Figure 21-2.

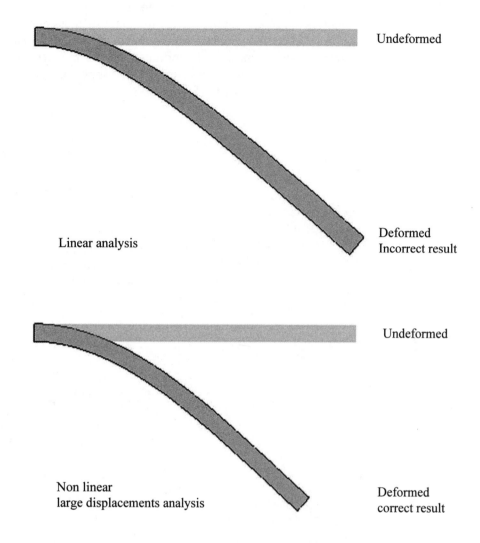

Undeformed

Linear analysis

Deformed
Incorrect result

Undeformed

Non linear
large displacements analysis

Deformed
correct result

Figure 21-2: A cantilever beam in bending. Incorrect results produced by a linear analysis (top). Correct results produced by a nonlinear, large displacement analysis (bottom).

Review studies in model BEAM for more information.

Similarly, analysis of a flat membrane under pressure requires a nonlinear analysis to account for the change in model stiffness during the deformation process (even though these displacements may be very small). Neglecting this fact and using a linear model formulation leads to a very serious and potentially more dangerous error than that shown in Figure 21-2 because results can look plausible (Figure 21-3).

Incorrect deformed shape result based on a linear model. Maximum displacement 21mm. Deformation shown in side view at a 1:1 scale.

Correct deformed shape result based on a nonlinear model. Maximum displacement 4.8mm. Deformation shown in side view at a 1:1 scale.

Figure 21-3: A thin plate subjected to a pressure load must be treated as a nonlinear large displacement problem.

For more information review studies 01 linear and 02 nonlinear in model ROUND PLATE NYLON.

A very serious yet common modeling error is using a model with stress singularities to find stress results in those singular locations (Figure 21-4).

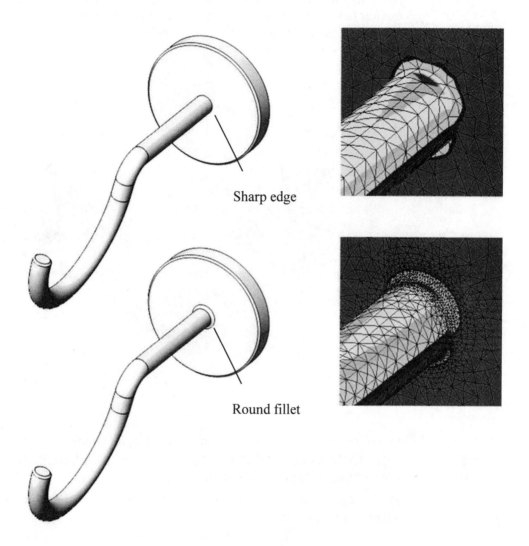

Sharp edge

Round fillet

Figure 21-4: Stress singularities caused by a sharp re-entrant edge (top). If stresses at the base of the cantilever are of interest, a fillet must be present in the analyzed geometry, no matter how small the fillet may be (bottom).

Review model SUPPORT for more information. A similar problem was illustrated in chapter 2 using model L BRACKET.

A mathematical model may also have more "trivial" errors such as incorrect loading or incorrect material properties. In the author's experience, errors are commonly found in the restraints definitions. For example, applying a rigid support to the entire back face of a support plate rather than to the bolt holes may lead to severe underestimation of stress (Figure 21-5).

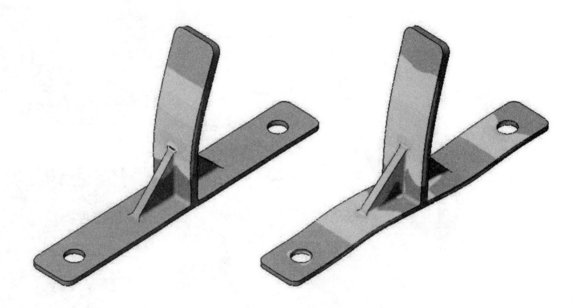

Figure 21-5: Errors caused by an incorrect restraint definition. Restraints are applied to the entire bottom face (left). Restraints applied to only the holes produce very different stress results (right).

Review model T FLAT for more information: study 01 back face support, and study 02 bolt support.

A mathematical model is never free of all errors. These unavoidable errors are known as the less intimidating term - simplifying assumptions. Every definition in making a mathematical model has some degree of simplifying assumptions which must be justified and are critical to the success of an analysis. It is our responsibility to assure that simplifying assumptions are not made "subconsciously" and that they do not prevent the model from providing trustworthy results.

Mathematical models are seldom simple enough to solve by hand and so we must use numerical techniques to solve them. FEA is one of these numerical techniques which due to its versatility and ease of use, has dominated the commercial market of engineering analysis software.

Step 2: Creation of an FEA model

As with any other numerical technique, FEA works with a discretized model. Therefore, in preparation for a solution with FEA, the mathematical model must be discretized. In discretization, a continuous mathematical model is split into finite elements in the process commonly known as meshing. While a meshed model is easy to depict graphically, this graphical representation may be confusing because it implies that a mesh is imposed on the model geometry. In fact there is nothing continuous left in the FEA model. Continuous geometry is replaced by discrete nodes, and the interaction between the nodes is defined by elements connecting these nodes. Finite elements define relations between nodes. It is conceptually important to remember that loads and restraints are also discretized. Discrete loads and discrete restraints are applied to nodes. The model's mass is no longer distributed continuously but rather, it is distributed among nodes. Unfortunately, FEA programs do not have graphical capabilities to show discretization of anything but geometry.

The process of discretization which converts the mathematical model into an FEA model does have problems that add to errors in the mathematical model. Every discretization brings with it discretization errors which may be analyzed (and controlled) in the convergence process where we analyze the effect of element size on the results. There are many "shades" of a convergence process. Most often a mesh is refined and the results are examined in terms of their sensitivity to the refinement. Many modern FEA programs have capabilities to perform a convergence processes automatically.

Discretization of an FEA model leads to the discretization of results. The result's nature depends on the type of elements used. The ability (or the lack of ability) of elements to model the real displacement and stress distribution very strongly impacts the results. A common error is to use too large of elements which are unable to capture local stress concentrations (Figure 21-6).

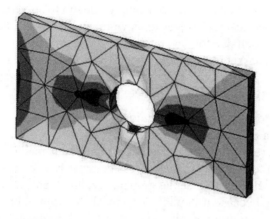

Too large of elements;
Maximum von Mises stress
304MPa

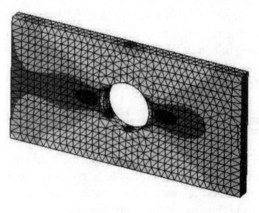

Correctly sized elements;
Maximum von Mises stress
378MPa

Figure 21-6 Errors caused by incorrect meshing.

You may use model HOLLOW BRACKET from chapter 2 to produce these results.

Problems depicted in Figure 21-6 are easy to catch by a trained eye and can all be rectified by mesh refinement. In fact, understanding the discrete nature of results will prevent the use of inadequate meshes. Even though discretization errors are easily preventable, experience indicates that they still plague analysis results.

Step 3: Solution

Once an FEA model has been created, its solution is just a matter of solving a large number of linear algebraic equations. This can be done by a variety of solvers. The solution introduces numerical errors which are usually very low.

Step 4: Interpretation of results

Finally, results must be analyzed and a design decision made. Incorrect interpretation of results is a topic for a separate article. Here we just mention a few common errors. Indiscriminate use of von Mises stress as a safety criterion is, in the author's opinion, on top of the list. Von Mises stress is a valid safety measure for materials showing distinct plasticity on a stress-strain curve. For example, using it to analyze results of a ceramic part is not valid.

Another mistake is the incorrect use of element versus nodal stress results, which results from a lack of understanding the difference between these two.

Each of the above steps takes us further away from the reality we are modeling. Errors can be made at each step, some of them are unavoidable such as errors inherent to the method, and others may be grave errors of FEA "malpractice".

We are now in the position to define the terms **verification** and **validation**.

Verification checks if the mathematical model, as submitted to be solved with FEA, has been correctly discretized and solved.

Validation determines if an FEA model correctly represents the reality from the perspective of the intended use of the model. It checks if results correctly describe the real life behavior of the analyzed object.

The difference between verification and validation is pictured in Figure 21-7.

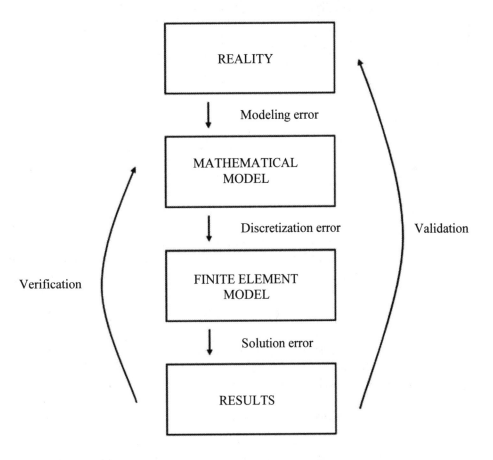

Figure 21-7 Verification and validation of FEA results.

A model with meshing errors would not pass the verification test. For example, having been discretized into too large of elements, the mathematical model would be solved incorrectly. Verification fails if discretization and/or solution errors invalidate results. Convergence analysis will usually reveal problems causing verification test failure and those problems can be treated by mesh refinement or by using higher order elements.

A model with incorrect load definitions would pass the verification test because verification only concerns itself with correctness of solution of the mathematical model, not if the mathematical model itself is correct.

Establishing the correctness of a mathematical model along with the correctness of its solution is the process of validation which should follow verification. Validation will fail because of conceptual errors in the definition of the mathematical model. These conceptual errors are much more dangerous than the errors of discretization. They may escape the modeler's attention, especially since there is no well-defined structured process to reveal conceptual errors. Our only protection is the true understanding of the analyzed problem.

FEA DRIVEN DESIGN PROCESS

We have already stated that FEA should be implemented early in the design process and be executed concurrently with design activities in order to help make more efficient design decisions. This concurrent CAD-FEA process is illustrated in Figure 21-8.

Notice that the design begins in CAD geometry and FEA begins in FEA-specific geometry. Every time FEA is used, the interface line is crossed twice: the first time when modifying CAD geometry to make it suitable for analysis with FEA, and the second time when implementing results.

This significant interfacing effort can be avoided if the new design is started and iterated in FEA-specific geometry. Only after performing a sufficient number of iterations can we switch to CAD geometry by adding all manufacturing specific features. This way, the interfacing effort is reduced to just one switch from FEA to CAD geometry as illustrated in Figure 21-8.

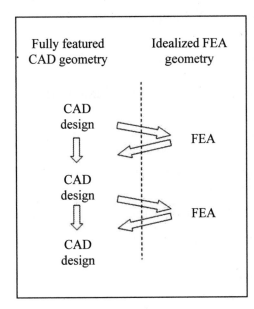
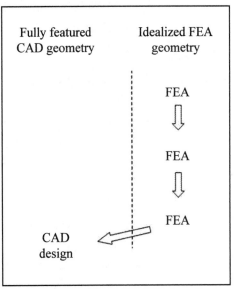

Concurrent CAD-FEA design process   FEA driven design process

Figure 21-8: Concurrent CAD-FEA product development processes (left) and FEA driven product development process (right).

The CAD-FEA design process is developed in CAD-specific geometry, while FEA analysis is conducted in FEA-specific geometry. Interfacing between the two geometries requires substantial effort and is prone to error.

CAD-FEA interfacing efforts can be significantly reduced if the differences between CAD geometry and FEA geometry are recognized and the design process starts with FEA-specific geometry.

FEA PROJECT MANAGEMENT

Now let us discuss the steps in an FEA project from a managerial point of view. The steps in an FEA project that require the involvement of management are marked with an asterisk (*).

Do I really need FEA? *

This is the most fundamental question to address before any analysis starts. FEA is expensive to conduct and consumes significant company resources to produce results. Therefore, a decision to use FEA should be well justified.

Providing answers to the following questions may help to decide if FEA is worthwhile:

- Can I use previous test results or previous FEA results?
- Is this a standard design, in which case no analysis is necessary?
- Are loads, supports, and material properties known well enough to make FEA worthwhile?
- Would a simplified analytical model do?
- Does my customer demand FEA?
- Do I have enough time to implement the results of FEA?

Should the analysis be done in house or should it be contracted out? *

Conducting analysis in-house versus using an outside consultant has advantages and disadvantages. Consultants usually produce results faster while analysis performed in house is conducive to establishing company expertise leading to long-term savings.

The following list of questions may help in answering this question:

- How fast do I need to produce results?
- Do I have enough time and resources in-house to complete FEA before design decisions must be made?
- Is in-house expertise available?
- Do I have software that my customer wants me to use?

Establish the scope of the analysis*

Now we decide what type of analysis is required. The following is a list of questions that may help in defining the scope of analysis.

Is this project:

❑ A standard analysis of a new product from an established product line?

❑ The last check of a production-ready new design before final testing?

❑ A quick check of a design in-progress to assist the designer?

❑ An aid to an R&D project (particular detail of a design, gauge, fixture etc.)?

❑ A conceptual analysis to support a design at an early stage of development (e.g. R&D project)?

❑ A simplified analysis (e.g. only a part of the structure) to help make a design decision?

Other questions to consider are:

❑ Is it possible to perform comparative analyses?

❑ What is the estimated number of model iterations, load cases, etc.?

❑ What are applicable criteria to evaluate results?

❑ How will I know whether the results can be trusted?

Establish a cost-effective modeling approach and define the mathematical model accordingly

Having established the scope of analysis, the FEA model must now be prepared. The best model is of course the simplest one that provides the required results with acceptable accuracy. Therefore, the modeling approach should minimize project cost and duration, but should account for the essential characteristics of the analyzed object.

We need to decide on acceptable idealizations of geometry. This decision may involve simplification of CAD geometry by defeaturing, or idealization by using surface or wire frame representations. The goal is to produce a meshable geometry properly representing the analyzed problem.

Create a Finite Element model and solve it

The Finite Element model is created by discretization (meshing) of a mathematical model. Although meshing implies that only geometry is discretized, discretization also affects loads and supports. Meshing and solving are both a largely automated step, but still require input, which depending on the software used, may include:

❑ Element type(s) to be used

❑ Default element size and size tolerance

❑ Definition of mesh controls (if any)

❑ Automesher type to be used

❑ Solver type and options to be used

Review results

FEA results must be critically reviewed prior to using them for making design decisions. This critical review includes:

❑ Verification of assumptions and assessment of results (an iterative step that may require several analysis loops to debug the model and to establish confidence in the results)

❑ Studying the overall mode of deformations and animating displacements to ensure that loads and restraints have been defined properly

❑ Checking for Rigid Body Motions

❑ Checking for overall stress levels (at least the order of magnitude) using analytical methods in order to verify the applied loads

❑ Checking for reaction forces and comparing them with free body diagrams

❑ A review of discretization errors (e.g. by comparing nodal and element stresses or performing a convergence process)

❑ Analysis of stress concentrations and the ability of the mesh to model them properly

❑ A review of results in difficult-to-model locations, such as thin walls, high stress gradients, etc.

❑ An investigation of the impact of element distortions on the data of interest

Analyze results*

The exact execution of this step depends, of course, on the objective of the analysis.

- ❑ Present displacement results (preferably animated)
- ❑ Present reaction force results supported by free body diagrams
- ❑ Present modal frequencies and associated modes of vibration (if applicable)
- ❑ Present stress results and corresponding factors of safety
- ❑ Consider modifications to the analyzed structure to eliminate excessive stresses and to improve material utilization and manufacturability
- ❑ Discuss results, and repeat iterations until an acceptable solution is found

Produce report*

- ❑ Produce a report summarizing the activities performed, including assumptions and conclusions
- ❑ Append the completed report with a backup of relevant electronic data

FEA PROJECT CHECKPOINTS

FEA project management requires the involvement of the manager during project execution. The correctness of FEA results cannot be established by only reviewing the analysis of the results. A list of progress checkpoints may help a manager stay in the loop and improve communication with the person performing the analysis. Several checkpoints are suggested in Figure 21-9.

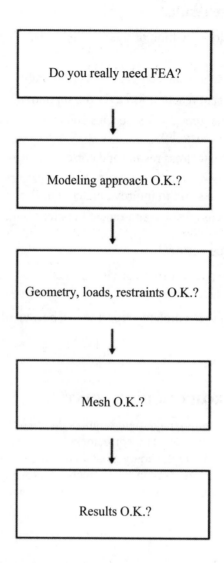

Figure 21-9: Checkpoints in an FEA project.

Using the proposed checkpoints, the project is allowed to proceed only after the manager/supervisor has approved each step.

FEA REPORT

Even though each FEA project is unique, the structure of an FEA report follows similar patterns. The following are the major sections of a typical FEA report and their contents.

Section	Content
Executive Summary	Objective of the project, part/assembly number, project number, essential assumptions, results and conclusions, software used, information on where project backup is stored, etc.
Introduction	Description of the problem: Why did the project require FEA? What kind of FEA? (static, contact stress, frequency, etc.) What were the data of interest?
Geometry **Material** **Loads** **Restraints**	Description and justification of any defeaturing and/or idealization of geometry Justification of the modeling approach (e.g. solids, shells, beams) Description of the material properties and applicable failure criteria Description of loads and restraints, including free body diagrams
Mesh	Description of the type of elements, global element size, mesh controls, number of elements, number of DOF, type of automesher used Justification of why this particular mesh is adequate to model the data of interest
Analysis type	Structural, thermal, linear, nonlinear, types of nonlinearities
Solver	Type of solver, adaptive method used
Analysis of results	Presentation of displacement, strain, stress, temperatures etc. results, including plots and animations Justification of the type of stress used to present results and failure criteria Discussion of errors in the results

Conclusions	Recommendations regarding structural integrity, necessary modifications, further studies needed
	Recommendations for follow-up testing procedure (e.g., strain-gauge test, fatigue life test)
	Recommendations on future similar analyses
Project documentation	Full documentation of the design, design drawings, FEA model explanations, and computer back-ups
	Notice that building in-house expertise requires very good documentation of the project besides the project report itself. Significant time should be allowed to prepare project documentation.
Follow-up	After the completion of tests, append the report with test results
	Discussion of the correlation between analysis results and test results
	Discussion of the corrective action taken in case the correlation is unsatisfactory (may involve a revised model and/or tests)

22: Glossary of terms

The following glossary provides short descriptions of selected terms used in this book.

Term	Definition
2D element	Depending on the type, 2D elements are intended for analysis of plane stress, plane strain and axi-symmetric problems. Nodes of 2D elements have 2 degrees of freedom.
Aspect ratio	Measure of element distortion (largest/smallest size)
Beam element	A beam element is intended for meshing wire frame geometry. Nodes of beam elements have 6 degrees of freedom.
Boundary Element Method	An alternative to the FEA method of solving field problems, where only the boundary of the solution domain needs to be discretized. Very efficient for analyzing compact 3D shapes, but difficult to use on more "spread out" shapes.
CAD	Computer Aided Design.
Clean-up	Removing and/or repairing geometric features that would prevent the automesher from creating a mesh or would result in an incorrect mesh.
Convergence criterion	A condition that must be satisfied in order for the convergence process to stop. In **SolidWorks Simulation** this applies to studies where an h-adaptive or a p-adaptive solution has been selected.

Term	Definition
Convergence process	This is a process of systematic changes in the mesh in order to see how the data of interest changes with the choice of the mesh and (hopefully) proves that the data is not significantly dependent on the choice of discretization. A convergence process can be performed as h-convergence or p-convergence.
	An h-convergence process is done by refining the mesh, i.e., by reducing the element size in the mesh and comparing the results before and after mesh refinement. Reduction of element size can be done globally, by refining the mesh everywhere in the model, or locally, by using mesh controls. An h-convergence analysis takes its name from the element characteristic dimension h, which changes from one iteration to the next.
	A p-convergence analysis does not affect element size. Elements stay the same throughout the entire convergence analysis process. Instead, element order is upgraded from one iteration to the next. A p-convergence analysis is done automatically in an iterative solution until the user-specified convergence criterion is satisfied.
	Sometimes, the desired accuracy cannot be achieved even with the highest available p-element order. In this case, the user has to refine the p-element mesh manually in a fashion similar to traditional h-convergence, and then re-run the iterative p-convergence solution. This is called a p-h convergence analysis.
Defeaturing	Defeaturing is the process of removing (or suppressing) geometric features in the CAD geometry in order to simplify the finite element mesh or make meshing possible.
Discretization	This defines the process of splitting up a continuous mathematical model into discrete "pieces" called elements. A visible effect of discretization is the finite element mesh. However, model mass, loads and restraints are also discretized.

Discretization error	This type of error affects FEA results because FEA works on an assembly of discrete elements (the mesh) rather than on a continuous structure. The finer the finite element mesh, the lower the discretization error, but the longer the solution time.
Element stress	This refers to stresses at Gauss points of a given element. Stresses at different Gauss points are averaged amongst themselves (but not with stresses reported by other elements) and one value is assigned to the entire element. Element stresses produce a discontinuous stress distribution in the model.
Finite Difference Method	This is an alternative to the FEA method of solving a field problem, where the solution domain is discretized into a grid. The Finite Difference Method is generally less efficient for solving structural and thermal problems, but is often used in fluid dynamics problems.
Finite Element	Finite elements are the building blocks of a mesh, defined by the position of their nodes and by functions approximating distribution of sought after quantities, such as displacements or temperatures.
Finite Volume Method	This is an alternative to the FEA method of solving a field problem, similar to the Finite Difference Method and is also often used in fluid dynamics problems.
Frequency analysis	Also called modal analysis, a frequency analysis calculates the natural frequencies of a structure as the associated modes (shapes) of vibration. Modal analysis does not calculate displacements or stresses.
Gaussian points	These points are locations in the element where stresses are calculated. Later, these stress results can be extrapolated to nodes.
h-adaptive solution	An iterative solution which involves mesh refinement. Iterations continue until convergence requirements are satisfied or the maximum number of iterations is reached.

h-element	An h-element is a finite element for which the order does not change during solution. Convergence analysis of the model using h-elements is done by refining the mesh and comparing results (like displacement, stress, etc.) before and after refinement. The name, *h-element*, comes from the element characteristic dimension *h*, which is reduced in consecutive mesh refinements.
Harmonic analysis	Dynamic analysis where excitation is a function of frequency.
Idealization	This refers to making simplifying assumptions in the process of creating a mathematical model of an analyzed structure. Idealization may involve geometry, material properties, loads and restraints. Representing a structure as a surface for shell element meshing or wireframe for beam element meshing are examples of idealization.
Idealization error	This type of error results from the fact that analysis is conducted on an idealized model and not on a real-life object. Geometry, material properties, loads, and restraints are all idealized in models submitted to FEA.
Jacobian	Measure of element curvilinear distortion.
Linear material	This is a type of material where stress is a linear function of strain.
Meshing	This refers to the process of discretizing the model geometry. As a result of meshing, the originally continuous geometry is represented by an assembly of finite elements.
Modal analysis	See Frequency analysis.
Modal Time History analysis	Dynamic analysis where excitation is an explicit function of time.
Modeling error	See Idealization error.
Nodal stresses	These stresses are calculated at nodes by extrapolating stress from Gauss points and then averaging stresses (coming from different elements) at nodes. Nodal stresses, by virtue of averaging, produce continuous stress distributions in the model.
Numerical error	This is round-off error accumulated by the solver.

p-element	P-elements are elements that do not have a pre-defined order. The solution of a p-element model requires several iterations while element order is upgraded until the difference in user-specified measures (e.g. total strain energy, RMS stress) becomes less than the requested accuracy. The name p-element, comes from the p-order of polynomial functions which defines the displacement field in the element. This order is upgraded during the iterative solution.
p-adaptive solution	This refers to an option available for static analysis with solid elements only. If the p-adaptive solution is selected (in the properties window of a static study), **SolidWorks Simulation** uses p-elements for an iterative solution. A p-adaptive solution provides results with narrowly specified accuracy.
Pre-load	A pre-load is a load that modifies the stiffness of a structure. A pre-load may be important in a static or frequency analysis if it significantly changes structure stiffness.
Power Spectral Density	A function describing random excitation, its argument is frequency.
Principal stress	Principal stress is the stress component that acts on the side of an imaginary stress cube in the absence of shear stresses. A general 3D state of stress can be represented either by six stress components (normal stresses and shear stresses) expressed in an arbitrary coordinate system or by three principal stresses and three angles defining the cube orientation in relation to that coordinate system.
Random analysis	The dynamic analysis of a system response to a random excitation.
Rigid body mode or Rigid body motion	A rigid body mode is the ability to move without elastic deformation. In the case of a fully supported structure, the only way it can move under load is by deforming its shape. If a structure is not fully supported, it can move as a rigid body without any deformation. A structure with no supports has six rigid body modes. Rigid body motions are only allowed in Frequency (modal) analysis.
RMS stress	Root Mean Square stress. RMS stress may be used as a convergence

	criterion if the p-adaptive solution method is used.
Shell element	Shell elements are intended for meshing surfaces. The shell element that is used in **SolidWorks Simulation** is a triangular shell element. Triangular shell elements have three corner nodes. If this is a second order triangular element, it also has mid-side nodes, making the total number of nodes equal to six. Each node of a shell element has 6 degrees of freedom.
Small Displacement assumption	Analysis based on small displacements assumes that displacements caused by loads are small enough to not significantly change the structure stiffness. Analysis based on this assumption of small deformations is also called a linear geometry analysis or a small displacement analysis. However, the magnitude of displacements is not the deciding factor in determining whether or not a small displacement solution will produce correct results. What matters is whether or not those displacements significantly change the stiffness of the analyzed structure.
Solid element	This is a type of element used for meshing solid geometry. The only solid element available in **SolidWorks Simulation** is a tetrahedral element. It has four triangular faces and four corner nodes. If used as a second order element (high quality) it also has mid-side nodes, making the total number of nodes equal to 10. Each node of a tetrahedral element has 3 degrees of freedom.
Steady state thermal analysis	Steady state thermal analysis assumes that heat flow has stabilized and no longer changes with time.
Structural stiffness	Structural stiffness is a function of shape, material properties, and restraints. Stiffness characterizes a structural response to an applied load.
Symmetry boundary conditions	These refer to displacement conditions defined on a flat model boundary allowing only for in-plane displacement and restricting any out-of-plane displacement components. Symmetry boundary conditions are very useful for reducing the model size if the model geometry, load, and supports are all symmetric.
Thermal analysis	Thermal analysis finds temperature distribution, temperature gradient and heat flux in a structure.

Transient thermal analysis	Transient thermal analysis is an option in a thermal analysis. It calculates temperature, temperature gradient and heat flow changes over time as a result of time dependent thermal loads and thermal boundary conditions.
Ultimate strength	The maximum stress that may occur in a structure. If the ultimate strength is exceeded, failure will take place (the part will break). Ultimate strength is usually much higher than the yield strength.
Vibration analysis	An analysis of oscillations of a model about its position of equilibrium.
von Mises stress	This is a stress measure that takes into consideration all six stress components of a 3D state of stress. Von Mises stress, also called Huber stress, is a very convenient and popular way of presenting FEA results because it is a scalar, non-negative value and because the magnitude of von Mises stress can be used to determine safety factors for materials exhibiting elasto-plastic properties, such as most types of steel and aluminum alloys.
Yield strength	The maximum stress that can be allowed in a model before plastic deformation takes place.

Notes:

23: Resources available to FEA users

Many sources of FEA expertise are available to users. Sources include, but are not limited to:

- Engineering textbooks

- Software manuals

- Engineering journals

- Professional development courses

- FEA user groups

- Government organizations

Readers of "Engineering Analysis with SolidWorks Simulation 2013" may wish to review the book "Finite Element Analysis for Design Engineers" which expands on many topics discussed in this book (Figure 23-1).

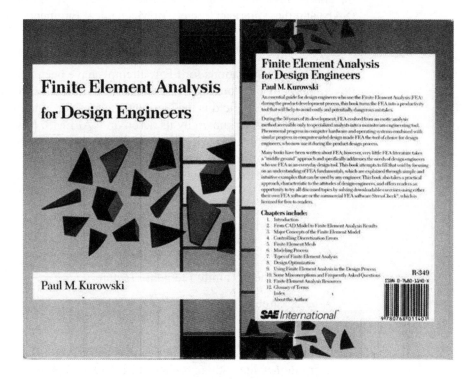

Figure 23-1: The "Finite Element Analysis for Design Engineers" book.

"Finite Element Analysis for Design Engineers" is available through the Society of Automotive Engineers website (www.sae.org).

Engineering literature offers a large selection of FEA-related books, a few of which are listed here:

1. Adams V., Askenazi A. "Building Better Products with Finite Element Analysis", OnWord Press, 1998.

2. Inman D., "Engineering Vibration" Prentice Hall 2007

3. Kim N.H., Sankar B.V. "Introduction to Finite Element Analysis and Design", John Wiley & Sons, Inc., 2009.

4. Logan D. "A First Course in the Finite Element Method", Brooks/Cole 2007

5. Spyrakos C. "Finite Element Modeling in Engineering Practice", West Virginia University Printing Services, 1994.

6. Szabo B., Babuska I. "Finite Element Analysis", John Wiley & Sons, Inc., 1991.

7. Zienkiewicz O., Taylor R. "The Finite Element Method", McGraw-Hill Book Company, 1989.

Several professional organizations like the Society of Automotive Engineers (SAE) and the American Society of Mechanical Engineers (ASME) offer professional development courses in the field of Finite Element Analysis. More information can be found at www.sae.org and www.asme.org.

With so many applications for FEA, attempts have been made to create a governing body overlooking FEA standards and practices. One of the leading organizations in this field is the National Agency for Finite Element Methods and Standards, better known by its acronym NAFEMS. It was founded in the United Kingdom in 1983 with the specific objective: "To promote the safe and reliable use of finite element and related technology." NAFEMS has published many FEA handbooks such as:

*   A Finite Element Primer

*   A Finite Element Dynamics Primer

*   Guidelines to Finite Element Practice

*   Background to Benchmarks

The full list of these excellent publications can be found at www.nafems.org. Another internet site with a number of FEA related publications is presented by Design Generator Inc. Publications related to FEA fundamentals, training, and implementation can be found at:

www.designgenerator.com

24: List of exercises

Chapter	Part	Assembly
1	BRACKET DEMO	
2	HOLLOW PLATE	
3	L BRACKET	
4	PIPE SUPPORT	
5	LINK	
6	TUNING FORK, PLASTIC PART	
7	PIPE CONNECTOR, HEATER	
8		HEAT SINK
9		HANGER
10		LOOP
11	I BEAM	
12	BRACKET	
13	RING	
14	NL002, CLIP, ROUND PLATE, LINK02, BRACKET NL, SPRING	
15	WHEEL	
16	ROPS, TRUSS	
17	END CAP, HOLLOW PLATE 2D, L BRACKET 2D	CONTACT
18		1DOF, 2DOF
19	HD HEAD	
20	MESH QUALITY 01, MESH QUALITY 02 NON UNIFORM LOAD, HELICOPTER ROTOR, CIRCULAR	GUSSET, SHRINK FIT, CRANE, STAND, PIPES, TUBE WELDMENT, BEARING SUPPORT, CLAMP, CLAMP2013
21	BEAM, ROUND PLATE NYLON, SUPPORT, T FLAT	

Notes: